AF801700

# Communications in Computer and Information Science 2414

Series Editors

Gang Li, *School of Information Technology, Deakin University, Burwood, VIC, Australia*
Joaquim Filipe, *Polytechnic Institute of Setúbal, Setúbal, Portugal*
Zhiwei Xu, *Chinese Academy of Sciences, Beijing, China*

**Rationale**
The CCIS series is devoted to the publication of proceedings of computer science conferences. Its aim is to efficiently disseminate original research results in informatics in printed and electronic form. While the focus is on publication of peer-reviewed full papers presenting mature work, inclusion of reviewed short papers reporting on work in progress is welcome, too. Besides globally relevant meetings with internationally representative program committees guaranteeing a strict peer-reviewing and paper selection process, conferences run by societies or of high regional or national relevance are also considered for publication.

**Topics**
The topical scope of CCIS spans the entire spectrum of informatics ranging from foundational topics in the theory of computing to information and communications science and technology and a broad variety of interdisciplinary application fields.

**Information for Volume Editors and Authors**
Publication in CCIS is free of charge. No royalties are paid, however, we offer registered conference participants temporary free access to the online version of the conference proceedings on SpringerLink (http://link.springer.com) by means of an http referrer from the conference website and/or a number of complimentary printed copies, as specified in the official acceptance email of the event.

CCIS proceedings can be published in time for distribution at conferences or as post-proceedings, and delivered in the form of printed books and/or electronically as USBs and/or e-content licenses for accessing proceedings at SpringerLink. Furthermore, CCIS proceedings are included in the CCIS electronic book series hosted in the SpringerLink digital library at http://link.springer.com/bookseries/7899. Conferences publishing in CCIS are allowed to use Online Conference Service (OCS) for managing the whole proceedings lifecycle (from submission and reviewing to preparing for publication) free of charge.

**Publication process**
The language of publication is exclusively English. Authors publishing in CCIS have to sign the Springer CCIS copyright transfer form, however, they are free to use their material published in CCIS for substantially changed, more elaborate subsequent publications elsewhere. For the preparation of the camera-ready papers/files, authors have to strictly adhere to the Springer CCIS Authors' Instructions and are strongly encouraged to use the CCIS LaTeX style files or templates.

**Abstracting/Indexing**
CCIS is abstracted/indexed in DBLP, Google Scholar, EI-Compendex, Mathematical Reviews, SCImago, Scopus. CCIS volumes are also submitted for the inclusion in ISI Proceedings.

**How to start**
To start the evaluation of your proposal for inclusion in the CCIS series, please send an e-mail to ccis@springer.com.

Wei-Ta Chu · Chih-Ya Shen · Hong-Han Shuai
Editors

# Technologies and Applications of Artificial Intelligence

## 29th International Conference, TAAI 2024
## Hsinchu, Taiwan, December 6–7, 2024
## Proceedings, Part I

Springer

*Editors*
Wei-Ta Chu
National Cheng Kung University
Tainan City, Taiwan

Chih-Ya Shen
National Tsing Hua University
Hsinchu City, Taiwan

Hong-Han Shuai
National Yang Ming Chiao Tung University
Hsinchu City, Taiwan

ISSN 1865-0929 ISSN 1865-0937 (electronic)
Communications in Computer and Information Science
ISBN 978-981-96-4588-6 ISBN 978-981-96-4589-3 (eBook)
https://doi.org/10.1007/978-981-96-4589-3

© The Editor(s) (if applicable) and The Author(s), under exclusive license
to Springer Nature Singapore Pte Ltd. 2025

This work is subject to copyright. All rights are solely and exclusively licensed by the Publisher, whether the whole or part of the material is concerned, specifically the rights of translation, reprinting, reuse of illustrations, recitation, broadcasting, reproduction on microfilms or in any other physical way, and transmission or information storage and retrieval, electronic adaptation, computer software, or by similar or dissimilar methodology now known or hereafter developed.
The use of general descriptive names, registered names, trademarks, service marks, etc. in this publication does not imply, even in the absence of a specific statement, that such names are exempt from the relevant protective laws and regulations and therefore free for general use.
The publisher, the authors and the editors are safe to assume that the advice and information in this book are believed to be true and accurate at the date of publication. Neither the publisher nor the authors or the editors give a warranty, expressed or implied, with respect to the material contained herein or for any errors or omissions that may have been made. The publisher remains neutral with regard to jurisdictional claims in published maps and institutional affiliations.

This Springer imprint is published by the registered company Springer Nature Singapore Pte Ltd.
The registered company address is: 152 Beach Road, #21-01/04 Gateway East, Singapore 189721, Singapore

If disposing of this product, please recycle the paper.

# Preface

Artificial intelligence has continued to push the boundaries of innovation, creativity, and interdisciplinary collaboration. Against this backdrop, the International Conference on Technologies and Applications of Artificial Intelligence (TAAI) has consistently provided a platform for advancing AI research and fostering meaningful dialogue. Since its inception in 1995, TAAI has served as a cornerstone of AI research in Taiwan and has gained recognition internationally. The 2024 edition of TAAI embraced the transformative advancements in Large Language Models (LLMs) and Generative AI, which have reshaped industries and fueled global collaboration. With the theme "Cross-domain Collaboration, Industry Co-creation," the conference highlighted the importance of breaking traditional boundaries to unlock the vast potential of AI. Hosted at National Tsing Hua University in Hsinchu, Taiwan, a city renowned for its vibrant science and technology ecosystem, TAAI 2024 brought together researchers, practitioners, and industry leaders to showcase their work and exchange ideas.

This year's conference received 147 submissions from contributors around the globe, reflecting the growing interest in AI's transformative capabilities. Each submission underwent a rigorous review by three reviewers in a single-blind process, overseen by an international panel of experts. A total of 49 papers were accepted for presentation. These proceedings capture a curated selection of high-quality research papers that combine theoretical advancements with innovative applications. The topics explored include cutting-edge work in data science, optimization techniques, ethical AI, and applications that address pressing societal challenges. A special highlight of this year's program was the significant engagement of young scholars, including a record number of submissions for the High School Session.

The successful organization of TAAI 2024 would not have been possible without the dedication and efforts of many individuals and organizations. We extend our heartfelt gratitude to the authors for their outstanding contributions and to the reviewers for their meticulous efforts in ensuring the quality and integrity of the selection process. We also wish to thank the organizing committee, including the Taiwanese Association for Artificial Intelligence (TAAI), National Tsing Hua University, and our esteemed sponsors and partners, for their unwavering support.

We hope these proceedings will serve as a valuable resource for researchers, practitioners, and students, inspiring further exploration and innovation in the field of artificial intelligence.

December 2024

Wei-Ta Chu
Chih-Ya Shen
Hong-Han Shuai

# Organization

## General Chairs

| | |
|---|---|
| Yi-Shin Chen | National Tsing Hua University, Taiwan |
| Wen-Chih Peng | National Yang Ming Chiao Tung University, Taiwan |
| Chuan-Kang Ting | National Tsing Hua University, Taiwan |

## Program Committee Chairs

| | |
|---|---|
| Wei-Ta Chu | National Cheng Kung University, Taiwan |
| Chih-Ya Shen | National Tsing Hua University, Taiwan |
| Hong-Han Shuai | National Yang Ming Chiao Tung University, Taiwan |

## Keynote Program Chair

| | |
|---|---|
| Chang-Shing Lee | National University of Tainan, Taiwan |

## Nectar Program Chair

| | |
|---|---|
| Hung-Yu Kao | National Tsing Hua University, Taiwan |

## Special Session Chairs

| | |
|---|---|
| Lieu-Hen Chen | National Chi Nan University, Taiwan |
| Yi-Hsin Ho | Takushoku University, Japan |

## Industrial Track and Sponsorship Chairs

| | |
|---|---|
| I-Heng Meng | Institute for Information Industry, Taiwan |
| Richie Tsai | Taiwan AI Academy, Taiwan |

## Publication Chairs

| | |
|---|---|
| Fernando Calderón | Fu Jen Catholic University, Taiwan |
| Te-Chuan Chiu | National Tsing Hua University, Taiwan |

## Financial Chair

| | |
|---|---|
| Rung-Tzuo Liaw | Fu Jen Catholic University, Taiwan |

## Publicity Chair

| | |
|---|---|
| Wei-Chen Chiu | National Yang Ming Chiao Tung University, Taiwan |

## Tutorial Chair and AI Competition Chair

| | |
|---|---|
| Tzong-Han Tsai | National Central University, Taiwan |

## Young Woman Star Session Chair

| | |
|---|---|
| Min-Chu Hu | National Tsing Hua University, Taiwan |

## Game Tournament Chair

| | |
|---|---|
| Shi-Jim Yen | National Dong Hwa University, Taiwan |

## Program Committee

| | |
|---|---|
| Albert Bakhtizinm | Russian Academy of Sciences, Russia |
| Been-Chian Chien | National University of Tainan, Taiwan |
| Bi-Ru Dai | National Taiwan University of Science and Technology, Taiwan |
| Bor-Shen Lin | National Taiwan University of Science and Technology, Taiwan |
| Che-Nan Kuo | CTBC Business School, Taiwan |

| | |
|---|---|
| Cheng-Te Li | National Cheng Kung University, Taiwan |
| Cheng-Zen Yang | Yuan Ze University, Taiwan |
| Chenn-Jung Huang | National Dong Hwa University, Taiwan |
| Chih-Chieh Hung | National Chung Hsing University, Taiwan |
| Chih-Chin Lai | National University of Kaohsiung, Taiwan |
| Ching-Hu Lu | National Taiwan University of Science and Technology, Taiwan |
| Chuang-Chieh Lin | National Taiwan Ocean University, Taiwan |
| Chun-Hao Chen | National Kaohsiung University of Science and Technology, Taiwan |
| Daw-Tung Lin | National Taipei University, Taiwan |
| Eri Shimokawara | Tokyo Metropolitan University, Japan |
| Frank Tseng | National Kaohsiung University of Science and Technology, Taiwan |
| Giuseppe D'aniello | Università degli Studi di Salerno, Italy |
| Hao-Shang Ma | National Taichung University of Science and Technology, Taiwan |
| Hong-Jie Dai | National Kaohsiung University of Science and Technology, Taiwan |
| Hsiao-Ping Tsai | National Chung Hsing University, Taiwan |
| Hsien-Chou Liao | Chaoyang University of Technology, Taiwan |
| Hsin-Min Wang | Academia Sinica, Taiwan |
| Hsiu Min Chuang | National Defense University, Taiwan |
| Hsua-Tien Lin | National Taiwan University, Taiwan |
| Hsu-Yung Cheng | National Central University, Taiwan |
| Hui-Ju Hung | National Central University, Taiwan |
| Hung-Yu Kao | National Cheng Kung University, Taiwan |
| I-Shyan Hwang | Yuan Ze University, Taiwan |
| Jenq-Haur Wang | National Taipei University of Technology, Taiwan |
| Jen-Tzung Chien | National Yang Ming Chiao Tung University, Taiwan |
| Jen-Wei Huang | National Cheng Kung University, Taiwan |
| Jr-Chang Chen | National Taipei University, Taiwan |
| Kazunori Mizuno | Takushoku University, Japan |
| Klaus Brinker | University of Applied Sciences Hamm-Lippstadt, Germany |
| Ko-Wei Huang | National Kaohsiung University of Science and Technology, Taiwan |
| Kun-Ta Chuang | National Cheng Kung University, Taiwan |
| Lung-Pin Chen | Tunghai University, Taiwan |
| Min-Chun Hu | National Tsing Hua University, Taiwan |
| Po-Ruey Lei | ROC Naval Academy, Taiwan |

| | |
|---|---|
| Po-Yuan Chen | Jinwen University of Science and Technology, Taiwan |
| Ramakrishna Garine | University of North Texas, USA |
| Rong-Ming Chen | National University of Tainan, Taiwan |
| Sai-Keung Wong | National Yang Ming Chiao Tung University, Taiwan |
| Shih-Hung Wu | Chaoyang University of Technology, Taiwan |
| Shi-Jim Yen | National Dong Hwa University, Taiwan |
| Shing-Tai Pan | National University of Kaohsiung, Taiwan |
| Show-Jane Yen | Ming Chuan University, Taiwan |
| Tao-Hsing Chang | National Kaohsiung University of Science and Technology, Taiwan |
| Tsaipei Wang | National Yang Ming Chiao Tung University, Taiwan |
| Tsung-Ting Kuo | University of California San Diego, USA |
| Tzu-Hsien Yang | National Cheng Kung University, Taiwan |
| Tzung-Pei Hong | National University of Kaohsiung, Taiwan |
| Wei-Min Liu | National Chung Cheng University, Taiwan |
| Wen-Hung Liao | National Chengchi University, Taiwan |
| Wen-Yang Lin | National University of Kaohsiung, Taiwan |
| Yasufumi Takama | Tokyo Metropolitan University, Japan |
| Yi-Chung Chen | National Yunlin University of Science and Technology, Taiwan |
| Yihsin Ho | Takushoku University, Japan |
| Yi-Hung Wu | Chung Yuan Christian University, Taiwan |
| Yi-Leh Wu | National Taiwan University of Science and Technology, Taiwan |
| Ying-ping Chen | National Yang Ming Chiao Tung University, Taiwan |
| Yi-Shin Chen | National Tsing Hua University, Taiwan |
| Yue-Shi Lee | Ming Chuan University, Taiwan |
| Yufei Xie | Wayve, USA |
| Yung-Chun Chang | Taipei Medical University, Taiwan |
| Shih-Cheng Hong | Chaoyang University of Technology, Taiwan |
| Yi-Jen Su | Shu-Te University, Taiwan |

# Contents – Part I

**Games**



**Machine Learning and Applications**



**AI Studies**

# Contents – Part II

# Data Robustness

# A Study on Synthesizing Expressive Violin Performances: Approaches and Comparisons

Tzu-Yun Hung, Jui-Te Wu, Yu-Chia Kuo, Yo-Wei Hsiao, Ting-Wei Lin, and Li Su(✉)

Institute of Information Science, Academia Sinica, Taipei, Taiwan

**Abstract.** Expressive music synthesis (EMS) for violin performance is a challenging task due to the disagreement among music performers in the interpretation of expressive musical terms (EMTs), the paucity of labeled recordings, and the limited generalization ability of the synthesis model. These challenges create trade-offs between model effectiveness, diversity of generated results, and controllability of the synthesis system, making it essential to conduct a comparative study on EMS model design. In this paper, we discuss two violin EMS approaches. First, the end-to-end approach is a modification of a state-of-the-art text-to-speech neural network. Second, the parameter-controlled approach is based on a simple parameter sampling process that can render note lengths and other parameters compatible with MIDI-DDSP. We systematically study the two approaches through both objective and subjective experiments and discuss several key issues of EMS based on the results.

**Keywords:** Expressive musical terms · Violin performance synthesis · Data analysis · Parameter-controlled

## 1 Introduction

Endowing music with expressive power is a major goal of the music generation task. Synthesizing music performances from symbolic music data (e.g., MIDI or musicXML formats) conditioned on a designated expressive music term (EMT)[1] represents a further step forward in emotion-conditioned music generation and further innovative techniques [27]. This task, named as the expression-conditioned music synthesis (EMS) task in this paper, is more than the traditional music synthesis task of generating real-world, human-like music

[1] In this paper, we refer to EMT as the Italian musical terms which describe an emotion, feeling, image, or metaphor of a section of music (e.g., the ten EMTs labeled in the SCREAM-MAC-EMT dataset [13]). To facilitate the discussion, we distinguish expressive music terms from the articulation marks (e.g., accent/staccato, tempo, and dynamics), although articulation marks are surely related to music expression. An EMT includes, but is not limited to music emotion.

© The Author(s), under exclusive license to Springer Nature Singapore Pte Ltd. 2025
W.-T. Chu et al. (Eds.): TAAI 2024, CCIS 2414, pp. 3–16, 2025.
https://doi.org/10.1007/978-981-96-4589-3_1

performance (called *performance generation*) [5,9,24]: the EMS task supports one to change the expression of music performance from one to another. The EMS task incorporates several technical targets, such as identifying the key features determining the expression of a musical performance, understanding the long-term dependency between EMTs and musical structure, high-quality EMT-conditioned music synthesis, and the extension to various musical genres and styles.

The EMS task is still a less-explored and challenging research topic due to several reasons. First, EMS requires audio recording data with EMT annotation, but such kinds of data are scarce. Even the largest dataset to our knowledge (i.e. the SCREAM-MAC-EMT dataset [13], which is used in this paper) still lacks diversity as there are only 10 short pieces of music being performed. This hinders the modeling of high-level concepts such as EMTs. Second, EMTs are highly subjective and context dependent. Both listeners and performers may disagree on the interpretation of EMT in music performance. Also, considering the potential of computer-human interaction, an EMS system should also support controllability, such as output editing, adding articulation on some specific notes, and different input formats. To summarize, EMS research still faces a few open problems, including the achievability of EMT-conditioned generation, the design of EMS inputs and outputs, diversity control, and the choice of models.

In this paper, we study these issues by exploring the performance of two EMS approaches in violin performance. First, the end-to-end approach is a modification of a state-of-the-art text-to-speech generator. Second, the parameter-controlled approach is based on a simple parameter sampling process that can render note lengths and parameters compatible with MIDI-DDSP [25]. Also, we consider a modified system that supports MusicXML file input and can have articulation symbols as input. From the results, we report some challenges in EMS compared to the task of generating human-like performance. Results indicate that judging some EMTs is even harder for human beings. Also, we notice that the parameter-controlled model performs better when the human performance is preferred, while the end-to-end model performs better when human and machine can not be distinguished easily.

## 2 Related Work

EMS is a multidisciplinary research topic which involves quite diverse tasks, ranging from analysis to generation. For the analysis part, analyzing the tempo or micro-timing in music performance is, therefore, a central topic in music performance analysis [1,4,12]. Previous research has mostly focused on studying how the *time-varying* behavior of tempo and inter-onset interval (IOI) related to different music structures and expressions, performers, and eras [8,20,21]. A systematic review regarding music performance analysis can be seen in [12]. A few previous works mentioned the importance of analyzing expressive violin performances. Molina-Solana *et al.* modeled Implication-Realization patterns [19] from audio data and utilized the patterns to classify 23 different violinists' performances [18]. Zhao *et al.* proposed a model that classified nine violinists using note-level timbre features and machine learning [28]. Marchini *et al.* analyzed three kinds of expressions (i.e., mechanical, normal, and exaggerated) in the performance of string quartets based on four sets of features (i.e., sound level, note lengthening, vibrato extent, and bow velocity) [16]. Li *et al.* firstly proposed a dataset and performed classification over 11 EMTs [13]. These works all emphasized the importance of extracting musically meaningful features in note-, phrase-, and other levels of music structure. While previous research assumes the dependency between EMT and musical structures [2,14] and styles [3], a recent study has shown that there may be some structure- and style-independent factors that determine the characteristics of EMT [10].

In the literature of music synthesis, a number of works mentioned music expressiveness, though the term expressive here usually refers to natural, human-like, or realistic performance rather than specific EMT. For example, Jonason *et al.* proposed a model based on bidirectional long-short memory (BLSTM) that generates pitch and loudness contours [11]. The MIDI-DDSP model considers 6 parameters to condition on the decoder [25]. Shih *et al.* considers note duration (ND), key overlap time (KOT), energy and vibrato rate (VR), and vibrato extent (VE) and uses them to imitate two violin maestros' (Heifetz and Oistrakh) playing style [22]. The traditional synthesizers used for expressive music performance include concatenative synthesis [15], phase vocoders, and others. Recently, end-to-end music synthesis models have caught wide attention. Dong *et al.* proposed a Transformer-based score-to-music synthesis for violin sounds [5]. There are quite limited works which use expressive musical terms as conditions. Yang *et al.* demonstrated an EMS model using note segmentation and manipulation of note duration, note vibrato, and phrase-level dynamics, taking the phase vocoder as the synthesizer [27].

## 3 Method

Given a symbolic music file (e.g., MIDI, musicXML), the objective of EMS is to generate an audio recording with a target EMT. Figure 1 illustrates the whole system diagram of our experiments. We consider two types of EMS models, the parameter-controlled one (lower part of Fig. 1) and the end-to-end one (upper part of Fig. 1). It should be noted that the parameter-controlled model has two variants, one taking the MIDI as input and the other taking musicXML as input. All the three models can be regarded as zero-shot music generation as they work for unseen data. These models will be discussed later on.

### 3.1 Data

We used the SCREAM-MAC-EMT dataset, the largest EMT dataset of violin performance to our knowledge, as the training dataset. The dataset comprises 40 violinists' performances on 10 pieces of music, and each piece is performed with five suitable EMTs. The dataset contains the performance recordings in 10 EMTs: *Tranquillo* (calm), *Grazioso* (graceful), *Scherzando* (playful), *Risoluto* (declarative), *Maestoso* (dignified), *Affettuoso* (affection), *Espressivo* (expressive), *Agitato* (restless), *Con Brio* (energetic), and *Cantabile* (like singing).

In addition to the five EMTs, every musician performed a non-expressive version (denoted as *None*) for each piece. As a result, the dataset contains 2400 excerpts, as each of the 10 classical music pieces was interpreted in 6 different versions by 40 violinists. More information about the dataset, such as the EMTs used in each piece of music, is provided in [13].

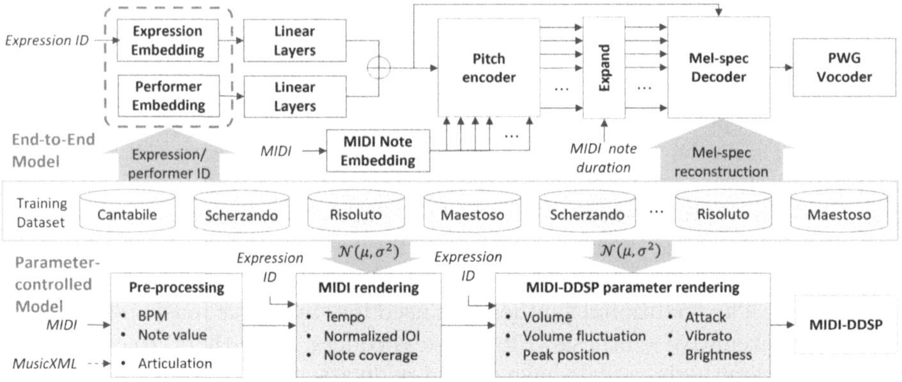


**Fig. 1.** Diagram of the end-to-end and the parameter-controlled EMS models. The training data are illustrated in blue and the bold blue arrows represent the actions in the training process. Italic texts represent the required inputs in the synthesis process. The two variants of the parameter-controlled model are illustrated as the solid-line and the dashed-line arrows in the lower left corner, where one represents MIDI input and the other is musicXML input (i.e., adding articulation). (Color figure online)

### 3.2 Model 1: Gaussian MIDI-DDSP

In the parameter-controlled model, we utilized a general symbolic-to-music synthesizer, MIDI-DDSP [25], based on Differentiable Digital Signal Processing (DDSP) [6], as our audio synthesizer at the final stage of the model. Our goal is then simplified to the generation of the MIDI-DDSP parameters. In our work, according to the target EMT, we aim to transform into, we consider a very simple way of parameter generation: we adjust the model of each MIDI-DDSP parameter as a Gaussian distribution, where the mean and the variance are directly derived from the distribution of that parameter in the training data. The generation process is then simplified into the rendering of Gaussian distributions of the independent parameters. This model is denoted as Gaussian MIDI-DDSP.

The pipeline of Gaussian MIDI-DDSP incorporates rendering both the MIDI and the MIDI-DDSP parameters (see the lower part of Fig. 1). In the step of MIDI parameter rendering, we consider the distribution of the three features:

tempo, normalized IOI, and note coverage (see discussion below). The sampled values are employed to modify the onset time and offset time of each note event in the input MIDI file. In MIDI-DDSP parameter rendering, we consider five major MIDI-DDSP features, namely the volume, volume fluctuation, peak position, vibrato, and brightness, to modify the MIDI file and the sampled parameters into MIDI-DDSP to obtain the final audio. Since the normalization and sampling process of these parameters are similar, they are introduced together as follows.

**Parameter Normalization.** First, denote $x_{ij}$ as the $j$th audio recording under the $i$th expression, only the tempo feature $T_{ij}$ is a piece-level feature. The rest seven features (normalized IOI, note coverage, volume, volume fluctuation, peak position, vibrato, and brightness) are all note-level features. For the $k$th note in the recording $x_{ij}$, the 7-dimensional features are represented as $z_{ijk} = \{\hat{I}_{ijk}, \hat{C}_{ijk}, \hat{V}_{ijk}, \hat{F}_{ijk}, \hat{P}_{ijk}\ , \hat{R}_{ijk}, \hat{B}_{ijk}\}$. It is noted that all the features in $z_{ijk}$ are dimensionless.

Given the pair of onset and offset time $(o_{ijk}, f_{ijk})$ (in second) and the note value[2] $n_{ijk}$ (in beat) for the $k$th note in $x_{ij}$, the tempo feature is described as

$$T_{ij} = \frac{\text{total length}}{\text{total beat}} = \frac{f_{ijK} - o_{ij1}}{\sum_k n_{ijk}}. \tag{1}$$

The inter-onset interval (IOI) for the $k$th note is $I_{ijk} = o_{ij(k+1)} - o_{ijk}$, and its *normalized IOI* (denoted as $\hat{I}_{ijk}$) is defined as

$$\hat{I}_{ijk} = \frac{\text{actual length}}{\text{standard length}} = \frac{I_{ijk}}{(1/K)\sum_k n_{ijk} I_{ijk}}, \tag{2}$$

where $K$ is the number of notes in $x_{ij}$. More specifically, $\hat{I}_{ijk}$ measures whether a note is longer (or shorter) than the notes of the same note value, on average.

The *note coverage* of the $k$th note $\hat{C}_{ijk}$ is the portion of the note duration (i.e., from the onset time to the offset time) in the IOI it occupies. Note coverage is therefore obtained by the following equation

$$\hat{C}_{ijk} = \frac{f_{ijk} - o_{ijk}}{I_{ijk}}. \tag{3}$$

The remaining five features are parameters for MIDI-DDSP. Applying the equations and methods in [25] to the $k$th note in $x_{ij}$, We then have 1) Volume $V_{ijk}$ (in dB), the mean amplitude of the $k$th note; 2) Volume fluctuation $F_{ijk}$ (in dB), the standard deviation of the amplitude curve; 3) Peak position $\hat{P}_{ijk}$, the normalized location of the highest volume in the $k$th note; 4) Vibrato $R_{ijk}$ (in Hz), the mean frequency of vibrato; and 5) Brightness $B_{ijk}$, spectral centroid of the harmonic distribution. It should be noted that we did not compute the attack

[2] Let's take a music piece in 4/4 m as an example: in this case, if the $k$th note is a quarter note, then we have $n_{ijk} = 1$ as it lasts for one beat. Similarly, if the $k$th note is an eighth note, then we have $n_{ijk} = 0.5$.

parameters ourselves; rather, we used the parameters generated by MIDI-DDSP as our synthesis parameter.

It is noted that $V_{ijk}$, $F_{ijk}$, $R_{ijk}$, and $B_{ijk}$ are performed with min-max normalization since MIDI-DDSP requires these features to be scaled within $[0, 1]$. In our experiments, the min-max pairs of these features are $[-80, \max_k(V_{ijk})]$, $[\min_k(F_{ijk}), \max_k(F_{ijk})]$, $[\min_k(R_{ijk}), \max_k(R_{ijk})]$, and $[\min_k(B_{ijk}), \max_k(B_{ijk}]$, respectively.

**Formulation of Gaussian Distribution.** To simplify our model, we assume the tempo feature $T_{ij}$ can be described as a sample from an independent Gaussian distribution $\mathcal{N}_i^T$, and the distribution only depends on the musical expression. In order to reconstruct the Gaussian distribution, we calculate the mean $\mu_i^T$ and the variance ${\sigma_i^T}^2$ from our data, and the Gaussian distribution for $T_{ij}$ is $\mathcal{N}_i^T = \mathcal{N}(\mu_i^T, \sigma_i^T)$. Likewise, we have a similar approach for all note-level features in the set $z_{ijk}$. Suppose, given a feature $\hat{X}_{ijk} \in z_{ijk}$, the Gaussian distribution for the feature $\hat{X}_{ijk}$ is $\mathcal{N}_i^{\hat{X}} = \mathcal{N}(\mu_i^{\hat{X}}, \sigma_i^{\hat{X}})$, where $\mu_i^{\hat{X}}$ and $\sigma_i^{\hat{X}}$ are the mean and standard deviation of the feature computed from the training data.

**MIDI-DDSP Inference.** Given any MIDI file $y$ with $K$ musical notes and $K$ sets of five parameters (volume, volume fluctuation, peak position, vibrato, and brightness) for all notes, the neural network MIDI-DDSP $f$ is capable of synthesizing an audio performance. To select proper parameters for the style of the $i$th expression, the process is similar to the MIDI pre-processing in the inference stage Section. We simply sample all features from their corresponding distribution $K$ times and concatenate all samples as the parameter input. To be more specific, the audio output can be described as $f(y', [p_k]_{k=1}^K)$, where $y'$ is our modified MIDI file and the $k$th set of parameters is defined as $p_k = \{\pi_k \sim \mathcal{N}_i^{\hat{X}} | \hat{X} \in \{\hat{V}, \hat{F}, \hat{P}, \hat{R}, \hat{B}\}\}$.

In practice, the distribution is adjusted to a truncated Gaussian distribution during every sampling process in MIDI pre-processing in the inference stage Section and MIDI-DDSP inference Section, which helps the stability of the output result. The upper bound and lower bound of the truncated Gaussian distribution is set to $[\mu + \sigma, \mu - \sigma]$.

**Table 1.** Mapping from dynamic markings to the volume parameter ($V_{ijk}$) in MIDI-DDSP.

| *ppp* | *pp* | *p* | *mp* | *mf* | *f* | *ff* | *fff* |
|---|---|---|---|---|---|---|---|
| .164 | .313 | .484 | .564 | .664 | .773 | .890 | 1.00 |

**Table 2.** Mapping from articulation symbols to the attack parameter in MIDI-DDSP.

| staccato | accent | marcato | tenuto | legato |
|---|---|---|---|---|
| .545 | .600 | .655 | .545 | .227 |

**MIDI Pre-processing in the Inference Stage.** Given the input MIDI file $y$, we can obtain its Tempo $T$ and the $k$th onset-offset pairs of its note events $(o_k, f_k)$. After sampling the targeted tempo $\tau \sim \mathcal{N}_i^T$, we need to scale the original tempo to the target one by setting new onset times and offset times for $y$ as $(o'_k, f'_k) = (\tau' o_k, \tau' f_k)$, where $\tau' = \frac{T}{\tau}$. Next, we adjust IOIs in $y$ by sampling normalized IOI $\iota_k \sim \mathcal{N}_i^{\hat{I}}$ $K$ times and resetting the new onset time as $o''_k = \iota_{k-1}(o'_k - o'_{k-1}) + S_{k-2}$, where $S_k = \sum_1^k o''_k$. Finally, the new offset time $f''_k$ is determined by the $k$th sample from the note coverage distribution $\kappa_k \sim \mathcal{N}_i^{\hat{C}}$ and set to $f''_k = o''_k + \kappa_k(o''_{k+1} - o''_k)$. The pairs of $(o''_k, f''_k)$ will be the onset-offset pair for the modified MIDI file $y'$.

### 3.3 Model 2: Gaussian MusicXML-DDSP

Using musicXML files as the input of a parameter-controlled EMS model has the advantage that the articulation symbols (which are omitted in the MIDI format) can be directly parsed into the system. That means the musicXML format can serve as an interface for users who want to designate articulation symbols to specific notes in the input. We have developed a musicXML parser that converts XML files into a user-friendly format, enabling users to upload their edited scores directly and extract the necessary data seamlessly. This model is denoted as Gaussian MusicXML-DDSP.

We built a simple, one-to-one mapping table which maps the articulation symbols to MIDI-DDSP parameters. The mappings are built according to domain knowledge. For example, Tables 1 and 2 outline the parameter ranges of dynamics and articulations. To map the values of the volume parameter, we have utilized Avid's Sibelius 5 [23], a notation software that offers default MIDI velocity values associated with dynamic markings and has normalized the velocity differences accordingly. Similarly, to map the values of the attack parameter, we have consulted the definition of articulation velocity in MuseScore instruments.xml and conducted experiments using the MIDI-DDSP system with the writer's knowledge of sound sense. This approach ensures that our simulation accurately captures the intricacies of musical expressions.

In the synthesis stage, a note without articulation/ dynamic symbols is simply processed with the parameters rendered from Gaussian MIDI-DDSP. If a dynamic marking exists, we need to take care of both the volume parameter from Gaussian MIDI-DDSP and the one from the mapping in Table 1. Here we adopt a scaling scheme with *mf* as the default volume. For example, if a note is rendered a value 0.661 and is marked with *p*, then the modified volume parameter becomes 0.661 (rendered volume)×0.484 (volume of *p*)/0.664 (volume of *mf*)=0.482.

### 3.4 Model 3: End-to-End Model

Unlike the previous method of using various low-level features as controllable inputs, the end-to-end model only takes MIDI and EMT as input and directly generates the final audio. The upper part of Fig. 1 shows the flowchart of the model. In view of the fact that such a task is very similar to multi-speaker text-to-speech (TTS) with text and speaker label as input, we adopted the architecture of state-of-the-art TTS model StyleSpeech [17] and made some adjustments such as to fit the purpose of our EMS task. The main four changes are as follows. First, the end-to-end model takes a sequence of midi pitches as input and converts them into note-level pitch embeddings. This part replaces the phoneme embedding in StyleSpeech. Second, we replaced the Mel-Style encoder, which was originally used for extracting speaker-dependent features, with performer embedding and expression embedding. The two embeddings are fed into several linear layers and then add up to form a style vector, which is used as a feature to control the intermediate layers of the encoder and decoder. It should be noted that the performer embedding is required only in the training stage. Third, Since the pitch and duration information is already provided by the MIDI input, we removed the variance adapters that were originally used to predict pitch, energy, and duration. In our preliminary experiments, we found that predicting energy did not improve overall generation results. Finally, we utilized Parallel WaveGAN (PWG) as the vocoder to convert mel-spectrogram to audio [26].

## 4 Experiment

### 4.1 Experiment Setup

To evaluate the performance of the EMS models, we consider two experiments: 1) an EMT classification task on the generated audio, serving as an objective evaluation method, and 2) a questionnaire-based subjective evaluation. The purpose of EMT classification is to understand the machine's ability to distinguish the performance of different EMTs. This also represents a first attempt in performing deep learning algorithms on EMT classification; the classification result will then be compared to the previously reported result based on the support vector machine (SVM) [13]. We report the result with a confusion table and the values of precision (P), recall (R), and F1-score (F1).

The subjective test of the EMS task is quite challenging. Executing a subjective test that covers all the EMTs in the dataset is unrealistic as the loading for the subjects is too much. Therefore, we have to select a subset of the EMTs rather than all in our questionnaire. Our questionnaire contains two parts. In the first part, we provided a few recordings from the SCREAM-MAC-EMT dataset and asked participants to guess the EMT that the performer interpreted in the recording. The questions were in the multiple-choice format: participants just need to select one out of the five choices. This part represents a background survey for us to understand the feasibility as well as the limitations of how humans judge the EMT.

In the second part of the questionnaire, for each question, we present four audio recordings, which are the same piece of music 1) from the dataset (i.e., Ground truth), 2) synthesized by the End-to-End model, 3) Gaussian MIDI-DDSP, and 4) Gaussian MusicXML-DDSP, all are with the same EMT. The name of the song and the corresponding EMT are presented to the participants. Participants are asked to listen to the recording and answer four questions (Q1) Which performance sounds most like the EMT? (Q2) Which performance sounds least like the EMT? (Q3) Which recording sounds most like a human performance? (Q4) Which recording sounds least like a human performance? Six sets of questions were given, and therefore 24 audio recordings from both humans and models were presented. Designing the questions in such an EMT-informed and comparative manner is to save participants' time, as judging the EMT of one recording at a time is somehow beyond human effort.

We selected five EMTs for the second part of the subject test (see Table 3). We removed the EMTs which are too similar to each other and difficult to distinguish. For example, Affettuoso is removed since it is hard to be distinguished from Cantabile according to our domain knowledge. Also, we select the EMTs according to the EMT classification results: the selected EMTs should contain the ones which achieve a high F1-score (e.g., Tranquillo) and the ones which perform badly (e.g., Cantabile). Two songs are taken to generate the audio recording: Theme of Twelve Variations on '*Ah vous dirai-je, Maman*' by W. A. Mozart, and *Élégie* by Gabriel Faureé. All the generated results are transported to the same key.

We calculate two evaluation metrics for each model in our subjective test: 1) EMS performance score, being the number of votes in Q1 minus the number of votes in Q2, and 2) human-like performance score, being the number of votes in Q3 minus the number of votes in Q4. For example, for the recordings synthesized with Scherzando, if 10 people said the recordings of model X is most like Scherzando while 3 people said model X is least like it, then the EMS performance score is $10 - 3 = 7$, the net votes for the model X. The higher the value, the better the model performs.

### 4.2 EMT Classification

In this section of our experiment, we use an expression classifier based on an Audio Spectrogram Transformer (AST) to evaluate the generated audio [7]. We took the pre-trained model from the official AST repo and replaced the last output layer with a linear layer that outputs 11 expression classes. We split the violin dataset into 9/1 train/valid, and fine tune the whole model for 5k steps. The batch size is set to 8, and we use the Adam optimizer with learning rate sets to 1e-5 for fine-tuning.

Figure 2 shows the confusion matrix of the 11 classes of EMTs. It can be seen that major confusions are in certain EMTs, demonstrated by the low recall in Cantabile, and the low precision Affetuoso and Grazioso. The left part of Table 3 lists the resulting precision, recall, and F1-score of selected EMT. Compared to

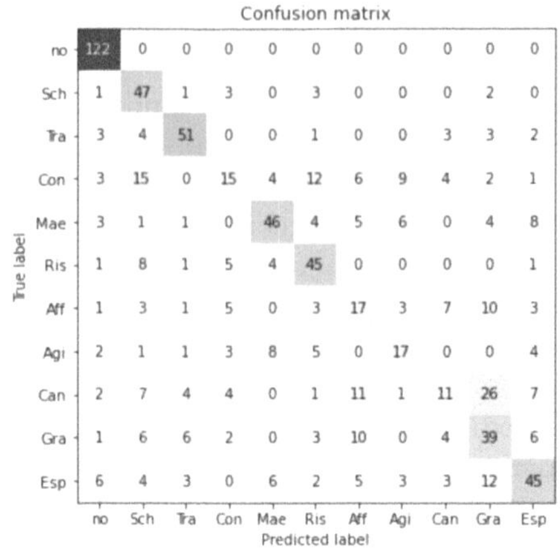


**Fig. 2.** Confusion matrix of EMT classification.

the results reported in [13], the classification model adopted in this work outperforms the SVM model in Expressivo and Maestoso, while still falling behind in Scherzando, Tranquilo, and Cantabile. Generally speaking, though the adopted deep learning model performs well in various audio classification tasks, it does not gain strong benefits in EMT classification.

### 4.3 Subjective Evaluation

**Results of the Pre-test.** The results of the first part of the subjective test reveal the challenges for humans to "guess the EMT" in a multiple-choice format. As an informal test, we just report two noteworthy observations. First, for the recordings in Scherzando, only 22% of the participants could guess them correctly, while 44% participants guessed Cantabile and 28% guessed Tranquillo. This is surprising when compared to the EMT classification result, where Scherzando actually achieves a high recall at 82.5%. We found that such a result is hard to discuss since it not only depends on the participant's understanding of Scherzando but also depends on their understanding of other EMTs listed in the question. The participant's choice turns unreliable in this case, as the definition of each EMT in their mind would be interdependent when putting multiple EMTs together.

Second, for the recordings in Tranquillo, 44% of participants correctly answered it, while 26% of them guessed them as Maestoso. Again, Tranquillo is an EMT which can be classified the best with machine learning models (Recall = 76.1%). This somehow indicates the limitation of our experiment scenario: some EMTs require more contextual information in order to be properly identified. Tranquillo is the EMT which highly depends on volume and the "tranquility" can be effectively perceived only when compared to other louder recordings. Apart from volume, there are arguably no strong features that can help to distinguish a Tranquillo performance from others. These observations suggest us not to use multiple-choice questions to study the subjective perception of EMTs.

**Table 3.** The experiment results, including the EMT classification (precision, recall, and F1-score) of EMT classification and the average EMS and human-like performance scores in the subject test. The four models under comparison are from the dataset (GT), end-to-end model (E2E), Gaussian MIDI-DDSP (MIDI), and Gaussian musicXML-DDSP (XML).

| | Objective test | | | | Subjective test | | | | | | | |
|---|---|---|---|---|---|---|---|---|---|---|---|---|
| | [13] | This work | | | EMS performance | | | | Human-like | | | |
| | F1 | Pre | Rec | F1 | GT | E2E | MIDI | XML | GT | E2E | MIDI | XML |
| Scherzando | .763 | .490 | .825 | .614 | 20.5 | −16 | −10 | **5.5** | 16.5 | −9 | **0** | −7 |
| Tranquillo | .800 | .739 | .761 | .750 | 30 | 0 | −29 | **1** | 21 | −15 | **−2** | −4 |
| Cantabile | .532 | .344 | .149 | .208 | 16 | **1** | −4 | −13 | 19 | −12 | **3** | −10 |
| Espressivo | .451 | .584 | .506 | .542 | 25 | −6 | −15 | **−4** | 24 | −12 | −7 | **−5** |
| Maestoso | .618 | .676 | .590 | .630 | 18 | **9** | −23 | −4 | 22 | −11 | **−3** | −8 |

**Model Comparison.** In the second part of the questionnaire, 32 participants (more than one-half have more than five years of music training experience) answered the questions, and the average scores of all the questions are summarized in the right part of Table 3. First, for EMS performance, although GT unsurprisingly outperforms other models, there are still differences in performance across different EMTs. For instance, the majority of participants voted GT for Tranquillo (EMS performance score = 30), while interestingly, for Cantabile the net votes for GT dropped to 16, only the number of half of the participants. In other words, listeners consider that the gap between human performance and the synthesized audio is not that wide for Cantabile, in comparison to Tranquillo. This is probably because that there is less consistency among humans in telling the exact meaning of the EMT. Such a gap between humans and machines is somehow related to the EMT classification results (see the left part of Table 3) though the relationship is not significant.

Second, we observe that when the EMS performance score of GT is lower, participants are more likely to take the End-to-End model as the best EMS model (see the case of Maestoso and Cantabile). Conversely, when the EMS performance score of GT is high, participants tend to select the Gaussian MusicXML-DDSP model as the best EMS model (see the case of Tranquillo and Espressivo). This implies that the features related to the GT-prevailing EMTs (e.g., Tranquillo and Expressivo) can be more explicitly described with the note-level features (e.g., IOI, volume, etc.) and the articulations. On the other hand, for those EMTs whose meanings are vague (e.g., Cantabile), end-to-end modeling could outperform parameter-controlled approaches. To summarize, the performance of different models on EMS highly depends on the target EMT.

Third, in the right part of Table 3, the resulting human-like performance scores behave quite differently from EMS performance scores. In general, people prefer Gaussian MIDI-DDSP, followed by Gaussian musicXML-DDSP and the end-to-end model, regardless of the chosen target EMT. To summarize, when discussing the music performance generation problem using state-of-the-art neural synthesizers, some models appear to be consistently better than others and the trend is independent from the target EMT. On the other hand, the EMS task is indeed more complicated than music performance generation as the ranks of different models depend on the target EMT.

Lastly, it should be mentioned that the inference time of the three models differs a lot. While generating a 40-s music clip using the end-to-end model costs less than 2 s with GPU, the inference time using either MIDI-DDSP or musicXML-DDSP models on the same clip takes around 3–4 min. This is probably because MIDI-DDSP is built upon the recurrent neural networks, which tend to be slower in the inference stage.

## 5 Concluding Remarks

The three EMS models we proposed in this paper cover several aspects related to the development of an EMS system, including the EMT ambiguities, note-level control, articulation, limitation of human listeners, and inference time. According to the experiment results, we conclude that none of the three models are found to be consistently superior to the others. Besides, we have also identified the trade-off between the inference time and the human-like performance score. We also observe that even considering the state-of-the-art models, EMT classification is still a task more challenging than general audio classification, and therefore, the EMS task is more challenging than the traditional music audio generation task.

Our experiments on EMS also indicate the sophisticated relation between the EMS performance, as well as the gap between humans and machines. Understanding the human-level limitations in interpreting and judging EMTs in performance could be as important as training a model that fits the data of human performance. Hence, future research in this area should include more human factors that may influence expressive performances.

**Disclosure of Interests.** The authors have no competing interests to declare that are relevant to the content of this article.

## References

1. Cancino-Chacón, C.E., Grachten, M., Goebl, W., Widmer, G.: Computational models of expressive music performance: a comprehensive and critical review. Front. Digit. Human. **5**, 25 (2018)
2. Chang, L.: A comparative statistical analysis of music styles (seventeenth-nineteenth centuries). Interdisc. Sci. Rev. **45**(4), 581–594 (2020)

3. De Poli, G., Rodà, A., Vidolin, A.: Note-by-note analysis of the influence of expressive intentions and musical structure in violin performance. J. New Music Res. **27**(3), 293–321 (1998)
4. Desain, P., Honing, H.: Does expressive timing in music performance scale proportionally with tempo? Psychol. Res. **56**(4), 285–292 (1994)
5. Dong, H.W., Zhou, C., Berg-Kirkpatrick, T., McAuley, J.: Deep performer: score-to-audio music performance synthesis. In: IEEE International Conference on Acoustics, Speech and Signal Processing (ICASSP), pp. 951–955 (2022)
6. Engel, J., Hantrakul, L., Gu, C., Roberts, A.: DDSP: differentiable digital signal processing. arXiv preprint arXiv:2001.04643 (2020)
7. Gong, Y., Chung, Y., Glass, J.R.: AST: audio spectrogram transformer. In: Interspeech 2021. 22nd Annual Conference of the International Speech Communication Association, pp. 571–575. Brno, Czechia (2021)
8. Honing, H.: Structure and interpretation of rhythm in music. In: The Psychology of Music, pp. 369–404 (2013)
9. Huang, C.Z.A., et al.: Music transformer. arXiv preprint arXiv:1809.04281 (2018)
10. Hung, T.Y., Hsiao, Y.W., Su, L.: Structure-independent factors in expressive timing: a preliminary study on violin solo performance. In: Proceedings of the 22nd International Society for Music Information Retrieval Conference (ISMIR). Online (2021)
11. Jonason, N., Sturm, B.L., Thomé, C.: The control-synthesis approach for making expressive and controllable neural music synthesizers. In: Joint Conference on AI Music Creativity (AIMC 2020) (2020)
12. Lerch, A., Arthur, C., Pati, A., Gururani, S.: An interdisciplinary review of music performance analysis. Trans. Int. Soc. Music Inf. Retrieval **3**(1), 221–245 (2020)
13. Li, P.C., Su, L., Yang, Y.H., Su, A.W., et al.: Analysis of expressive musical terms in violin using score-informed and expression-based audio features. In: Proceedings of the 16th International Society for Music Information Retrieval Conference (ISMIR), pp. 809–815 (2015)
14. Lindström, E.: Impact of melodic organization on perceived structure and emotional expression in music. Music Sci. **10**(1), 85–117 (2006)
15. Maestre, E., Ramírez, R., Kersten, S., Serra, X.: Expressive concatenative synthesis by reusing samples from real performance recordings. Comput. Music. J. **33**(4), 23–42 (2009)
16. Marchini, M., Ramirez, R., Papiotis, P., Maestre, E.: The sense of ensemble: a machine learning approach to expressive performance modelling in string quartets. J. New Music Res. **43**(3), 303–317 (2014)
17. Min, D., Lee, D.B., Yang, E., Hwang, S.J.: Meta-stylespeech: multi-speaker adaptive text-to-speech generation. In: International Conference on Machine Learning, pp. 7748–7759 (2021)
18. Molina-Solana, M., Arcos, J.L., Gomez, E.: Using expressive trends for identifying violin performers. In: ISMIR, pp. 495–500 (2008)
19. Narmour, E.: The Analysis and Cognition of Melodic Complexity: The Implication-Realization Model. University of Chicago Press, Chicago (1992)
20. Povel, D.J.: Temporal structure of performed music: some preliminary observations. Acta Physiol. (Oxf) **41**(4), 309–320 (1977)
21. Rector, M.: Historical trends in expressive timing strategies: Chopin's etude, op. 25 no. 1. Empir. Musicol. Rev. **15**(3–4), 176–201 (2021)
22. Shih, C.C., et al.: Analysis and synthesis of the violin playing style of Heifetz and oistrakh. In: Proceedings of the 20th International Conference on Digital Audio Effects (DAFx-17) (2017)

23. Technology, A.: Sibelius reference (2022). https://resources.avid.com/SupportFiles/Sibelius/2022.5/Sibelius_Reference.pdf. Accessed 9 Feb 2023
24. Wang, B., Yang, Y.H.: Performancenet: score-to-audio music generation with multi-band convolutional residual network. In: Proceedings of the AAAI Conference on Artificial Intelligence, vol. 33, pp. 1174–1181 (2019)
25. Wu, Y., et al.: Midi-DDSP: detailed control of musical performance via hierarchical modeling. arXiv preprint arXiv:2112.09312 (2021)
26. Yamamoto, R., Song, E., Kim, J.: Parallel WaveGAN: a fast waveform generation model based on generative adversarial networks with multi-resolution spectrogram. In: Proceedings of the IEEE International Conference on Acoustics, Speech and Signal Processing (ICASSP), pp. 6199–6203 (2020)
27. Yang, C.H., Li, P.C., Su, A.W., Su, L., Yang, Y.H., et al.: Automatic violin synthesis using expressive musical term features. In: Proceedings of the 19th International Conference on Digital Audio Effects (DAFx). Brno, Czech Republic (2016)
28. Zhao, Y., Fazekas, G., Sandler, M.: Violinist identification using note-level timbre feature distributions. In: IEEE International Conference on Acoustics. Speech and Signal Processing (ICASSP), pp. 601–605. Milano, Italy (2022)

# Towards User Autonomy in Electricity Market by Evaluating Incentive Sufficiency for Demand Response Participation

He-Teng Cao, Bo-Heng Chen, and Kun-Ta Chuang(✉)

Department of Computer Science and Information Engineering, National Cheng Kung University, Tainan, Taiwan
{htcao,bhchen}@netdb.csie.ncku.edu.tw, ktchuang@mail.ncku.edu.tw

**Abstract.** With the continuous growth of electricity demand during peak times, demand response (DR) programs have emerged as an effective tool for load management. However, incentive-based DR programs often face issues of instability and uncertainty. Traditional methods typically involved direct control of user equipment to reduce electricity use, but this approach is not feasible for households without controllable devices. As such, this paper discusses how to evaluate the existing instability and uncertainty of incentive-based DR by only providing load reduction incentives and signals to households and proposes an algorithm to find feasible plans. We propose an innovative 2-phase Monte Carlo Simulation Genetic Algorithm (2P-MCSGA) designed to maximize the likelihood of achieving load reduction within a specific budget. Our approach integrates Monte Carlo simulation with genetic algorithms, employing constraint relaxation and gene repair techniques to enhance solution feasibility and algorithm efficiency. This method ensures both the practicality and effectiveness of the DR plan, offering a novel solution to the challenges of incentive-based demand response.

**Keywords:** Demand Response · Genetic Algorithm · Constraint Relaxation · Monte Carlo Simulation

## 1 Introduction

### 1.1 Background

To date, global electricity consumption is currently increasing at an unprecedented rate. To meet the high demand during peak periods, expanding power plant capacity is a practical solution. However, it is important to note that peak periods constitute only a small portion of total operational time, suggesting that

© The Author(s), under exclusive license to Springer Nature Singapore Pte Ltd. 2025
W.-T. Chu et al. (Eds.): TAAI 2024, CCIS 2414, pp. 17–32, 2025.
https://doi.org/10.1007/978-981-96-4589-3_2

the power resources allocated for these temporary spikes are underutilized most of the time.[1]

Demand response offers an alternative solution. Specifically, demand response is a strategy that encourages users to reduce their electricity consumption during peak periods or shift it to off-peak periods through economic incentives or price signals [12]. This approach not only alleviates peak demand pressure, but also enhances the economic and environmental performance of the power system. Industrial and commercial users have been widely applied in numerous countries. Recent studies indicate that residential consumption accounts for almost 40[2], suggesting that the potential to use demand response in residential users is feasible. Exploring residential demand response will provide more flexible and diverse options for the implementation of demand response.

Numerous studies [15] indicate that incentive-based demand response can directly manage household loads, such as controlling home appliances through automated systems. These studies suggest that such direct control demand response programs may also lead to low participation rates or cause users to opt out due to prolonged scheduling requirements.

### 1.2 Overview of Electricity Market

Because individual residential units offer minimal reduction capacity, a position called a load aggregator exists in the day-ahead electricity market [15]. Load aggregators are pivotal in the demand response market as they combine several small loads into a single larger, manageable load and engage in market transactions for these loads.

The electricity market plays a vital role in power system operations by maintaining the balance between electricity supply and demand and optimizing the distribution of electricity resources. The day-ahead market forms an essential segment of the electricity market, where transactions are conducted a day or more in advance. As illustrated in Fig. 1, in the day-ahead market, electricity producers and buyers engage in trading based on anticipated demand, typically through auctions held the previous day, allowing generators to ready themselves for production[3] [5].

### 1.3 Feasible Demand Response Plans

A viable demand response plan is essential for load aggregators, involving tasks such as determining the bid amount, bid capacity, and methods to encourage

[1] Ministry of Economic Affairs, "Promoting Demand Bidding Management Is a Global Trend, Which Is More Economical and Environmentally Friendly than Increasing the Number of Peak-Load Units," available at: https://www.moea.gov.tw/Mns/populace/news/News.aspx?kind=1&menu_id=40&newsid=108056.

[2] U.S Energy Information Administration, "Use of Electricity", available at: https://www.eia.gov/energyexplained/electricity/use-of-electricity.php.

[3] California ISO, "Demand Response - Proxy Demand Resource," available at: https://www.caiso.com/library/demand-response-proxy-demand-resource.

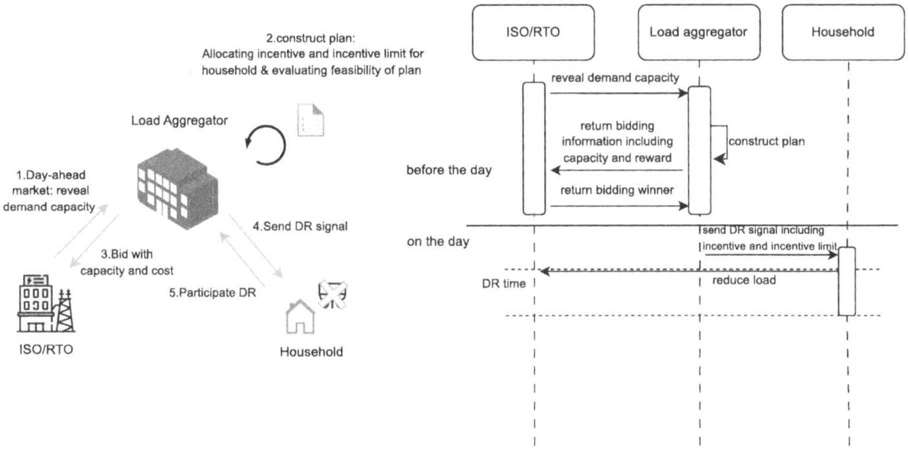


**Fig. 1.** Overview of day-ahead market.

residents to decrease their load. Load aggregators incur penalties if they do not achieve the bid capacity.

To encourage homeowners to get involved in demand response initiatives and to harness the potential for residential demand response, this article examines methods to create demand response strategies that do not involve direct control over household loads. In this context, homeowners maintain authority over their power consumption and decrease their load when they receive demand response notifications. Consequently, homeowners are not exposed to any financial risk.

Despite the inherent unpredictability of residential load reduction, aggregators face the risk of fluctuating responses. To the best of our knowledge, this is the first study to focus on evaluating and alleviating the risks encountered by aggregators in these conditions.

## 2 Related Works

**Demand Response.** Formally, [15] adopts an incentive-based demand response strategy to reduce the expenses of electricity procurement in the wholesale market by managing user devices. Despite this, [11] highlights that direct load control struggles with low customer signup rates and significant dropout rates. [1] constructs a model of user preferences and suggests optimal appliance usage schedules according to predicted prices. In the work of [10], deep neural networks are employed to forecast prices, and reinforcement learning is utilized to adjust incentive rates to enhance benefits for both service providers and customers. [9] employs RL to learn operation policy of electricity market to maximize the profit of load service providers.

Furthermore, [2] carried out preliminary experiments on demand response driven by incentives and evaluated different reward strategies, documenting the outcomes. According to pilot trial report[4] a significant challenge is to ensure that residential customers meet the anticipated load reduction targets.

Most studies focused on incentive-based demand response do not consider the risks encountered by load aggregators when they bid for load reduction capacity in the electricity market. This paper provides a comprehensive examination of how to assess the effectiveness of residential load reduction without the need to directly control loads or appliances, allowing load aggregators to develop and assess plans as well as their viability within bid capacity and budget limits prior to bidding.

**Stochastic Knapsack Problem**
In this paper, the problem of formulating plans is transformed into the stochastic knapsack problem. The stochastic knapsack problem is regarded as a classical NP-HARD combinatorial optimization problem [3]. Numerous studies have proposed solutions for the stochastic knapsack problem. For example, [3] introduced a heuristic algorithm to address the "zero return if broken" scenario, while [8] presented an exhaustive-like algorithm to tackle a variant known as the Constrained Knapsack Problem. However, most studies assume that the weights of items are revealed once placed into the knapsack, which is different from the context of this paper. Some research addresses variants of the stochastic knapsack problem that are orthogonal to the scenario described in this study. Therefore, heuristic algorithms must be developed to address the unique context discussed in this paper.

**Genetic Algorithms**
Inspired by the principles of natural selection and genetics, genetic algorithms are heuristic search methods. Their strong global search abilities have led to their application in a variety of domains [4,7,17]. In this paper, we utilize GA to iteratively optimize demand response strategies. By leveraging its global search ability, we refine plans to enhance the likelihood of achieving higher success rates within the given budget constraints.

# 3 Problem Formulation

## 3.1 Preliminary

In the electricity market, load aggregators evaluate demand response schemes implemented for household and decide on the bid reduction amount and budget for market bidding. This paper proposes a heuristic algorithm to compute the most feasible scheme, maximizing the probability of achieving the target load reduction within a given budget. During the formulation process, the algorithm allocates rewards and reward caps for each household, evaluating the feasibility of the scheme and ultimately providing a plan for the load aggregator to execute. Before proceeding, some necessary symbols and definitions are set as follows:

[4] "Energy conversation initiatives", SoftBank Power, available at: https://www.sbpower.co.jp/action/sdgs/demand-response/?lang=ja.

**Definition 1 (Set of Residences):** The group of residences gathered by the load aggregator to participate in the demand response program. Denoted as $U = \{u_1, u_2, \ldots, u_p\}$.

**Definition 2 (Set of Rewards):** To incentivize different behaviors of residences, the load aggregator should define a set of rewards. During the formulation process of plan, an element from the set is allocated to specific residences. The unit is dollar/kWh. Denoted as $R = \{r_1, r_2, \ldots, r_k\}$.

**Definition 3 (Rewarded Load Reduction Upper Bound Set):** Due to limited profit from bidding, the load aggregator should defines a set of rewarded load reduction upper bound. During the formulation process, an element from the set is allocated to specific residences. Load reductions beyond the cap do not receive rewards, whereas reductions within the cap are rewarded based on the reduction amount multiplied by the allocated reward. Denoted as $D = \{d_1, d_2, \ldots, d_n\}$.

**Definition 4 (Budget):** The budget $B$ provided by the load aggregator for the demand response program. The maximum total budget for executing the incentive plan must not exceed this amount.

**Definition 5 (Target Load Reduction):** The target load reduction $M$ set by the load aggregator, theoretically equivalent to the actual bid reduction amount.

### 3.2 Problem Statement

According to [16], the stochastic knapsack problem is defined as finding the optimal $y$ that maximizes the probability of exceeding a threshold. This paper corresponds the problem to the multi-choice stochastic knapsack problem. The problem is expressed in Eq. (1).

$$\begin{aligned}
\max_{y} \quad & P\left(\sum_{i=1}^{p}\sum_{j=1}^{n*k} l_{ij}y_{ij} \geq M\right) \\
\text{s.t.} \quad & \sum_{i=1}^{p}\sum_{j=1}^{n*k} c_{ij}y_{ij} \leq B \\
& \sum_{j} y_{ij} = 1, \forall i \in U \\
& y_{ij} \in \{0, 1\}, \forall i \in U, j \in R \times D
\end{aligned} \tag{1}$$

$l_{ij}$ is a known random vector. In this paper, the random vector of household responses is established using historical demand response data. $y_{ij}$ represents a binary indicator indicating whether an item is selected. In the context of this problem, the plan formulation process requires selecting a specific set of rewards and reward caps for each household. $M$ is the given threshold, corresponding to

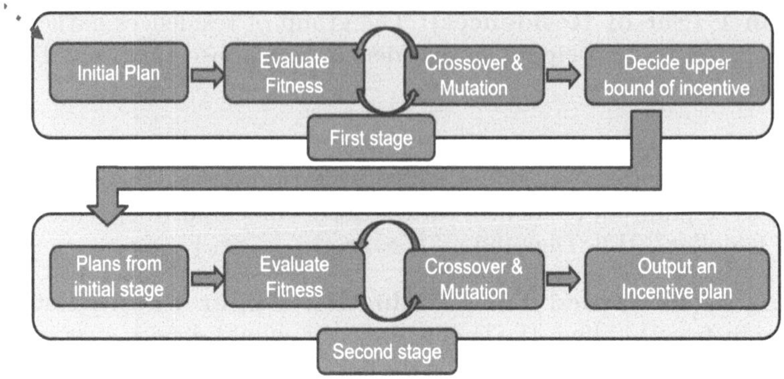


**Fig. 2.** Overview of Two-stage genetic algorithm.

the target reduction. $c_{ij}$ represents the weight of the item, determined by the product of the rewarded load reduction upper bound and the reward. $B$ is the given constraint, considered as the budget of the load aggregator. Ultimately, the objective is aiming to find a plan which has the maximum probability of achieving the target load reduction within the budget, which will be executed by the load aggregator.

# 4 Methodology

This study introduces a two-phase genetic algorithm to create and refine customized incentive schemes for load aggregators. Initially, constraint relaxation strategies are employed to formulate the preliminary plans, which are then optimized to stay within budget. Figure 2 shows the workflow, and this section details each component.

## 4.1 Gene Design

In this study, each gene represents a customer and contains two main pieces of information:

1. **Incentive Level**: The element selected from set of rewards.
2. **Rewarded Load Reduction Upper Bound**: The element selected from rewarded load reduction upper bound set.

The gene is represented as:

$$\text{Gene} = (\text{Incentive Level}, \text{Rewarded Load Reduction Upper Bound})$$

For example, a gene might be represented as (1, 3), indicating that the customer will receive one dollar for each unit of reduced load, with a maximum rewarded reduction of three units.

A chromosome is composed of all genes, with the size equal to the set of customers. Each chromosome represents a complete incentive plan. This means a chromosome contains the incentive level and maximum rewarded load reduction for all customers.

The chromosome is represented as:

$$\text{Chromosome} = [\text{Gene}_1, \text{Gene}_2, \ldots, \text{Gene}_c]$$

where $\text{Gene}_i$ represents the information for the $i$-th customer. This design allows each chromosome to flexibly represent different incentive plans and find the optimal reward allocation through the genetic algorithm.

### 4.2 Fitness Function

In a genetic algorithm, the fitness function evaluates the quality of each individual based on the problem's specific requirements. In this study, the fitness function is designed to find the demand response plan with the highest probability of achieving the total load reduction without exceeding the budget, as described in Eq. (1).

Prior to assessing the overall success probability of a plan, it is essential to evaluate each customer's load reduction. Initially, this study employs historical demand response data from residences to determine the likelihood of each customer attaining various load reductions at different incentive levels.

For example, for a residential customer, a table is established based on the customer's historical records, representing the frequency of load reductions achieved at different incentive levels. The size of the table is the product of the size of the reward set $k$ and the size of the rewarded load reduction upper bound set $n$. During the table creation, historical load reductions are discretized. To avoid overestimation of the load reduction, we truncate the decimal values.

To understand the behavior of residences at specific incentive levels, the frequency of achieving a specific load reduction for a customer is divided by the total number of times the load aggregator assigned that incentive level to the customer, as shown in Eq. (2) below:

$$p_k(d = d_n, r = r_{k,j}) = \frac{x_{k,j,n}}{\sum_{i=1}^{m} x_{k,j,i}}. \tag{2}$$

Here $p_k(d = d_n, r = r_{k,j})$ represents the probability that the $k$-th residence reduces a specific amount $d_n$ of electricity usage at the incentive level $r_{k,j}$. In addition, $x_{k,j,n}$ denotes the historical count of instances where the $k$-th residence achieved a load reduction of $d_n$ at the incentive level $r_{k,j}$. The term $\sum_{i=1}^{m} x_{k,j,i}$ denotes the total count of instances where the $k$-th residence achieved any reduced load $d_i$ under the incentive level $r_{k,j}$, also indicating the total instances the load aggregator allocated that incentive level to the residence.

Next, we illustrate with an example where there are three households and three load reduction levels. The overall success rate of the plan can be estimated, which can be expressed by the following Eq. (3):

$$
\begin{aligned}
&P(D_1 + D_2 + D_3 \geq D) = \\
&P(D_1 = d_3, D_2 = d_3, D_3 = d_3) + P(D_1 = d_3, D_2 = d_3, D_3 = d_2) + \\
&P(D_1 = d_3, D_2 = d_3, D_3 = d_1) + P(D_1 = d_3, D_2 = d_2, D_3 = d_3) \\
&+ \cdots
\end{aligned} \tag{3}
$$

This equation represents all possible combinations where the sum of $D_1 + D_2 + D_3$ is at least the target value $D$. Each probability $P(D_i = d_j)$ represents the probability of the $i$-th residence achieving a specific load reduction at a given incentive level.

However, when there are $k$ residences and the size of combination of the rewarded load reduction upper bound set and reward set is $n$, we will have $n^k$ terms to calculate. The vast amount of calculation terms results in extremely high computational overhead, rendering it infeasible to perform.

Therefore, directly enumerating all possible combinations to calculate the overall plan success rate is infeasible. An alternative algorithm or approximation technique is required to address this issue more efficiently.

To address the issue of high computational complexity, this study employs the Monte Carlo Simulation method. Monte Carlo simulation is an approach that estimates outcomes through random sampling, making it particularly effective for managing high-dimensional and intricate probability issues [6, 14]. Specifically, the Monte Carlo simulation is used to estimate the probability of achieving the total load reduction target $D$ without exceeding the budget. The basic steps of the Monte Carlo simulation method are as follows:

1. **Random Sampling**: Based on the historical data of each customer, generate a random set of load reductions for the customers. These load reductions are sampled according to the previously mentioned probability tables.
2. **Calculate Total Load Reduction**: For each sampling, calculate the total load reduction for all customers.
3. **Evaluate Target Achievement**: Determine whether the total load reduction meets or exceeds the target $D$. If it does, record a successful iteration.
4. **Repeat Steps 1–3**: Repeat the above steps multiple times to obtain sufficient sample data.
5. **Estimate Success Probability**: Finally, the number of successful iterations is divided by the total number of simulations to obtain the estimated probability of achieving the total load reduction target $D$ under the given incentive plan, as shown in Eq. (4):

$$
F(S) = \frac{\text{Number of successful iterations}}{\text{Total number of iterations}} \tag{4}
$$

### 4.3 Constraint Relaxation

Since the initial solutions are generated randomly, it is possible that the whole population might have zero fitness values, as they do not fulfill all the constraints.

To address this issue, we introduce constraint relaxation techniques [13]. By relaxing some constraints in the initial stage, we can generate some initial feasible solutions with non-zero fitness values under the relaxed constraints. As the algorithm advances, we reinstate the original constraints, leading the solutions to comply with all the original restrictions, ultimately identifying the best incentive plan within the budget and reduction requirements.

In the first phase, a constraint relaxation technique is adopted. Specifically, the budget constraint is changed from a hard constraint to a soft constraint, and a static penalty function $G(S)$ is adopted. This penalty function is incorporated into the fitness evaluation, as shown below:

$$F^*(S) = F(S) - G(S), \tag{5}$$

where $G(S) = \frac{t}{T}$, and $T$ represents the total number of Monte Carlo simulations, and $t$ represents times of both load reduction and budget are exceeded in simulations. This penalty function implies that while the budget is no longer strictly enforced, any violations of the budget constraint are accounted for during the simulation process.

In the first stage, because the overall plan cost limit is not considered, the Rewarded Load Reduction Upper Bound for each customer does not need to be determined, thereby reducing the search space. Therefore, the upper bound for each gene is defined as the maximum value in the set of rewarded load reduction upper bounds. This approach enables us to more effectively identify initial viable solutions and reintroduce budget limits in later stages to achieve the optimal solution. Specifically, in the first stage, our objective function and constraints can be expressed as:

$$\max_{y} P\left(\sum_{i=1}^{p}\sum_{j=1}^{k} l_{ij}y_{ij} \geq M, \sum_{i=1}^{p}\sum_{j=1}^{k} c_{ij}y_{ij} \leq B\right). \tag{6}$$

In this stage, we relax the budget constraint, allowing solutions to exceed the budget limit but still considering the budget impact when evaluating fitness. This method of relaxation facilitates the generation of initial solutions and prevents a situation where every initial solution has zero fitness, thereby promoting the efficient functioning of the genetic algorithm.

In the second stage, we gradually restore the budget constraint, ensuring that the final solution meets all the original constraints. This includes determining each customer's Rewarded Load Reduction Upper Bound and finding the optimal incentive plan within the budget.

By using this two-stage approach, we effectively address optimization problems under high-dimensional and strict constraints. The application of the constraint relaxation technique in the first stage not only increases the probability of finding feasible solutions in the initial stage but also ensures that the algorithm gradually converges to the optimal solution in subsequent stages.

## 4.4 Strategy of Gene Repair

After using the constraint relaxation technique in the first stage, the generated solutions may become infeasible due to the relaxed budget constraints. These solutions cannot meet the strict budget limits. Therefore, a mechanism is needed to repair these infeasible solutions and convert them into feasible solutions. This study presents a gene repair method to address this issue.

Formally, gene repair is a method used to modify genetic information in chromosomes to satisfy certain requirements. In the demand response plan, the purpose of gene repair is to ensure that all generated solutions meet the budget constraints while still achieving the total load reduction target.

In this study, the following steps are used to repair infeasible solutions generated in the first stage:

1. **Initial Simulation**: Run several simulations for each chromosome in the population and record the load reduction of customers in each simulation.
2. **Identify Key Customers**: Find the customer with the lowest times where the load reduction is greater than or equal to the reward upper bound.
3. **Adjust Reward Upper Bound**: Reduce the reward upper bound for these key customers.
4. **Evaluate Cost**: Determine if the adjusted total cost exceeds the budget threshold. If so, repeat steps 2 through 4 until the total cost is within the budget.

This gene repair strategy ensures that the final solution meets the budget constraints while not excessively compromising the probability of achieving the target load reduction. Effectively applying this approach allows us to transform initially infeasible solutions from the first stage into viable ones, thus enhancing both the algorithm's efficiency and the final solution's quality.

As illustrated in Fig. 3, to summarize, the gene repair method is essential in the genetic algorithm for the demand response strategy. It not only repairs infeasible solutions generated in the initial stage but also ensures that the probability of achieving the target load reduction is maximized while meeting the budget constraints. This approach allows the algorithm to run more efficiently and ultimately achieve the desired goals.

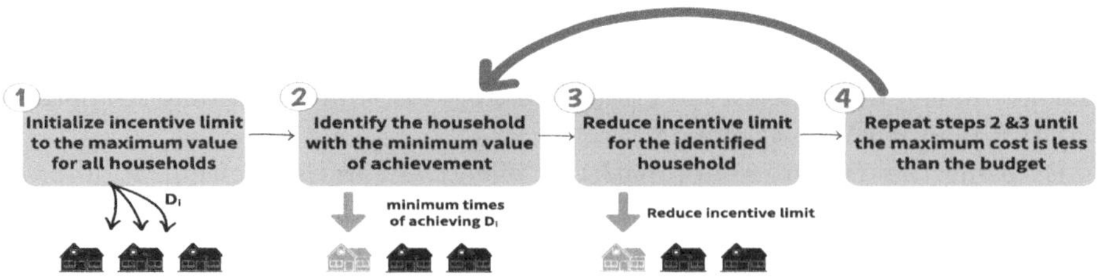


**Fig. 3.** Flow of gene repairing.

### 4.5 Algorithm Summary

In this paper, we proposed an innovative algorithm for optimizing load reduction incentive plans, namely the 2-phase Monte Carlo Simulation Genetic Algorithm (2p-MCSGA). This algorithm aims to maximize the probability of achieving load reductions within a given budget by optimizing incentive plans. The incentive and reward upper limits for each household can be derived from the expected values obtained from the historical data. We combine plans formed through initialization with those derived from expected values and subsequently proceed with optimization towards the objective.

The primary contribution of this study is the integration of Monte Carlo simulation with genetic algorithms, effectively addressing optimization problems under high-dimensional and strict constraints. By introducing constraint relaxation and gene repair techniques, we successfully tackled the issue of zero fitness values in randomly generated initial solutions, ensuring the convergence and efficiency of the algorithm.

## 5 Experiments

**Dataset:** The dataset comes from the customer trial data of the Australian government's smart grid city trial[5]. It contains data related to peak response events, including customer electricity consumption prior to, during, and the rewards received from the event. This experiment selects the top fifty users based on the number of responses.

**Experimental Setup:** In the experiment, we use three columns: *ACTUAL_KWH*, *BASELINE_KWH*, and *REBATE_AMOUNT*. Specifically, *BASELINE_KWH* represents the recognized electricity usage before the response event. *ACTUAL_KWH* is the average electricity usage during the response event, and *REBATE_AMOUNT* represents the incentive received during the event. Since the difference between *ACTUAL_KWH* and *BASELINE_KWH* is seven kWh for most of the data, we divide the data ranging from zero to seven kWh

**Table 1.** Summary of Experiment settings

| Parameter | Range |
|---|---|
| Rewarded Load Reduction Upper Bound Set | $\{0, 1, \ldots, 7\}$ kWh |
| Reward Set | $\{1.0, 1.25, 1.5\}$ per kWh |
| Times of Monte-Carlo Simulation | 150 |
| Crossover Rate | 0.2 |
| Mutation Rate | 0.03 |

[5] Australian Government, Smart-Grid Smart-City Customer Trial Data, available at:https://data.gov.au/dataset/ds-dga-4e21dea3-9b87-4610-94c7-15a8a77907ef/details.

into intervals of one, establishing these as the upper bounds for rewarded load reduction. The incentive per kWh generally ranges from 1 to 1.5; therefore, we segment this data into intervals of 0.25 to form the reward set. Finally, simulated demand response events will be generated based on each customer's load reduction distribution. For better understanding, data settings are outlined in Table 1.

### 5.1 Experimental Studies on Demand Response

In this study, we created simulated demand response events ranging from 100 to 300 as historical data for the specified residential environments, with intervals set at 100 events. Using the historical data provided, we calculated the probability of successfully executing one hundred demand response events and compared the success rates across varying quantities of historical data. As the amount of historical data increases, the success rate also improves, because more data allows the Monte Carlo simulation evaluation to better approximate real-world conditions. Due to the stochastic nature of the optimization process in genetic algorithms, each generated plan may have different fitness levels. Considering that Load Aggregators (LA) might not execute plans with low fitness, we adjusted various thresholds in this experiment. When the threshold is set higher, only plans with higher fitness are considered for execution, resulting in a higher success rate. Plans falling below the threshold were excluded, suggesting that LA can filter out plans with low fitness by establishing appropriate thresholds. The experimental results are shown in Fig. 4.

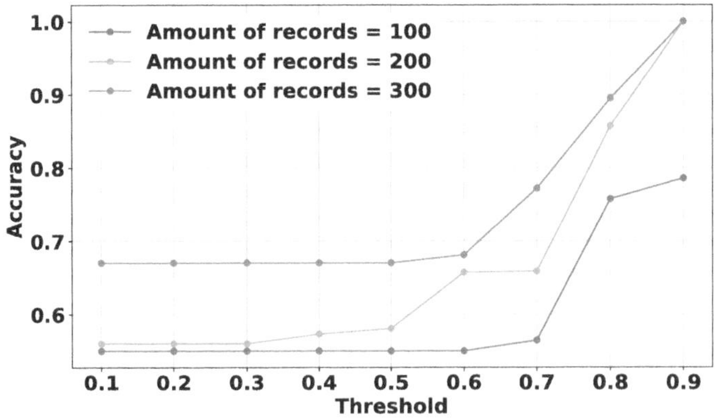


**Fig. 4.** Success Rate Based On Different Amount of Records.

It is clear that the volume of data input into the algorithm has a substantial impact on the quality of the plans produced. As the amount of data increases, the behavior distribution of the households can be captured more accurately. It is evident that plans generated with less historical data are less effective compared to those created with a larger amount of historical data inputs.

### 5.2 Performance Comparison

We compare the proposed method with two greedy algorithms. In particular, greedy algorithms choose the incentive level with the greatest expected reduction in load based on historical data and set the upper bound for rewarded reduction according to the historical average load reduction. When the total cost of the plan exceeds the budget, each method adjusts differently:

- Adjust Upper Bound: This method identifies the household with the highest cost and lowers its rewarded reduction upper bound, repeating the process until the total cost is within the budget.
- Adjust Incentive Level: This method identifies the household with the highest cost and lowers its incentive level, repeating the process until the total cost is within the budget.

The experimental results are shown in Table 2. $R$ represents different load reduction targets, and this experiment evaluates various load reduction targets. Note that due to the stochastic nature of the optimization process in genetic algorithms, the final plan may have low fitness. Load aggregators will not implement plans with fitness below 0.8. Therefore, plans with fitness below 0.8 are excluded from consideration in this experiment. As can be seen, the proposed method demonstrates a higher success rate across different load reduction targets compared to other methods, indicating superior planning performance. In contrast, the Greedy approach shows a significant drop in success rate when R = 135. This decline occurs because the Greedy method does not account for the success rate of the plans it selects. Specifically, when the load reduction target reaches a certain threshold, the plans selected by the Greedy algorithm fail to meet the required success criteria, resulting in a reduced success rate.

**Table 2.** Success rates for different methods and reduction target

| Method | R | | |
|---|---|---|---|
| | 135 | 130 | 125 |
| Greedy with adjusting upper bound | 0.43 | 0.96 | 1.0 |
| Greedy with adjusting incentive | 0.49 | 0.86 | 1.0 |
| 2P-MCSGA | 0.894 | 0.96 | 1.0 |

**Table 3.** Sensitivity Analysis of Different Decision Thresholds

| Threshold | R = 135 | | R = 130 | | R = 125 | |
|---|---|---|---|---|---|---|
| | Succ. rate | Part. rate | Succ. rate | Part. rate | Succ. rate | Part. rate |
| 0.6 | 0.67 | 0.95 | 0.96 | 1.0 | 1.0 | 1.0 |
| 0.7 | 0.75 | 0.60 | 0.96 | 1.0 | 1.0 | 1.0 |
| 0.8 | 0.894 | 0.19 | 0.96 | 1.0 | 1.0 | 1.0 |
| 0.9 | 1.0 | 0.04 | 0.96 | 1.0 | 1.0 | 1.0 |

### 5.3 Sensitivity Analysis

In this study, the participation rate is identified as the proportion of plans whose fitness values surpass the decision threshold. In this experiment, the participation rate and success rate for different decision thresholds are compared.

Table 3 demonstrates the importance of selecting decision threshold. It can be observed that as the decision threshold increases, the performance of the method also increases, while the participation rate decreases. Since the participation rate represents the proportion of strategies formulated by the method that exceed the threshold, it is expected that the higher the threshold is set, the lower the participation rate will be. A higher threshold indicates that the plans selected are more optimal; therefore, it can be expected that as the decision threshold increases, the success rate will also increase.

### 5.4 Numerical Analysis

**Impact of Times of Monte-Carlo Simulation:** In this experiment, we analyzed the impact of different numbers of Monte Carlo simulations on the accuracy of the demand response plan. Specifically, we performed simulations in sets of 50, 100, and 150, each repeated ten times and the outcomes averaged to ensure robustness. As indicated in Fig. 5(a), the precision of the plan notably enhances with the rise in the number of simulations, suggesting that a higher number of simulations yields a more dependable estimation of the optimal load reduction strategy.

**Comparison with Optimal Solution:** Due to the computational complexity, it is nearly impossible to generate an optimal plan for a large number of households with modern computer capabilities. Thus, we limited the number of participants to 5 in this experiment and employed an exhaustive search to identify the optimal solution. In this experiment, 300 historical data points were provided. We used this historical data to generate the plan with the highest probability in the distribution and compared it with the plan generated by 2P-MCSGA. The comparison results are shown in Fig. 5(b).

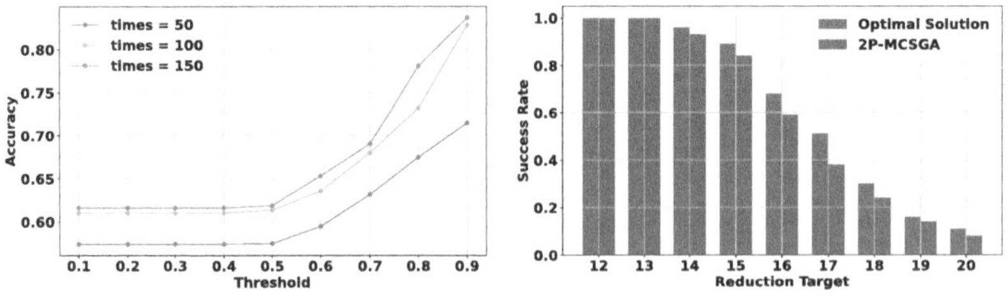


(a) Success Rate Based On Different Amount of Monte-Carlo Simulation (b) Comparison with Optimal Solution

**Fig. 5.** Results of Numerical Analysis.

In this experiment, we executed 100 simulated DR events using plans generated by both the 2P-MCSGA and the optimal solution. The 2P-MCSGA closely approaches the performance of the optimal solution. A major benefit of the 2P-MCSGA is its relatively low computational complexity, which allows it to effectively produce viable plans on a larger scale. The effectiveness of 2P-MCSGA makes it a valuable tool for practical DR planning, as it can attain results close to optimal with much lower computational demands.

## 6 Conclusions

Previous studies have made significant advancements in incentive-based demand response via direct control, successfully implementing it in various industrial and commercial settings. However, the utilization of direct control techniques in regular residential environments is uncommon. Due to the varied circumstances in residential areas, direct control-based DR schemes are difficult to accept. This study delves into aspects not covered in earlier research for the first time, suggesting methods to assess the likelihood of meeting load reduction goals and identifying feasible plans. It is expected that future incentive-based DR could be extended to ordinary households, thus unlocking their considerable load reduction potential.

**Acknowledgment.** This paper was supported in part by National Science and Technology Council (NSTC), R.O.C., under Contract 112-2221-E-006-158, 113-2622-8-006-011-TD1 and 113-2221-E-006-203-MY2.

## References

1. Bintoudi, A.D., Bezas, N., Zyglakis, L., Isaioglou, G.: Incentive-based demand response framework for residential applications: design and real-life demonstration. Energies **14** (2021)
2. Bradley, P., Coke, A., Leach, M.: Financial incentive approaches for reducing peak electricity demand, experience from pilot trials with a UK energy provider. Energy Policy **98**, 108–120 (2016)
3. Chen, K., Ross, S.M.: An adaptive stochastic knapsack problem. Eur. J. Oper. Res. **239**(3), 625–635 (2014)
4. Chen, R., Yang, B., Li, S., Wang, S.: A self-learning genetic algorithm based on reinforcement learning for flexible job-shop scheduling problem. Comput. Ind. Eng. **149** (2020)
5. Gkatzikis, L., Koutsopoulos, I., Salonidis, T.: The role of aggregators in smart grid demand response markets. IEEE J. Sel. Areas Commun. **31**(7), 1247–1257 (2013)
6. Guan, L., Abbasi, A., Ryan, M.: A simulation-based risk interdependency network model for project risk assessment. Decis. Support Syst. **148** (2021)
7. Jo, S., et al.: Hybrid genetic algorithm with k-nearest neighbors for radial distribution network reconfiguration. IEEE Trans. Smart Grid **15**(3), 2614–2624 (2024)
8. Kosuch, S., Lisser, A.: Upper bounds for the 0–1 stochastic knapsack problem and a b&b algorithm. Ann. Oper. Res. **176**(1), 77–93 (2010)

9. Liu, D., Qin, Z., Hua, H., Ding, Y., Cao, J.: Incremental incentive mechanism design for diversified consumers in demand response. Appl. Energy **329** (2023)
10. Lu, R., Hong, S.H.: Incentive-based demand response for smart grid with reinforcement learning and deep neural network. Appl. Energy **236**, 937–949 (2019)
11. Parrish, B., Heptonstall, P., Gross, R., Sovacool, B.K.: A systematic review of motivations, enablers and barriers for consumer engagement with residential demand response. Energy Policy **138** (2020)
12. Qdr, Q.J.U.D.E.: Benefits of demand response in electricity markets and recommendations for achieving them. Technical report, US Dept. Energy, Washington, DC, USA (2006)
13. Rahimi, I., Gandomi, A.H., Chen, F., Mezura-Montes, E.: A review on constraint handling techniques for population-based algorithms: from single-objective to multi-objective optimization. Arch. Comput. Methods Eng. **30**(3), 2181–2209 (2023)
14. Tokdemir, O.B., Erol, H., Dikmen, I.: Delay risk assessment of repetitive construction projects using line-of-balance scheduling and Monte Carlo simulation. J. Constr. Eng. Manag. **145**(2) (2019)
15. Wang, F., Ge, X., Li, K., Mi, Z.: Day-ahead market optimal bidding strategy and quantitative compensation mechanism design for load aggregator engaging demand response program. IEEE Trans. Ind. Appl. **55**(6), 5564–5573 (2019)
16. Woodruff, D.L.: Advances in Computational and Stochastic Optimization, Logic Programming, and Heuristic Search (1998)
17. Zheng, T., Li, H., He, H., Lei, Z., Gao, S.: An adaptive strategy-incorporated integer genetic algorithm for wind farm layout optimization. J. Bionic Eng. **21**(3), 1522–1540 (2024)

# Graph-Based Syntactic Analysis for Cross-Domain Fraud Messages Detection

Nai-Chien Hsu(✉) and Yi-Shin Chen

Institute of Information Systems and Applications, National Tsing Hua University, Hsinchu, Taiwan
abc554488@gmail.com

**Abstract.** Given the surge in digital communication, the spread of fraud messages across various communication platforms poses an increasingly significant threat to the public due to their accessibility and ubiquity. Existing fraud detection methodologies predominantly focus on recognized fraud tactics, thus diminishing their effectiveness against unfamiliar or evolving deceptive strategies, a challenge known as domain adaptation. To address this issue, we introduce a novel approach, Graph-Based Syntactic Structure Generation, capable of autonomously learning common syntactic structures within fraud messages without the need for predefined fraud patterns. This method leverages co-occurrence graphs and graph auto-encoder techniques to extract connection state features of each token from extensive texts, thereby acquiring global information essential for identifying complex syntactic structures indicative of fraud messages. Further, we employ an attention-based model for syntactic structure transformation of texts, converting each token into *word*, *part of speech (POS)*, or *# (fixed valued)* to facilitate effective syntactic pattern recognition. This approach not only enhances the model's understanding of textual syntactic structures but also enriches semantic information for subsequent large language model analysis. Experiments conducted on datasets sourced from Cofacts and the 165 anti-fraud platform demonstrate our method's robust recognition performance on cross-domain datasets, even with limited training data, surpassing traditional methods' limitations when confronting newly emerged fraud tactics.

**Keywords:** Fraud messages detection · Syntactic analysis · Graph-based · Cross-domain · Attention-base

## 1 Introduction

The rise of digital communication has brought convenience but also an alarming increase in fraudulent activities, leading to financial losses and privacy breaches, which erode trust in online interactions [10]. Fraudulent messages, in particular, are pervasive and indiscriminate, making them a significant threat to the general public [24,25].

© The Author(s), under exclusive license to Springer Nature Singapore Pte Ltd. 2025
W.-T. Chu et al. (Eds.): TAAI 2024, CCIS 2414, pp. 33–48, 2025.
https://doi.org/10.1007/978-981-96-4589-3_3

Existing fraud detection methods often rely on identity-based approaches, analyzing social network connections or behavioral patterns [5,17]. However, these methods struggle when fraudsters change identities or when they are close to the victim. Content-based approaches have become increasingly popular, analyzing the textual content of messages to identify fraud through specific phrases, grammatical patterns, or topic-based features [11,14,15]. Machine learning techniques, such as Doc2Vec, have been used to embed these features into vectors for more effective detection [12,13].

Despite advancements, content-based methods face challenges as fraud tactics evolve, leading to model inefficiency over time. While large language models like GPT-4 [23] show promise, they often focus on local context, missing global relationships crucial for detecting complex fraud schemes [3]. This limitation hampers their ability to adapt to increasingly sophisticated fraud techniques.

The susceptibility to cross-domain failure in fraud detection can be exacerbated by the undue influence of embeddings for words irrelevant to the main theme. As in Fig. 1, in fraud message identification, two fraudulent statements such as 'Win a free phone, click now!' and 'Get your free phone, click here!' may exhibit closely similar embeddings during training. Yet, they remain vulnerable to the impact of embeddings from words unrelated to the fraudulent intent. Consider a non-fraudulent sentence 'Your phone is here!', which shares several words with the aforementioned fraudulent messages. This similarity could cause a misleadingly close overall sentence embedding, potentially leading to false positives. Although accumulating extensive datasets can mitigate this issue, it often necessitates the collection of numerous similar cases prone to misjudgment.

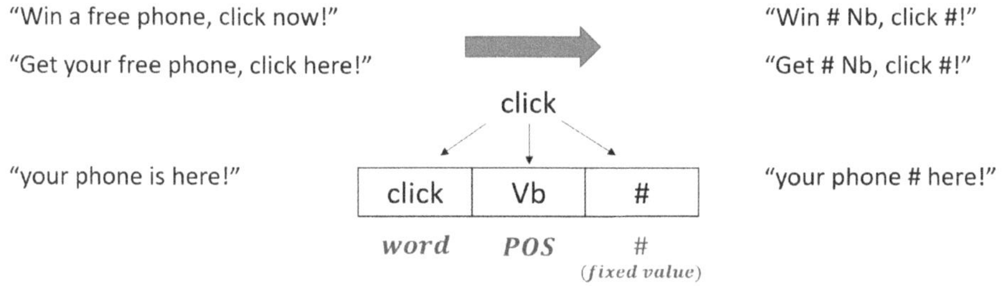


**Fig. 1.** Syntactic Structure Transformation via Categorization into *word*, *POS*, or # for Enhanced Cross-Domain Fraud Messages Detection.

Our model extends the capability to incorporate perspectives that transcend the mere lexical meanings of words. Within our innovative framework, each token is afforded the opportunity to embody one of three distinct categories: its conventional *word* meaning, its *part-of-speech (POS)* classification, or a fixed value, denoted by #. Therefore, a token such as 'click' can be modeled to represent the direct action linked to the term'click', to fall under the verb category as per its POS, or to assume a constant fixed value.

After such transformation, the example fraudulent messages might be converted by the model into 'Win # Nb, click #!' and 'Get # Nb, click #!'. Such a restructuring could ensure a closer alignment of the embeddings for these two sentences, enhancing the precision of fraud detection.

In order to address the challenges of cross-domain fraud messages detection, we propose a method capable of capturing fraudulent syntactic structures. Our contributions are outlined as follows:

- **Integration of graph-based feature extraction:** We leverage co-occurrence graph and graph auto-encoder to generate global informative features for each token, facilitating the representation of inter-token relationships.
- **Development of Attention-based syntactic pattern recognition:** Through an attention-based model, we extract syntactic patterns from the graph-generated features, enabling the identification of key linguistic structures indicative of fraudulent messages.
- **Superior Performance in Cross-domain Fraud Messages Detection:** Demonstrating commendable detection efficacy on cross-domain datasets with limited training data, our approach overcomes the limitations faced by traditional methods when encountering newly emerged scam tactics.

## 2 Related Work

### 2.1 Fraud Messages Detection

Identity-based approaches, using social network analysis and behavioral patterns, have been traditionally employed to detect fraudulent activities [5,17]. However, these methods often struggle with rapidly changing fraud tactics and scenarios involving close relationships between victims and fraudsters.

Content-based analysis has gained traction for its ability to analyze textual content for fraud indicators using natural language processing (NLP) techniques [11]. Deep learning methods have also been effective in embedding linguistic features for automated detection [12,13]. Recent work has focused on specific fraudulent communications, such as smishing SMS and spam SMS, employing supervised learning techniques like TF-IDF and feature extraction to classify spam with high accuracy [19,20].

Despite these advances, challenges remain in adapting to evolving fraud tactics and integrating global semantic information. To address this, our method combines graph-based feature extraction with attention-based syntactic pattern recognition, enhancing cross-domain fraud detection.

### 2.2 Graph Auto-encoder

Graph Auto-Encoder (GAE) is a framework for unsupervised learning on graphs, utilizing Graph Neural Networks (GNNs) to encode graph topology and node features into compact representations for tasks like link prediction and node classification [6,18,21]. GAE focuses on preserving graph structure and node content [30].

Building on GAE, Variational Graph Auto-Encoder (VGAE) incorporates a variational Bayes framework to learn probabilistic node embeddings, introducing Gaussian priors and reparameterization for better generalization and robustness in sparse graph data [21]. This approach has led to improved graph representation learning models.

Adversarially Regularized Graph Auto-Encoder (ARGAE) extends VGAE by adding adversarial training to further refine embeddings [7], aligning latent distributions with a Gaussian prior, which boosts model performance in link prediction. In this work, we apply ARGAE to co-occurrence graphs, capturing complex interactions between entities.

### 2.3 Syntactic Pattern Construction

Syntactic Pattern Construction is crucial for improving model adaptability across domains [1,2]. Previous studies have shown that syntactic patterns can identify domain-specific items like emotions and misinformation by constructing co-occurrence graphs from large text collections and calculating metrics like clustering coefficients to differentiate between Topical Words (TW) and Connector Words (CW).

These methods highlight the importance of cross-domain syntactic patterns for tasks such as emotion classification and fake news detection. However, limitations arise from the use of fixed graph metrics and manually curated pattern dictionaries. Our work addresses these challenges by introducing Graph-Based Syntactic Structure Generation, using graph auto-encoder techniques to capture node structures and extract patterns from fraud-related messages. This structural data is fed into an attention-based model to enhance the detection of fraudulent messages, improving cross-domain performance.

## 3 Methodology

In this section, we will introduce our proposed model, **G**raph-Based **S**yntactic Analysis for **C**ross-Domain **F**raud Messages **D**etection (**GSC-FD**). As shown in Fig. 2, there are two main parts: Graph-based Embedding Synthesis and Syntactic Structure Generation. For Graph-based Embedding Synthesis, there are two sub-components: Co-occurrence Graph Construction and Graph Encoder Module (GEM). Similarly, the Syntactic Structure Generation consists of two sub-components: Pattern Construction Module (PCM) and Fraud Prediction Module (FPM). We will now introduce the architecture and purpose of each block in detail.

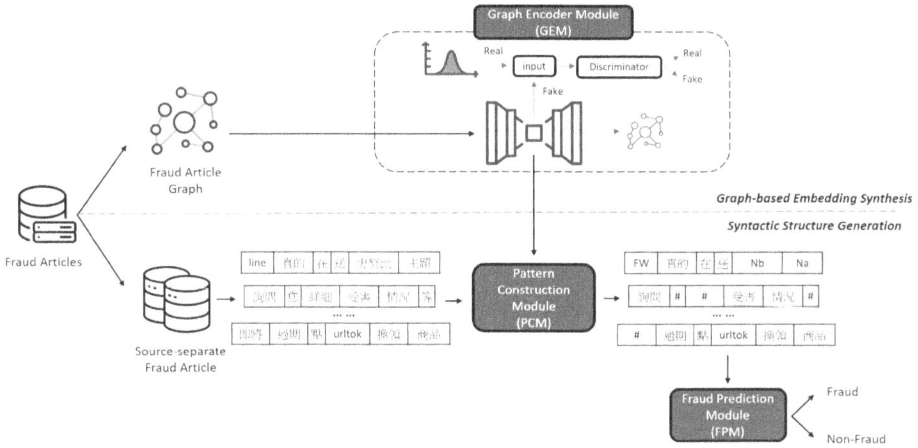


**Fig. 2.** The proposed Framework of GSC-FD.

### 3.1 Thesis Statement

This study proposes a Graph-Based Syntactic Structure Generation method that enhances fraud message detection by integrating global syntactic information through co-occurrence graphs and attention-based models, aiming for robust performance across diverse domains.

### 3.2 Problem Statement

**Definition 1.** *Cross-Domain fraud messages detection aims to learn syntactic structure patterns to achieve the identification of messages utilizing new scam techniques. Given a labeled fraud dataset* $D = \{(M_i, y_i)\}, i = 1, 2, 3, ..., n$, *where* $M_i$ *denotes i-th messages,* $y_i$ *denotes the corresponding label (if message is fraudulent, labeled 1, otherwise 0) and* $n$ *denotes the number of messages in D. Our goal is to predict labels of testing samples which is cross-domain using a model* $f$ *trained on* $D$.

### 3.3 Graph-Based Embedding Synthesis

There are two main steps in this part - the Co-occurrence Graph Construction and Graph Encoder Module (GEM).

One fundamental challenge addressed here is the lack of semantic distinction for words with multiple meanings, which can lead to ambiguous connections in the graph. For instance, without context, the word 'bear' in 'It's a bear.' and 'I can't bear being bored.' would be indistinguishably linked, despite their different meanings. Furthermore, relying solely on the graph topology could result in capturing only surface-level connections among tokens, failing to indicate with which tokens each one is associated. To overcome these challenges, our objective is to enrich the graph structure by incorporating Part-of-Speech (POS) tags and semantic information, thereby creating a more nuanced and informative representation that reflects both the lexical and syntactic relationships within the data.

**Co-occurrence Graph Construction.** The Co-occurrence Graph $G$ is defined as followed:

**Definition 2 (Co-occurrence Graph).** *An undirected co-occurrence graph is denoted as*

$$G = (V, E), \tag{1}$$

*where $V$ is the set of vertices, with each vertex representing a pair that consists of a unique word from a collection of articles and its corresponding part-of-speech (POS) tag, denoted as (word, POS). The set $E$ comprises edges that indicate the co-occurrence relationships between pairs of vertices. An edge $(v_i, v_j) \in E$ if and only if the corresponding words for $v_i$ and $v_j$ appear within a predefined window size of one another in any article. Specifically, the window size for determining co-occurrence is set to 1, meaning that an edge is formed between two words if and only if they are adjacent in the text.*

The feature vector for each vertex in the graph is constructed by merging the embeddings of both the word and its corresponding part-of-speech (POS) tag. This design choice is motivated by the intent to capture both the semantic aspects of the words and the syntactic roles as indicated by their POS tags, the latter of which is explicitly modeled through the use of part-of-speech embeddings. As defined, the POS embedding for a tag is the average of embeddings of all tokens that share this tag within a co-occurrence graph, enabling a nuanced representation that encapsulates both lexical and grammatical patterns.

**Definition 3 (Part-of-speech embedding).** *Given a set of tokens $T = \{t_1, t_2, ..., t_n\}$ with corresponding POS tags $P = \{p_1, p_2, ..., p_n\}$ and their embeddings $E = \{e_{word}(t_1), e_{word}(t_2), ..., e_{word}(t_n)\}$ within a co-occurrence graph, the POS embedding for a tag $p$ is defined as the average of embeddings of all tokens that share this tag:*

$$e_{POS}(p) = \frac{1}{|T_p|} \sum_{t_i \in T_p} e_{word}(t_i) \tag{2}$$

*where $T_p = \{t_i | p_i = p, t_i \in T\}$ is the set of tokens with the POS tag $p$ and $|T_p|$ is the number of such tokens.*

**Definition 4 (Node Feature).** *Given a vertex $v_i = (t_i, p_i)$ in the graph where $t_i$ is a token and $p_i$ is its corresponding part-of-speech (POS) tag. , the feature vector of the vertex, denoted as $feature(v_i)$, is constructed by concatenating the word embedding of $t_i$ and the POS embedding of $p_i$:*

$$feature(v_i) = e_{word}(t_i) \oplus e_{POS}(p_i) \tag{3}$$

*where $e_{word}(t_i)$ is the embedding of the token $t_i$, $e_{POS}(p_i)$ is the POS embedding of the tag $p_i$, and $\oplus$ denotes the concatenation operation.*

This dual perspective not only reveals the structural relationships between nodes but also elucidates the frequent lexical and grammatical patterns among closely associated terms. Such an enriched node representation becomes crucial in subsequent phases, as it enables the selection of fraud patterns that are more effective in recognizing fraud messages.

**Graph Encoder Module (GEM).** The Graph Encoder Module (GEM) enriches node embeddings with semantic and syntactic information by processing co-occurrence graphs. This module employs the Adversarial Regularized Graph Autoencoder (ARGAE) to achieve a dual objective: capturing the intricate topology of co-occurrence graphs and integrating lexical attributes along with part-of-speech (POS) tags into the embeddings. The architecture of GEM primarily comprises three components: the Encoder, the Decoder, and the Discriminator.

The encoder leverages a Graph Convolutional Network (GCN) to encode node features into a latent space. Given a graph $G = (V, E)$ with node features $X$, the encoding process at the $l$-th layer can be mathematically described as:

$$H^{(l+1)} = \sigma(\tilde{D}^{-\frac{1}{2}}\tilde{A}\tilde{D}^{-\frac{1}{2}}H^{(l)}W^{(l)}), \tag{4}$$

where $H^{(0)} = X$ is the input feature matrix, $\tilde{A} = A + I_N$ is the adjacency matrix $A$ of the graph with added self-connections $I_N$, $\tilde{D}$ is the degree matrix of $\tilde{A}$, $W^{(l)}$ is the weight matrix for the $l$-th layer, and $\sigma$ represents a non-linear activation function such as ReLU. The final output $H^{(L)}$ after $L$ layers serves as the encoded node representations $Z$.

The decoder aims to reconstruct the adjacency matrix $\hat{A}$ from the encoded representations $Z$, using the following equation:

$$\hat{A} = \sigma(ZZ^T), \tag{5}$$

where $\sigma$ is typically a sigmoid function applied element-wise, converting the dot product of latent representations into probabilities indicating the likelihood of edge existence between node pairs.

The discriminator is tasked with distinguishing between real and synthesized node embeddings. Given a real node embedding $z_{real}$ and a fake node embedding $z_{fake}$, generated by sampling from a prior distribution, the discriminator's objective can be formalized as:

$$\min_{D_\psi} - \mathbb{E}_{z_{\text{real}} \sim p_{\text{data}}}[\log D_\psi(z_{\text{real}})] \qquad - \mathbb{E}_{z_{\text{fake}} \sim p_z}[\log(1 - D_\psi(z_{\text{fake}}))],$$

where $D_\psi$ denotes the discriminator parameterized by $\psi$, and $p_{data}$ and $p_z$ represent the distributions of real and fake embeddings, respectively.

The overall objective combines the reconstruction loss $\mathcal{L}_{recon}$, typically the cross-entropy between $A$ and $\hat{A}$, and the adversarial loss $\mathcal{L}_{adv}$ as follows:

$$\mathcal{L} = \mathcal{L}_{recon}(A, \hat{A}) + \lambda\mathcal{L}_{adv}(D_\psi, Z), \tag{6}$$

where $\lambda$ is a regularization coefficient balancing the contribution of the adversarial loss.

Upon completion of the unsupervised learning process within the Graph Encoder Module (GEM), we obtain the embedding matrix Z. This matrix integrates the semantic information of individual nodes, the semantics of adjacent words, and the connectivity details within the graph, providing a rich, contextual representation of the textual data. Z is subsequently utilized as input for the Pattern Construction Module (PCM), enabling the model to access global information crucial for the effective detection of fraudulent messages. This approach ensures that the model is well-equipped to recognize fraud patterns by leveraging both the syntactic and semantic intricacies captured in the embeddings, thereby enhancing its ability to identify fraudulent messages across various domains.

### 3.4 Syntactic Structure Generation

There are two main steps in this part - the Pattern Construction Module (PCM) and Fraud Prediction Module (FPM).

The challenge addressed here involves detecting dispersed and fragmentary patterns within text, which often elude traditional analysis methods. Traditional techniques typically capture patterns with adjacent elements, overlooking non-contiguous sequences that are also indicative of fraud, such as the fragmented pattern "click...urltok" found in fraudulent messages. To address this issue, our objective is to develop a model that comprehends the full context of a text. This allows for the accurate determination of each word's syntactic role, thereby identifying and understanding both contiguous and dispersed fraudulent patterns.

Additionally, this section leverages the global information of each token derived from the Graph-based Embedding Synthesis, along with the messages to be identified, guiding the model in learning to select the most appropriate category for each token: *word* (representing its inherent meaning), *POS* (denoting its part-of-speech), or # (a fixed value). This strategy allows the model to dynamically adapt its representation of tokens, enhancing its ability to distinguish between different syntactic roles and meanings, thereby improving the overall accuracy of fraud detection.

**Pattern Construction Module (PCM).** The Pattern Construction Module (PCM) harnesses the global information within the embedding matrix $Z$, originating from the Graph Encoder Module (GEM). The primary objective of PCM is to utilize this global context, provided by $Z$, within an advanced attention-based model to interpret the semantics and syntactic roles of tokens in incoming messages. Attention-based models, renowned for their superior performance in text comprehension tasks, allow PCM to effectively discern the intricate relationships between words, thereby enhancing the model's ability to identify patterns indicative of fraud across diverse domains.

Given an incoming message $m$ with a sequence of tokens $\{t_1, t_2, ..., t_n\}$, the Pattern Construction Module (PCM) initiates by extracting relevant embeddings for each token from the embedding matrix $Z$. For a token $t_i$, its embedding $e(t_i)$ is retrieved based on the corresponding node ID in the graph, formalized as:

$$e(t_i) = Z[id(t_i)]$$

where $id(t_i)$ denotes the node ID associated with token $t_i$, and $Z[id(t_i)]$ represents the embedding of the node from the embedding matrix $Z$.

Subsequently, to compile an embedding matrix for the entire message $m$, embeddings for all tokens are aggregated to form $E_m$, where each row corresponds to the embedding of a token:

$$E_m = [e(t_1); e(t_2); ...; e(t_n)]$$

For instance, an incoming message, say "click this link", the PCM begins by extracting the relevant embeddings for each token from $Z$. $e_{\text{click}}$, $e_{\text{this}}$, $e_{\text{link}}$ denote the embeddings for "click", "this", and "link" respectively.

The retrieved embeddings are then fed into a Multi-head Attention (MHA) module. The MHA module allows the model to focus on different segments of the input sequence for a comprehensive understanding. The mathematical representation of the MHA operation is:

$$\text{MHA}(Q, K, V) = \text{Concat}(\text{head}_1, \ldots, \text{head}_h)W^O \tag{7}$$

$$\text{where head}_i = \text{Attention}(QW_i^Q, KW_i^K, VW_i^V) \tag{8}$$

$$\text{Attention}(Q, K, V) = \text{softmax}\left(\frac{QK^T}{\sqrt{d_k}}\right)V \tag{9}$$

Here, $Q$, $K$, $V$ represent the queries, keys, and values matrices derived from the input embeddings, $W^O$, $W_i^Q$, $W_i^K$, $W_i^V$ are parameter matrices, and $h$ is the number of attention heads. $d_k$ is the dimensionality of the keys, ensuring the softmax operates over a normalized scale. The assembled embedding matrix $E_m$ is then utilized as $Q$, $K$, and Value $V$ in MHA layer.

The output from the MHA module undergoes a linear transformation, projecting the attention-enhanced features into a space of three values per token. These values correspond to the probabilities of the token representing a *word*, *part of speech (POS)*, or # (denote a predetermined fixed value). This step is formalized as:

$$L_i = W_l \cdot \text{MHA}_i + b_l \tag{10}$$

$$P_i = \text{softmax}(L_i) \tag{11}$$

where $L_i$ is the linear transformation of the $i$-th token's output from MHA, $W_l$ and $b_l$ are the weights and bias of the Linear module, and $P_i$ is the resulting probability distribution after applying the softmax function.

PCM concludes by selecting the highest probability category for each token and weighting its embedding by this probability, formalizing the representation for fraud prediction:

$$C_i = \text{argmax}(P_i) \tag{12}$$

$$E'_i = P_i(C_i) \cdot embed(C_i) \tag{13}$$

where *embed* is determined by the category $C_i$:

- $embed(C_i)$ is the original token $i$ embedding if $C_i$ is *word*,
- $embed(C_i)$ is the part-of-speech embedding of the token $i$ if $C_i$ is *part of speech*,
- $embed(C_i)$ is a predetermined fixed embedding if $C_i$ is $\#$.

Furthermore, $C_i$ is the category with the highest probability for the $i$-th token, indicative of its role as either a *word*, a *part of speech*, or a fixed value denoted by $\#$. $E'_i$ represents the final weighted embedding for the $i$-th token, meticulously prepared and optimized for input into the Fraud Prediction Module (FPM).

Through this sophisticated architecture, the PCM not only enriches the semantic and syntactic analysis of text but also bridges the gap between raw textual data and actionable insights for fraud detection. This module, therefore, constitutes an essential component of our framework, underscoring our novel approach to tackling the challenge of cross-domain fraud messages detection.

**Fraud Prediction Module (FPM).** The Fraud Prediction Module (FPM) primarily focusing on classifying messages into fraudulent or legitimate categories. It operates by receiving a sequence of final weighted embeddings from the Pattern Construction Module (PCM). These embeddings are rich in semantic and syntactic information, making them highly informative for the fraud detection task at hand.

Given a sequence of weighted embeddings $\mathbf{E}' = E'_1, E'_2, \ldots, E'_n$ for an input message, where $n$ denotes the number of token in the message. The FPM utilizes BERT to compute the probability of the message being fraudulent. The process can be mathematically represented as follows:

$$P(\text{Fraud} \mid E'_1, E'_2, \ldots, E'_n) = \text{BERT}(E'_1, E'_2, \ldots, E'_n) \tag{14}$$

where $P(\text{Fraud} \mid E'_1, E'_2, \ldots, E'_n)$ denotes the conditional probability of the message being fraudulent given the sequence of embeddings. The BERT function encapsulates the forward pass through the BERT model, resulting in a classification output based on the aggregated contextual embeddings.

## 4 Experiment and Results

### 4.1 Datasets and Settings

**Datasets.** To evaluate the model's cross-domain capability and proficiency in identifying unfamiliar fraudulent techniques or descriptions, this work constructs datasets from two sources: Cofacts Open Datasets and 165 Anti-fraud System Datasets. These datasets include articles labeled as fraudulent by users on online reporting platforms, providing a rich and diverse array of scenarios for robust model assessment. The details of each dataset are described in the following sections.

*Cofacts Open Datasets.* Collected from the 'Cofacts Real or Not' platform, a crowd-sourced fact-checking platform that uses chatbot technology to verify suspicious messages [26]. The platform allows users to scrutinize and discuss each message's validity, categorizing them into different types including those labeled as fraudulent. Along with the submitted articles, the dataset includes replies from the community, facilitating a collective verification process to ascertain the relevance and accuracy of each article with respect to the identified themes, including fraud. We collected a total of 2023 fraud data entries by September 17, 2022.

*165 Anti-fraud System Datasets.* The 165 Anti-fraud System Datasets are derived from the 165 Anti-fraud System, an initiative established by the National Police Agency under the Ministry of the Interior [27]. This system serves as a pivotal platform for the public to report fraudulent activities directly to law enforcement authorities. Given its purpose of facilitating official investigations, the system prompts individuals to provide detailed information about their experiences with fraud. This includes specifying the channels through which the fraud was perpetrated, as well as the particular tactics employed by the fraudsters. The richness and specificity of the data collected through this system make the 165 Anti-fraud System Datasets a valuable resource for developing and refining models designed to detect and understand fraudulent activities in a comprehensive manner. We collected a total of 12818 fraud data entries by June, 2023.

**Experimental Setup.** We compare GSC-FD method with some state-of-the-art baselines in which input only contains fraud content, including:

- **URL Presence.** Many users rely on simple heuristics, such as the presence of a URL within the message, to flag potential fraud. To benchmark our model against such intuitive approaches, we conducted an additional evaluation where messages containing URL were labeled as fraudulent across both seen and unseen sources. This heuristic, denoted as 'URL Presence' in our performance Table 3, did not involve any model training and solely relied on the textual feature.
- **LSTM** [8] excels at processing sequential data, making them particularly suited for analyzing text where the context and order of words are crucial for understanding content. Their ability to remember information over long sequences can be leveraged to detect subtle cues of deceptive language often found in fraud messages.
- **Random Forest** [9] is an ensemble learning method for classification, has been applied to detect phishing emails and fraud content due to its robustness and ability to handle high-dimensional data.

- **CNN** [8] is not only powerful for image processing but also effective for text classification due to their ability to detect local patterns and automatically learn feature hierarchies. In fraud detection, CNN can identify local textual patterns or phrases commonly associated with deceptive intent, even in varying linguistic contexts.
- **BERT** [31] is a pre-trained model, brings the advantage of leveraging vast amounts of general language knowledge, which can then be fine-tuned for the specific task of fraud detection. Its deep understanding of language context and nuances allows for the identification of sophisticated scams that may rely on subtle manipulations of language to deceive the recipient.

Given the predominance of Traditional Chinese in our dataset, tokenization and part-of-speech tagging were conducted using CKIPLab [28] to capture the linguistic nuances. A subset of CKIPLab's part-of-speech tags and their corresponding names in both English and Chinese are adapted from CKIPLab's "Tokenization and POS Tagging Guidelines" [29].

Unlike English, where token embeddings are readily available, Traditional Chinese does not have direct embeddings for tokens but only for individual Chinese characters. Therefore, to compute the embedding for Traditional Chinese tokens, we averaged the BERT embeddings of all characters constituting each token. This process is encapsulated by the following equation:

$$E(T) = \frac{1}{n}\sum_{i=1}^{n} \text{BERT}(c_i) \tag{15}$$

where $E(T)$ denotes the embedding for the token $T$, $\text{BERT}(c_i)$ represents the BERT embedding for the $i^{th}$ character within the token $T$, and $n$ is the total number of characters in the token $T$. By averaging the embeddings of each character, we achieve a composite embedding that integrates both the granular details of each character and the broader contextual significance of the entire token.

### 4.2 Overall Performance

For our experimental assessment, we utilized data classified as fraudulent from the Cofacts platform as a seen source for training model, detailed in Table 1. Concurrently, we deployed data aggregated from the 165 Anti-fraud System as an unseen source to evaluate the model's cross-domain adaptability, detailed in Table 2. Non-fraud message data for both seen and unseen sources were exclusively drawn from the non-fraudulent categories of the Cofacts platform.

Table 3 shows the performance of the GSC-FD method and all the compared methods on seen/unseen source. In Table 3, "Seen" indicates training and testing on the Cofacts dataset, while "Unseen" denotes training on Cofacts and testing on the 165 Anti-fraud dataset. The table reveals that GSC-FD's performance on the Seen source is closely competitive with the best-performing baseline model,

**Table 1.** Statistics for Seen Source (from Cofacts)

| Data Split (from Cofacts) | Count | Fraud Count | Fraud Average number of tokens | Non-Fraud Count | Non-Fraud Average number of tokens |
|---|---|---|---|---|---|
| Training | 2734 | 1393 | 47.13 | 1341 | 129.31 |
| Validation | 586 | 316 | 41.01 | 270 | 140.96 |
| Testing | 586 | 314 | 46.13 | 272 | 156.07 |

**Table 2.** Statistics for Unseen Source (from 165)

| Data Split (from 165) | Count | Fraud Count | Fraud Average number of tokens | Non-Fraud Count | Non-Fraud Average number of tokens |
|---|---|---|---|---|---|
| Testing | 12818 | 6400 | 34.83 | 6418 | 127.62 |

BERT. Notably, while other models experience significant performance degradation (a substantial drop rate) on the Unseen source, GSC-FD maintains consistent performance, indicative of its strong cross-domain effectiveness.

**Table 3.** Fraud detection performance on Seen: Cofacts → Cofacts/Unseen: Cofacts → 165

| Methods | Accuracy | Precision | Recall | F1 | AUC |
|---|---|---|---|---|---|
| URL Presence: Seen | 0.603 | 0.626 | 0.580 | 0.602 | 0.604 |
| URL Presence: Unseen | 0.489 | 0.483 | 0.342 | 0.400 | 0.489 |
| LSTM: Seen | 0.563 | 0.537 | 0.705 | 0.609 | 0.567 |
| LSTM: Unseen | 0.631 | 0.755 | 0.359 | 0.487 | 0.624 |
| Random Forest: Seen | 0.690 | 0.814 | 0.498 | 0.618 | 0.691 |
| Random Forest: Unseen | 0.545 | 0.582 | 0.232 | 0.332 | 0.537 |
| CNN: Seen | 0.609 | 0.607 | 0.678 | 0.641 | 0.607 |
| CNN: Unseen | 0.627 | 0.752 | 0.350 | 0.478 | 0.620 |
| BERT: Seen | **0.881** | **0.892** | 0.851 | **0.871** | 0.880 |
| BERT: Unseen | 0.693 | **0.847** | 0.451 | 0.589 | 0.660 |
| GSC-FD: Seen | 0.841 | 0.788 | **0.965** | 0.868 | **0.954** |
| GSC-FD: Unseen | **0.809** | 0.745 | **0.939** | **0.831** | **0.876** |

## 5 Conclusion and Future Work

Our proposed model, GSC-FD, adeptly identifies syntactic patterns indicative of fraudulent messages by leveraging global information. It uniquely allows each token the autonomy to represent either its inherent word meaning (*word*), its grammatical part-of-speech (*POS*), or a predetermined fixed value (#). Experimental results affirm that GSC-FD achieves the highest recognition rates on unseen datasets, with a significantly lower performance drop compared to alternative approaches. Remarkably, this substantial cross-domain adaptability was achieved with a dataset comprising just about 2,700 training examples, highlighting the model's efficient learning capability.

For future work, we plan to refine our approach by incorporating the frequency of token co-occurrences within the same texts as edge weights in the Co-occurrence Graphs to further enrich the global information.

## References

1. Huang, Y.-H., Liu, T.-W., Lee, S.-R., Calderon Alvarado, F.H., Chen, Y.-S.: Conquering cross-source failure for news credibility: learning generalizable representations beyond content embedding. In: Proceedings of the Web Conference 2020, pp. 774–784. ACM, New York (2020). https://doi.org/10.1145/3366423.3380158
2. Saravia, E., Liu, H.-C. T., Huang, Y.-H., Wu, J., Chen, Y.-S.: CARER: contextualized affect representations for emotion recognition. In: Riloff, E., Chiang, D., Hockenmaier, J., Tsujii, J. (eds.) Proceedings of the 2018 Conference on Empirical Methods in Natural Language Processing, pp. 3687–3697. ACL, Brussels (2018). https://doi.org/10.18653/v1/D18-1404
3. Yang, Y., Cui, Q., Ji, L., Cheng, Z.: Graph convolution word embedding and attention for text classification. In: Proceedings of the 2022 6th International Conference on Machine Learning and Soft Computing, pp. 160–166. ACM, New York (2022). https://doi.org/10.1145/3523150.3523175
4. Sailusha, R., Gnaneswar, V., Ramesh, R., Rao, G.R.: Credit card fraud detection using machine learning. In: 2020 4th International Conference on Intelligent Computing and Control Systems (ICICCS), pp. 1264–1270. IEEE, Madurai (2020). https://doi.org/10.1109/ICICCS48265.2020.9121114
5. Hu, J., et al.: Collaborative fraud detection: how collaboration impacts fraud detection. In: Proceedings of the 31st ACM International Conference on Multimedia, pp. 8891–8899. ACM, New York (2023). https://doi.org/10.1145/3581783.3613780
6. Naddaf, P., Nejad, E.M.A., Zahirnia, K., Jaeger, M., Schulte, O.: Joint link prediction via inference from a model. In: Proceedings of the 32nd ACM International Conference on Information and Knowledge Management, pp. 1877–1886. ACM, New York (2023). https://doi.org/10.1145/3583780.3614941
7. Pan, S., Hu, R., Long, G., Jiang, J., Yao, L., Zhang, C.: Adversarially regularized graph autoencoder for graph embedding. In: Proceedings of the 27th International Joint Conference on Artificial Intelligence, pp. 2609–2615. IJCAI, Stockholm (2018)
8. Heryadi, Y., Warnars, H.L.H.S.: Learning temporal representation of transaction amount for fraudulent transaction recognition using CNN, stacked LSTM, and CNN-LSTM. In: 2017 IEEE International Conference on Cybernetics and Computational Intelligence (CyberneticsCom), pp. 84–89. IEEE, New York (2017). https://doi.org/10.1109/CYBERNETICSCOM.2017.8311689
9. Xuan, S., Liu, G., Li, Z., Zheng, L., Wang, S., Jiang, C.: Random forest for credit card fraud detection. In: 2018 IEEE 15th International Conference on Networking, Sensing and Control (ICNSC), pp. 1–6. IEEE, New York (2018). https://doi.org/10.1109/ICNSC.2018.8361343
10. Button, M., Lewis, C., Tapley, J.: Not a victimless crime: the impact of fraud on individual victims and their families. Secur. J. **27**, 36–54 (2014). https://doi.org/10.1057/sj.2012.11
11. Li, Q., Cheng, M., Wang, J., Sun, B.: LSTM phishing detection for big email data. IEEE Trans. Big Data **8**(1), 278–288 (2022). https://doi.org/10.1109/TBDATA.2020.2978915

12. Salloum, S., Gaber, T., Vadera, S., Shaalan, K.: A systematic literature review on phishing email detection using natural language processing techniques. IEEE Access **10**, 65703–65727 (2022). https://doi.org/10.1109/ACCESS.2022.3183083
13. Doshi, J., Parmar, K., Sanghavi, R., Shekokar, N.: A comprehensive dual-layer architecture for phishing and spam email detection. Comput. Secur. **133**, 103378 (2023). https://doi.org/10.1016/j.cose.2023.103378
14. Alhogail, A., Alsabih, A.: Applying machine learning and natural language processing to detect phishing email. Comput. Secur. **110**, 102414 (2021). https://doi.org/10.1016/j.cose.2021.102414
15. Gangavarapu, T., Jaidhar, C.D., Chanduka, B.: Applicability of machine learning in spam and phishing email filtering: review and approaches. Artif. Intell. Rev. **53**, 5019–5081 (2020)
16. Xiang, S., et al.: Semi-supervised credit card fraud detection via attribute-driven graph representation. In: Proceedings of the AAAI Conference on Artificial Intelligence, vol. 37, no. 12, pp. 14557–14565 (2023). https://doi.org/10.1609/aaai.v37i12.26702
17. Liu, Y., Sun, Z., Zhang, W.: Improving fraud detection via hierarchical attention-based graph neural network. J. Inf. Secur. Appl. **72**(C), 103399 (2023). https://doi.org/10.1016/j.jisa.2022.103399
18. Wu, H., Tian, L., Wu, Y., Zhang, J., Ng, M.K., Long, J.: Transferable graph auto-encoders for cross-network node classification. Pattern Recogn. **150**, 110334 (2024). https://doi.org/10.1016/j.patcog.2024.110334
19. Mishra, S., Soni, D.: DSmishSMS-a system to detect smishing SMS. Neural Comput. Appl. , 1–18 (2021). https://doi.org/10.1007/s00521-021-06305-y
20. Abid, M.A., Ullah, S., Siddique, M.A., Mushtaq, M.F., Aljedaani, W., Rustam, F.: Spam SMS filtering based on text features and supervised machine learning techniques. Multimed. Tools Appl. **81**(28), 39853–39871 (2022). https://doi.org/10.1007/s11042-022-12991-0
21. Zhang, H., Li, P., Zhang, R., Li, X.: Embedding graph auto-encoder for graph clustering. IEEE Trans. Neural Netw. Learn. Syst. **34**(11), 9352–9362 (2023). https://doi.org/10.1109/TNNLS.2022.3158654
22. Yu, H.H.: Scenario Analysis of Fraud Victim. Unpublished (2011)
23. OpenAI: GPT-4 Technical report. arXiv preprint arXiv:2303.08774 (2023). https://arxiv.org/abs/2303.08774
24. National Police Agency, Ministry of the Interior: Police Statistics Bulletin (Week 50 of the year 2023). https://www.npa.gov.tw/ch/app/data/doc?module=wg057&detailNo=1184012029187330048&type=s. Accessed 14 Jan 2024
25. Ministry of Justice: Statistical Analysis of Fraudulent Crime Cases. https://www.rjsd.moj.gov.tw/RJSDWEB/common/WebListFile.ashx?list_id=1802. Accessed 17 Jan 2024
26. Cofacts: Cofacts Open Datasets. https://github.com/cofacts/opendata. Accessed 23 Jan 2024
27. National Police Agency, Ministry of the Interior: 165 Anti-fraud Reporting System. https://165.npa.gov.tw/#/report/statement. Accessed 23 Jan 2024
28. Institute of Information Science, Academia Sinica: CKIP Lab Chinese Word Segmentation Tool. https://ckip.iis.sinica.edu.tw/project/ws. Accessed 13 Mar 2024

29. Academia Sinica, Institute of Information Science: Tokenization and POS Tagging Guidelines. https://ckip.iis.sinica.edu.tw/CKIP/tr/9305_2013
30. Kipf, T.N., Welling, M.: Variational graph auto-encoders. arXiv preprint arXiv:1611.07308 (2016). https://arxiv.org/abs/1611.07308
31. Sahmoud, T., Mikki, M.: Spam Detection Using BERT. arXiv preprint arXiv:2206.02443 (2022). https://arxiv.org/abs/2206.02443

# Image Analysis

# Dynamically Searching and Classifying Images by Using Neural Networks and Reinforcement Learning with the Grid Table

I-Fan Lee and Ying-Ping Chen(✉)

Department of Computer Science, National Yang Ming Chiao Tung University, Hsinchu, Taiwan
{ivanlee.cs11,ypchen}@cs.nycu.edu.tw

**Abstract.** Since the advent of the Transformer, there have been numerous significant studies in the language domain, and it has also impacted the visual domain, where many visual studies integrating Transformers have achieved remarkable performance. A classic example is the Vision Transformer (ViT). ViT utilizes a global self-attention mechanism, allowing any block in the image to interactively compute with other blocks. However, in many images, non-critical information occupies most of the blocks, and in reality, excluding these blocks from computation has minimal impact on decision-making outcomes. Therefore, we developed a method based on a patch-based approach, utilizing global information through a grid table, abbreviated as GT-RAM. Through training methods from reinforcement learning, GT-RAM only collects samples from certain blocks for image classification. In experiments using the Mnist and Fashion datasets, compared with different computational approaches like CNN and ViT, GT-RAM's accuracy exceeded the former two methods, demonstrating that even with only key blocks sampled, the model can perform well. The sampling efficiency also surpassed similar architectures such as RAM and DT-RAM. This research confirms the effectiveness of the patch-based sampling method, and the straightforward approach of GT-RAM, which avoids redundant sampling, contributes to future studies on cooperative sampling among multiple agents.

**Keywords:** Reinforcement learning · pixel-wise · patch-based · Classification · RNN · LSTM · ViT

## 1 Introduction

Since the advent of the Transformer [3], the multi-head self-attention mechanism has significantly impacted and transformed the field of natural language processing (NLP). This influence has subsequently permeated the vision domain. In comparison to the limitations of convolutional neural networks (CNNs), the

© The Author(s), under exclusive license to Springer Nature Singapore Pte Ltd. 2025
W.-T. Chu et al. (Eds.): TAAI 2024, CCIS 2414, pp. 51–65, 2025.
https://doi.org/10.1007/978-981-96-4589-3_4

Transformer enhances overall computational capabilities, enabling comprehensive interaction among all image patches. This leads to substantial improvements across various neural network methodologies in the vision domain. However, it is noteworthy that in many images, only a few key feature patches are essential. Building upon the Recurrent Attention Model (RAM), this study introduces the Grid-Table RAM (GT-RAM) method, which incorporates a grid table to facilitate patch-based sampling on images, ultimately producing image classification predictions. It shows the process flow diagram is presented in Fig. 1. Our experiments on the Fashion dataset reveal that GT-RAM achieves higher accuracy than ViT-large, utilizing less than one-tenth of the parameters.

Since its introduction in 2020, the Vision Transformer (ViT) [4] has achieved numerous breakthroughs in various vision tasks. Compared to CNNs, the global attention mechanism fully leverages the information across the entire image, resulting in significant advancements in image classification [6], object detection [2], image segmentation [9], and other vision applications. This represents a substantial improvement over traditional convolutional networks, which are constrained by fixed kernel sizes for image processing.

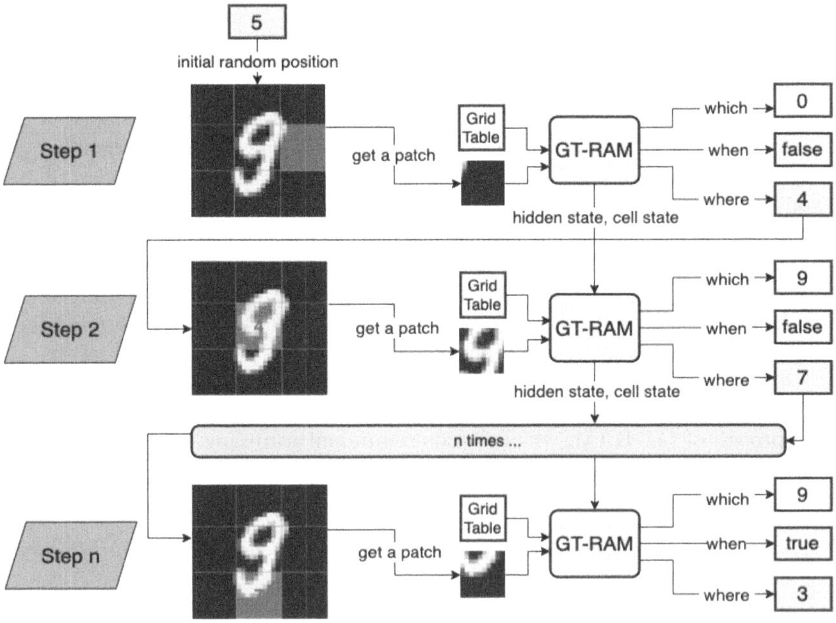


**Fig. 1.** The diagram presents an example flowchart for GT-RAM. Initially, the model randomly selects one patch from the image, then feeds the selected patch along with the grid table into GT-RAM. At that moment, the model outputs three actions: Which category does this image belong to (which)? Should sampling stop at this moment (when)? Where should it move next (where)? The new patch and updated grid table are inputted into the model to generate new actions. This process is repeated until the model outputs true for the 'when' action or reaches the maximum step limit.

The self-attention architecture allows the model to focus on specific patches, enabling a comprehensive analysis. However, this approach presents a challenge: the global attention mechanism necessitates the participation of all patches in the computation, despite the fact that crucial information is often confined to a limited number of localized patches. Consequently, many patches contribute little to the overall computation.

Previous studies, such as RAM [8] and DT-RAM [7], have employed memory models like RNNs to implement local attention mechanisms. These approaches utilize reinforcement learning to identify and predict the locations of critical information based on prior knowledge. Local detection is facilitated through reinforcement learning methods and reward mechanisms, guiding the effective sampling process. Additionally, DT-RAM enables the model to autonomously determine when to cease sampling, thereby reducing the average number of samples required.

In the sampling methodologies of both RAM and DT-RAM, the model collects patches at the pixel level across the entire image. However, it has been observed that many sampling steps exhibit significant overlap, leading to resource inefficiency. For instance, even after identifying key features, the model may move only one or two pixels per sampling step to reach the optimal position.

Building on the foundations of RAM models, we propose the Grid-Table RAM (GT-RAM) method, designed to facilitate patch-based sampling on images. Our experimental results indicate that utilizing LSTM models is more effective for patch-based sampling. Furthermore, we have modified the reward function originally employed in RAM to accommodate patch-based data. By defining diverse data using grid characteristics and consolidating them into a grid table, we have enhanced the sampling performance. The primary contributions of this study, abbreviated as GT-RAM in this paper, are as follows:

1. The design of GT-RAM to enable patch-based sampling on images.
2. The development of a reward function suitable for GT-RAM.
3. The provision of a grid-table to enhance GT-RAM's sampling efficiency.

Our experimental results demonstrate that GT-RAM outperforms previous methodologies, including RAM and DT-RAM, in both sampling efficiency and error rates. In experiments conducted on the Fashion dataset, GT-RAM exceeds the performance of ViT-small with an equivalent number of parameters and achieves a lower error rate than ViT-large, which has more than ten times the number of parameters.

This paper demonstrates the effectiveness of the patch-based sampling method through image classification experiments. In the future, this well-structured, conflict-free approach may serve as a foundational study for implementing multi-agent image classification.

## 2 Related Work

The concept of recurrent attention was first introduced in RAM [8]. DT-RAM [7] added a Stopper model to decide when to stop sampling. Based on RAM, other studies integrated RAM methods to design applications such as drawing [5] and house number recognition [1].

Since AlexNet in 2012, Convolutional Neural Networks (CNNs) have demonstrated excellent capabilities in various research and applications. Thanks to their ability to reduce computational complexity and to effectively analyze images in a two-dimensional space, CNNs are almost indispensable in various image recognition competitions.

Since the introduction of the Transformer, many new breakthroughs have emerged in the NLP field. Global self-attention has proven its advantages over many classic models, whether in language translation, article writing, or sentiment analysis. In the vision domain, by using patch-based image segmentation, images can be analyzed using the Transformer framework. ViT [4] represents a successful example, especially under conditions of large parameters and large datasets, where it outperforms traditional CNN models.

Based on the Markov chain, models in the settings of reinforcement learning (RL) can interact with the environment. The model inputs the state information provided by the environment and then outputs an action, which ultimately affects the environment. Following this cycle, the model needs to learn to maximize the cumulative reward in the environment. The reward comes from a user-designed reward function, which influences the model's training. Through this interactive framework, the model can be trained until it finds a local optimal solution.

RAM proposes a method to implement an attention mechanism in the spatial dimension by utilizing Deep Neural Networks (DNN) in combination with Reinforcement Learning (RL). This approach enables the model to autonomously control the movement of a detection window within an image, thereby capturing a image patch. For instance, using images from the MNIST dataset, where each image has a size of $28 \times 28$ pixels, the detection window is set to a size of $8 \times 8$ pixels. Additionally, the current position of the detection window, denoted as x-pos and y-pos, is inputted into the model. The positional information is normalized to a range between $-1$ and 1. For example, if the detection window initially appears at the center, the positional information provided is (14,14), which is then normalized to (0.0, 0.0). The image patch and positional information are processed by a DNN, and the output is then passed to an RNN. The RNN utilizes the output from the DNN along with the memory from the previous time step (t-1) and produces outputs for two downstream DNNs. The first DNN outputs the classification prediction, while the second DNN controls the movement of the detection window. This entire process realizes a method for locating image patches. The classification DNN is trained using a cross-entropy loss, while the movement control DNN is trained using a reward system, where the model receives a reward if the prediction after movement is correct. This reward is then used to optimize the parameters.

A DNN model was integrated into DT-RAM to control whether the model continues sampling. The difference from RAM is that RAM only uses A DNN to control model movement, but the number of samples is fixed. DT-RAM can decide whether to stop during the sampling process, thereby increasing sampling efficiency and reducing the average number of sampling steps. Ultimately, DT-RAM demonstrated that it could achieve a lower error rate than RAM with a similar number of sampling steps.

# 3 Methods

The main difference of this proposal from RAM and DT-RAM is that the sampling process has been changed from pixel-wise to patch-based. Additionally, the original input, which only consisted of the detection box position, has been changed to a grid table format for the model. However, experiments showed that the original design using patch-based sampling was less effective. Therefore, we designed the model, a reward function, and a training method to make GT-RAM, which conducts patch-based sampling, ultimately showing that GT-RAM outperforms RAM and DT-RAM in sampling efficiency and error rates.

## 3.1 Grid Table

In the past pixel-wise methods, the detection box could move freely within the $w \times h$ image. In the patch-based method, $w \times h$ is divided into $n \times n$ patches of $p \times p$. This characteristic allows the entire image to be represented by an $n \times n$ table, which is called a grid table in this study. We devised four kinds of information to provide to the model.

The grid table is composed of four maps: the current map, history map, class map, and prob map. These maps respectively store the current position of the detection window, the movement history including both current and past information, the predicted class information, and the probabilities associated with the predicted classes. Each map has the same size and is divided into $n$ equal parts along both the length and width, forming an $n \times n$ map. Here is an example in Fig. 2: suppose the model took three steps in a sampling process. In the chart on the right, the symbol $s$ represents a step, with a total of three steps in the process. At step 3, the detection window is located at (1,1), so the current map indicates the current location of the window. The history map shows the movement records for all sampling steps. $H$ denotes the maximum limited step. The history map shows that positions (1,1), (1,2), and (3,1) have been visited, each recorded as $1/H$ because they were visited only once. The class map and prob map represent the classes and probabilities predicted by the detection window in the past. At step 1, the model predicted class 9 with a probability of 0.9, and at step 2, the model predicted class 3 with a probability of 0.4.

The design of the grid table enhances the model's performance in movements, classification, and stopping actions. This table serves as a simple method for information compression, allowing the model to reference past data at time $t$. Within the History map, we introduce a hyperparameter $H$, defined as the maximum number of movements allowed for the model. In this study, $H$ is set to 10. Once the number of movements reaches 10, the exploration is forcibly terminated, thus ending the entire sampling process.

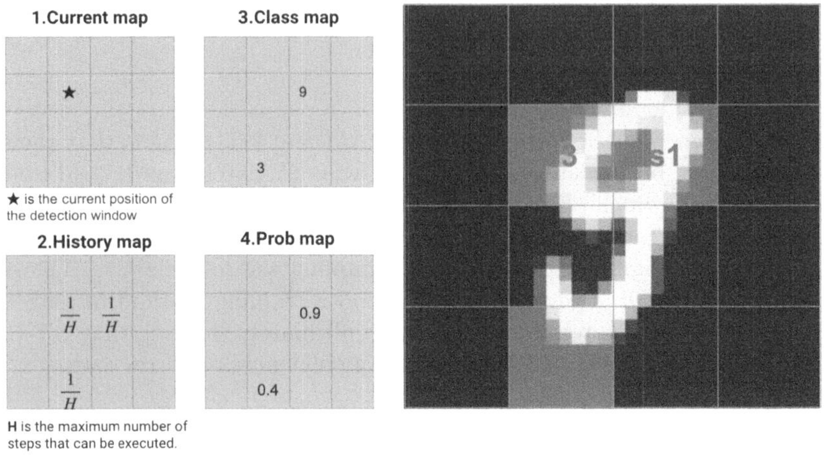


**Fig. 2.** The grid table provides four types of maps: (1) Current map: the current position of the detection window, (2) History map: the records of the current and past movements of the detection window, (3) Class map: the records of the predicted classes by the classifier, and (4) Prob map: the records of the predicted probabilities.

We organized information from four maps and expanded each map into a one-dimensional vector before inputting it into the model. Assuming the length and width of each map are $n$, after flattening, each becomes a vector of $n^2$. Finally, these four vectors are concatenated to form a vector of size $4n^2$, which is then input into the model as auxiliary information.

### 3.2 Model Design

In GT-RAM, the model's input consists of two types of data: the patch data and the grid table information. The patch data go through the Encoder, and the grid table information goes to the Location. The output information is then combined with the Encoder's output, goes through a ReLU layer, and is input to the Memory model. The Memory model receives the combined information from the Encoder and Location, along with the previous memory at time $t-1$, and then outputs. Finally, the Memory output goes to the Classifier, Mover, and Stopper, allowing the model to perform classification, movement, and stopping. The entire model architecture is illustrated in Fig. 3.

**Reinforcement Learning.** In GT-RAM, we apply reinforcement learning to train the model. Initially, we allow the model to move continuously, but its performance is poor due to the random initial parameters. The environment provides a reward value if the model successfully predicts the image. This reward is then used to perform gradient ascent on the actions, enabling the model to learn how to move more efficiently toward critical patches. By repeating this process iteratively, the model's performance improves step by step.

**Encoder.** The Encoder model consists of two linear layers with a ReLU in between. Before the patch input, the $1 \times 8 \times 8$ image is first converted to $1 \times 64$, which the Encoder can process.

**Location.** The Location model consists of two linear layers with a ReLU in between. Compared to previous methods, it only had $x$-pos and $y$-pos information. However, with the patch-based structure, the results produced by the model can be fully segmented each time. Therefore, in the grid table content, we provide the current position information, the exploration history, and the predicted class, and probability values for each step, making full use of the patch-based characteristics to utilize the past information.

**Memory.** In previous methods, RAM used RNN to compute the current information along with past memory. However, it was observed that in the pixel-based sampling process, due to the non-overlapping content in each sampling instance, a more robust capability was required to manage the highly variable information. Compared to RAM, the error rate in GT-RAM significantly increased when using RNN. Consequently, LSTM was adopted instead. Experimental results demonstrated that GT-RAM with LSTM outperformed GT-RAM with RNN.

**Mover.** The Mover is a neural network constructed with two hidden layers, utilizing the tanh activation function. Its purpose is to predict the next sampling location on an $n \times n$ grid after incorporating values supplied by the Memory and additional grid table information. Upon output, Mover uses PyTorch's Categorical distribution to randomly generate a probability distribution, from which it selects a value to determine the next movement location.

During the training of the Mover, our aim is for it to explore as extensively as possible. Discovering more key tiles leads to higher overall rewards. Consequently, the probability of participating in an action during the sampling process increases with higher total rewards and decreases otherwise. The design incorporates the REINFORCE algorithm [10] to optimize this behavior.

**Stopper.** The Stopper is a neural network comprising two hidden layers, with tanh as the activation function in the middle layers. The primary function of the Stopper is to input values from Memory and incorporate grid table information, then establish a Bernoulli distribution using PyTorch. Based on this probability distribution, it outputs a value of 0 or 1, which determines whether to stop the entire sampling process.

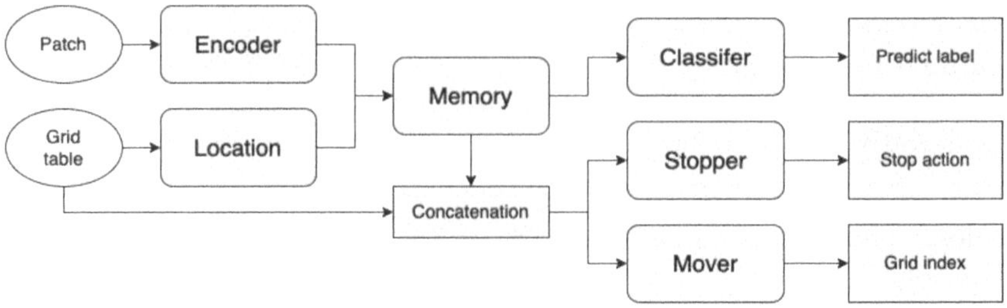


**Fig. 3.** The architecture of GT-RAM

During the training of the Stopper, the reward value is multiplied by $\gamma^t$, where $\gamma = 0.99$. The reward diminishes as the step $t$ increases due to this multiplication. If sampling stops too early, leading to incorrect predictions, a reward of 0 is returned. Therefore, the Stopper needs to learn whether sufficient information has been obtained during the Mover's sampling process to allow the Classifier to make an accurate prediction. If so, it must stop as soon as possible; otherwise, it allows the Mover to continue sampling. Similar to the Mover, the Stopper also employs the REINFORCE algorithm [10], where a greater reward value increases the probability of that action being taken.

### 3.3 Cumulative Reward

The reward function design for the Mover in both RAM and DT-RAM involves checking whether the Classifier's output matches the label at the final step. If it does, the Mover receives a reward of 1 for each action taken from the first step to the last step. In DT-RAM, the Stopper's reward is further multiplied by a decay factor $\gamma$ based on the number of steps.

In GT-RAM experiments, we initially tried the same reward function as that was adopted in existing studies but obtained inferior results. Analyzing specific samples revealed that some important features of certain images were divided into several patches. These divided patches contained equally important information, making it unclear which patch should be the final step. In this situation, our expectation is that all patches with important features are collected rather than focusing on one specific patch. The original reward design assumes that in pixel-wise sampling, the detection box center moves to the most critical feature step by step. However, our observations revealed that important features might be divided into multiple patches. Therefore, in such cases, all these patches should be sampled, not just one.

Therefore, we designed a cumulative reward mechanism. As long as the Classifier successfully predicts at any step, the function records and accumulates a reward of 1. At the end, all actions receive the same reward. The key idea is that some images have rich features with several key patches, while others have only one key patch. The core idea of the patch-based method is to encourage the Mover to collect all key information as much as possible and to speculate the importance of different patches based on the information obtained at the time, starting with the most important patches.

During our experiments, after switching to cumulative rewards, we discovered a new problem: if important features are concentrated in one grid, the Mover may leave this grid and then return to collect it again in later steps, causing repetitive sampling.

To address this issue, we designed a filled map to record which areas have been rewarded. If repetitive sampling occurs, the reward will not be accumulated.

### 3.4 Slight Disturbance

During the experiment, we found that compared to RAM, the GT-RAM method is prone to overfitting. The reason is that the pixel-wise and patch-based methods differ significantly in the amount of data they can capture. In RAM and DT-RAM, pixel-wise sampling results in a total of (height - detection box height + 1) $\times$ (width - detection box width + 1) samples. For example, with a $32 \times 32$ image and an $8 \times 8$ detection box, there are 625 samples. However, with the patch-based method adopted by GT-RAM, sampling from grids cut from integers results in only 16 samples for $(32/8) \times (32/8)$. In comparison, pixel-wise sampling provides more samples, which is why GT-RAM is more prone to overfitting during training.

To solve this problem, we used a data augmentation method, randomly offsetting each image by 1 pixel in four directions. Although it is a small disturbance, the effect is significant (Table 7). To ensure fairness in our experiments, we also applied the same data augmentation to RAM, ViT, and CNN during training in the experimental section.

### 3.5 Loss Function

In GT-RAM model training, we need to optimize six parts: Encoder, Location, Memory, Classifier, Mover, and Stopper. Additionally, there are two Critic models to reduce reward variance.

For each classification training, we use cross-entropy loss for the Encoder, Location, Memory, and Classifier based on the predicted and true labels.

$$L = -\sum_{c=1}^{C} y_c \log(\hat{y}_c) \tag{1}$$

For the Mover, we use reinforcement learning methods. When the model receives a positive reward, all actions taken in $t$ steps will be increased in probability distribution using gradient ascent. Equation (2) is derived from Eq. (1) in the RAM paper [8].

Next is the reward estimation function. To reduce the variance impact during Mover training, we designed a model to estimate the reward value. We optimized this estimation function with the mean squared error. The output value, denoted as '$b$', is then used in the training of the Mover.

$$\nabla_\theta J = \sum_{t=1}^{T} \mathbb{E}_{p(s1:T;\theta)}[\nabla_\theta \log \pi(u_t|s_{1:t};\theta)R] \approx \frac{1}{M}\sum_{i=1}^{M}\sum_{t=1}^{T} \nabla_\theta \log \pi(u_t^i|s_{1:t}^i;\theta)(R_t^i - b_t) \tag{2}$$

For the Stopper, we use the same calculation method as the Mover, and additionally add entropy loss to increase its probability distribution's randomness.

$$H(x) = -\sum_{i=1}^{n} P(x_i)\log_e P(x_i) \tag{3}$$

### 3.6 Planning Exploration

During the model sampling process, due to certain regional features, the Classifier's convergence speed is slow, causing some local areas to easily gain rewards and making exploration confined in some specific areas, entering a vicious cycle. For example, in handwritten digit recognition, it is easy to linger in the middle and not move to the edges, resulting in fewer samples and poor Classifier predictions for the edges, causing the Mover to sample only specific patches. Generally, the Classifier must converge to a certain degree on the patches so that the Mover can progressively sample patches. If the Mover is confined to sampling in certain areas, the overall performance will degrade.

To address this issue, we designed a pre-training process where the Mover and Stopper do not participate. Before each pre-training, a movement path is obtained, with each step in this path not repeating. Then, it is randomly shuffled and provided for model training. This allows the Classifier to learn all patches in the image, equipping it with prior knowledge of the entire image, reducing the problem of the Mover being confined to specific areas during exploration.

## 4 Experiments

The experiments are divided into three parts to evaluate the performance of GT-RAM, namely steps, error rates, and weights. The subjects of the experiment are the MNIST and Fashion datasets.

For the subsets, each of the training, validation, and test sets has 50,000, 10,000, and 10,000 samples, respectively. In each experiment, a unique timestamp is used as a random seed to ensure the independence of each experiment. Each experiment was conducted for 30 independent runs, and the mean and standard deviation were recorded as the final experimental outcome. For model comparison, we utilized RAM and DT-RAM, as well as CNN, ViT small, and ViT large, for performance evaluation. To design the CNN, we referred to the RAM paper. The first layer is a convolutional network consisting of 8 filters of size $10 \times 10$ with a stride of 5. A hidden layer with 256 units follows this, and ReLU activation functions follow both layers. The first layer of the ViT small employs a fully connected layer with 256 units, while the second layer is a VisionEncoder with 8 attention heads and a 256 embedding dimension. The ViT large is the same as the ViT small, except that the second layer consists of three VisionEncoder layers with a 512 embedding dimension.

### 4.1 Steps and Error Rate Comparison

Table 1 compares the steps and error rates between RAM, DT-RAM, and GT-RAM. The step count indicates that the smaller the number, the fewer steps are needed to complete the detection on average. Since RAM does not have a Stopper to decide when to stop, the steps for RAM are fixed. We also refer to DT-RAM's data [5] to compare sampling efficiency.

Since the code for DT-RAM is in Lua Torch, which has not been updated since 2018, we directly include the data from the DT-RAM paper. Kevin Zakka provided a PyTorch implementation of RAM [11], and we use this project for obtaining the experimental data. In the MNIST dataset, RAM's best performance in the paper is an error rate 1.07% for 7 steps, and in our experiment, RAM's best performance is an error rate of 1.05% at 8 steps.

We also experimented with the Fashion dataset in Table 2. The best RAM version has an error rate of 11.18% for 7 steps, while our version is 8.98%, showing that GT-RAM has a lower error rate.

**Table 1.** Comparison of steps and error rates on MNIST. (*): Due to the fact that the open-source code for this method has not been maintained for a long time and the torch framework implemented in Lua poses significant difficulties in reproduction, we only use the data from the paper for comparison. For the above reasons, DT-RAM did not incorporate the method of slight disturbance. $\mu \pm \sigma$(-): $\mu$ represents the mean, $\sigma$ represents the standard deviation, and (-) indicates that the results are statistically significantly inferior to **0.86Âś0.1** by using the t-test with a 95% confidence interval.

| Method (size = $8 \times 8$) | Error (%) | |
|---|---|---|
| | RNN | LSTM |
| RAM 2 steps | $9.08 \pm 1.30$(-) | $8.65 \pm 0.44$(-) |
| RAM 3 steps | $2.82 \pm 1.47$(-) | $2.40 \pm 0.22$(-) |
| RAM 4 steps | $1.64 \pm 0.53$(-) | $1.43 \pm 0.26$(-) |
| RAM 5 steps | $2.03 \pm 4.69$(-) | $1.23 \pm 0.31$(-) |
| RAM 6 steps | $1.26 \pm 1.02$(-) | $1.11 \pm 0.21$(-) |
| RAM 7 steps | $1.07 \pm 0.45$(-) | $1.19 \pm 0.38$(-) |
| RAM 8 steps | $1.05 \pm 0.27$(-) | $1.28 \pm 1.18$(-) |
| RAM 9 steps | $1.13 \pm 0.74$(-) | $1.55 \pm 1.37$(-) |
| DT-RAM 5.2 steps(*) | 1.12 | |
| GT-RAM $3.9 \pm 0.1$ steps | $2.1 \pm 0.22$(-) | |
| GT-RAM $4.4 \pm 0.18$ steps | | $\mathbf{0.86 \pm 0.1}$ |

**Table 2.** Comparison of steps and error rates on Fashion. $\mu \pm \sigma(\text{-})$: $\mu$ represents the mean, $\sigma$ represents the standard deviation, and (-) indicates that the results are statistically significantly inferior to $\mathbf{8.98 \pm 0.23}$ by using the t-test with a 95% confidence interval.

| Method (size = $8 \times 8$) | Error (%) | |
|---|---|---|
| | RNN | LSTM |
| RAM 2 steps | $20.69 \pm 1.29$(-) | $20.52 \pm 0.82$(-) |
| RAM 3 steps | $16.43 \pm 2.66$(-) | $15.08 \pm 1.14$(-) |
| RAM 4 steps | $13.70 \pm 2.49$(-) | $13.20 \pm 1.09$(-) |
| RAM 5 steps | $12.48 \pm 1.32$(-) | $12.28 \pm 1.47$(-) |
| RAM 6 steps | $11.96 \pm 1.47$(-) | $12.24 \pm 1.85$(-) |
| RAM 7 steps | $11.18 \pm 1.33$(-) | $12.63 \pm 3.87$(-) |
| RAM 8 steps | $11.91 \pm 2.59$(-) | $11.91 \pm 2.52$(-) |
| RAM 9 steps | $11.89 \pm 1.97$(-) | $12.12 \pm 3.55$(-) |
| GT-RAM $3.7 \pm 0.1$ steps | $13.40 \pm 0.77$(-) | |
| GT-RAM $5.5 \pm 0.23$ steps | | $\mathbf{8.98 \pm 0.23}$ |

### 4.2 Error Rate Comparison

We also compared error rates with RAM, GT-RAM, CNN and ViT in Tables 3 and 4. Since the steps and error rates comparison shows that LSTM performs better than RNN, we selected the LSTM version and tried experiments with 3, 5, 7, and 9 steps. To fairly compare the capabilities of GT-RAM, RAM, and ViT, we set the patch size of GT-RAM and RAM to $7 \times 7$ for a comparison with ViT. In the MNIST and Fashion experiments, both GT-RAM and ViT used $28 \times 28$ images, with a patch size of $7 \times 7$, resulting in 16 patches.

### 4.3 Weight Comparison

Both GT-RAM and ViT are patch-based methods, so we experimented with MNIST and Fashion datasets. Additionally, we designed two versions of ViT, small and large, to examine weights and error rates in Tables 5 and 6.

In the MNIST experiment, the ViT large error rate is lower than GT-RAM, but in the Fashion dataset, GT-RAM requires less than 1/10 of the parameters and has a lower error rate than ViT-large.

### 4.4 Ablation Study

We also conducted an ablation study on the GT-RAM model for observation and investigation of each component after ablation in Table 7.

**Table 3.** Comparison on the MNIST. $\mu \pm \sigma$(-): $\mu$ represents the mean, $\sigma$ represents the standard deviation, and (-) indicates that the results are statistically significantly inferior to $\mathbf{0.92 \pm 0.09}$ by using the t-test with a 95% confidence interval.

| Method (size = $7 \times 7$) | Error (%) |
|---|---|
| RAM 3 steps, LSTM | $3.69 \pm 0.69$(-) |
| RAM 5 steps, LSTM | $1.94 \pm 1.02$(-) |
| RAM 7 steps, LSTM | $2.16 \pm 2.13$(-) |
| RAM 9 steps, LSTM | $1.77 \pm 2.25$(-) |
| Conv | $1.42 + 0.83$(-) |
| ViT | $1.24 + 0.07$(-) |
| GT-RAM $4.7 \pm 0.1$ steps | $\mathbf{0.92 \pm 0.09}$ |

**Table 4.** Comparison on the Fashion. $\mu \pm \sigma$(-): $\mu$ represents the mean, $\sigma$ represents the standard deviation, and (-) indicates that the results are statistically significantly inferior to $\mathbf{8.72 \pm 0.29}$ by using the t-test with a 95% confidence interval.

| Method (size = $7 \times 7$) | Error (%) |
|---|---|
| RAM 3 steps, LSTM | $17.17 \pm 3.47$(-) |
| RAM 5 steps, LSTM | $14.62 \pm 3.70$(-) |
| RAM 7 steps, LSTM | $11.85 \pm 2.99$(-) |
| RAM 9 steps, LSTM | $11.28 \pm 1.95$(-) |
| Conv | $9.96 \pm 2.73$(-) |
| ViT | $10.22 \pm 0.20$(-) |
| GT-RAM $5.6 \pm 0.19$ steps | $\mathbf{8.72 \pm 0.29}$ |

**Table 5.** MNIST experiment

| Method | Error | Parameter |
|---|---|---|
| ViT small | $1.24 + 0.07$ | 0.81M |
| ViT large | $\mathbf{0.87 + 0.08}$ | 9.49M |
| GT-RAM $7 \times 7$ | $0.92 + 0.09$ | 0.69M |

**Table 6.** Fashion experiment

| Method | Error | Parameter |
|---|---|---|
| ViT small | $10.22 \pm 0.20$ | 0.81M |
| ViT large | $9.3 \pm 0.18$ | 9.49M |
| GT-RAM $7 \times 7$ | $\mathbf{8.72 \pm 0.29}$ | 0.69M |

## 5 Conclusion and Future Work

In conclusion, we summarize the research findings and experimental results and discuss potential future directions.

### 5.1 Conclusions

In our experiments, we began by exploring the principle of the Vision Transformer's (ViT) global computations on image patches, approaching the problem from a data-centric perspective. This enabled the model to autonomously select patches and make predictions. Building upon the design of the Recurrent Attention Model (RAM), we modified the sampling method from a pixel-wise approach to a patch-based approach, resulting in the design of Grid-Table RAM (GT-RAM). Various methods for input data, training methodologies, and reward functions were experimented with in order to address the challenges inherent in patch-based sampling.

Our experiments demonstrated that GT-RAM achieved superior sampling efficiency and lower error rates in image classification tasks compared to the existing methods such as RAM and DT-RAM. Furthermore, comparisons with CNN and ViT models, which have architectures similar to RAM, revealed that GT-RAM exhibited superior performance on the MNIST and Fashion datasets.

**Table 7.** Ablation

| Without | Error (%) | Glimpse |
|---|---|---|
| Cumulative-reward and filled map | $1.04 \pm 0.09$ | $4.7 \pm 0.26$ |
| Grid table for location | $0.89 \pm 0.09$ | $4.8 \pm 0.9$ |
| Concatenation for mover and stopper | $1.03 \pm 0.12$ | $4.3 \pm 0.1$ |
| Slight disturbance | $2.53 \pm 0.38$ | $5.1 \pm 1.1$ |
| Planning exploration | $1.09 \pm 0.1$ | $4.5 \pm 0.2$ |
| Entropy loss | $1.07 \pm 0.12$ | $5.2 \pm 0.7$ |
| GT-RAM | $0.86 \pm 0.01$ | $4.4 \pm 0.2$ |

Additionally, a comparison between the parameter-heavy ViT-large and GT-RAM indicated that, in the Fashion dataset experiments, GT-RAM outperformed ViT-large while utilizing less than one-tenth of the parameters.

### 5.2 Future Work

Our experiments have demonstrated that sequential patch sampling on a grid can outperform RAM and DT-RAM, on the MNIST and Fashion datasets. Future research may focus on developing a multi-agent approach based on the GT-RAM architecture. This approach will enable agents to collaborate in sampling and classification, replacing the need to process the entire image with a more flexible, patch-based method for downstream tasks. Furthermore, if image complexity can be assessed during the detection process, dynamically determining the number of agents may offer a flexible solution for practical resource utilization. Recently, multi-agent systems have been extensively researched and applied in language models. We anticipate that multi-agent systems will similarly provide a more flexible and versatile research direction in the field of image detection.

**Acknowledgments.** The work was supported in part by the National Science and Technology Council of Taiwan under Grant NSTC 113-2221-E-A49-156.

## References

1. Ba, J., Mnih, V., Kavukcuoglu, K.: Multiple object recognition with visual attention. arXiv preprint arXiv:1412.7755 (2014)
2. Carion, N., Massa, F., Synnaeve, G., Usunier, N., Kirillov, A., Zagoruyko, S.: End-to-end object detection with transformers. In: European Conference on Computer Vision, pp. 213–229. Springer, Cham (2020)
3. Devlin, J., Chang, M., Lee, K., Toutanova, K.: BERT: pre-training of deep bidirectional transformers for language understanding. CoRR abs/1810.04805 (2018). http://arxiv.org/abs/1810.04805
4. Dosovitskiy, A., et al.: An image is worth 16x16 words: transformers for image recognition at scale. arXiv preprint arXiv:2010.11929 (2020)

5. Gregor, K., Danihelka, I., Graves, A., Rezende, D., Wierstra, D.: Draw: a recurrent neural network for image generation. In: International Conference on Machine Learning, pp. 1462–1471. PMLR (2015)
6. He, K., Chen, X., Xie, S., Li, Y., Dollár, P., Girshick, R.: Masked autoencoders are scalable vision learners. In: Proceedings of the IEEE/CVF Conference on Computer Vision and Pattern Recognition, pp. 16000–16009 (2022)
7. Li, Z., Yang, Y., Liu, X., Zhou, F., Wen, S., Xu, W.: Dynamic computational time for visual attention. In: 2017 IEEE International Conference on Computer Vision Workshops (ICCVW), pp. 1199–1209 (2017). https://doi.org/10.1109/ICCVW.2017.145
8. Mnih, V., Heess, N., Graves, A., Kavukcuoglu, k.: Recurrent models of visual attention. In: Ghahramani, Z., Welling, M., Cortes, C., Lawrence, N., Weinberger, K. (eds.) Advances in Neural Information Processing Systems, vol. 27. Curran Associates, Inc. (2014), https://proceedings.neurips.cc/paper_files/paper/2014/file/09c6c3783b4a70054da74f2538ed47c6-Paper.pdf
9. Strudel, R., Garcia, R., Laptev, I., Schmid, C.: Segmenter: transformer for semantic segmentation. In: Proceedings of the IEEE/CVF International Conference on Computer Vision, pp. 7262–7272 (2021)
10. Williams, R.: Simple statistical gradient-following algorithms for connectionist reinforcement learning. Mach. Learn. **8**, 229–256 (1992)
11. Zakka, K.: Github source code:recurrent-visual-attention. https://github.com/kevinzakka/recurrent-visual-attention. Accessed 4 May 2024

# MLDN-Net: Multi-Level Denoising Neural Network for Wet Fingerprint via Cyclic Multi-Variate Function

Chao-Lin Kuo[1], Ching-Te Chiu[1], and Mao-Hsiu Hsu[2(✉)]

[1] Department of Computer Science, National Tsing Hua University, Hsinchu, Taiwan
ctchiu@cs.nthu.edu.tw

[2] Department of Electro-Optical Engineering, National Formosa University, Huwei, Taiwan
maohsiuhsu@gmail.com,mh.hsu@nfu.edu.tw

**Abstract.** The fingerprint identification system is widely used for personnel identity confirmation. However, fingerprint contamination, such as sweat, reduces accuracy. We proposed MLDN-Net, which employs a recurrent neural network with a KNN classifier and CoordConv layers, enabling adaptation to wet fingerprints. Tested on the Nasic9395 1018 dataset, MLDN-Net reduced FRR from 19.6% to 9.2%, outperforming state-of-the-art denoising models.

**Keywords:** Wet fingerprint denoising · Real noise · Cyclic neural network

## 1 Introduction

Fingerprints are unique patterns used in biometric authentication, yet contamination from sweat, moisture, and oil reduces recognition accuracy.

We collected fingerprint data using the FT9395 capacitive sensor Fig. 1, which captures smaller, lower-quality images ($36 \times 176$ pixels), making identification more challenging. As noted in [6], sensor quality significantly impacts image quality and recognition, thus emphasizing the need for denoising while preserving fingerprint features.

In recent years, some of studies employ CNN-based method for image denoising. For example, UNet [14], CVF-SID [12] are for real world image denoising. In addition, FingerNet [9], PFENet [16] and FPDM-Net [1] are specific for the fingerprint denoising. However, these methods will over-restore the pattern of the fingerprint, leading to recognition failure.

Based on the recognition results in the Table 7, we can observe that CVF-SID [12] performs better in fingerprint recognition. Because CVF-SID uses the self-supervised manner, it does not need ground truth, which means that it is denoising based on the original image. In addition, with cyclic function and its related loss function, the structure of its output and input can be kept similar.

© The Author(s), under exclusive license to Springer Nature Singapore Pte Ltd. 2025
W.-T. Chu et al. (Eds.): TAAI 2024, CCIS 2414, pp. 66–76, 2025.
https://doi.org/10.1007/978-981-96-4589-3_5

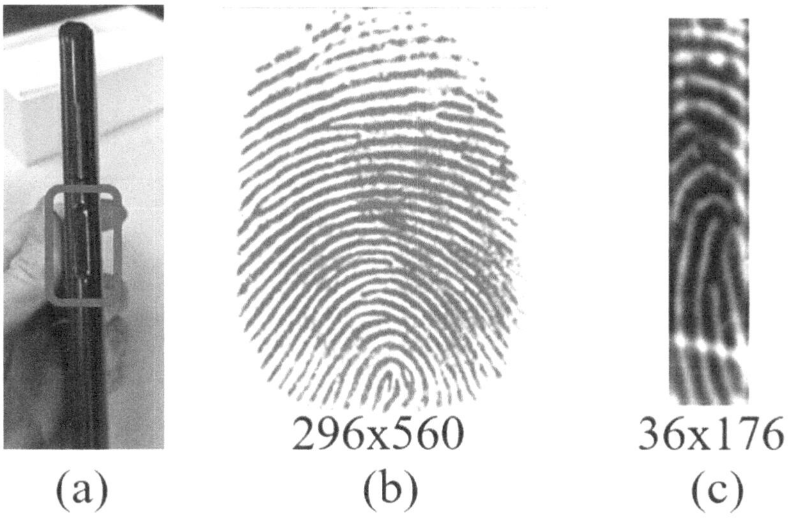


**Fig. 1.** (a) Sensor on the side of a mobile phone that collects fingerprints. (b) FVC2000 DB2 example image in full size, (c) example image collected by side sensor on phone.

Therefore, in order to solve the problem of wet fingerprint denoising, we decide to utilize CVF-SID as our base model.

In this work, we proposed MLDN-NET can be used for wet fingerprints denoising and preserve its features via cyclic multi-variant function. The proposed model can reduce the FRR of the Nasic9395_testset from 19.60% to 9.20%. Also, our model outperforms state-of-the-art network models on the performance of fingerprint recognition.

## 2 Proposed Architecture

This section introduces the main components of MLDN-Net, including KNN classifier, cyclic multi-variant function, deformable convolution, CoordConv layer, and optimized loss function.

### 2.1 MLDN-NET Architecture

The process of MLDN-Net is illustrated in the Fig. 2. Initially, the input of a wet fingerprint, denoted as $I_n$, passes through our MLDN block. Subsequently, three outputs are generated: $\hat{I}_c$, $\hat{N}_d$, and $\hat{N}_i$. Here, $I_n$ represents the wet fingerprint, $\hat{I}_c$ represents the restored clean image, $\hat{N}_d$ and $\hat{N}_i$ stands for dependent noise and independent noise. Then these three outputs are recombined as inputs, which are subsequently fed through the MLDN block for training. Each MLDN block consists of two main components: a clean generator and a noise generator.

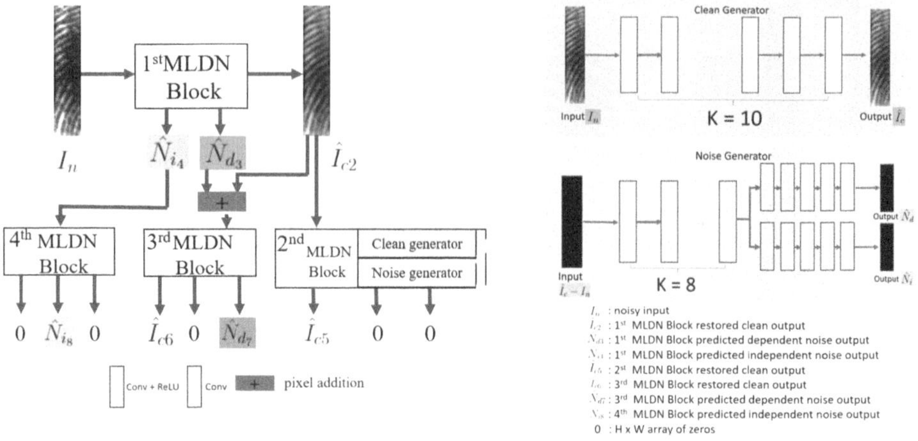


**Fig. 2.** The overall architecture of the proposed MLDN-NET.

## 2.2 Cyclic Multi-Variant Function Framework

The are two stages in the cyclic multi-variant function(CVF) which is illustrated in Fig. 3. In first stage the input will through the 1st MLDN Block and decompose to $\hat{I}_c$, $\hat{N}_d$ and $\hat{N}_i$. In the second stage, the outputs from the first stage are utilized as the new inputs in the three MLDN Block.

## 2.3 MLDN Block Architecture

The MLDN block consists of three parts, KNN classifier, clean generator and noise generator, the KNN classifier is for noise input classification, the clean image is for image restoration and the noise generator is for noise prediction. The MLDN block architecture is shown in Fig. 4.

The dataflow about the MLDN block. The input wet fingerprint image is first sent through KNN classifier to predict its image quality. Then it is fed into the corresponding clean generator to get the restored output. Finally, we use the input $I_n$ to subscribe the output $\hat{I}_c$ to predict the noise $\hat{N}_d$ and $\hat{N}_i$.

**KNN Classifier Architecture.** The KNN classifier [7,15,17,18] is to split the noise input into several classes. First, the noisy input is sent to the power spectrum weights blocks [2] and smudge noise quality estimator block [3] to compute the power spectrum and smudge noise quality value. Afterward, it will employ a K-Nearest Neighbors (KNN) classifier to categorize the image into levels 0 and 1. Higher numbers represent better quality fingerprints and lower numbers represent poorer quality. The KNN classifier architecture is shown in Fig. 5.

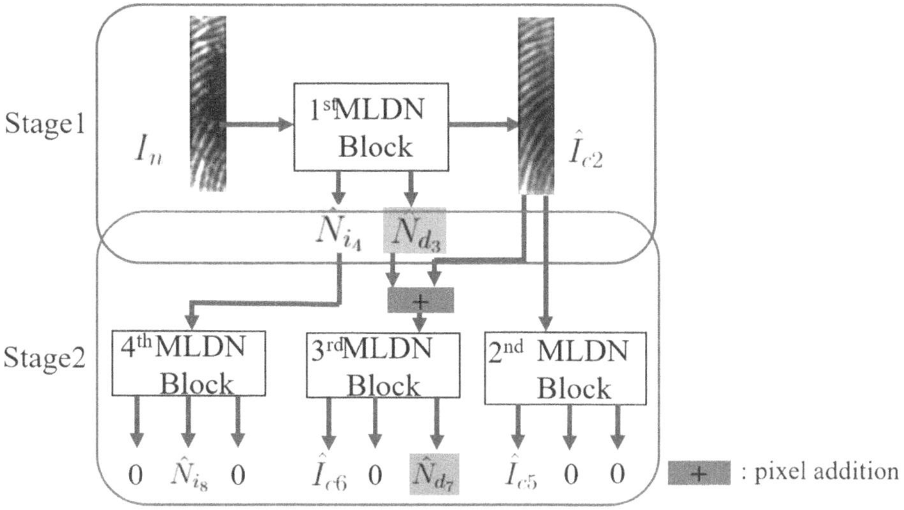


**Fig. 3.** The framework of cyclic multi-variant function.

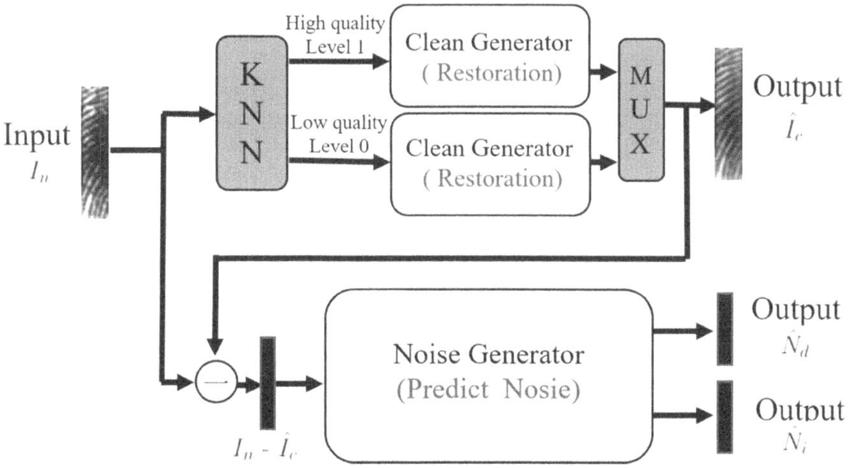


**Fig. 4.** The architecture of MLDN block.

**Clean Generator Architecture.** The clean generator consists of 10 convolution layers with ReLU activation to produce a restored fingerprint image, as shown in Fig. 6.

**Noise Generator Architecture.** The noise generator contains 8 convolution layers with ReLU and branches into two outputs: dependent noise and independent noise, targeting fingerprint ridges and background, respectively (Fig. 7).

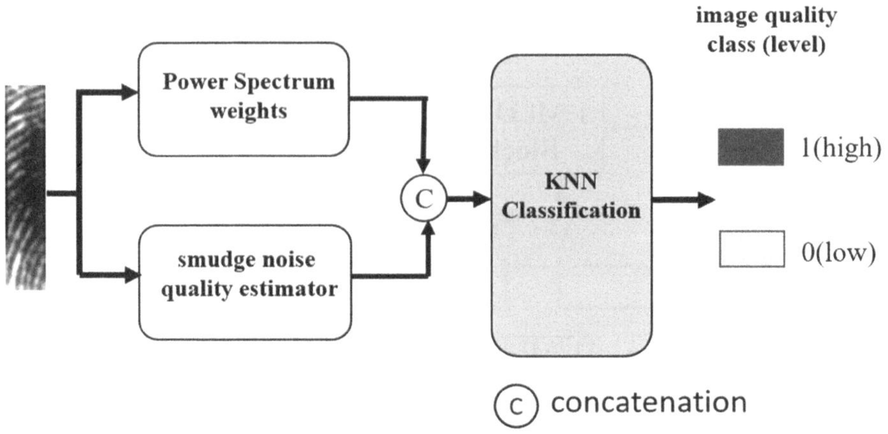


**Fig. 5.** The architecture of KNN classifier.

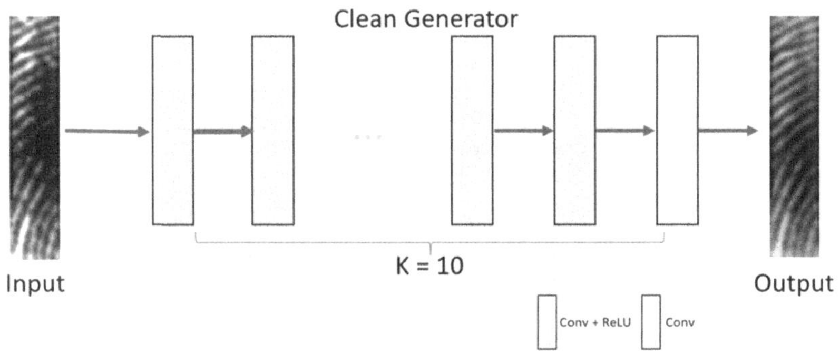


**Fig. 6.** Architecture of the Clean Generator.

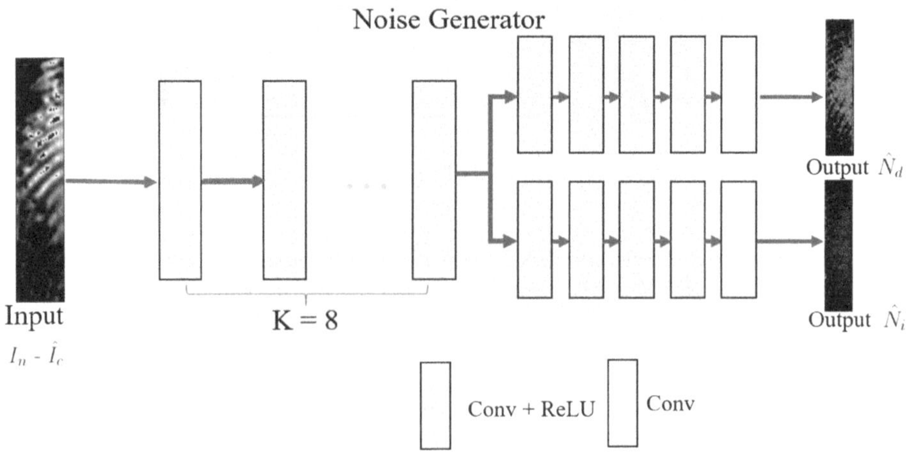


**Fig. 7.** Architecture of the Noise Generator.

### 2.4 Deformable Convolution

Deformable convolution [4] is a convolution layer for offset learning, each pixel does the convolution with the offset coordinate, which can adapt to the local feature.

### 2.5 CoordConv

The CoordConv layer [10] architecture. First, use the SIFT [5,11,13] algorithm to generate matching point coordinate. Second, concatenate the SIFT coordinate map then do convolution. We replace the basic Conv with deformable convolution and CoordConV in our clean generator for ablation study.

### 2.6 Loss Function

To optimize denoising and feature preservation, we employ multiple loss functions. The L2 norm $\|\cdot\|$ is used to compute Mean Squared Error (MSE) loss across all functions, where image dimensions are $H \times W$.

- **Consistency Loss** ($L_{con}$): Ensures that the combined outputs converge to the noisy input $I_n$:

$$L_{con} = \| I_n - (\hat{I}_{c_2} + \hat{N}_{d_3} + \hat{N}_{i_4}) \| \tag{1}$$

- **Identity Loss** ($L_{id}$): Enforces similarity among corresponding terms, maintaining image consistency:

$$L_{id} = \| \hat{I}_{c_2} - \hat{I}_{c_5} \| + \| \hat{I}_{c_2} - \hat{I}_{c_6} \| + \| \hat{N}_{d_3} - \hat{N}_{d_7} \| + \| \hat{N}_{i_4} - \hat{N}_{i_8} \| \tag{2}$$

- **Reconstruct Loss** ($L_{rec}$): Measures the difference between the restored image $\hat{I}_{c_2}$ and ground truth $I_c$:

$$L_{rec} = \| I_c - \hat{I}_{c_2} \| \tag{3}$$

- **Match Loss** ($L_{match}$): Compares SIFT values between $I_c$ and both $I_n$ and $\hat{I}_{c_2}$. Higher SIFT values for $\hat{I}_{c_2}$ indicate better restoration:

$$L_{\text{match}} = \begin{cases} 0, \text{ if SIFT}(\hat{I}_{c_2}, I_c) > \text{SIFT}(I_n, I_c), \\ 1, \text{ if SIFT}(\hat{I}_{c_2}, I_c) = \text{SIFT}(I_n, I_c), \\ 2, \text{ if SIFT}(\hat{I}_{c_2}, I_c) < \text{SIFT}(I_n, I_c) \end{cases} \tag{4}$$

The total loss function is applied differently for high-quality and low-quality images:

- **Total Loss for High-Quality Images**:

$$L_{total\_h} = L_{con} + 0.4 \cdot L_{id} + 0.5 \cdot L_{rec} \tag{5}$$

- **Total Loss for Low-Quality Images**:

$$L_{total\_l} = L_{con} + 0.4 \cdot L_{id} + 1.25 \cdot L_{rec} \quad (6)$$

When using CoordConv, the total loss includes the match loss ($L_{match}$):

- **Total Loss with CoordConv for High-Quality Images**:

$$L_{total\_h} = L_{con} + 0.4 \cdot L_{id} + 0.5 \cdot L_{rec} + 0.03 \cdot L_{match} \quad (7)$$

- **Total Loss with CoordConv for Low-Quality Images**:

$$L_{total\_l} = L_{con} + 0.4 \cdot L_{id} + 1.25 \cdot L_{rec} + 0.03 \cdot L_{match} \quad (8)$$

# 3 Experimental Results

## 3.1 Dataset

We use the Nasic9395_1018 dataset for training. The dataset is divided into training, validation, and testing. It is described in Table 1. Dataset consists 8 people's fingerprints of a pair of blurry wet and ground-truth fingerprint images.

**Table 1.** The detail of the dataset Nasic9395_1018.

| Dataset | Scanner | Training Images | Validation Images | Testing Images |
|---|---|---|---|---|
| Nasic9395_1018 | Capacitive | 25639 | 3204 | 3204 |

The Nasic9395_testset contains fingerprints from three people with different fingers. The following Table 2 summarizes the information of the dataset and their corresponding FRR when the denoising algorithm is not utilized. Enroll fingerprints is to capture fingerprint biometrics samples, processing them to create a template.Identify fingerprints is to compare with the templates stored in the database.

**Table 2.** The detail of the dataset Nasic9395_testset.

| Dataset | Enroll | Identify | Success | FRR (%) |
|---|---|---|---|---|
| Nasic9395_testset | 251 | 500 | 402 | 19.6 |

## 3.2 Implementation Details

We select Nasic9395_1018 as training dataset, the Nasic9395_test as test dataset. In the training step, our batch size is set to 32 and we use the Adam optimizer training for 50 epochs. Our experiment is conducted using NVIDIA 3090Ti GPU and 6-core Intel(R) 12400 CPU with PyTorch implementation.

### 3.3 Recontruct Loss

The reconstruct loss is aimed at achieving a balance between fingerprint denoising and preserving details. Therefore, we first experiment our MLDN-Net without the KNN classifier and with only one clean generator (Table 3).

**Table 3.** Ablation study on adding reconstruct loss to MLDN-Net.

| Model | reconstruct loss value($\lambda$) | # of successful images | FRR (%) |
|---|---|---|---|
| MLDN-Net w/o KNN classifer | 0 | 411 | 17.8 |
| | 0.25 | 428 | 14.4 |
| | 0.5 | **450** | **10.0** |
| | 1.0 | 430 | 14.0 |
| | 1.5 | 429 | 14.2 |
| No enhance | | 402 | 19.6 |

### 3.4 Single-Stage vs Cyclic (Two-Stage and Three Stage

In our MLDN-Net have two stage, we conducted the following experiment to compare the difference between single-stage and two- stage. In single stage MLDN-Net only has one MLDN block. Therefore total loss will become:

$$L_{total} = L_{con} + L_{rec} * 0.5 \tag{9}$$

The Table 4 shows the recognition performance of MLDN-Net on single-stage and two-stage. The result shows that single-stage MLDN-Net worse than the no enhance fingerprint.

### 3.5 KNN Classifier

The experiment is to demonstrate KNN classifier can improve the MLDN-NET recognition performance. Without the KNN, MLDN-NET only has one clean generator and total loss as follow:

$$L_{total} = L_{con} + L_{con} * 0.4 + L_{rec} * 0.5 \tag{10}$$

With the KNN, MLDN-NET has two clean generators and total loss are same as Eq. 5 and Eq. 6 (Table 5).

**Table 4.** Ablation study on single-stage and cyclic for MLDN-Net.

| Model | Stage | # of successful images | FRR (%) |
|---|---|---|---|
| MLDN-Net | Single-stage | 388 | 24.4 |
| | Two-stage | **450** | **10.0** |
| | Three-stage | 449 | 10.2 |
| No enhance | | 402 | 19.6 |

**Table 5.** Ablation study on KNN classifier on MLDN-Net.

| Model | # of successful images | FRR (%) |
|---|---|---|
| MLDN-Net w/o KNN classifier | 450 | 10.0 |
| MLDN-Net w/ KNN classifier | **452** | **9.6** |
| No enhance | 402 | 19.6 |

### 3.6 Convolution Type

The experiment different type of convolution on MLDN-NET clean generator, basic Conv, deformable Conv and CoordConv. The Table 6 shows the recognition performance of different types of convolution on MLDN-NET clean generator, MLDN-NET with the CoordConv has the better recognition performance.

**Table 6.** Ablation study on single-stage and cyclic for MLDN-Net.

| Model | Conv Type | # of successful images | FRR(%) |
|---|---|---|---|
| MLDN-Net | Basic Conv | 452 | 9.6 |
| | Deformable Conv | 436 | 12.8 |
| | CoordConv | **454** | **9.2** |
| No enhance | | 402 | 19.6 |

The following table summarizes the recognition performance compared with related works mentioned above.

**Table 7.** The recognition results of the image denoising models.

| Model | Flops | Training dataset | # of Identify image | Successful recognition | FRR (%) |
|---|---|---|---|---|---|
| DenseUNet [2] | 79.09G | Nasic9395 _1018 | 500 | 209 | 58.2 |
| XYDeblur [8] | 7.25G | | | 205 | 59 |
| CVF-SID [12] | 5.38G | | | 409 | 18.2 |
| FingerNet [9] | 3.54G | | | 323 | 35.4 |
| Residual M-net [3] | 3.41G | | | 269 | 46.2 |
| FPDMNet [1] | 1.01G | | | 295 | 41 |
| MLDN-Net (Ours) | 3.99G | | | **454** | **9.2** |
| No enhance | | | | 402 | 19.6 |

The below Fig. 8 shows that our MLDN-Net compare with SOTA models, in the above fingerprint DenseUNet and FPDMet connect ridge that don't exist. FingerNet and Residual M-net over clean the ridge. In the below fingerprint, DenseUNet and FPDMet, Residual M-net and FingerNet over-restore the ridge.

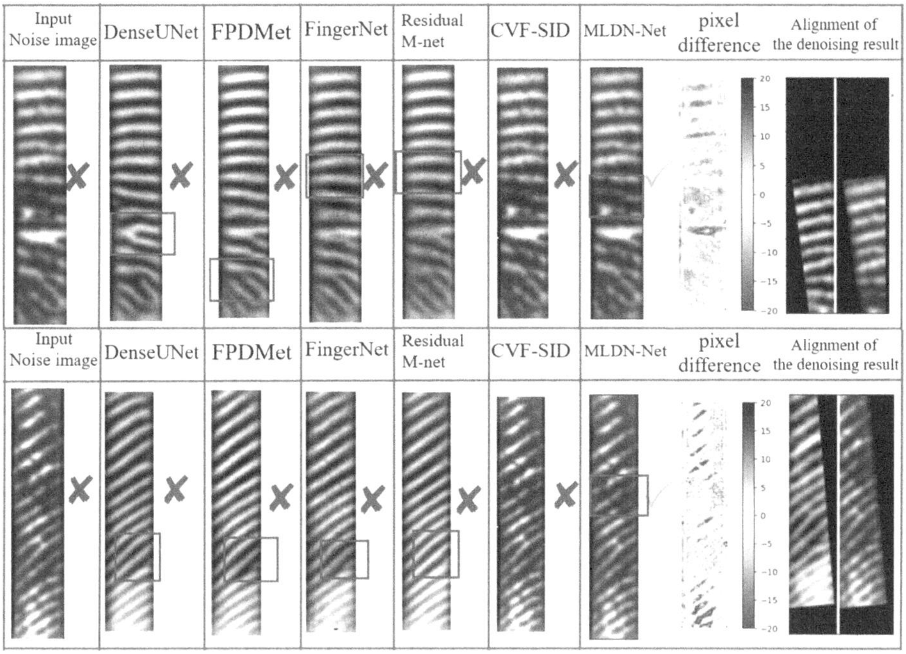


**Fig. 8.** The key points matching using the SIFT algorithm.

## 4 Conclusion

In this work, we presented MLDN-Net for fingerprint denoising. MLDN-Net uses MLDN blocks as the fundamental structures. In the MLDN block, we apply KNN classifier for different level noise fingerprint. In addition, we modified the CoordConv architecture to feed the SIFT information to the network. We conduct the experiment on the Nasic9395_1018 to demonstrate our MLDN-Net recognition performance, the FRR is reduced from 19.2% to 9.2% and outperforms other SOTA methods.

## References

1. Adiga, V.S., Sivaswamy, J.: FPD-m-net: fingerprint image denoising and inpainting using m-net based convolutional neural networks. In: Inpainting and Denoising Challenges, pp. 51–61. Springer, Cham (2019)
2. Cai, S., Tian, Y., Lui, H., Zeng, H., Wu, Y., Chen, G.: Dense-unet: a novel multiphoton in vivo cellular image segmentation model based on a convolutional neural network. Quant. Imaging Med. Surg. **10**(6) (2020). https://qims.amegroups.org/article/view/43519
3. Cunha, N.D.S., Gomes, H.M., Batista, L.V.: Residual m-net with frequency-domain loss function for latent fingerprint enhancement. In: 2022 35th SIBGRAPI Conference on Graphics, Patterns and Images (SIBGRAPI), vol. 1, pp. 198–203 (2022). https://doi.org/10.1109/SIBGRAPI55357.2022.9991793

4. Dai, J., et al.: Deformable convolutional networks. In: 2017 IEEE International Conference on Computer Vision (ICCV), pp. 764–773 (2017). https://doi.org/10.1109/ICCV.2017.89
5. Hendre, M., Patil, S., Abhyankar, A.: Biometric recognition robust to partial and poor quality fingerprints using distinctive region adaptive sift keypoint fusion. Multimedia Tools Appl. **81** (2022). https://doi.org/10.1007/s11042-021-11686-2
6. Hsu, M.H., Hsu, Y.C., Chiu, C.T.: Tiny partial fingerprint sensor quality assessment. IEEE Sens. Lett. **8**(5), 1–4 (2024). https://doi.org/10.1109/LSENS.2024.3387419
7. Javid, J., Mughal, M.A., Karim, M.: Using KNN algorithm for classification of distribution transformers health index. In: 2021 International Conference on Innovative Computing (ICIC), pp. 1–6 (2021).https://doi.org/10.1109/ICIC53490.2021.9693013
8. Ji, S.W., et al.: Xydeblur: divide and conquer for single image deblurring. In: 2022 IEEE/CVF Conference on Computer Vision and Pattern Recognition (CVPR), pp. 17400–17409 (2022). https://doi.org/10.1109/CVPR52688.2022.01690
9. Li, J., Feng, J., Kuo, C.C.J.: Deep convolutional neural network for latent fingerprint enhancement. Sig. Process. Image Commun. **60**, 52–63 (2018)
10. Liu, R., et al.: An intriguing failing of convolutional neural networks and the coordconv solution (2018)
11. Lowe, D.G.: Distinctive image features from scale-invariant keypoints. Int. J. Comput. Vision **60**(2), 91–110 (2004). https://doi.org/10.1023/B:VISI.0000029664.99615.94
12. Neshatavar, R., Yavartanoo, M., Son, S., Lee, K.M.: CVF-SID: cyclic multi-variate function for self-supervised image denoising by disentangling noise from image. In: IEEE/CVF Conference on Computer Vision and Pattern Recognition (CVPR) (2022)
13. Park, U., Pankanti, S., Jain, A.K.: Fingerprint verification using sift features. In: SPIE Defense + Commercial Sensing (2008). https://api.semanticscholar.org/CorpusID:18315414
14. Ronneberger, O., Fischer, P., Brox, T.: U-net: convolutional networks for biomedical image segmentation. In: International Conference on Medical Image Computing and Computer-assisted Intervention, pp. 234–241. Springer, Cham (2015)
15. Shang, T., Xia, X., Jun, Z.: Mime-KNN: Improve KNN classifier performance include classification accuracy and time consumption. DEStech Trans. Comput. Sci. Eng. (2018). https://doi.org/10.12783/dtcse/csse2018/24490
16. Shen, Z., Xu, Y., Lu, G.: CNN-based high-resolution fingerprint image enhancement for pore detection and matching. In: 2019 IEEE Symposium Series on Computational Intelligence (SSCI), pp. 426–432 (2019). https://api.semanticscholar.org/CorpusID:211242597
17. Taunk, K., De, S., Verma, S., Swetapadma, A.: A brief review of nearest neighbor algorithm for learning and classification. In: 2019 International Conference on Intelligent Computing and Control Systems (ICCS), pp. 1255–1260 (2019). https://doi.org/10.1109/ICCS45141.2019.9065747
18. Zang, B., Huang, R., Wang, L., Chen, J., Tian, F., Wei, X.: An improved KNN algorithm based on minority class distribution for imbalanced dataset. In: 2016 International Computer Symposium (ICS), pp. 696–700 (2016). https://doi.org/10.1109/ICS.2016.0143

# Training-Free Zero-Shot Composed Image Retrieval via Weighted Modality Fusion and Similarity

Ren-Di Wu, Yu-Yen Lin, and Huei-Fang Yang(✉)

National Sun Yat-sen University, Kaohsiung 804201, Taiwan
{b104020009,m124020039}@student.nsysu.edu.tw,
hfyang@mail.cse.nsysu.edu.tw

**Abstract.** Composed image retrieval (CIR), which formulates the query as a combination of a reference image and modified text, has emerged as a new form of image search due to its enhanced ability to capture user intent. However, training a CIR model in a supervised manner typically requires labor-intensive collection of (reference image, text modifier, target image) triplets. While existing zero-shot CIR (ZS-CIR) methods eliminate the need for training on specific downstream datasets, they still require additional pretraining on large-scale image datasets. In this paper, we introduce a training-free approach for ZS-CIR. Our approach, **Wei**ghted **Mo**dality fusion and similarity for **CIR** (WeiMo-CIR), operates under the assumption that image and text modalities can be effectively combined using a simple weighted average. This allows the query representation to be constructed directly from the reference image and text modifier. To further enhance retrieval performance, we employ multimodal large language models (MLLMs) to generate image captions for the database images and incorporate these textual captions into the similarity computation by combining them with image information using a weighted average. Our approach is simple, easy to implement, and its effectiveness is validated through experiments on the FashionIQ and CIRR datasets. Code is available at https://github.com/whats2000/WeiMoCIR.

**Keywords:** Composed image retrieval · Zero-shot composed image retrieval · Multimodal large language model · Vision-language model

## 1 Introduction

Given a reference image and a textual description, composed image retrieval (CIR) is to find a target image, that visually resembles the reference image and also incorporates modifications specified by the text, from an image database. Compared to using a single modality (e.g., images or texts alone), which could have limited expressiveness in capturing users' preferences, CIR allows users to better express their preferences with multimodal queries. Consequently, recent years have witnessed significant research efforts in CIR [2,3,14,17].

© The Author(s), under exclusive license to Springer Nature Singapore Pte Ltd. 2025
W.-T. Chu et al. (Eds.): TAAI 2024, CCIS 2414, pp. 77–90, 2025.
https://doi.org/10.1007/978-981-96-4589-3_6

Multimodal queries pose a unique challenge to image retrieval because the retrieval algorithms need to understand what to retain in the visual content and what to modify based on finer details expressed in the natural language. Previous studies [3,13] have tackled this by training CIR models on large-scale (reference image, text modifier, target image) triplets to learn how to fuse the reference image and the text modifier into a query representation for retrieval. However, collecting such triplets requires substantial human effort, and the supervised approaches usually exhibit limited performance on unseen data due to being tuned on specific datasets. Consequently, zero-shot CIR (ZS-CIR), capable of performing CIR without supervised learning on downstream data, has gained attention. However, existing ZS-CIR methods, such as Pic2Word [17] and SEARLE [2], still require training on large image datasets to learn mappings for converting images into pseudo-word tokens, which are then combined with textual descriptions for text-to-image retrieval. This additional training can be resource-intensive.

In this paper, we introduce a training-free approach for ZS-CIR. Our approach leverages existing vision-language models (VLMs) and multimodal large language models (MLLMs). Specifically, we use a VLM, such as CLIP [15], to obtain visual features from the reference image and textual features from the text modifier. Given that images and texts are aligned within a shared space in the VLMs, we assume that the fused query representation can be obtained through a weighted combination of the visual and textual representations. During retrieval, unlike previous methods that rely solely on comparing the query feature and database image features for retrieval, our method also incorporates the textual information of the database images for similarity computation. This is achieved by using an MLLM, such as Gemini [7], to generate captions for each database image. To capture different aspects of the image content, multiple descriptions are generated for each database image. By incorporating these generated descriptions, our approach considers both the similarities between the query and visual features of the database images and the similarities between the query and textual features of database images through a weighted average. We term our approach WeiMoCIR, which stands for **Wei**ghted **Mo**dality fusion and similarity for **CIR**.

Our contributions are summarized as follows:

- We introduce a training-free ZS-CIR approach that does not require any resource-intensive training by leveraging pretrained VLMs and MLLMs.
- We show that a simple weighted fusion of the image and text modalities is sufficient to generate an effective fused query feature, and incorporating additional textual information further enhances retrieval performance.
- Our method is simple, easy to implement and achieves results comparable to or better than existing methods on FashionIQ [22] and CIRR [13].

## 2 Related Work

*Composed Image Retrieval.* In CIR, the query comprises two modalities-a reference image and a text modifier-with the goal of retrieving images that satisfy the conditions specified in the query. Earlier CIR methods [3,6,21] have focused on developing multimodal fusion techniques to combine the visual features and textual features to obtain the query representation. For instance, CLIP4CIR [3] trains a combiner to fuse the information from two modalities. However, these methods require triplets for specific downstream applications for model training, and collecting such triplets is labor-intensive. As a result, recent research has explored ZS-CIR. Representative methods, like Pic2Word [17] and SEARLE [2], learn to project images into the textual space using large-scale image datasets. With the learned mappings from images to texts, the projected pseudo-word tokens are then combined with the text modifier for text-to-image retrieval without needing to train on downstream datasets. CIReVL [10] further eliminates the need for additional training to learn the image-to-text mappings and achieves training-free ZS-CIR. It utilizes a pretrained VLM [11,15] to generate a textual description for the reference image. This description and the text modifier are fed into an LLM [4,16] to produce a textual description of the desired image for text-to-image retrieval. LDRE [23] leverages a pretrained image captioner to generate multiple descriptions for the reference images and employs an LLM to reason based on these descriptions and the modified text. This approach demonstrates that multiple image captions can capture the diverse semantics of the composed result, thereby enhancing performance.

Similar to CIReVL and LDRE, our approach is training-free but differs in two key aspects: (1) our method composes the query representation from both visual and text representation while CIReVL and LDRE translate images to texts; and (2) our method utilizes an MLLM to generate captions for the database images and considers both visual and textual information during retrieval. In contrast, CIReVL and LDRE only consider the visual features of database images.

*Vision-Language Models.* VLMs [11,15], pretrained on large datasets of image-text pairs, are capable of processing both the visual and textual modalities. One of the earliest VLMs is CLIP [15]. Having learned the association between images and texts, CLIP has demonstrated strong generalization capabilities and been applied to various vision-language tasks such as zero-shot classification [15], image generation [5], and event classification [12]. Beyond vision-language understanding tasks, BLIP [11] further extends the capability of the VLMs to generation tasks and can perform tasks such as image captioning [20] and VQA [1].

In our work, VLMs are leveraged as feature extractors. Built upon the VLM's joint space where images and texts are aligned, our approach utilizes a weighted approach to fuse the two modalities to achieve ZS-CIR without any training.

# 3 Method

Our goal is to retrieve a target image from an image database $\mathcal{D} = \{\boldsymbol{I}_n\}_{n=1}^{N}$ that reflects the relevant visual elements of the reference image $\boldsymbol{I}$ along with the modifications specified in the text $\boldsymbol{T}$, all without the need for additional training. Figure 1 gives an overview of the proposed WeiMoCIR. It consists of three modules: the weighted modality fusion module constructs the query representation from the visual and text features; the enhanced representations module improves database image representations with MLLM-generated image captions; and the weighted modality similarity module considers both image and textual information for retrieval. We elaborate on each module in the following.

*Weighted Modality Fusion for Query Composition.* We utilize a pretrained VLM, such as CLIP or BLIP, which includes a vision encoder and a text encoder as feature extractors. For the reference image $\boldsymbol{I}$, the vision encoder $f_\theta$ extracts its visual representation as $\boldsymbol{v} = f_\theta(\boldsymbol{I}) \in \mathbb{R}^{d\times 1}$, where $d$ is the feature dimension. For the text modifier $\boldsymbol{T}$, the text encoder $f_\phi$ extracts a textual representation $\boldsymbol{t} = f_\phi(\boldsymbol{T}) \in \mathbb{R}^{d\times 1}$.

To find relevant images in the database, an intuitive approach is to use a merger function $\mathcal{M}$ that combines both the reference image and the text and yields a query representation $\boldsymbol{q} = \mathcal{M}(\boldsymbol{v}, \boldsymbol{t})$ for retrieval. Although the merger

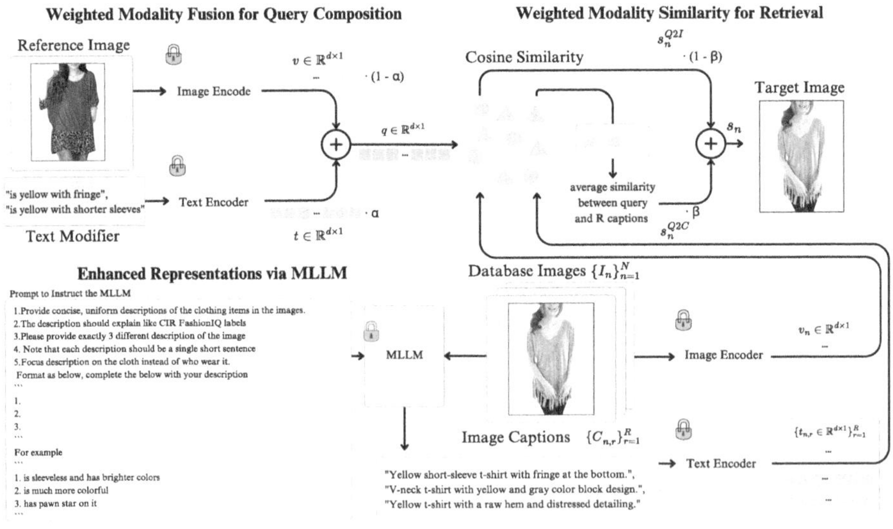


**Fig. 1.** Overview of the proposed WeiMoCIR, a training-free approach for zero-shot composed image retrieval (ZS-CIR). Leveraging pretrained VLMs and MLLMs, our method comprises three modules: weighted modality fusion for query composition, enhanced representations through MLLM-generated image captions, and weighted modality similarity, which integrates both query-to-image and query-to-caption similarities for retrieval.

function could be complex, we assume that since the images and the texts are aligned in a common space within the VLMs, a simple weighted sum of the visual and textual features can produce a representation with sufficient expressiveness. Thus, we obtain the query feature $\boldsymbol{q}$ as:

$$\boldsymbol{q} = (1 - \alpha) \cdot \boldsymbol{v} + \alpha \cdot \boldsymbol{t}, \tag{1}$$

where $\alpha$ controls the weighting between the two modalities.

*Enhanced Representations via MLLM-Generated Image Captions.* While directly comparing the query feature $\boldsymbol{q}$ to images in the database by computing query-to-image similarity can yield desired results, we propose leveraging the descriptive power of language to enhance retrieval performance. Language can convey concepts that may be difficult to capture with images alone. To capture different aspects of each database image $\boldsymbol{I}_n$ in the database, we utilize an MLLM, such as Gemini, to generate a set of $R$ captions, $\{\boldsymbol{C}_{n,r}\}_{r=1}^{R}$, describing the image content from multiple perspectives.

*Weighted Modality Similarity for Retrieval.* Similar to the reference image, for each database image $\boldsymbol{I}_n$, the vision encoder extracts its visual representation as $\boldsymbol{v}_n = f_\theta(\boldsymbol{I}_n) \in \mathbb{R}^{d \times 1}$, and the text encoder is used to obtain its textual representations $\{\boldsymbol{t}_{n,r}\}_{r=1}^{R}$, where $\boldsymbol{t}_{n,r} = f_\phi(\boldsymbol{C}_{n,r}) \in \mathbb{R}^{d \times 1}$.

Since the query representation should be close to both the visual representation of the target image and its textual descriptions, we consider both query-to-image and query-to-caption similarities for retrieval. Specifically, the query-to-image similarity measures the similarity between the query $\boldsymbol{q}$ and the visual representation of a database image $\boldsymbol{I}_n$:

$$s_n^{Q2I} = \text{sim}(\boldsymbol{q}, \boldsymbol{v}_n),$$

where sim denotes cosine similarity. The query-to-caption similarity is the average similarity between the query and the $R$ textual representations of a database image $\boldsymbol{I}_n$:

$$s_n^{Q2C} = \frac{1}{R} \sum_{r=1}^{R} \text{sim}(\boldsymbol{q}, \boldsymbol{t}_{n,r}).$$

The final similarity $s_n$ between the query $\boldsymbol{q}$ and database image $\boldsymbol{I}_n$ is computed as a weighted average of the query-to-image similarity $s_n^{Q2I}$ and the query-to-caption similarity $s_n^{Q2C}$:

$$s_n = (1 - \beta) \cdot s_n^{Q2I} + \beta \cdot s_n^{Q2C}, \tag{2}$$

where $\beta$ controls the influence between two types of similarities.

To find the desired images, the database images are sorted by their similarity scores with respect to the query, and the top $K$ images are returned.

## 4 Experiments

In this section, we first describe the experimental setup, followed by the experimental results and ablation studies to analyze the effects of the design choices. Finally, qualitative results are presented.

### 4.1 Experimental Benchmarks and Protocols

*Datasets.* We use FashionIQ [22] and CIRR [13] to validate the effectiveness of the proposed method. **FashionIQ** [22] is a dataset focused on fashion apparel, sourced from real-world online data. It contains 30,134 triplet data points from 77,684 images. The dataset is divided into three categories: *Dress*, *Shirt*, and *Toptee*. Each triplet is accompanied by two human-generated annotations. **CIRR** [13] is a dataset that features a real-world wider range of domains, with more complex descriptive characteristics compared to FashionIQ. The dataset is derived from the NLVR2 [19] dataset and contains 21,552 images.

*Metrics.* The evaluation metric is the top K retrieval results (R@K). For FashionIQ, we compute R@K for each of the three categories and their average. Since the test set is no longer available for evaluation, we follow previous studies [2,8–10,17,24] and report results on the validation set. For CIRR, we evaluate full-set ranking results using R@1, R@5, R@10, and R@50 metrics. For the subset group, we assess performance using R@1, R@2, and R@3. We use the validation set to select hyperparameters $\alpha$ and $\beta$ and report the results on the Test1 set.

### 4.2 Implementation Details

We use the CLIP model pretrained on LAION-2B English subset of LAION-5B [18] as the feature extractor to obtain visual representations from the images and textual representations from the text modifiers and captions. For the MLLMs, due to the experiments being conducted at different times, we employed Google Gemini Pro Vision to generate captions for the FashionIQ dataset and Google Gemini 1.5 Flash for the CIRR dataset. We set $\alpha$ to 0.1 and $\beta$ to 0.8. All experiments were conducted on a single RTX 3090 GPU with Conda Python 3.8 and PyTorch 2.3.0.

*Prompts to Instruct the MLLM to Generate Captions.* During retrieval, as the captions of the database images are incorporated into the similarity computation, their quality could impact performance. Our experiments show that when the generated captions are more closely aligned with the text modifiers, our method produces more favorable results. For FashionIQ, the MLLM is instructed to describe the characteristics of the clothes while explicitly avoiding any mention of the person wearing the clothes. For CIRR, we employ a role-playing instruction to guide the MLLM to provide concise descriptions and exclude any descriptions unrelated to the images. For both datasets, we provide a defined output format and a set of example descriptions, and specify that the output should consist of $R$ captions, with $R$ set to 3.

### 4.3 Main Experimental Results

*Results on FashionIQ.* Table 1 shows the comparison of our approach with other ZS-CIR methods, including those requiring additional pretraining and those that are training-free. It is observed that the zero-shot methods with additional pretraining, such as MagicLens [24] and LinCIR [9], achieve the best performance. This superior performance is primarily due to the additional pretraining that adapts the model to be more suitable for the CIR task.

It is worth noting that the training-free approaches sometimes outperform some methods that involve additional training, demonstrating that favorable results can be achieved by leveraging pretrained models and a well-designed retrieval pipeline. Our method consistently surpasses the other training-free

**Table 1.** R@K results on FashionIQ. The best scores for each backbone are highlighted in **bold**. The pretrained CLIP is used as the feature extractor.

| Backbone | Method | Shirt | | Dress | | Toptee | | Average | |
|---|---|---|---|---|---|---|---|---|---|
| | | R@10 | R@50 | R@10 | R@50 | R@10 | R@50 | R@10 | R@50 |
| *Methods that need an additional pre-traning step* | | | | | | | | | |
| ViT L/14 | Pic2Word [17] | 26.20 | 43.60 | 20.00 | 40.20 | 27.90 | 47.40 | 24.70 | 43.70 |
| | SEARLE-XL-OTI [2] | 30.37 | 47.49 | 21.57 | 44.47 | 30.90 | 51.76 | 27.61 | 47.90 |
| | CompoDiff [8] | **37.69** | 49.08 | **32.24** | **46.27** | **38.12** | 50.57 | **36.02** | 48.64 |
| | LinCIR [9] | 29.10 | 46.81 | 20.92 | 42.44 | 28.81 | 50.18 | 26.28 | 46.49 |
| | MagicLens [24] | 32.70 | **53.80** | 25.50 | 46.10 | 34.00 | **57.70** | 30.70 | **52.50** |
| ViT H/14 | Pic2Word [17] | **36.90** | 55.99 | 28.01 | 51.51 | 40.18 | 62.01 | 35.03 | 56.50 |
| | SEARLE [2] | 36.46 | 55.45 | 28.46 | 51.07 | 38.81 | 60.89 | 34.57 | 55.80 |
| | LinCIR [9] | **36.90** | **57.75** | **29.80** | **52.11** | **42.07** | **62.52** | **36.26** | **57.46** |
| ViT G/14 | Pic2Word [17] | 33.17 | 50.39 | 25.43 | 47.65 | 35.24 | 57.62 | 31.28 | 51.89 |
| | SEARLE [2] | 36.46 | 55.35 | 28.16 | 50.32 | 39.83 | 61.45 | 34.81 | 55.71 |
| | CompoDiff [8] | 41.31 | 55.17 | 37.78 | 49.10 | 44.26 | 56.41 | 39.02 | 51.71 |
| | LinCIR [9] | **46.76** | **65.11** | **38.08** | **60.88** | **50.48** | **71.09** | **45.11** | **65.69** |
| *Training-free methods* | | | | | | | | | |
| ViT B/32 | CIReVL [10] | 28.36 | **47.84** | 25.29 | **46.36** | 31.21 | 53.85 | 28.29 | 49.35 |
| | LDRE [23] | 27.38 | 46.27 | 19.97 | 41.84 | 27.07 | 48.78 | 24.81 | 45.63 |
| | WeiMoCIR (Ours) | **29.20** | 47.15 | **26.23** | 46.31 | **34.17** | **55.99** | **29.86** | **49.82** |
| ViT L/14 | CIReVL [10] | 29.49 | 47.40 | 24.79 | 44.76 | 31.36 | 53.65 | 28.55 | 48.57 |
| | LDRE [23] | 31.04 | **51.22** | 22.93 | 46.76 | 31.57 | 53.64 | 28.51 | 50.54 |
| | WeiMoCIR (Ours) | **32.78** | 48.97 | **25.88** | **47.30** | **35.95** | **56.71** | **31.54** | **50.99** |
| ViT H/14 | WeiMoCIR (Ours) | 36.56 | 53.58 | 28.76 | 48.98 | 39.72 | 59.87 | 35.01 | 54.14 |
| ViT G/14 | CIReVL [10] | 33.71 | 51.42 | 27.07 | 49.53 | 35.80 | 56.14 | 32.19 | 52.36 |
| | LDRE [23] | 35.94 | **58.58** | 26.11 | 51.12 | 35.42 | 56.67 | 32.49 | 55.46 |
| | WeiMoCIR (Ours) | **37.73** | 56.18 | **30.99** | **52.45** | **42.38** | **63.23** | **37.03** | **57.29** |

**Table 2.** R@K results on CIRR. The best scores for each backbone are highlighted in **bold**. The pretrained CLIP is used as the feature extractor.

| Backbone | Method | Recall@K | | | | $Recall_{Subset}@K$ | | |
|---|---|---|---|---|---|---|---|---|
| | | R@1 | R@5 | R@10 | R@50 | R@1 | R@2 | R@3 |
| *Methods that need an additional pretraining step* | | | | | | | | |
| ViT L/14 | Pic2Word [17] | 23.90 | 51.70 | 65.30 | 87.80 | 53.76 | 74.46 | 87.08 |
| | SEARLE-XL-OTI [2] | 24.87 | 52.31 | 66.29 | 88.58 | 53.80 | 74.31 | 86.94 |
| | CompoDiff [8] | 18.24 | 53.14 | 70.82 | 90.25 | 57.42 | 77.10 | 87.90 |
| | LinCIR [9] | 25.04 | 53.25 | 66.68 | - | 57.11 | 77.37 | 88.89 |
| | MagicLens [24] | **30.10** | **61.70** | **74.40** | **92.60** | **68.10** | **84.80** | **93.20** |
| ViT H/14 | Pic2Word [17] | 32.94 | 63.11 | 73.86 | - | 62.22 | 81.35 | 91.23 |
| | SEARLE [2] | **34.00** | **63.98** | 75.25 | - | **64.63** | **83.21** | **92.77** |
| | LinCIR [9] | 33.83 | 63.52 | **75.35** | - | 62.43 | 81.47 | 92.12 |
| ViT G/14 | Pic2Word [17] | 30.41 | 58.12 | 69.23 | - | **68.92** | **85.45** | 93.04 |
| | SEARLE [2] | 34.80 | 64.07 | 75.11 | - | 68.72 | 84.70 | **93.23** |
| | CompoDiff [8] | 26.71 | 55.14 | 74.52 | 92.01 | 64.54 | 82.39 | 91.81 |
| | LinCIR [9] | **35.25** | **64.72** | **76.05** | - | 63.35 | 82.22 | 91.98 |
| *Training-free methods* | | | | | | | | |
| ViT B/32 | CIReVL [10] | 23.94 | 52.51 | 66.00 | 86.95 | 60.17 | 80.05 | 90.19 |
| | LDRE [23] | 25.69 | 55.13 | 69.04 | 89.90 | **60.53** | **80.65** | **90.70** |
| | WeiMoCIR (Ours) | **26.31** | **57.69** | **70.36** | **91.01** | 53.35 | 75.57 | 87.76 |
| ViT L/14 | CIReVL [10] | 24.55 | 52.31 | 64.92 | 86.34 | 59.54 | 79.88 | 89.69 |
| | LDRE [23] | 26.53 | 55.57 | 67.54 | 88.50 | **60.43** | **80.31** | 89.90 |
| | WeiMoCIR (Ours) | **30.94** | **60.87** | **73.08** | **91.61** | 58.55 | 79.06 | **90.07** |
| ViT H/14 | WeiMoCIR (Ours) | 29.11 | 59.76 | 72.34 | 91.18 | 57.23 | 79.08 | 89.76 |
| ViT G/14 | CIReVL [10] | 34.65 | 64.29 | 75.06 | 91.66 | 67.95 | 84.87 | 93.21 |
| | LDRE [23] | **36.15** | **66.39** | **77.25** | **93.95** | **68.82** | **85.66** | **93.76** |
| | WeiMoCIR (Ours) | 31.04 | 60.41 | 72.27 | 90.89 | 58.84 | 78.92 | 89.64 |

approaches across most of the metrics. Furthermore, our results improve with the use of larger CLIP models on this dataset. These results validate that leveraging pretrained VLMs and MLLMs, employing a simple weighted fusion of the reference image and text features, and incorporating the textual information into similarity computation are effective strategies for CIR.

*Results on CIRR.* Table 2 shows the results. Similar to the findings on FashionIQ, the methods requring additional pretraining, particularly those utilizing larger CLIP models, generally have an advantage over the training-free methods. However, unlike the results on FashionIQ, our method does not consistently yield better results with larger models. Hence, as can be seen, our approach yields results comparable to the other training-free methods with smaller CLIP models but underperforms with the larger CLIP ViT-G/14. This could be due to two reasons: (1) although larger models generally have stronger generalization capabilities, their performance on specific datasets may not always exceed that of smaller models, and (2) our approach relies heavily on pretrained VLMs for feature extraction, and the choice of VLM can significantly impact retrieval performance, as confirmed by the ablation study presented next.

**Table 3.** Ablation study on the impact of different pretrained VLMs with different backbones on retrieval performance.

| **FashionIQ** | | | Shirt | | Dress | | Toptee | | Average | |
|---|---|---|---|---|---|---|---|---|---|---|
| Backbone | $\alpha$ | $\beta$ | R@10 | R@50 | R@10 | R@50 | R@10 | R@50 | R@10 | R@50 |
| CLIP ViT L/14 | 0.80 | 0.10 | 32.78 | 48.97 | 25.88 | 47.30 | 35.95 | 56.71 | 31.54 | 50.99 |
| CLIP ViT H/14 | 0.80 | 0.10 | 36.56 | 53.58 | 28.76 | 48.98 | 39.72 | 59.87 | 35.01 | 54.14 |
| CLIP ViT G/14 | 0.80 | 0.10 | **37.73** | **56.18** | **30.99** | **52.45** | **42.38** | **63.23** | **37.03** | **57.29** |
| BLIP w/ ViT-B | 0.95 | 0.20 | 23.16 | 37.00 | 20.48 | 38.62 | 25.14 | 47.37 | 22.93 | 41.00 |
| BLIP w/ ViT-B$^{\dagger}$ | 0.95 | 0.20 | 27.09 | 43.72 | 24.29 | 44.12 | 33.10 | 53.24 | 28.16 | 47.03 |
| BLIP w/ ViT-B$^{\ddagger}$ | 0.95 | 0.20 | 30.52 | 48.33 | 25.33 | 45.46 | 34.63 | 55.89 | 30.16 | 49.90 |
| BLIP w/ ViT-L | 0.95 | 0.20 | 20.95 | 37.63 | 17.20 | 34.95 | 23.81 | 40.85 | 20.66 | 37.81 |
| BLIP w/ ViT-L$^{\dagger}$ | 0.95 | 0.20 | 29.15 | 45.73 | 22.86 | 42.89 | 31.11 | 51.56 | 27.70 | 46.72 |
| BLIP w/ ViT-L$^{\ddagger}$ | 0.95 | 0.20 | 28.95 | 45.83 | 21.22 | 42.44 | 30.55 | 50.33 | 26.91 | 46.20 |
| **CIRR** | | | Recall@K | | | | $Recall_{Subset}$@K | | | |
| Backbone | $\alpha$ | $\beta$ | R@1 | R@5 | R@10 | R@50 | R@1 | R@2 | R@3 | |
| CLIP ViT L/14 | 0.80 | 0.10 | 30.94 | 60.87 | 73.08 | 91.61 | 58.55 | 79.06 | 90.07 | |
| CLIP ViT H/14 | 0.80 | 0.10 | 29.11 | 59.76 | 72.34 | 91.18 | 57.23 | 79.08 | 89.76 | |
| CLIP ViT G/14 | 0.80 | 0.10 | 31.04 | 60.41 | 72.27 | 90.89 | 58.84 | 78.92 | 89.64 | |
| BLIP w/ ViT-B | 0.95 | 0.20 | 25.16 | 52.55 | 64.94 | 86.96 | 56.58 | 77.40 | 88.75 | |
| BLIP w/ ViT-B$^{\dagger}$ | 0.95 | 0.20 | 33.37 | 62.63 | 73.30 | 92.19 | 63.98 | 82.46 | 91.81 | |
| BLIP w/ ViT-B$^{\ddagger}$ | 0.95 | 0.20 | **36.51** | **66.75** | **77.88** | 93.45 | **65.06** | **82.63** | **92.60** | |
| BLIP w/ ViT-L | 0.95 | 0.20 | 24.46 | 53.04 | 66.70 | 88.99 | 50.92 | 73.78 | 86.65 | |
| BLIP w/ ViT-L$^{\dagger}$ | 0.95 | 0.20 | 30.94 | 61.64 | 73.49 | 92.60 | 57.88 | 78.53 | 90.02 | |
| BLIP w/ ViT-L$^{\ddagger}$ | 0.95 | 0.20 | 32.07 | 63.08 | 75.28 | **93.49** | 58.63 | 79.13 | 90.53 | |

$^{\dagger}$ Finetuned on Flickr30k $^{\ddagger}$ Finetuned on COCO

## 4.4 Ablation Study

*Impact of Different Pretrained VLMs with Different Backbones* In Table 3, we study the impact of pretrained VLMs on retrieval performance. The effectiveness of CLIP versus BLIP varies by dataset: CLIP outperforms BLIP on FashionIQ, while both models exhibit comparable performance on CIRR. When using the BLIP models

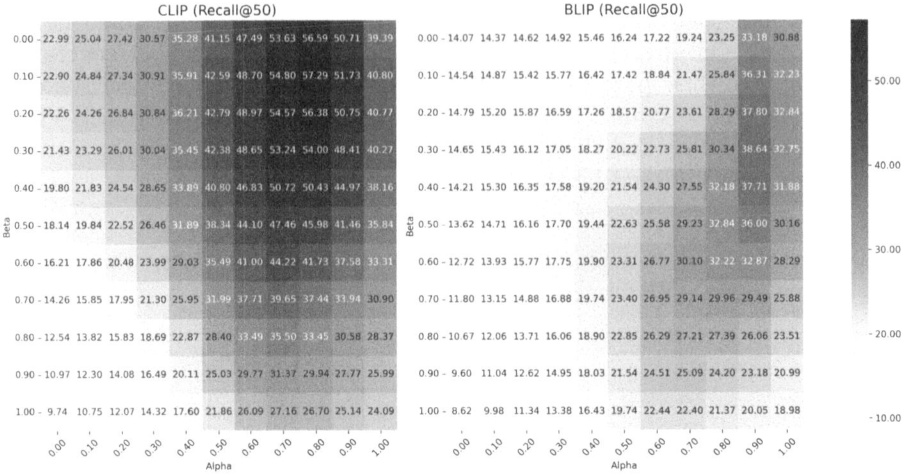


**Fig. 2.** Effects of $\alpha$ and $\beta$ on retrieval performance on FashionIQ. Left: average R@50 using CLIP ViT G/14. Right: average R@50 using BLIP ViT-B.

**Table 4.** Impact of MLLM-generated captions on retrieval performance on the FashionIQ validation set. $\boldsymbol{t}_{n,r}$ denotes the $r$the generated caption for the database image $\boldsymbol{I}_n$.

| Captions ($\boldsymbol{t}_{n,r}$) | CLIP | | BLIP | |
|---|---|---|---|---|
| | R@10 | R@50 | R@10 | R@50 |
| $\boldsymbol{t}_{n,1}$ | 31.44 | 50.82 | 22.48 | 40.21 |
| $\boldsymbol{t}_{n,2}$ | 30.77 | 50.18 | 21.33 | 39.48 |
| $\boldsymbol{t}_{n,3}$ | 30.84 | 49.96 | 22.07 | 38.80 |
| $\boldsymbol{t}_{n,1} \cup \boldsymbol{t}_{n,2}$ | 31.84 | 50.94 | 22.79 | 40.83 |
| $\boldsymbol{t}_{n,2} \cup \boldsymbol{t}_{n,3}$ | 31.05 | 50.12 | 22.39 | 40.15 |
| $\boldsymbol{t}_{n,1} \cup \boldsymbol{t}_{n,3}$ | **31.77** | 50.98 | **22.95** | 40.50 |
| $\boldsymbol{t}_{n,1} \cup \boldsymbol{t}_{n,2} \cup \boldsymbol{t}_{n,3}$ | 31.54 | **50.99** | 22.93 | **41.00** |

that have been further finetuned on COCO or Flickr30k, our method achieves significantly better results on both datasets compared to using the BLIP model without additional finetuning. This improvement is likely due to the high relevance of COCO and Flickr30k images to FashionIQ and CIRR images. These findings suggest a strong correlation between the VLMs' pretraining strategies and datasets and their performance on specific downstream datasets. As our method is training-free, it offers the flexibility to easily employ different VLMs depending on the datasets and applications.

*Effects of $\alpha$ and $\beta$ on Performance.* In Eq. (1), $\alpha$ controls the balance between the visual and textual influence in the query, with higher $\alpha$ values giving more weight to the textual representation. Similarly, in Eq. (2), higher $\beta$ values place greater emphasis on the query-to-caption similarity during retrieval.

We analyze the effects of $\alpha$ and $\beta$ on performance using FashionIQ and show the performance heatmaps in Fig. 2. As observed, regardless of the pretrained VLMs used, better retrieval performance is consistently exhibited in the upper-right regions, which correspond to relatively higher $\alpha$ values and lower $\beta$ values. This suggests that the query representation contains more textual information than visual information. In the CIR task, where users explicitly specify the desired aspects of the target images through the text modifiers, increasing the influence of textual information in the query representation can lead to more satisfactory retrieval results.

In contrast, the query-to-image similarity is a dominant factor in retrieving the target images, but adding a small amount of information from the query-to-caption similarity can enhance performance. We attribute the improvement to the reason that the MLLM-generated captions might provide information not fully captured within the visual representations of the database images.

(a) Retrieval results of example queries from FashionIQ.

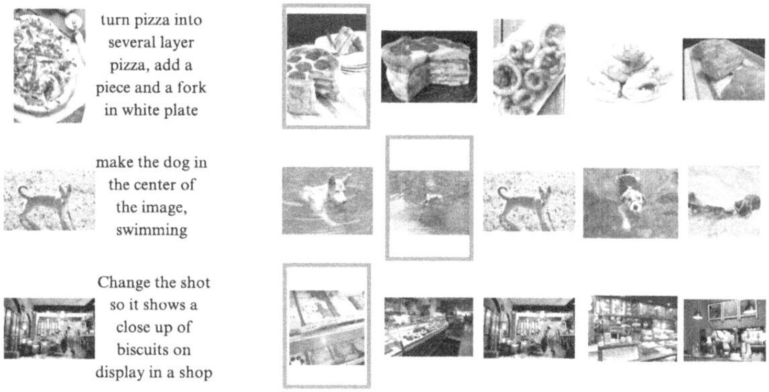


(b) Retrieval results of example queries from CIRR.

**Fig. 3.** Retrieval results of example queries from FashionIQ and CIRR. Our method with CLIP ViT L/14 successfully retrieves the desired images, highlighted with green boxes, demonstrating its ability to perform CIR for a wide variety of text modifiers. (Color figure online)

*Effects of MLLM-Generated Captions.* In our experiments, three captions are generated for each database image. We assess the impact of these MLLM-generated captions on the retrieval performance in Table 4, where $\boldsymbol{t}_{n,r}$ denotes the $r$th generated caption for the database image $\boldsymbol{I}_n$.

As observed, when only a single image caption is included in the similarity computation, the first caption generated by the MLLM yields better results than the other two, suggesting it captures the image content more effectively. Incorporating multiple captions further enhances retrieval performance, mainly because combining more captions provides a more complete description of the image. We emphasize that the performance gains from including multiple captions is achieved by guiding MLLMs with well-designed prompts, without any additional human annotations.

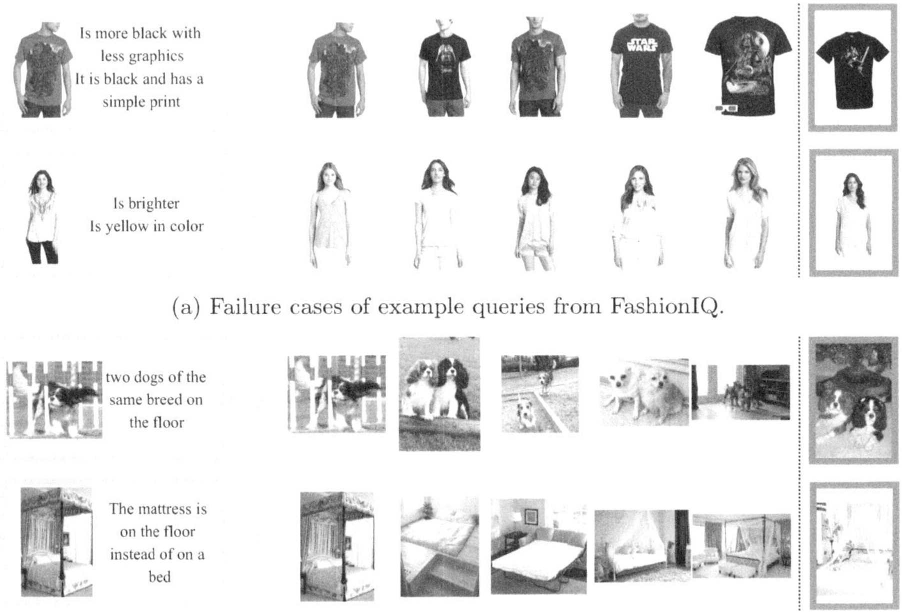


(a) Failure cases of example queries from FashionIQ.

(b) Failure cases of example queries from CIRR.

**Fig. 4.** Failure cases of our method with CLIP ViT L/14 on example queries from FashionIQ and CIRR. Target images are highlighted with green boxes in the last column. As observed, the failures stem from difficulties in capturing more abstract concepts like 'simple print' and recognizing specific 'dog breeds'.(Color figure online)

## 4.5 Qualitative Results

Figure 3 shows the CIR results from our method on example queries from FashionIQ and CIRR. The text modifiers cover a range of modifications, from color and style adjustments in fashion images to complex modifications in scenes, objects, and actions in natural images. Our method accurately interprets user intent and retrieves the desired images.

While our method yields promising results, it has certain limitations. As shown in Fig. 4, although our method can retrieve images that align well with most user requirements, it sometimes struggles to capture the full semantics of complex multimodal queries, such as understanding abstract concepts like 'simple print' (1st row of Fig. 4a), differentiating subtle differences like dog breeds (1st row of Fig. 4b), or determining relative object positioning (2nd row of Fig. 4b). These limitations indicate a need for mechanisms to enhance our method's ability to interpret nuanced queries.

## 5 Conclusion

We have presented a training-free approach for ZS-CIR. By leveraging pretrained VLMs and MLLMs, our approach integrates information from different modalities via a weighted average. This results in an easy approach to construct the query representation and allows for the incorporation of textual information into the similarity computation. Our approach performs CIR without any training and hence has the flexibility to use different VLMs and MLLMs depending on the datasets and applications. Experiments and analyses on two datasets demonstrate the effectiveness of our method. Future work will focus on enhancing our method's ability to interpret nuanced queries.

**Acknowledgments.** This work was supported in part by the National Science and Technology Council, Taiwan under Grant NSTC 113-2640-E-110-002, 112-2221-E-110-047-MY3, and 112-2634-F-006-002.

## References

1. Antol, S., et al.: VQA: visual question answering. In: ICCV, pp. 2425–2433 (2015)
2. Baldrati, A., Agnolucci, L., Bertini, M., Del Bimbo, A.: Zero-shot composed image retrieval with textual inversion. In: ICCV, pp. 15338–15347 (2023)
3. Baldrati, A., Bertini, M., Uricchio, T., Del Bimbo, A.: Effective conditioned and composed image retrieval combining clip-based features. In: CVPR, pp. 21466–21474 (2022)
4. Brown, T., et al.: Language models are few-shot learners. In: NeurIPS, pp. 1877–1901 (2020)
5. Cimino, M.G.C.A., Galatolo, F.A., Vaglini, G.: Generating images from caption and vice versa via clip-guided generative latent space search. In: IMPROVE, pp. 166–174 (2021)
6. Delmas, G., Rezende, R.S., Csurka, G., Larlus, D.: Artemis: attention-based retrieval with text-explicit matching and implicit similarity. In: ICLR (2022)
7. Gemini Team: Anil, R., et al.: Gemini: a family of highly capable multimodal models. arXiv preprint arXiv:2312.11805 (2023)
8. Gu, G., Chun, S., Kim, W., Jun, H., Kang, Y., Yun, S.: CompoDiff: versatile composed image retrieval with latent diffusion. TMLR (2024)
9. Gu, G., Chun, S., Kim, W., Kang, Y., Yun, S.: Language-only training of zero-shot composed image retrieval. In: CVPR, pp. 13225–13234 (2024)

10. Karthik, S., Roth, K., Mancini, M., Akata, Z.: Vision-by-language for training-free compositional image retrieval. In: ICLR (2024)
11. Li, J., Li, D., Xiong, C., Hoi, S.: BLIP: bootstrapping language-image pre-training for unified vision-language understanding and generation. In: ICML, pp. 12888–12900 (2022)
12. Li, M., et al..: Clip-event: connecting text and images with event structures. In: CVPR, pp. 16420–16429 (2022)
13. Liu, Z., Rodriguez-Opazo, C., Teney, D., Gould, S.: Image retrieval on real-life images with pre-trained vision-and-language models. In: ICCV, pp. 2125–2134 (2021)
14. Liu, Z., Sun, W., Hong, Y., Teney, D., Gould, S.: Bi-directional training for composed image retrieval via text prompt learning. In: WACV, pp. 5753–5762 (2024)
15. Radford, A., et al.: Learning transferable visual models from natural language supervision. In: ICML, pp. 8748–8763 (2021)
16. Radford, A., et al.: Language models are unsupervised multitask learners. OpenAI Blog, p. 9 (2019)
17. Saito, K., et al.: Pic2Word: mapping pictures to words for zero-shot composed image retrieval. In: CVPR, pp. 19305–19314 (2023)
18. Schuhmann, C., et al.: LAION-5B: an open large-scale dataset for training next generation image-text models. In: NeurIPS, pp. 25278–25294 (2022)
19. Suhr, A., Zhou, S., Zhang, A., Zhang, I., Bai, H., Artzi, Y.: A corpus for reasoning about natural language grounded in photographs. In: NeurIPS, pp. 6418–6428 (2019)
20. Vinyals, O., Toshev, A., Bengio, S., Erhan, D.: Show and tell: lessons learned from the 2015 mscoco image captioning challenge. IEEE TPAMI, pp. 652–663 (2016)
21. Vo, N., et al.: Composing text and image for image retrieval - an empirical odyssey. In: CVPR, pp. 6439–6448 (2019)
22. Wu, H., et al.: Fashion IQ: a new dataset towards retrieving images by natural language feedback. In: CVPR, pp. 11307–11317 (2021)
23. Yang, Z., Xue, D., Qian, S., Dong, W., Xu, C.: LDRE: LLM-based divergent reasoning and ensemble for zero-shot composed image retrieval. In: SIGIR, pp. 80–90 (2024)
24. Zhang, K., et al.: Magiclens: self-supervised image retrieval with open-ended instructions. arXiv preprint arXiv:2403.19651 (2024)

# Uncertainty-Error Correlations in Evidential Deep Learning Models for Biomedical Segmentation

Hai Siong Tan[1(✉)], Kwancheng Wang[2], and Rafe McBeth[3]

[1] Gryphon Center for A.I. and Theoretical Sciences, Singapore, Singapore
haisiong.tan@gryphonai.com.sg
[2] Georgia Institute of Technology, Atlanta, GA, USA
[3] Perelman School of Medicine, Department of Radiation Oncology, University of Pennsylvania, Philadelphia, USA

**Abstract.** In this work, we examine the effectiveness of an uncertainty quantification framework known as Evidential Deep Learning applied in the context of biomedical image segmentation. This class of models involves assigning Dirichlet distributions as priors for segmentation labels, and enables a few distinct definitions of model uncertainties. Using the cardiac and prostate MRI images available in the Medical Segmentation Decathlon for validation, we found that Evidential Deep Learning models with U-Net backbones generally yielded superior correlations between prediction errors and uncertainties relative to the conventional baseline equipped with Shannon entropy measure, Monte-Carlo Dropout and Deep Ensemble methods. We also examined these models' effectiveness in active learning, finding that relative to the standard Shannon entropy-based sampling, they yielded higher point-biserial uncertainty-error correlations while attaining similar performances in Dice-Sørensen coefficients. These superior features of EDL models render them well-suited for segmentation tasks that warrant a critical sensitivity in detecting large model errors.

**Keywords:** Uncertainty Quantification in A.I. · Evidential Deep Learning · Biomedical segmentation

## 1 Introduction

This paper examines the effectiveness of an uncertainty quantification (UQ) framework known as Evidential Deep Learning (EDL) applied in the context of U-Net-based segmentation of biomedical images. In particular, we scrutinize the nature of uncertainty-error correlations inherited by this model, comparing them to two major categories of UQ frameworks in the current literature[1]: (i) Monte-Carlo (MC) Dropout (ii) Deep Ensemble method.

[1] A general survey can be found in [2] whereas comprehensive recent reviews in the field of medical imaging can be found in [15] and [27].

© The Author(s), under exclusive license to Springer Nature Singapore Pte Ltd. 2025
W.-T. Chu et al. (Eds.): TAAI 2024, CCIS 2414, pp. 91–105, 2025.
https://doi.org/10.1007/978-981-96-4589-3_7

The fundamental principle of EDL lies in asserting a higher-order Bayesian prior over the probabilistic neural network output, embedding it within the loss function and subsequently generating uncertainty heatmaps upon completion of model training. There are two major variants of it proposed in the seminal works of Sensoy et al. in [20] and Amini et al. in [3], with the former being more relevant for our work here. In EDL, these parameters are incarnated as part of the model output which are thus naturally obtained when training is completed. They are then used to furnish estimates of model uncertainty. This is in contrast to MC Dropout and Deep Ensemble techniques. For MC Dropout [8], one typically inserts stochastic dropout variables at various points of the neural networks, and after model is trained, a number of feedforward passes are performed to evaluate mean and variance of the output. The latter is then regarded as the model uncertainty. For Deep Ensemble method [9,14], one typically sets up a list of models sharing the main network structure but differing in initial weight values and possibly model hyperparameters so that the final output is obtained as the average over this ensemble, and the uncertainty defined as the variance of the set of outputs.

In this paper, a primary focus lies in examining the degree to which uncertainty estimates are correlated with model prediction errors. If there exists a robust uncertainty-error correlation for the UQ model, it implies that one can leverage the uncertainty distribution to discover potential regions of model errors, and thus enable efficient human expert intervention as part of a reliable A.I.-guided workflow. This feature can be crucial for certain real-life biomedical segmentation tasks that warrant a higher sensitivity in detecting model errors. For example, in the radiotherapy clinic, if the autosegmentation of a lesion target in CT images suffers from a serious error made by the model, it may lead to harmful radiation dose being deposited on organs-at-risk. An uncertainty-aware segmentation model yields uncertainty heatmaps that can warn the medical team against potential large model errors. This in turn relies on the premise that the model inherits a strong *uncertainty-error correlation* – which is the primary focus of our work here.

To our knowledge, applications of EDL in the context of biomedical segmentation have previously appeared in [12,16,21,28]. However, none of these earlier works (and including others, e.g. [4,17,23,26] devoted to applications outside the domain of segmentation) demonstrated any direct evidence that uncertainty estimates correlate well with the actual model errors characterizing predictions made on the testing dataset. It is thus unknown how different UQ models compare against one another in this aspect. Our work fills this gap. Using two different MRI datasets drawn from the Medical Segmentation Decathlon [22], we furnished contextual definitive evidence that EDL models exhibit stronger uncertainty-error correlations for the segmentation task while attaining similar Dice coefficients compared to the more conventional MC Dropout and Deep Ensemble methods. We found that the uncertainty heatmaps generated by EDL models can act as useful visual aids towards identifying potential regions of model errors. Further, we found highly suggestive evidence of how EDL-based uncertainty sampling can furnish an excellent active learning method, attaining higher uncertainty-error correlations while converging to the same optimal Dice coefficient (associated with the full training set) compared to Shannon entropy-based uncertainty sampling.

## 2 Preliminaries

Before elaborating on our model implementation, we would like to briefly review some fundamental aspects of the theoretical framework underlying Evidential Deep Learning (EDL), in particular, with a focus on how it contains a few different notions of uncertainties; this has been missed by most of the works using EDL (e.g. [16,21,28]).

We can consider segmentation of an organ on some medical image as a set of Bernoulli trials defined separately for each pixel. For a binary class segmentation, let $p_2$ be the probability of the pixel belonging to the foreground (part of the organ) and $p_1 = 1 - p_2$ that of it being part of the image background. A neural network adapted for this task will typically generate softmax final outputs corresponding to these probability parameters. A key feature of EDL is the notion of specifying a prior distribution for the Bernoulli or more generally the categorical distribution, i.e. that $p_1, p_2$ themselves are random variables following a 'higher-order' distribution. In Bayesian language, the prior distribution is some assumed probability distribution before any observational evidence is taken into account. A common prior or 'evidential' distribution adopted for a general multi-class segmentation tasks in EDL is the Dirichlet distribution

$$D(\boldsymbol{p}|\boldsymbol{\alpha}) = \frac{1}{B(\boldsymbol{\alpha})}\prod_{i=1}^{K} p_i^{(\alpha_i-1)}, \qquad \sum_{i=1}^{K} p_i = 1, \qquad B(\boldsymbol{\alpha}) = \frac{\prod_{i=1}^{K}\Gamma(\alpha_i)}{\Gamma(\sum_{i=1}^{K}\alpha_i)}, \tag{1}$$

where $K$ is the number of class labels, $\boldsymbol{\alpha}$ are hyperparameters and $B(\boldsymbol{\alpha})$ is the multivariate beta function. For binary segmentation ($K = 2$), the Dirichlet distribution reduces to the beta distribution

$$D(p_1, p_2|(\alpha, \beta)) = \frac{1}{B(\alpha, \beta)} p_1^{\alpha-1} p_2^{\beta-1}, \quad p_2 = 1 - p_1, \quad B(\alpha, \beta) = \frac{\Gamma(\alpha)\Gamma(\beta)}{\Gamma(\alpha+\beta)}, \tag{2}$$

where we have defined $\boldsymbol{\alpha} = (\alpha, \beta)$. Since $p_j$ is a random variable of the Dirichlet distribution, we can compute the expectation values of their moments. We define the aleatoric and epistemic uncertainties associated with each class label $i$ in this evidential distribution as follows.

$$u_a = \mathrm{E}_{Diri}[\mathrm{Var}_{bernoulli}] = \mathrm{E}_{Diri}\left(p_i(1-p_i)\right), \tag{3}$$

$$u_e = \mathrm{Var}_{Diri}[\mathrm{E}_{bernoulli}] = \mathrm{Var}_{Diri}\left(p_i\right). \tag{4}$$

Using the integral identity

$$\int_0^1 dx\; x^a\,(1-x)^b = \frac{\Gamma(1+a)\Gamma(1+b)}{\Gamma(a+b+2)},$$

we can simplify (3) and (4) to read

$$u_a = \frac{\alpha_i(S-\alpha_i)}{S(S+1)}, \quad u_e = \frac{\alpha_i(S-\alpha_i)}{S^2(S+1)}, \quad S = \sum_{i=1}^{K} \alpha_i. \tag{5}$$

For binary segmentation ($K = 2, \boldsymbol{\alpha} \equiv (\alpha, \beta)$), these expressions reduce to

$$u_a = \frac{\alpha\beta}{S(S+1)}, \quad u_e = \frac{\alpha\beta}{S^2(S+1)}, \quad S = \alpha + \beta, \tag{6}$$

where the foreground and background labels share identical uncertainties with $u_a, u_e$ symmetric under the exchange $\alpha \leftrightarrow \beta$. Now in the original formulation of EDL by Sensoy et al. [20], the authors alluded to a different notion of uncertainty called 'Dempster uncertainty' that is defined within the framework of Dempster-Shafer-Theory of Evidence [18] and the formalism of Subjective Logic [1]. This notion of uncertainty is commonly invoked in works related to EDL.

The Dempster-Shafer Theory of Evidence (DST) is a generalization of the Bayesian theory to subjective probabilities [18]. It assigns 'belief functions' and an overall uncertainty $u_d$ to the set of exclusive possible states, e.g., in our context, the set of possible class labels for pixels of a medical image. These quantities which measure the reliability of the model satisfy the following sum rule

$$u_d + \sum_{j=1}^{K} b_j = 1, \quad b_j = \frac{e_j}{S}, \quad S = \sum_{j=1}^{K} (e_j + 1), \tag{7}$$

where $e_j$ is the 'evidence function' derived for class $j$, $u_d$ is the overall Dempster uncertainty and $b_j$ are the 'belief functions' that correspond to a subjective opinion measuring the amount of data support in favor of an input to be classified into a definite class. The uncertainty $u_d$ and evidence functions are connected to the parameters of the Dirichlet distribution $\boldsymbol{\alpha}$ as follows.

$$e_j = \alpha_j - 1, \quad u_d = \frac{K}{\sum_{i=1}^{K} \alpha_i} = \frac{K}{S}. \tag{8}$$

Further, Eq. (8) implies that we can relate the Dempster uncertainty $u_d$ to the aleatoric and epistemic uncertainties $u_a, u_e$ as follows.

$$u_d = \frac{K u_e}{u_a}. \tag{9}$$

Thus, up to an overall scaling factor $K$ which is the number of class labels, the Dempster uncertainty $u_d$ is the epistemic uncertainty $u_e$ in units of the aleatoric uncertainty $u_a$. In Subjective Logic [1], the Dempster uncertainty $u_d$ represents the overall degree of vacuity of evidence with respect to the Dirichlet distribution. As reviewed in e.g. [13], the aleatoric uncertainty $u_a$ is representative of the stochasticity attributable to the image data uncertainty/noise. On the other hand, epistemic uncertainty is more of an uncertainty related to the limitation of the underlying neural network. This limitation can be due to an underlying inadequacy of the model's structure with respect to the data distribution and/or some fundamental insufficiency of the training data. There are thus different notions of uncertainties $\{u_d, u_a, u_e\}$ at a more granular level as explained above.

When implemented on a neural network, as originally proposed in [20], the model's final output variables are the evidence variables

$$e_i = \alpha_i - 1 = f_{model}(\boldsymbol{x}_i|\boldsymbol{w}), \tag{10}$$

where $f_{model}$ denotes the output function of the neural network, $\boldsymbol{w}$ denotes the weight vectors of the neural network, and $\boldsymbol{x}_i$ denotes the model's inputs, Once $\boldsymbol{e}$ and thus $\boldsymbol{\alpha}$ are obtained, we can make an inference of the pixel's class through the model's prediction of class probabilities. Taking expectation values with respect to the Dirichlet distribution (whose parameters $\boldsymbol{\alpha}$ have been learned), the mean class probabilities are

$$\langle p_k \rangle = \int_0^1 dp_k\, p_k \left( \frac{1}{B(\boldsymbol{\alpha})} \prod_{i=1}^{K} p_i^{(\alpha_i - 1)} \right) = \frac{\alpha_k}{\sum_{i=1}^{K} \alpha_i} \equiv \frac{\alpha_k}{S}, \quad k = 1, 2, \ldots, K. \tag{11}$$

# 3 Methodology

## 3.1 On Datasets, Model Structure and Loss Function

Open-source datasets were employed for our model validations. In this work, we chose to use two MRI image datasets drawn from the Medical Segmentation Decathlon [22]: cardiac (left atrium) mono-modal MRI and prostate (combining central gland and peripheral zone) MRI (T2 and apparent diffusion coefficient (ADC) modes), both of which were described in [22] to display large inter-subject variability. The ground truth images were annotated by medical experts in Radboud University, Nijmegen Medical Centre for the prostate dataset and those in King's College London for cardiac dataset [22].

For our neural network architecture, we adopted a 2D U-Net backbone with a 2-channel convolution layer as the final layer, the output variables being the evidence variables of eqn. (10) related to the Dirichlet distribution parameters $\alpha, \beta$ as follows.

$$e_1 = \alpha - 1, \quad e_2 = \beta - 1, \quad e_i \geq 0. \tag{12}$$

Inference on the binary class of each pixel is determined by the relative magnitude of the mean class probabilities

$$\hat{p}_1 = \frac{\alpha}{S}, \quad \hat{p}_2 = \frac{\beta}{S}, \quad S = \alpha + \beta, \tag{13}$$

where $\hat{p}_{1,2}$ refer to the probabilities of the pixel belonging to background and foreground respectively, these quantities being averaged over the Dirichlet distribution parametrized by $\alpha, \beta$. Our U-Net has the following structure:

- a 320 × 320 voxel image with N = 1 (cardiac) or 2 (prostate) channels;
- each downsampling level consists of two convolutional layers each with a (3 × 3) kernel, ReLU activation and equipped with a dropout unit with rate 0.1, followed by maximum pooling with kernel size (2 × 2);
- the downsampling operation is performed 4 times, with the number of convolutional filters for each layer being $\{32, 64, 128, 256\}$ respectively;
- at each of the four upsampling levels, features from the contraction path are concatenated with the corresponding upsampled (bilinear) features;
- the final 2-channel pointwise convolution layer yields the non-negative evidence variables $e_1, e_2$ which are used to infer pixel class via Eq. (13);

This model contained about $2 \times 10^6$ free weight parameters. We also took it to be the 'baseline model' after replacing the final layer's activation function with softmax function and using a Dice loss function for training.

For EDL model's loss function, among the few types proposed in [20], we found the Bayes risk function obtained by averaging mean-squared error over the Dirichlet distribution to be most effective. It reads

$$\mathcal{L}_{Bayes} = \int ||\boldsymbol{p} - \boldsymbol{y}||^2 \frac{1}{B(\boldsymbol{\alpha})} \prod_{l=1}^{K} p_l^{\alpha_l - 1} dp = \sum_{j=1}^{K} (y_j - \hat{p}_j)^2 + \frac{\hat{p}_j(1-\hat{p}_j)}{S+1}, \quad (14)$$

where $\hat{p}_j$ are the model's probabilistic prediction for the pixel's label defined in eqn. (13) earlier. This also needs to be augmented by a regularizer-type loss term that shifts the Dirichlet distributions for incorrectly-labeled pixels towards uniform distributions so that the errors are characterized by higher uncertainties. As formulated in [20], it reads

$$\mathcal{L}_{KL} = \log\left(\frac{\Gamma(\sum_j \tilde{\alpha}_j)}{\Gamma(K)\prod_j \Gamma(\tilde{\alpha}_j)}\right) + \sum_{j=1}^{K} (\tilde{\alpha}_j - 1)\left[\psi(\tilde{\alpha}_j) - \psi(\sum_j \tilde{\alpha}_j)\right], \quad (15)$$

where $\tilde{\alpha}$ are the $\alpha$'s of the incorrectly labeled pixels. This loss term is proportional to the Kullback-Leibler divergence (see e.g. [7]) between the Dirichlet and uniform distribution. In many or our ablation experiments, the sum of the loss terms (14) and (15) led to an effective segmentation model with good uncertainty-error correlations, but we found that for many choices of hyperparameters, it attained Dice coefficients which were markedly inferior to the baseline U-Net. This deficiency was resolved after adding another focal Dice loss term defined as follows.

$$\mathcal{L}_{Dice} = 1 - \left(\frac{2\frac{1}{N}\sum_{i=1}^{N} y_t^i y_p^i}{\frac{1}{N}\sum_{i=1}^{N}(y_t^i + y_p^i)}\right)^3, \quad (16)$$

where $y_t^i, y_p^i$ denote the ground truth label and model's prediction for pixel $i$ and $N$ is the total number of pixels. The final form of our loss function is the sum

$$\mathcal{L} = \mathcal{L}_{Bayes} + \lambda_{KL}\mathcal{L}_{KL} + \lambda_{Dice}\mathcal{L}_{Dice}, \quad (17)$$

where $\lambda$'s are hyperparameters of which optimal values we found to be $\lambda_{KL} = 0.20, \lambda_{Dice} = 0.15$ for cardiac dataset and $\lambda_{KL} = 0.20, \lambda_{Dice} = 0.01$, for prostate dataset.[2] Towards comparing the EDL model against more common approaches of uncertainty quantification in literature, we implemented a Deep Ensemble model and MC Dropout model for the same datasets. Each of the 5 neural networks used in the Deep Ensemble model share the same U-Net architecture with random weight initialization performed via the *He*-uniform initializer [10] to induce different initial conditions. For the MC Dropout model, the same base model was used for passing 30 forward passes with the dropout layers activated for model prediction. All models were trained on a NVIDIA A100 GPU for 800 epochs with a learning rate of $10^{-4}$ using Adam optimizer (implemented in Tensorflow).

### 3.2 On Active Learning

Towards the goal of incorporating EDL in real-time clinical workflow which often involves evolving large-scale datasets, we also performed a preliminary study of whether/how the predicted uncertainties can be useful for active learning.

Let the training dataset be split into a labeled set $\mathcal{D}_L$ and an unlabeled set $\mathcal{D}_U$. At any iteration, only the labeled set is used to train the model. Each iteration of active learning involves picking a number ($N_u$) of images $\tilde{X}$ from the unlabeled set $\mathcal{D}_U$ using some 'acquisition/query' function $\mathcal{Q}$,

$$\{\tilde{X}_1, \tilde{X}_2, \ldots, \tilde{X}_{N_u}\} = \mathcal{Q}\left(\{X : X \in \mathcal{D}_U\}\right), \tag{18}$$

which represents a selection criterion such that a small subset of the unlabeled pool can be added to expand the labeled pool for model training, formally, $\mathcal{D}_U \to \mathcal{D}_U \setminus \{\tilde{X}_1, \ldots, \tilde{X}_{N_u}\}, \quad \mathcal{D}_L \to \mathcal{D}_L \cup \{\tilde{X}_1, \ldots, \tilde{X}_{N_u}\}$. The acquisition function $\mathcal{Q}$ ranges from simply a random choice to more complicated selection strategies. As mentioned in [6,24,25], uncertainty sampling has proven to be one of the best active learning technique, with $\mathcal{Q}$ defined as the subset with highest uncertainty. A common measure is the Shannon entropy. In our work here, we explore the effectiveness of using the different uncertainties in EDL: Dempster, epistemic and aleatoric for defining the query function $\mathcal{Q}$.

$$\mathcal{Q} = \underset{\{\tilde{X}_1, \ldots \tilde{X}_{N_U}\}}{\arg\max} \sum_{i \in \tilde{X}} U_i, \qquad U_i \in \{U_{shannon}, u_d, u_e, u_a\}, \tag{19}$$

where $i$ is the pixel index, $U_{shannon} \equiv -\sum_{j=1}^{K} p_j \log p_j$, and $u_d, u_e, u_a$ are defined in eqns. (9) and (5). The active learning algorithm follows mostly that implemented in [6,24]. For the prostate dataset (481 training samples), each active

[2] The optimal coefficients were found with validation data arising from a 4:1 split of the training dataset, excluding a hold-out testing set that comprises of 20% of the entire dataset. The higher $\lambda_{KL}/\lambda_{Dice}$ ratio required for the prostate (vs cardiac) dataset may be related to it presenting a higher level of difficulty for segmentation as reflected in Table 1.

learning round involves 10 training epochs with $N_u = 6$ samples with the highest uncertainties acquired. For the larger cardiac dataset (1817 training samples), we took each iteration to involve 20 training epochs with $N_u = 20$. With these hyperparameters, the validation Dice coefficient converged at the $50^{\text{th}}$ iteration. Compatible with results obtained in [24], 0.68 and 0.75 of the entire training data were required to attain similar Dice coefficients achieved by using the full training data for the cardiac and prostate datasets respectively.

### 3.3 On Measures of Uncertainty-Error Correlations

A major goal of this work is to scrutinize the degree of correlation between uncertainty measures and model errors. Among the spectrum of indices we used, two of them are more discriminative and sensitive in detecting such a correlation. The first is the point-biserial coefficient between the dichotomous variable (true/false label prediction) and the continuous uncertainty measure. The other is the Kolmogorov-Smirnov statistic (see e.g. [19]) measuring the discrepancy between the empirical cumulative distribution functions of the two separate sets of true/false labels. For both these coefficients, we computed them for each 2D slice[3] of the MRI image since many biomedical applications involving segmentation operate at this scale, and then averaged over the testing dataset to obtain a representative score for each deep learning model.

For any uncertainty-aware model, the Brier score [5] and negative log likelihoods (NLL) [11] are two commonly used proper scoring rules in Decision Theory to measure how well-calibrated the probabilistic model predictions are. For each 2D slice, we computed the average Brier score, NLL, Dice and accuracy values as well as the average uncertainty measure. The Spearman's rank coefficient between the averaged uncertainty estimates and these various scores were then collected to probe whether 2D-image-averaged uncertainties correlated with the degree of calibration of each model.

## 4 Results

### 4.1 EDL Showed the Strongest Uncertainty-Error Correlation

Overall, our results demonstrated that EDL models exhibited the most significant correlation between uncertainties and errors, as measured by the point-biserial coefficient and the Kolmogorov-Smirnov statistic differentiating between the eCDFs of correctly and falsely labeled voxels. Detailed numerical results are collected in Table 1 for the both datasets, with the highlighted cells showing the most relevant ones for the strongest uncertainty-error correlations.

In terms of the Dice coefficient, EDL achieved the same performance relative to all the other models for both datasets, indicating that segmentation accuracy was not compromised while having a more robust uncertainty quantification. Our

[3] The 2D slices are defined along the axial plane for the prostate and the sagittal plane for the cardiac dataset.

experimental results also suggested that it is generally useful to consider the three subtypes of evidential uncertainties as we found aleatoric uncertainty to have the highest point-biserial coefficient (0.54) for cardiac dataset, while Dempster and epistemic uncertainties attained the highest value (0.51) for prostate dataset.

**Table 1.** Collection of correlation indices and Dice coefficients. **Abbrev**: Demp, Epis, Alea: Dempster, epistemic and aleatoric uncertainties, NLL: negative log-likelihood, K.S.:Kolmogorov-Smirnov statistic, Pt-Biserial: point-biserial coefficient between error and uncertainty, Spearman (...): Spearman's coefficient between uncertainty (U) and (i) Brier Score (B), (ii) negative log-likelihood (NLL), (iii) Dice coefficient (D), (iv) Accuracy (A).

| Prostate Dataset | **EDL** | | | **Baseline** | **MC Dropout** | **Deep Ensemble** |
|---|---|---|---|---|---|---|
| | Demp | Epis | Alea | Entropy | [Std.Dev.] | [Std.Dev.] |
| **Dice Coef.** | 0.81 | | | 0.80 | 0.80 | 0.80 |
| **Brier Score** | $3.8 \times 10^{-3}$ | | | $4.0 \times 10^{-3}$ | $3.4 \times 10^{-3}$ | $2.9 \times 10^{-3}$ |
| **NLL** | 0.031 | | | 0.055 | 0.035 | 0.023 |
| **K.S. statistic** | 0.94 | | | 0.62 | 0.56 | 0.68 |
| **Pt-Biserial** | 0.51 | 0.51 | 0.48 | 0.16 | 0.38 | 0.45 |
| **Spearman(B,U)** | 0.89 | 0.90 | 0.87 | 0.73 | 0.77 | 0.77 |
| **Spearman(NLL,U)** | 0.90 | 0.90 | 0.89 | 0.68 | 0.67 | 0.59 |
| **Spearman(D,U)** | -0.42 | -0.45 | -0.38 | -0.44 | -0.53 | -0.62 |
| **Spearman(A,U)** | -0.77 | -0.79 | -0.75 | -0.73 | -0.80 | -0.77 |
| Cardiac Dataset | | | | | | |
| | Demp | Epis | Alea | Entropy | [Std.Dev.] | [Std.Dev.] |
| **Dice Coef.** | 0.95 | | | 0.94 | 0.94 | 0.94 |
| **Brier Score** | $1.8 \times 10^{-4}$ | | | $2.4 \times 10^{-4}$ | $1.9 \times 10^{-4}$ | $1.6 \times 10^{-4}$ |
| **NLL** | 0.0051 | | | 0.0034 | 0.0018 | 0.0012 |
| **K.S. statistic** | 0.98 | | | 0.59 | 0.67 | 0.76 |
| **Pt-Biserial** | 0.53 | 0.51 | 0.54 | 0.17 | 0.45 | 0.48 |
| **Spearman(B,U)** | 0.94 | 0.94 | 0.93 | 0.84 | 0.87 | 0.93 |
| **Spearman(NLL,U)** | 0.93 | 0.92 | 0.92 | 0.84 | 0.84 | 0.85 |
| **Spearman(D,U)** | -0.80 | -0.80 | -0.79 | -0.72 | -0.77 | -0.79 |
| **Spearman(A,U)** | -0.90 | -0.91 | -0.90 | -0.82 | -0.90 | -0.89 |

In Table 1, we have also collected coarse-grained indices which quantify 2D image-averaged correlations. The relevant indices are the Spearman's rank coefficient between mean uncertainty measures and each of Brier score, NLL, Dice and accuracy scores. Results for both datasets indicated that 2D-slice-averaged uncertainty measures of EDL inherited higher correlations with Brier score and NLL relative to the other models, though there was no significant advantage over other methods in terms of their correlations with the Dice coefficient.

For a more holistic view on the uncertainty distributions, we examined plots of the empirical cumulative distribution functions (eCDF) of each element of the 'confusion matrix': True Positive, True Negative, False Positive, False Negative. In Fig. 1, one can discern the eCDFs for the correctly labeled voxels (True Positive and Negative) from the falsely labeled ones (False Positive and Negative), with the segregation most apparent for the EDL model. Formally, although simple visual inspection of Fig. 1 gave us sufficient insight, we can invoke the Kolmogorov-Smirnov statistic as a numerical representative index. We found that for both datasets, this statistic was significantly higher for EDL relative to all other methods. Collectively, our various results demonstrated that among all models considered here, EDL showed the strongest uncertainty-error correlation.

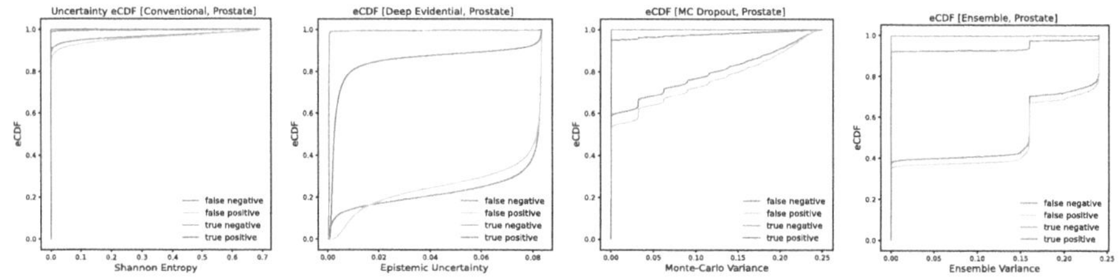


(a) (b) (c) (d)

**Fig. 1.** Empirical cumulative distribution functions (eCDF) of uncertainties in various models trained for prostate segmentation. Highly similar trends were also observed for eCDFs pertaining to the cardiac (left atrium) segmentation.

### 4.2 On Uncertainty Heatmaps

Visual inspection of the uncertainty heatmaps generated by EDL models suggests that they are useful towards discovering potential regions of model errors. In Figs. 2 and 3, we present a few illustrative images and their uncertainty heatmaps for each dataset as modeled by the EDL framework.

For the images of the cardiac dataset depicted in Fig. 2, (b) and (c) are examples of contours with small model errors in the neighborhood of the boundary curve. We note how discrepancies between the model-predicted (red curve) and ground truth (yellow mask) are often captured by elevated uncertainty regions. (a) and (d) are examples of cases where isolated components of the model-predicted contour contain no foreground pixels; these false-positive areas are marked by elevated uncertainty regions. For the prostate dataset depicted in Fig. 3, (a) and (b) are examples of contours with small model errors in the neighborhood of the boundary curve. (c) and (d) are examples of cases where the model-predicted contour misses the ground truth region completely; the elevated uncertainty regions are filled in the interior and extends to actual ground truth regions.

The basis for an effective uncertainty heatmap is a robust uncertainty-error correlation. Among the different measures, we found that the difference between eCDF plots of true and false labels stood out as the most consistent way of determining the usefulness of uncertainty heatmaps towards discovering model errors. Models which yielded uncertainty heatmaps that mirrored segmentation errors more effectively were always those which showed eCDF trends similar to Fig. 1b, with clear geometric deviations between eCDFs of true and false labels.

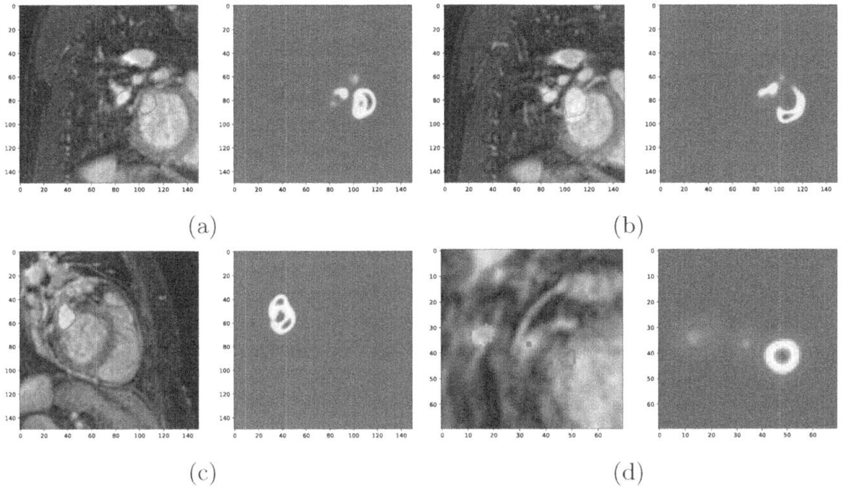

**Fig. 2.** Aleatoric uncertainty heatmaps for segmentation of the left atrium in sagittal T1-weighted cardiac MRI images. Red curves pertain to model-predicted contours overlaid on ground truth masks in yellow. (Color figure online)

### 4.3 On Active Learning

In Table 2, we collect various results for our study of active learning with EDL and a conventional model with uncertainty sampling via Shannon entropy. We found that while attaining similar Dice coefficient as random and uncertainty sampling, EDL-based uncertainty sampling yielded a much higher point-biserial coefficient and Kolomogorov-Smirnov statistic at the end of active learning iterations. Like our previous results using the conventional model training scheme, aleatoric and epistemic uncertainy-based active learning worked best for the cardiac and prostate dataset respectively. We note that all models converged to the optimal Dice coefficient at the end of the $50^{\text{th}}$ iteration with 0.68 and 0.75 of the full training dataset size required. Using EDL uncertainty-based sampling did not speed up the convergence (which would have led to greater training dataset reduction). Nonetheless, the much superior uncertainty-error correlation was still inherited by EDL models relative to standard random and uncertainty-based sampling algorithms (Fig. 4).

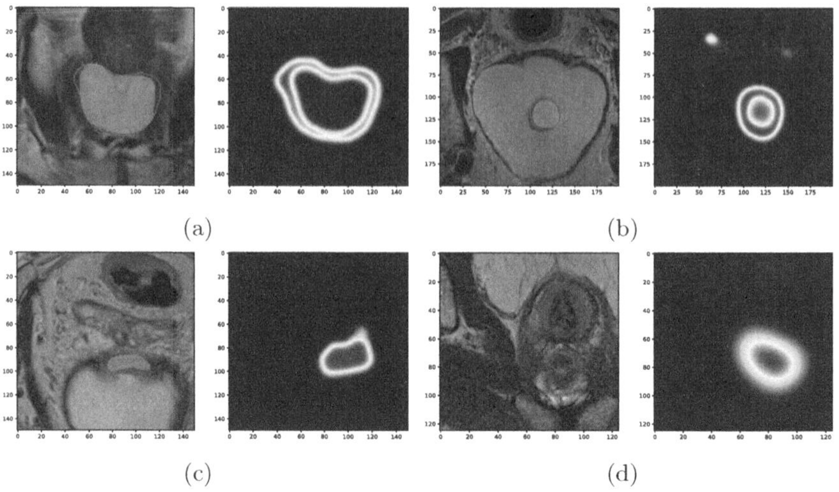


**Fig. 3.** Epistemic uncertainty heatmaps for segmentation of the central and peripheral zones of the prostate in axial T2-weighted MRI images. Note how elevated redder regions of each heatmap appear to mirror deviations between ground truth masks in yellow and their model-predicted contours in red. (Color figure online)

**Table 2.** Results for active learning algorithms. **Abbrev**: Demp, Epis, Alea: uncertainty sampling via higher mean Dempster, epistemic and aleatoric uncertainties respectively.

| | Cardiac dataset | | | | | Prostate dataset | | | | |
|---|---|---|---|---|---|---|---|---|---|---|
| | Demp | Epis | Alea | Random | Entropy | Demp | Epis | Alea | Random | Entropy |
| **Dice Coef.** | 0.94 | 0.94 | 0.94 | 0.93 | 0.94 | 0.81 | 0.81 | 0.80 | 0.80 | 0.80 |
| **Pt-Biserial** | 0.43 | 0.39 | **0.48** | 0.23 | 0.22 | 0.48 | **0.52** | 0.46 | 0.27 | 0.26 |
| **K.S. statistic** | | 0.96 | | 0.41 | 0.41 | | 0.95 | | 0.40 | 0.44 |

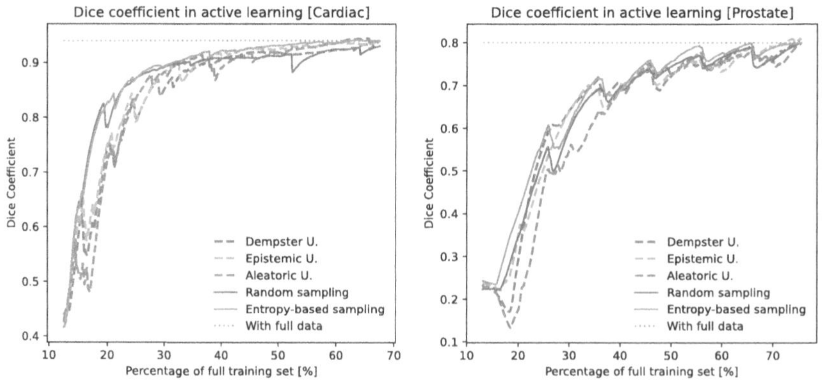


**Fig. 4.** Evolution of Dice coefficient during active training.

## 5 Discussion

Collectively, the various results of our work demonstrated that EDL models exhibited the most significant correlation between uncertainties and errors, as measured by the point-biserial coefficient and the Kolmogorov-Smirnov statistic differentiating between the eCDFs of correctly and falsely labeled voxels. In terms of the Dice coefficient, EDL attained the same performance relative to all the other models for both datasets, showing that segmentation accuracy was not compromised while having a more robust uncertainty quantification. Our experimental results also suggested that generally, it would be useful to consider the three subtypes of evidential uncertainties for generating uncertainty heatmaps, as we found aleatoric uncertainty to have the highest point-biserial coefficient (0.54) for cardiac dataset, while Dempster and epistemic uncertainties attained the highest value (0.51) for prostate dataset. A more global picture of the error-uncertainty relationship can be visualized using the eCDFs in each model. As depicted in Fig. 1, the EDL models exhibited the most significant deviation between eCDFs of correctly and falsely labeled voxels, and yielded the highest Kolmogorov-Smirnov statistic parametrizing the differences in eCDFs of uncertainty estimates.

Ultimately, we would like our model to yield uncertainty heatmaps that are effective in identifying potential regions of model errors so that the human expert (e.g. dosimetrist) can intervene and rectify the contours whenever necessary. Visual inspection of the uncertainty heatmaps generated by our EDL model in Figs. 2 and 3 suggests that they are useful towards realizing this goal.

Adapting EDL for active learning by using the various notions of uncertainties for defining the query function, we found that while attaining similar Dice coefficient as random and uncertainty sampling, EDL-based uncertainty sampling yielded a much higher point-biserial coefficient and Kolomogorov-Smirnov statistic at the end of active learning iterations. Like our previous results using the conventional model training scheme, aleatoric and epistemic uncertainty-based active learning worked best for the cardiac and prostate dataset respectively.

## 6 Conclusion

Using the cardiac and prostate MRI images of the Medical Segmentation Decathlon [22] for validation, we found that Evidential Deep Learning (EDL) models with U-Net backbones yielded superior correlations between prediction errors and uncertainties relative to the conventional baseline equipped with Shannon entropy measure, MC Dropout and Deep Ensemble methods. We also examined EDL's effectiveness in active learning, finding that relative to the standard entropy-based uncertainty sampling, they yielded higher point-biserial correlations while attaining similar performances in Dice coefficients. Our spectrum of results furnished novel contextual evidence that EDL models supersede MC Dropout and Deep Ensemble methods in terms of uncertainty-error correlation, and they yield uncertainty heatmaps that are useful for indicating potential regions of model errors. These superior features of EDL models render them particularly suitable as uncertainty-aware models for segmentation tasks that warrant a higher sensitivity in detecting large model errors.

**Disclosure of Interests.** The authors have no competing interests to declare that are relevant to the content of this article.

## References

1. Jøsang, A.: Subjective Logic: A Formalism for Reasoning Under Uncertainty. Springer (2016)
2. Abdar, M., et al.: A review of uncertainty quantification in deep learning: techniques, applications and challenges. Inf. Fusion **76**, 243–297 (2021)
3. Amini, A., Schwarting, W., Soleimany, A., Rus, D.: Deep evidential regression. In: Proceedings of the 34th International Conference on Neural Information Processing Systems. NIPS '20, Curran Associates Inc. (2020)
4. Bao, W., Yu, Q., Kong, Y.: Evidential deep learning for open set action recognition. In: Proceedings of the IEEE/CVF International Conference on Computer Vision (ICCV), pp. 13349–13358 (2021)
5. Brier, G.W.: Verification of forecasts expressed in terms of probability. Monthly Weather Rev. **78**(1), 1–3 (1950)
6. Burmeister, J.M., et al.: Less is more: a comparison of active learning strategies for 3D medical image segmentation (2022)
7. Cover, T.M., Thomas, J.A.: Elements of Information Theory (Wiley Series in Telecommunications and Signal Processing). Wiley-Interscience, USA (2006)
8. Gal, Y., Ghahramani, Z.: Dropout as a bayesian approximation: representing model uncertainty in deep learning. In: Balcan, M.F., Weinberger, K.Q. (eds.) Proceedings of The 33rd International Conference on Machine Learning. Proceedings of Machine Learning Research, vol. 48, pp. 1050–1059. PMLR, New York, New York, USA (2016)
9. Ganaie, M., Hu, M., Malik, A., Tanveer, M., Suganthan, P.: Ensemble deep learning: a review. Eng. Appl. Artif. Intellig. **115**, 105151 (2022)
10. He, K., Zhang, X., Ren, S., Sun, J.: Delving deep into rectifiers: surpassing human-level performance on imagenet classification. In: 2015 IEEE International Conference on Computer Vision (ICCV), pp. 1026–1034 (2015)
11. James, G., Witten, D., Hastie, T., Tibshirani, R.: An Introduction to Statistical Learning: with Applications in R. Springer (2013)
12. Jones, C.K., Wang, G., Yedavalli, V., Sair, H.: Direct quantification of epistemic and aleatoric uncertainty in 3D U-net segmentation. J Med Imaging (Bellingham) **9**(3), 034002 (2022)
13. Kendall, A., Gal, Y.: What uncertainties do we need in Bayesian deep learning for computer vision? In: Proceedings of the 31st International Conference on Neural Information Processing Systems. NIPS'17, Red Hook, NY, USA, pp. 5580–5590. Curran Associates Inc. (2017)
14. Lakshminarayanan, B., Pritzel, A., Blundell, C.: Simple and scalable predictive uncertainty estimation using deep ensembles. In: Proceedings of the 31st International Conference on Neural Information Processing Systems. NIPS'17, pp. 6405–6416. Curran Associates Inc. (2017)

15. Lambert, B., Forbes, F., Doyle, S., Dehaene, H., Dojat, M.: Trustworthy clinical AI solutions: a unified review of uncertainty quantification in deep learning models for medical image analysis. Artif. Intell. Med. **150**, 102830 (2024)
16. Li, H., Nan, Y., Ser, J.D., Yang, G.: Region-based evidential deep learning to quantify uncertainty and improve robustness of brain tumor segmentation (2022). https://arxiv.org/abs/2208.06038
17. Lou, J., Liu, W., Chen, Z., Liu, F., Cheng, J.: ELFNet: evidential local-global fusion for stereo matching (2023). https://arxiv.org/abs/2308.00728
18. P., D.A.: A generalization of Bayesian inference. J. Roy. Stat. Soc. **B**(10), 205–247 (1968)
19. Pratt, J.W., Gibbons, J.D.: Kolmogorov-Smirnov Two-Sample Tests, pp. 318–344. Springer, New York(1981)
20. Sensoy, M., Kaplan, L., Kandemir, M.: Evidential deep learning to quantify classification uncertainty. In: Advances in Neural Information Processing Systems, vol. 31 (2018)
21. Shi, R., Duan, L., Huang, T., Jiang, T.: Evidential uncertainty-guided mitochondria segmentation for 3D EM images. In: Proceedings of the AAAI Conference on Artificial Intelligence, vol. 38, no. 5, pp. 4847–4855 (2024)
22. Simpson, A.L., et al.: A large annotated medical image dataset for the development and evaluation of segmentation algorithms (2019)
23. Soleimany, A.P., Amini, A., Goldman, S., Rus, D., Bhatia, S.N., Coley, C.W.: Evidential deep learning for guided molecular property prediction and discovery. ACS Cent. Sci. **7**(8), 1356–1367 (2021)
24. Tan, H.S., Wang, K., Mcbeth, R.: Exploring UMAP in hybrid models of entropy-based and representativeness sampling for active learning in biomedical segmentation. Comput. Biol. Med. **176**, 108605 (2024)
25. Tharwat, A., Schenck, W.: A survey on active learning: State-of-the-art, practical challenges and research directions. Mathematics **11**(4) (2023)
26. Tong, Z., Xu, P., Denœux, T.: Fusion of evidential CNN classifiers for image classification. In: International Conference on Belief Functions, pp. 168–176. Springer (2021)
27. Zou, K., Chen, Z., Yuan, X., Shen, X., Wang, M., Fu, H.: A review of uncertainty estimation and its application in medical imaging. Meta-Radiol. **1**(1), 100003 (2023)
28. Zou, K., Yuan, X., Shen, X., Wang, M., Fu, H.: Tbrats: trusted brain tumor segmentation. In: Medical Image Computing and Computer Assisted Intervention - MICCAI 2022: 25th International Conference. Singapore, September 18–22, 2022, Proceedings, Part VIII, pp. 503–513. Springer, Heidelberg (2022)

# Knowledge Representation and Management

# Causality-Driven Patent Valuation: Integrating Domain Knowledge and Language Models in a Structured Interview-Like Selection Process

Chuan-Wei Kuo[1], Wen-Chih Peng[1(✉)], and Hsin-Ning Su[2]

[1] Department of Computer Science, National Yang Ming Chiao Tung University, No. 1001, University Road, Hsinchu 300, Taiwan
auberonkuo.cs07@nycu.edu.tw, wcpeng@cs.nycu.edu.tw

[2] Institute of Management of Technology, National Yang Ming Chiao Tung University, No. 1001, University Road,Hsinchu 300, Taiwan
ningsu@nycu.edu.tw

**Abstract.** Patents are essential for securing market leadership and protecting intellectual property, but traditional valuation methods often fail to fully capture their strategic value. This paper introduces a causality-driven framework for patent valuation that integrates domain expertise with advanced language models in a structured interview-like process. By analyzing semiconductor patents filed between 1997 and 2007-a pivotal period of technological transformation-our approach employs Directed Acyclic Graphs (DAGs) and Structural Equation Models (SEMs) to reveal causal relationships, providing precise value attribution. This integration enhances the analysis of complex patent data, offering a powerful tool for aligning technological innovation with market and legal strategies.

**Keywords:** Patent Valuation · Causality-Driven Analysis · Structured Interview Process · Pre-Trained Language Models · Semiconductor Industry

## 1 Introduction

In today's rapidly advancing technological landscape, patents have become indispensable assets, functioning as both defensive shields and competitive weapons [8,11] in the global marketplace. They not only safeguard a company's intellectual property but also serve as crucial indicators of innovation and market leadership [2,17]. Despite their importance, conventional methods of patent valuation [17] often fall short of capturing the full strategic value and potential impact of these assets, resulting in a disconnect between their legal standing and their true market worth. To address this gap, this paper introduces a novel framework for patent valuation that merges causality-driven analytics with a human-centric approach, inspired by the precision of structured interviews [5,6,14,19,30,36].

© The Author(s), under exclusive license to Springer Nature Singapore Pte Ltd. 2025
W.-T. Chu et al. (Eds.): TAAI 2024, CCIS 2414, pp. 109–123, 2025.
https://doi.org/10.1007/978-981-96-4589-3_8

Our approach is founded on the premise that patents, much like candidates in a structured interview, should be evaluated with a level of scrutiny and depth that goes beyond traditional quantitative metrics [6,30]. Each patent is treated as a unique entity, possessing its own narrative and latent value [17]. By adopting a structured, interview-like methodology, we aim to uncover the intrinsic potential of patents, moving beyond surface-level assessments to fully understand their capacity to drive innovation.

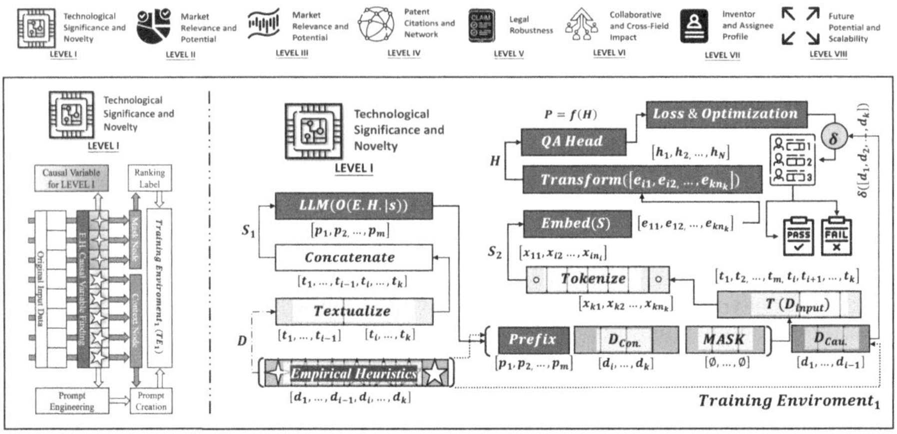


**Fig. 1.** The proposed methodological framework for patent valuation. This framework integrates causality-driven analysis, domain knowledge, and language models to provide a comprehensive and nuanced evaluation of patents, simulating a structured interview-like selection process.

Our analysis centers on semiconductor patents filed between 1997 and 2007 by nine leading companies in the industry. This period marks a critical juncture in the evolution of patents, as they transitioned from mere legal protections to strategic assets integral to technological advancement [3,8,11,12,28]. By examining this extensive dataset, we aim to develop valuation strategies that are not only applicable within the semiconductor industry but also extendable to other sectors. To further strengthen our valuation framework, we integrate financial metrics with patent analytics, offering a holistic perspective that considers both technological significance and market perceptions [17].

Inspired by the structured interview process [5,14], our proposed valuation methodology is both meticulous and exhaustive. Each patent is subjected to a thorough evaluation, analogous to a series of interviews, where its technological relevance, market influence, and innovative contribution are systematically assessed. In the era of big data, the sheer volume of patent-related information [22,31] demands advanced analytical tools. To meet this need, we incorporate state-of-the-art language models [4,13,15,20,21,29,32,35] alongside expert human judgment, enabling a level of analysis that is both deep and comprehensive.

This paper presents a transformative approach to patent valuation, combining data-driven analytics with expert judgment, and integrating financial considerations with technological insights. Our methodology is not merely a new tool for evaluation; it represents a paradigm shift in how we understand and assess the value of innovation, offering previously unattainable insights. Central to our approach is the proposed methodological framework, which seamlessly blends causality-driven analysis [24], domain expertise, and language models [4,13,15,20,21,29,32,35] to deliver a thorough and nuanced evaluation of patents, as depicted in Fig. 1. This framework simulates a structured interview-like selection process [5,6], ensuring that each patent is evaluated with the depth and rigor required to reveal its true potential.

## 2 Literature Review

The valuation of patents has long been a critical area of research, with traditional methods focusing primarily on quantitative metrics such as patent citation counts, family size, and claims analysis [10,17,28]. These approaches, while useful, often fall short in capturing the nuanced and multifaceted value that patents can represent, particularly in industries like semiconductors where technological advancements and market dynamics are closely intertwined. Recent advancements in the field have seen a shift towards more sophisticated analytical techniques [1,7,33], with a growing emphasis on integrating domain knowledge and machine learning to enhance the accuracy and depth of patent valuation.

Causality-driven approaches in patent analysis have been relatively unexplored in existing research, positioning our work at the forefront of this emerging field. These methods seek to uncover the underlying mechanisms that influence patent value, providing a more comprehensive view of the factors involved. By focusing on causal relationships rather than traditional correlation-based analyses, causality-driven approaches offer a more robust framework for patent valuation. In recent years, language models [9,18,34,37] have proven to be powerful tools across various domains, particularly in processing and understanding complex textual data at scale. Although their potential has been demonstrated in other fields [9,16,23,27], their application in patent valuation is still in its early stages. Our research introduces the integration of language models into patent analysis, leveraging their capabilities to handle and interpret intricate patent texts, thereby advancing the methodology in this domain.

Our work builds on these foundations by proposing a novel framework that combines causality-driven analysis with a structured interview-like methodology, augmented by domain knowledge and advanced language models. This approach not only addresses the limitations of traditional methods but also introduces a new paradigm for patent valuation that is both comprehensive and adaptable to the evolving technological landscape. By drawing parallels between the structured interview process and patent evaluation, we aim to capture the latent value of patents in a manner that reflects their true potential for driving innovation and market leadership. Furthermore, our focus on semiconductor patents filed between 1997 and 2007 allows us to examine a pivotal period in the industry's development, providing insights that are not only relevant to the semiconductor sector but also applicable to broader contexts [11]. The integration of financial metrics into our analysis further enhances the robustness of our framework, offering a more holistic view of patent value that aligns technological significance with market perceptions.

In summary, our literature review highlights the evolution of patent valuation methodologies, from traditional quantitative approaches to more advanced, causality-driven, and language model-enhanced frameworks. Our proposed methodology represents a significant advancement in this field, offering a nuanced and comprehensive approach to understanding and assessing the value of patents.

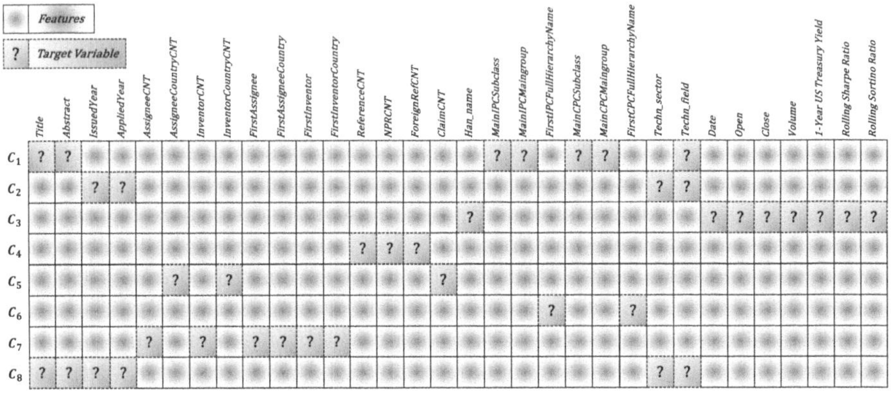


**Fig. 2.** The causal model used for patent valuation. Directed Acyclic Graphs (DAGs) and Structural Equation Models (SEMs) are employed to capture the complex interdependencies among patent variables, enabling a precise and defensible attribution of value.

## 3 Methodological Framework

In the realm of patent valuation, the inherent complexity and multifaceted nature of patents necessitate a methodological framework that is both rigorous and adaptable. Our approach is built upon a foundation of causality-driven analysis [24,25], seamlessly integrated with domain knowledge and augmented by the power of language models. This tripartite methodology enables a nuanced understanding of patents, transcending conventional valuation techniques to uncover the intrinsic value of intellectual property.

The causality-driven approach anchors our framework, employing advanced statistical tools to untangle the intricate web of factors influencing patent value. The integration of domain knowledge ensures that our analysis is grounded in the realities of the patent landscape, while the adoption of language models facilitates the extraction of insights from complex patent texts.

### 3.1 Causality-Driven Approach to Patent Valuation

In the pursuit of a robust patent valuation methodology, we adopt a causality-driven approach that transcends traditional correlation-based analyses. This paradigm shift is motivated by the need to discern the underlying causal mechanisms that significantly influence a patent's market and technological value.

Our methodology is undergirded by a causal inference framework that systematically disentangles the confounding factors often encountered in patent datasets. By leveraging the potential outcomes model and directed acyclic graphs (DAGs), we establish a structured causal model (SCM) that captures the complex interdependencies and directionalities within patent variables, as illustrated in Fig. 2.

The Expert Knowledge Corpus (EKC) serves as the foundational bedrock of our approach, aggregating domain-specific insights from a curated selection of seminal literature. The synthesis of this knowledge with the data-driven inferences drawn from our corpus enriches the process with a dual-layered understanding-balancing empirical evidence with theoretical acumen.

We delineate causal paths through the employment of counterfactual reasoning, enabling us to estimate the patent's value by answering "what-if" questions that simulate interventions. The Heuristic Knowledge Blueprint (HKB) augments this process by injecting experientially-derived heuristics into the model, ensuring that each valuation is not only data-compliant but also domain-aware.

The process of causal discovery is further enhanced by the Structured Interview Prompt Repository (SIPR), which systematically archives queries and responses crafted through the PTLM. These prompts are designed to interrogate the patent data, probing for causal insights that can elucidate the multifaceted nature of patent valuation.

$$\mathbf{Do}(X = x) \rightarrow Y = y \mid \mathcal{H}, \mathrm{EKC} \tag{1}$$

Here, $\mathbf{Do}(X = x)$ represents an intervention on a patent characteristic $X$ set to a particular value $x$, and $Y = y$ denotes the potential outcome of interest-such as the patent's market value. This is conditional on the heuristic set $\mathcal{H}$ and the domain expertise embodied in the EKC.

By integrating Directed Acyclic Graphs (DAGs) for causal modeling with Structural Equation Models (SEMs), as shown in Fig. 2, we ascertain the impact of latent variables and control for endogeneity. This facilitates a more precise and defensible attribution of value to the patent in question.

### 3.2 Integration of Domain Knowledge

In the orchestration of our methodological innovations, we intricately weave the tapestry of domain expertise into the generative process of our language model. We extract salient knowledge points from the seminal works of experts and scholars, forming a corpus that informs our heuristic framework for the generation of prefix prompts (questions and answers).

The corpus of domain expertise, henceforth referred to as the *Expert Knowledge Corpus* (EKC), is an amalgamation of pivotal research findings from various domains pertinent to our investigation. Alongside the EKC, we delineate a structured document, designated as the *Heuristic Knowledge Blueprint* (HKB), which encapsulates purpose-driven heuristics for each segment of the patent evaluation interview process. Within the HKB, we detail eight experiential heuristics $h_1, h_2, \ldots, h_8$ each mapping to a facet of knowledge within the overarching heuristic set $\mathcal{H}$.

In concert with the EKC, the Pre-Trained Language Model (PTLM), such as ChatGPT, is employed to construct prefix prompts that resonate with the real-world intricacies of patent assessment. The PTLM, guided by the HKB, crafts these prompts to reflect the nuanced requirements of the evaluation process. The resultant prompts are systematically archived in a compendium known as the *Structured Interview Prompt Repository* (SIPR).

The generation of the prefix prompts is mathematically modeled as:

$$p_i = \text{PTLM}(h_i \mid \text{EKC}, \text{HKB}) \tag{2}$$

where $p_i$ is the resultant prefix prompt, specifically tailored to elucidate the value of a patent through a series of structured queries and informed responses.

This integration of domain knowledge ensures that the PTLM-generated prompts are not only contextually enriched but also precisely targeted to elicit the most revealing insights from the underlying patent data. The subsequent application of these prompts within the framework of our pre-trained model facilitates a patent analysis that is deeply informed and meticulously nuanced.

### 3.3 Adoption of Language Models

Within the framework of our patent valuation task, we employ a synergetic interaction between two artificial intelligences: a Pre-Trained Language Model (PTLM) like ChatGPT for generating contextually-informed prefix prompts, and a general pre-trained model (GPTM) that leverages the prompts to yield specific insights on patents.

To begin, let $\mathcal{H}$ denote the heuristic set embodying the expert's experiential wisdom, which steers the PTLM towards generating prompts that resonate with the domain-specific exigencies. The PTLM, thus guided, synthesizes a prefix prompt $p_i \in \mathcal{P}$ that amalgamates a pertinent question $q_i \in \mathcal{Q}$ with its corresponding informed answer $a_i \in \mathcal{A}$. Formally, we capture this as:

$$p_i = \text{PTLM}(q_i, a_i \mid \mathcal{H}) \tag{3}$$

Here, $p_i$ emerges not merely as a blend of query and response but as a distilled epitome of contextual relevance, sculpted through the PTLM's nuanced understanding and the heuristic influence of $\mathcal{H}$.

Upon acquiring $p_i$, we engage a General Pre-Trained Model (GPTM), a model-agnostic entity, capable of adapting the learned representations from various pre-trained models to specific tasks. The GPTM undertakes the task of analyzing the patent document $d_j \in \mathcal{D}$, scrutinizing it under the lens of the generated prompt. The resulting judgment $r_i$ is a testament to the efficacy of the prefix prompt in highlighting the document's salient features $\mathcal{F}_j \subseteq \mathcal{F}$:

$$r_i = \text{GPTM}(p_i, d_j) \tag{4}$$

Each judgment $r_i$ is an output pivoting on the axis of the question-answer duo presented in $p_i$, revealing insights that are deeply entrenched in the patent's essence.

The ensuing optimization cycle is an iterative process seeking the parameter set $\Theta$ that minimizes the loss function $\mathcal{L}$, which quantifies the discrepancy between the GPTM's judgments and a corpus of veritable ground truths:

$$\Theta^* = \arg\min_{\Theta} \mathcal{L}(r_i, \mathcal{A}) \tag{5}$$

Thus, $\Theta^*$ represents the optimized parameters that align the model's inferences with empirical reality, a confluence of precision and contextuality.

This bipartite methodology, leveraging both the generative capabilities of an PTLM and the analytical prowess of a GPTM, crowned with expert heuristics, forms the cornerstone of our approach to patent analysis. It is a tapestry woven from the threads of artificial intelligence and human insight, offering a vantage point that stands at the intersection of computational efficiency and domain fidelity.

### 3.4 Structured Interview-Like Selection Process

Central to our causality-driven approach to patent valuation is the structured interview-like selection process [5], a novel methodology inspired by the rigor of structured employment interviews [6]. This process is designed to systematically evaluate patents through a series of meticulously crafted questions and answers, akin to an interview, with each level probing different dimensions of a patent's value.

The process unfolds across multiple levels, each corresponding to a specific aspect of the patent evaluation framework outlined in the Heuristic Knowledge Blueprint (HKB). At each level, the Pre-Trained Language Model (PTLM), informed by the Expert Knowledge Corpus (EKC) and heuristic experiences, generates context-aware prefix prompts. These prompts are tailored to extract insights on various facets such as technological innovation, market potential, legal robustness, and financial indicators.

The evaluation begins with an assessment of the patent's technological significance and novelty, gradually delving into its market relevance, financial performance indicators, legal strength, and cross-disciplinary impact. This hierarchical structure ensures a comprehensive appraisal of the patent, with each level building upon the insights gained from the previous one.

For each patent document $d_j \in \mathcal{D}$, the General Pre-Trained Model (GPTM) processes the responses to the PTLM-generated prompts, yielding a series of judgments $r_i$. These judgments encapsulate the patent's performance across the different evaluative criteria:

$$r_i = \text{GPTM}(p_i, d_j \mid \mathcal{H}, \text{EKC}, \text{HKB}) \tag{6}$$

The final valuation of the patent is derived from an aggregation of these judgments, providing a multifaceted view of the patent's worth. This structured interview-like selection process not only brings a systematic approach to patent valuation but also allows for a dynamic and adaptable framework that can evolve with emerging trends and technologies in the patent landscape.

In essence, this methodology mirrors the depth and precision of structured interviews, offering a robust and nuanced assessment of patents that is grounded in causality and enriched by domain expertise.

## 4 Result and Discussion

Our study leverages a comprehensive dataset of 24,853 patents sourced from the United States Patent and Trademark Office (USPTO), covering the period from 1997 to 2007. These patents were meticulously selected from nine semiconductor industry leaders, chosen based on their ranking among the top 20 companies by the number of patent applications filed during the 1997–2007 and 2007–2017 periods. The companies represented in this dataset include Texas Instruments Incorporated, Micron Technology, Inc., United Microelectronics Corp., Taiwan Semiconductor Manufacturing Company, Ltd., Sony Corporation, Intel Corporation, International Business Machines Corporation, Applied Materials, Inc., and Infineon Technologies AG. To accurately assess the value and future impact of these patents, we developed an innovative structured interview-like selection process, implemented across eight sequential stages. In each stage, candidate patents were evaluated through a series of ten questions, designed and generated by pre-trained language models [4,13,15,20,21,29,32,35] informed by domain-specific knowledge. These questions aimed to probe various dimensions of patent quality and potential impact. Patents were filtered through these stages, with approximately 50% of candidates being eliminated at each stage, leading to a final selection of around 100 patents deemed to have high potential value.

It is important to note that the primary objective of this study is not to identify or develop the optimal pre-trained language model, but rather to leverage the capabilities of these models to enhance the accuracy and depth of patent valuation. The focus is on how these tools can be integrated into a structured process to provide more nuanced and reliable insights into patent quality and potential impact. The final selection process involved a rigorous evaluation of citation strength, serving as a proxy for patent value. Additionally, we conducted a detailed analysis of the effect of question length on the quality of patent selection at each stage, providing insights into the relationship between question complexity and response accuracy.

The entire experimental framework was executed over a 28-day period, utilizing a combination of widely available hardware and software tools. The questions and answers for each stage were crafted using ChapGPT [4], with prompts generated based on expert domain knowledge. In addition, we analyze the performance of various natural language inference (NLI) models using our proposed causality-driven patent valuation framework. We evaluate the models based on the Normalized Discounted Cumulative Gain (NDCG) [26] metric across different levels of K, providing a detailed comparative analysis of the results.

**Table 1. Comparative NDCG@K Scores for PTLMs and Machine Learning Models.** The table presents NDCG@K scores for various PTLMs and traditional machine learning models at different cut-off points (K), highlighting the highest (**bold**), second-highest (underline), and lowest (*italic*) values per column, offering a clear comparison of model performance in relevance ranking.

| Model | @1 | @3 | @5 | @10 | @20 | @50 | @100 | @150 |
|---|---|---|---|---|---|---|---|---|
| distilBART-CNN | 0.4000 | 0.3000 | 0.2314 | 0.1711 | 0.1732 | **0.4346** | **0.7527** | 0.8846 |
| MiniLM-Cross | 0.2000 | 0.2235 | 0.1907 | 0.1598 | 0.1339 | 0.2724 | 0.5164 | 0.7577 |
| DeBERTa-Cross | 0.1000 | 0.1531 | 0.1661 | 0.1423 | 0.1543 | 0.3012 | 0.5807 | 0.7739 |
| RoBERTa-Cross | 0.1000 | 0.1000 | 0.0985 | 0.0639 | 0.0818 | 0.2572 | 0.5500 | 0.8577 |
| BART-Large | *0.0000* | 0.0235 | 0.0301 | *0.0413* | *0.0554* | *0.0899* | *0.1825* | *0.2684* |
| distilRoBERTa | 0.3000 | 0.1877 | 0.1503 | 0.1189 | 0.1363 | 0.3907 | 0.6855 | 0.8910 |
| Contriever | *0.0000* | 0.0296 | 0.0491 | 0.0525 | 0.0751 | 0.2286 | 0.4623 | 0.6673 |
| E5-Base | 0.2000 | 0.1173 | 0.0848 | 0.0686 | 0.0662 | 0.2034 | 0.4778 | 0.6860 |
| distilBERT | 0.1000 | 0.1000 | 0.0869 | 0.0760 | 0.1267 | 0.3653 | 0.6938 | **0.9270** |
| MobileBERT | 0.1000 | 0.1000 | 0.0854 | 0.0687 | 0.1391 | 0.3005 | 0.5776 | 0.8053 |

### 4.1 NDCG@K Scores Across Different Models

Figure 3 presents the box plots of NDCG@K scores for various NLI models across a range of K values, from 3 to 150. The results indicate a general trend where pretrained language models (PTLMs) tend to struggle when tasked with accurately ranking a smaller number of top candidates (patents). This is reflected in the lower NDCG scores at smaller K values, suggesting that these models may find it challenging to precisely identify the most relevant patents when the number of selected candidates is limited. However, as K increases-meaning as we consider a larger number of top candidate patents-the performance of these models generally improves, reflecting their ability to better capture relevant information when a broader selection of candidates is evaluated.

Focusing on the higher K values, distilBART-CNN [20] demonstrates strong performance, particularly at K = 50 and K = 100, where it achieves the highest NDCG scores, indicating its robustness in accurately ranking a larger set of

**Table 2. NDCG Scores at Different Interview Levels for Pre-Trained Language Models.** The table shows NDCG scores for various PTLMs across eight interview levels, highlighting the top (**bold**) and second-best (<u>underline</u>) scores per level, providing a clear comparison of model performance in patent relevance filtering.

| Model | I | II | III | IV | V | VI | VII | VIII |
|---|---|---|---|---|---|---|---|---|
| distilBART-CNN | 0.9367 | **0.9320** | **0.9247** | 0.9144 | 0.9026 | 0.8897 | 0.8738 | 0.8601 |
| MiniLM-Cross | 0.9317 | 0.9289 | 0.9191 | 0.9105 | 0.9057 | 0.8804 | 0.8800 | **0.8658** |
| DeBERTa-Cross | <u>0.9370</u> | 0.9288 | 0.9207 | **0.9153** | 0.9020 | 0.8846 | 0.8725 | 0.8615 |
| RoBERTa-Cross | 0.9362 | 0.9298 | 0.9227 | 0.9125 | 0.9035 | 0.8902 | **0.8817** | 0.8630 |
| BART-Large | 0.9353 | 0.9176 | 0.9100 | 0.9081 | <u>0.9060</u> | <u>0.8921</u> | 0.8631 | 0.8257 |
| distilRoBERTa | **0.9409** | 0.9292 | 0.9224 | 0.9144 | 0.9043 | 0.8900 | 0.8736 | 0.8601 |
| Contriever | 0.9355 | 0.9287 | 0.9224 | 0.9117 | 0.9007 | 0.8909 | 0.8737 | 0.8542 |
| E5-Base | 0.9323 | 0.9261 | 0.9205 | **0.9153** | 0.8998 | **0.9007** | 0.8785 | 0.8637 |
| distilBERT | 0.9369 | <u>0.9310</u> | <u>0.9241</u> | <u>0.9146</u> | <u>0.9060</u> | 0.8919 | <u>0.8814</u> | <u>0.8656</u> |
| MobileBERT | 0.9366 | 0.9281 | 0.9200 | 0.9134 | **0.9075** | 0.8884 | 0.8795 | 0.8612 |

candidate patents. However, at $K = 150$, distilBERT [29] surpasses distilBART-CNN, achieving the highest NDCG score of 0.9270, which suggests that distilBERT may be more effective in scenarios where an even broader context-evaluating a larger pool of candidate patents-is required, as shown in Table 1.

## 4.2 Impact of Question Length and Model Robustness

Figure 4 provides heatmaps of mean NDCG@K scores for each combination of model and best sequence across different interview levels. Each heatmap illustrates the impact of varying the question length on the performance of different models at each stage of the interview process. The analysis covers the entire experiment, encompassing 8 levels with 10 different question lengths per level, resulting in a comprehensive evaluation. The heatmaps reveal that question lengths of 7–9 sentences consistently yield higher NDCG scores, indicating better quality in filtering and selecting the most relevant patents. This suggests that providing a moderate level of detail in the questions is crucial for optimizing model performance during the selection process.

From Table 2, it is evident that while the NDCG scores slightly decline as the number of candidate patents is reduced across successive interview levels, the overall decrease remains within an acceptable range. This indicates that the models maintain a robust performance throughout the interview process, ensuring consistent and reliable patent selection. Notably, models like distilBART-CNN and distilRoBERTa exhibit strong and stable performance across all levels, with only minor fluctuations in NDCG scores. This stability is particularly important in structured interview-like selection processes, where consistent evaluation is crucial for reliable outcomes.

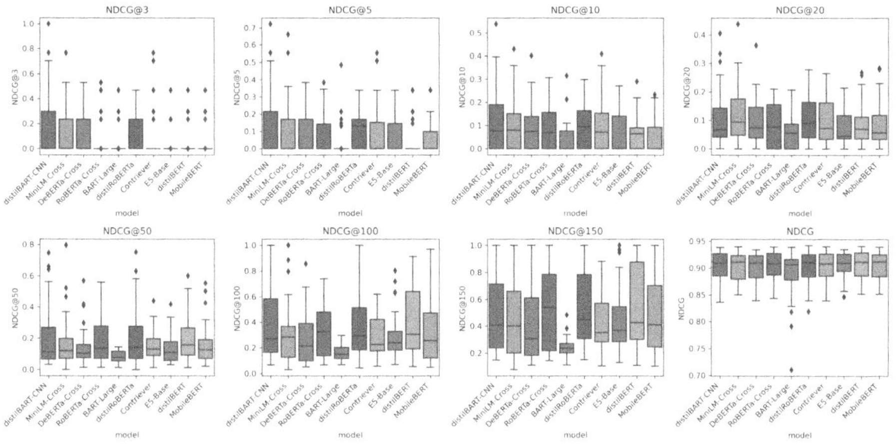


**Fig. 3.** Box Plots of NDCG@K Scores for Different NLI Models Across Various K Values. Each box plot represents the distribution of NDCG@K scores for a specific model, with K values ranging from 3 to 150. The box plots provide insights into the variability and central tendency of the NDCG@K scores for each model, facilitating a comparison of their performance across different levels of result rankings.

### 4.3 Discussion

The results of this study highlight the strength of our causality-driven patent valuation framework, which effectively integrates domain expertise with advanced language models to tackle the complexities of patent assessment. Through a structured interview-like selection process, we systematically filtered patents to identify those with the highest potential value, showcasing the robustness of our approach across various dimensions of patent quality, including technical innovation, market potential, and legal robustness.

A key insight from this research is the utility of causal inference techniques, such as Directed Acyclic Graphs (DAGs) and Structural Equation Models (SEMs), in disentangling the intricate interdependencies among patent variables. This causality-driven approach allows for a more refined understanding of the factors that contribute to patent value, beyond the traditional reliance on citation metrics. In industries like semiconductors, where patents often represent complex technological advancements with substantial market implications, the ability to model these causal relationships offers a significant advantage.

Moreover, our analysis reveals the importance of question complexity within the structured selection process. We found that moderate question lengths, between 7–9 sentences, tend to yield the most accurate patent evaluations. This suggests that striking a balance between detail and brevity is crucial for effectively assessing patent quality. The performance of various models used in the framework demonstrates that while challenges exist in ranking smaller subsets of patents (at lower K values), their efficacy improves with broader context and larger candidate pools. This highlights the importance of considering the

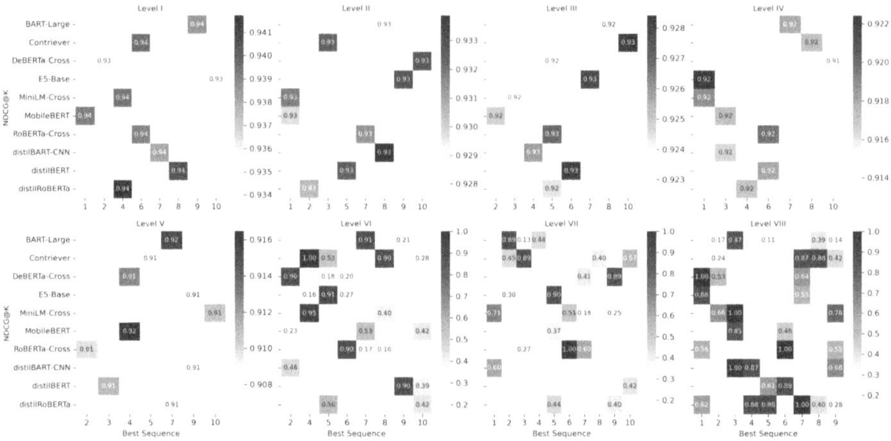


**Fig. 4.** Heatmaps of Mean NDCG@K Scores by Best Sequence and Model at Different Levels. Each heatmap corresponds to a specific level, with rows representing different NLI models and columns representing the best sequences. The color intensity indicates the mean NDCG@K score, with darker shades representing higher scores. The heatmaps provide insights into the performance of each model-sequence combination at various levels of evaluation.

broader technological and market landscape in patent evaluation. In conclusion, the methodological framework we have developed not only achieves a high degree of accuracy and reliability in patent valuation but also offers a scalable approach adaptable to various industries and datasets. The integration of causal inference with advanced language models provides a powerful tool for patent analysis, with potential applications extending beyond the semiconductor sector. Future work could explore the application of this framework to other high-technology domains and investigate the inclusion of additional data sources to further enhance the robustness and generalizability of the approach.

## 5 Conclusion

This study introduces a novel causality-driven framework for patent valuation that effectively integrates domain expertise with advanced language models in a structured interview-like selection process. By focusing on semiconductor patents from a critical period of technological transformation, our approach demonstrates the capability to uncover the latent value of patents by disentangling the complex causal relationships among patent variables. The incorporation of Directed Acyclic Graphs (DAGs) and Structural Equation Models (SEMs) provides a more nuanced understanding of the factors contributing to patent value, beyond traditional citation-based metrics.

Our findings highlight the importance of question complexity and sequence in optimizing the accuracy and robustness of patent evaluations. The structured process allows for a systematic and reliable selection of high-value patents, ensuring that the assessments are both comprehensive and scalable. This methodology, while demonstrated in the semiconductor industry, has potential applications across various sectors, offering a powerful tool for aligning technological innovation with market and legal strategies. The framework we have developed represents a significant advancement in the field of patent valuation, providing a scalable and adaptable approach that can be extended to broader datasets and different industries. Future research could further enhance this framework by integrating additional data sources and exploring its applicability in other high-technology domains, ensuring that the valuation of intellectual property remains robust and relevant in an ever-evolving technological landscape.

## References

1. Artz, K.W., Norman, P.M., Hatfield, D.E., Cardinal, L.B.: A longitudinal study of the impact of r&d, patents, and product innovation on firm performance. J. Product Innov. Manag. **27**(5), 725–740 (2010). https://doi.org/10.1111/j.1540-5885.2010.00747.x, https://doi.org/10.1111/j.1540-5885.2010.00747.x
2. Bessen, J.: The value of U.S. patents by owner and patent characteristics. Boston University Law & Economics Research Paper Series (2006). https://api.semanticscholar.org/CorpusID:15170032
3. Bloom, N., Reenen, J.V.: Patents, real options and firm performance. Econ. J. (2002). https://api.semanticscholar.org/CorpusID:56068613
4. Brown, T.B., et al.: Language models are few-shot learners (2020). https://arxiv.org/abs/2005.14165
5. Campion, M.A., Palmer, D.K., Campion, J.E.: A review of structure in the selection interview. Personnel Psychol. **50**, 655–702 (1997). https://api.semanticscholar.org/CorpusID:14327965
6. Campion, M.A., Pursell, E.D., Brown, B.K.: Structured interviewing: raising the psychometric properties of the employment interview. Personnel Psychol. **41**, 25–42 (1988). https://api.semanticscholar.org/CorpusID:145583680
7. Chung, P., Sohn, S.Y.: Early detection of valuable patents using a deep learning model: case of semiconductor industry. Technol. Forecast. Soc. Change **158**, 120146 (2020). https://api.semanticscholar.org/CorpusID:225253208
8. Cohen, W.M., Nelson, R.R., Walsh, J.P.: Protecting their intellectual assets: appropriability conditions and why U.S. manufacturing firms patent (or not). In: Working Paper 7552, National Bureau of Economic Research (2000). https://doi.org/10.3386/w7552, http://www.nber.org/papers/w7552
9. Devlin, J., Chang, M.W., Lee, K., Toutanova, K.: Bert: pre-training of deep bidirectional transformers for language understanding. In: North American Chapter of the Association for Computational Linguistics (2019). https://api.semanticscholar.org/CorpusID:52967399
10. Hall, B.H., Jaffe, A.B., Trajtenberg, M.: The NBER patent citation data file: lessons, insights and methodological tools. In: Working Paper 8498, National Bureau of Economic Research (2001). https://doi.org/10.3386/w8498, https://www.nber.org/papers/w8498
11. Hall, B.H., Ziedonis, R.H.: The patent paradox revisited: an empirical study of patenting in the U.S. semiconductor industry, 1979-1995. RAND J. Econ. **32**(1),

101–128 (2001). https://doi.org/10.2307/2696400, https://www.jstor.org/stable/2696400
12. Hasan, I., Tucci, C.L.: The innovation-economic growth nexus: global evidence. Res. Pol. **39**, 1264–1276 (2010). https://api.semanticscholar.org/CorpusID:15901440
13. He, P., Liu, X., Gao, J., Chen, W.: Deberta: decoding-enhanced Bert with disentangled attention. In: International Conference on Learning Representations (2020). https://arxiv.org/abs/2006.03654
14. Huffcutt, A.I., Arthur, W.: Hunter and hunter (1984) revisited: interview validity for entry-level jobs. J. Appl. Psychol. **79**, 184–190 (1994). https://api.semanticscholar.org/CorpusID:145232265
15. Izacard, G., et al.: Unsupervised dense information retrieval with contrastive learning (2022). https://arxiv.org/abs/2112.09118
16. Kojima, T., Gu, S.S., Reid, M., Matsuo, Y., Iwasawa, Y.: Large language models are zero-shot reasoners. Neural Inf. Process. Syst. abs/2205.11916 (2022). https://api.semanticscholar.org/CorpusID:249017743
17. Lanjouw, J.O., Schankerman, M.A.: Patent quality and research productivity: measuring innovation with multiple indicators. Econ. J. (2004). https://api.semanticscholar.org/CorpusID:54495150
18. Lester, B., Al-Rfou, R., Constant, N.: The power of scale for parameter-efficient prompt tuning. In: Conference on Empirical Methods in Natural Language Processing (2021). https://api.semanticscholar.org/CorpusID:233296808
19. Levashina, J., Hartwell, C.J., Morgeson, F.P., Campion, M.A.: The structured employment interview: narrative and quantitative review of the research literature. Personnel Psychol. **67**, 241–293 (2014). https://api.semanticscholar.org/CorpusID:26368968
20. Lewis, M., et al.: Bart: denoising sequence-to-sequence pre-training for natural language generation, translation, and comprehension. In: Annual Meeting of the Association for Computational Linguistics (2019). https://aclanthology.org/2020.acl-main.703/
21. Liu, Y., et al.: Roberta: a robustly optimized Bert pretraining approach (2019). https://arxiv.org/abs/1907.11692
22. Maurand, R., et al.: A CMOS silicon spin qubit. Nat. Commun. **7** (2016). https://api.semanticscholar.org/CorpusID:17966572
23. Nie, Y., Nguyen, N.H., Sinthong, P., Kalagnanam, J.: A time series is worth 64 words: Long-term forecasting with transformers. In: International Conference on Learning Representations, abs/2211.14730 (2022). https://api.semanticscholar.org/CorpusID:254044221
24. Pearl, J.: Causal diagrams for empirical research. Biometrika **82**, 669–688 (1995). https://api.semanticscholar.org/CorpusID:10023329
25. Pearl, J.: Causality: Models, Reasoning, and Inference. Cambridge University Press (2000)
26. Qin, T., Liu, T.Y., Li, H.: A general approximation framework for direct optimization of information retrieval measures. Information Retrieval **13**, 375–397 (2010). https://api.semanticscholar.org/CorpusID:3018043
27. Raffel, C., et al.: Exploring the limits of transfer learning with a unified text-to-text transformer. J. Mach. Learn. Res. **21**, 140:1–140:67 (2019). https://api.semanticscholar.org/CorpusID:204838007
28. Rosenkopf, L., Almeida, P.: Overcoming local search through alliances and mobility. Manag. Sci. **49**, 751–766 (2003). https://api.semanticscholar.org/CorpusID:30625106

29. Sanh, V., Debut, L., Chaumond, J., Wolf, T.: Distilbert, a distilled version of Bert: smaller, faster, cheaper and lighter. Neural Inf. Process. Syst. abs/1910.01108 (2019). https://api.semanticscholar.org/CorpusID:203626972
30. Schmidt, F.L., Hunter, J.E.: The validity and utility of selection methods in personnel psychology: practical and theoretical implications of 85 years of research findings. Psychological Bulletin **124**, 262–274 (1998). https://api.semanticscholar.org/CorpusID:16429503
31. Somaschi, N., et al.: Near-optimal single-photon sources in the solid state. Nature Photonics **10**, 340–345 (2015). https://api.semanticscholar.org/CorpusID:119281960
32. Sun, Z., Yu, H., Song, X., Liu, R., Yang, Y., Zhou, D.: Mobilebert: a compact task-agnostic Bert for resource-limited devices. In: Annual Meeting of the Association for Computational Linguistics (2020). https://api.semanticscholar.org/CorpusID:215238853
33. Trappey, A.J.C., Trappey, C.V., Govindarajan, U.H., Sun, J.J.H.: Patent value analysis using deep learning models–the case of IoT technology mining for the manufacturing industry. IEEE Trans. Eng. Manag. **68**, 1334–1346 (2021). https://api.semanticscholar.org/CorpusID:213012437
34. Vaswani, A., et al.: Attention is all you need. In: Neural Inf. Process. Syst. (2017). https://api.semanticscholar.org/CorpusID:13756489
35. Wang, W., Wei, F., Dong, L., Bao, H., Yang, N., Zhou, M.: MiniLM: deep self-attention distillation for task-agnostic compression of pre-trained transformers. Neural Inf. Process. Syst. (2020). https://dl.acm.org/doi/abs/10.5555/3495724.3496209
36. Wiesner, W.H., Cronshaw, S.F.: A meta?analytic investigation of the impact of interview format and degree of structure on the validity of the employment interview*. J. Occupat. Psychol. **61**, 275–290 (1988). https://api.semanticscholar.org/CorpusID:12867877
37. Zhao, W.X., et al.: A survey of large language models. arXiv:abs/2303.18223 (2023). https://api.semanticscholar.org/CorpusID:257900969

# Rationale-Driven Predictions for Stock Movements: A Multi-model Integration and Stack Generalization Approach

Chong-Yi Chong and Hung-Yu Kao(✉)

Department of Computer Science and Information Engineering, National Cheng Kung University, Tainan City, Taiwan
hykao@mail.ncku.edu.tw

**Abstract.** With the advancement of computational power, large language models (LLMs) have rapidly developed in various fields. However, predicting stock price fluctuations remains a significant challenge, mainly due to the following two aspects:

1. Lack Interpretability: Traditional methods usually lack interpretability, making it difficult for people to understand why the model predicts a rise or fall in stock prices. In the highly volatile financial market, since people often need to rely on professional judgment when making decisions, the quality of the reasoning provided by the model can sometimes be even more important than the accuracy of the model's predictions.
2. Model prediction bias: When generating rationales, models tend to favor a certain label, causing the final output of the model to lack reference significance.

To address these challenges, we propose a new framework. We independently trained two models, TechGPT and SentiGPT, to analyze stock price data and text data from community platforms, respectively. By combining the outputs of TechGPT and SentiGPT, we developed a comprehensive model named IntegraGPT. During the training data collection process, we used In-Context Learning to require multiple large language models to generate reasoning rationales, avoiding reliance on a single large language model for reasoning. This approach addresses the issues of insufficient interpretability and model prediction bias.

**Keywords:** Natural Language Processing · Stock Movement Prediction · Large Languange Model

## 1 Introduction

### 1.1 Background

Stock Movement Prediction is a crucial task in the financial domain aimed at forecasting the future price movements of stocks. This task holds significant

© The Author(s), under exclusive license to Springer Nature Singapore Pte Ltd. 2025
W.-T. Chu et al. (Eds.): TAAI 2024, CCIS 2414, pp. 124–138, 2025.
https://doi.org/10.1007/978-981-96-4589-3_9

importance for investors and financial institutions as accurate predictions can lead to substantial investment gains.

The primary objective of stock movement prediction is to forecast the price trend of specific stocks over a future period, typically predicting whether the price will rise or fall. Advanced models may also predict the magnitude of price changes.

### 1.2 Motivation

The rapid evolution of financial markets, characterized by increasing volatility and the infusion of vast quantities of data, presents both challenges and opportunities for predictive analytics.

Recent advancements in artificial intelligence, particularly in the field of Large Language Models (LLMs), offer promising new avenues for financial forecasting. LLMs [3] like GPT, Llama, and Mistral have demonstrated remarkable capabilities in text understanding and generation, suggesting their potential utility in decoding complex market dynamics from unstructured data sources. However, the direct application of LLMs to financial prediction often lacks the necessary specificity and adaptability to the volatile nature of stock markets.

Our investigations have revealed that different LLMs exhibit unique preferences in their predictive patterns. These preferences reflect the models' underlying training paradigms and inherent biases, which tend to skew their predictions toward certain outcomes.

Traditional approaches in stock market predictions using LLMs have been effective to a degree but often lack transparency in their decision-making processes. Most existing models generate predictions without rationales, making it difficult for users to understand or trust the model's reasoning. This limitation is significant in financial contexts where stakeholders require clear explanations to justify investment decisions and strategy adjustments.

In fact, the primary purpose of generating rationales in our model is to address the investors' focus on understanding the model's insights into the data rather than its mere accuracy. Given that accuracy levels in current models are often not exceptionally high, it is crucial that the models provide sufficient professional advice.

### 1.3 Our Works

Our study employs a structured pipeline that integrates the analytical capabilities of advanced Large Language Models (LLMs) to enhance stock movement prediction. The pipeline consists of two main phases: model development and integration.

We develop two specialized models: TechGPT and SentiGPT. Each fine-tuned for a distinct aspect of market analysis. TechGPT is designed to process and analyze technical stock market data, while SentiGPT focuses on extracting and interpreting sentiments from social media. Both models are fine-tuned using

LoRA technique to optimize their performance for specific data types while maintaining the comprehensive learning capabilities of their base LLM structures.

The insights generated by TechGPT and SentiGPT are synthesized by a third model, IntegraGPT, which combines their predictions and rationales to provide a holistic view of market trends.

In summary, our pipeline offers the following contributions:

1. By identifying and understanding the unique preferences of different LLMs, we have implemented stacked generalization to effectively merge their strengths. This approach leverages the distinct tendencies of each model to predict certain outcomes, using stacked generalization to harmonize these outputs into a unified prediction model.
2. Our methodology ensures each model generates rationales for its predictions, thereby increasing the transparency and interpretability of our analytical process. This feature is particularly important in financial applications where stakeholders value understanding the reasoning behind predictive analytics.

# 2 Related Work

## 2.1 Stock Movement Prediction with Deep Learning Methods

Astock leverages Natural Language Processing (NLP) and financial factors, combining stock-specific financial news with Semantic Role Labeling Pooling (SRLP) and a self-supervised learning strategy to enhance prediction accuracy and generalization, achieving superior performance in real trading scenarios.

StockNet [7] combines textual data from tweets and quantitative historical stock prices to predict stock movements. The Stocknet model consists of three main components: the Market Information Encoder (MIE), which processes and encodes tweets and stock prices; the Variational Movement Decoder (VMD), which predicts stock movements; and the Attentive Temporal Auxiliary (ATA), which uses an attention mechanism to integrate temporal losses.

## 2.2 Stock Movement Prediction with Large Language Model

The application of Large Language Models in financial markets has gained significant traction, driven by their advanced capabilities in processing and generating language-based data. These models have been at the forefront, due to their ability to interpret complex financial jargon and convert unstructured data into actionable insights.

A notable example of this application is the study by Lopez-Lira et al. [2], which explores the utility of ChatGPT, a prominent LLM, in predicting stock market movements based on news headlines. The research demonstrates that ChatGPT can effectively assess the sentiment of news headlines as positive, negative, or neutral and establish a significant correlation between these assessments and subsequent daily stock returns.

In the realm of stock movement prediction using Large Language Models, several notable studies provide insights into innovative methodologies. Pixiu [6] develops a domain-specific model tailored, FinMA for financial contexts, effectively integrating structured and unstructured data to handle complex financial queries. Ploutos [4] advances the application of dynamic token weighting and rearview mirror prompting techniques, significantly boosting the precision of financial predictions by adapting to market changes. AlphaFin [1], a retrieval-augmented stock-chain framework, enhances Large Language Models (LLMs) with improved retrieval and reasoning capabilities, integrating real-time financial knowledge to increase the accuracy and interpretability of stock trend predictions and financial question answering.

## 3 Methodology

This study employs a comprehensive approach to predict stock market movements by integrating both quantitative and qualitative data through the use of Large Language Models (LLMs) and advanced data processing techniques. The methodology consists of several key phases, each contributing uniquely to the final predictive model's development and performance.

### 3.1 Preprocess

The initial phase of the study, which shows in Fig. 1 involves the systematic collection and preprocessing of two distinct types of data: price data and textual data from tweets.

*Technical Data Processing.* The price data, which includes daily open, close, high, low, adjusted close prices and volume, is processed to extract key features that are crucial for understanding market dynamics. A rigorous alpha mining [5] process is employed where 293 technical indicators are initially considered. These indicators are derived from the price data through various computational techniques that analyze market trends, volatility, momentum, and other financial metrics. From this extensive set, the 10 most relevant indicators to stock movement are selected based on their correlation with market movements. This selection is critical as it ensures that the features used in model training are highly predictive and relevant to the outcomes being forecasted.

During the preprocessing of technical data, we select alphas based on the Pearson correlation with stock price movements. Out of 293 alphas, we specifically choose the top five alphas with the highest positive correlations and the top five with the most negative correlations, resulting in a refined selection of 10 alphas.

*Sentiment Data Processing.* Concurrently, the textual data from tweets is subjected to sentiment analysis. Each tweet is categorized as positive, neutral, or negative. A neutral filter is applied to refine the dataset by removing tweets that do not exhibit a clear sentiment, either positive or negative. This step is essential to enhance the quality of the sentiment analysis, focusing the model training on data that provides a more definitive emotional gauge of public market perception.

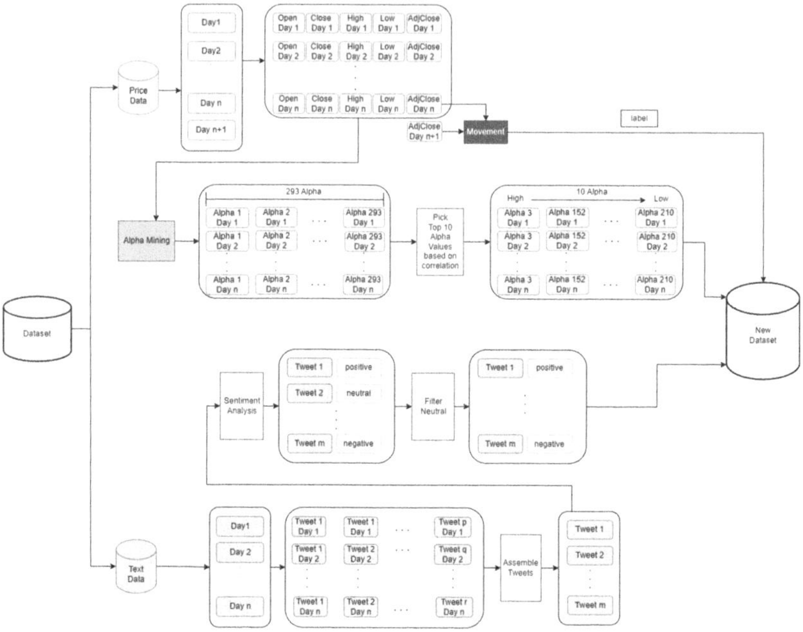


**Fig. 1.** Workflow of technical and sentiment data preprocessing

### 3.2 Training Data Collection

Building upon the principles of stacked generalization, this study employs a refined approach to collect and prepare training data for predicting stock movements. The process begins by leveraging a newly created dataset comprising both technical and sentiment data, which is depicted in Fig. 2.

The outputs from both technical and sentiment analyses are then fed into a decision-making process to determine their relevance and potential impact on market movements. The rationale provided by each LLM is crucial for understanding the context and reasoning behind each prediction.

When predictions from the LLMs align accurately with actual market movements, all such correct predictions are prioritized and incorporated directly into the training dataset. This ensures that the most reliable data influences the training process, enhancing the predictive accuracy of the models. In cases where all predictions from the LLMs are incorrect, rather than discarding these outcomes, they are collectively included in the data selection as well. This approach allows the models to learn from inaccuracies, providing a comprehensive dataset that includes both successes and failures.

To further illustrate the data collection process, the following two tables provide examples of the prompts given to the Language Learning Models (LLMs) for technical and sentiment analysis.

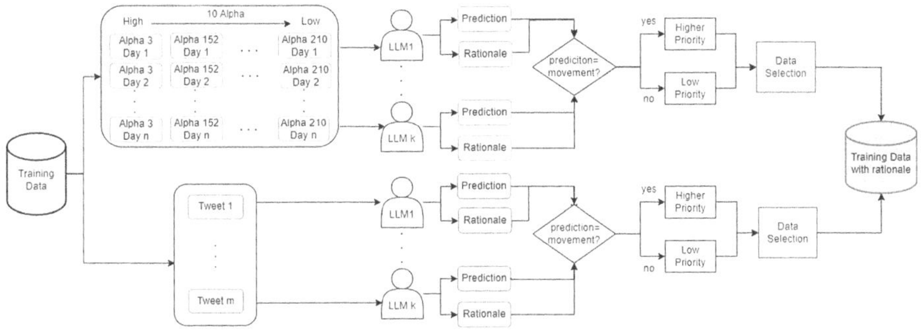


**Fig. 2.** Training data collection

## 3.3 Model Training Process

In this study, we employ a structured approach to develop and train three specialized models: TechGPT, SentiGPT, and IntegraGPT, which depicted in Fig. 3. Each based on Llama-2 and fine-tuned using the LoRA training method. This approach ensures that each model is optimally trained to handle specific aspects of the stock prediction task, with a focus on technical data analysis, sentiment analysis, and integration of insights, respectively.

TechGPT is trained on technical indicators derived from stock market data, specifically the 10 most predictive alpha signals selected through a rigorous alpha mining process. The model utilizes these features to predict stock market movements and generate rationales that explain the predictions, enhancing the interpretability of its outputs.

SentiGPT is trained on sentiment data extracted from tweets related to the stock market. Similar to TechGPT, SentiGPT also provides rationales alongside its predictions, which helps in understanding the influence of public sentiment on stock movements.

IntegraGPT serves as the integrative model that combines the outputs of TechGPT and SentiGPT. The training data for IntegraGPT consists of the predictions and rationales generated by these two models, offering a holistic view of the factors influencing stock prices.

Each of these models is fine-tuned using the LoRA method, which enables efficient adaptation of the pre-trained Llama-2 backbone to specific tasks without extensive retraining. For TechGPT and SentiGPT, LoRA's efficient parameter updates enable rapid adaptation to the highly dynamic datasets derived from stock market indicators and social media sentiments. For IntegraGPT, which synthesizes the outputs from both models, LoRA ensures that the integration is resource-efficient, maintaining a balance between performance and computational overhead.

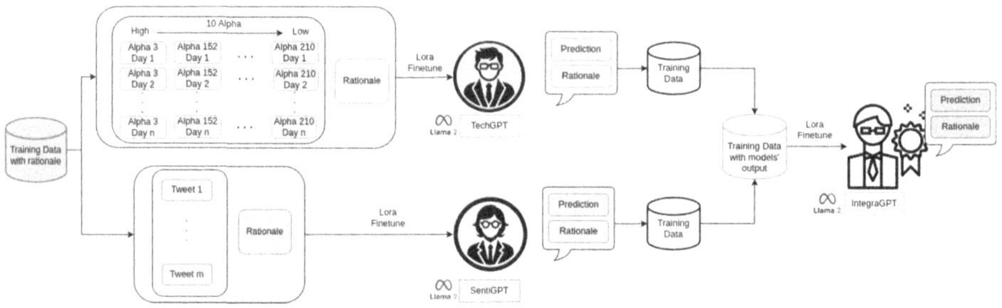


**Fig. 3.** Model training

## 3.4 Inference Process

The inference process, shown in Fig. 4 begins with the organization of testing data, which includes stock market data and tweets collected.

Technical data from the testing dataset is fed into TechGPT, a model that has been previously trained to analyze such data. TechGPT processes this information to generate predictions about stock movements based on historical and current market data. Alongside predictions, TechGPT also provides rationales, explaining the reasoning behind each prediction.

Concurrently, sentiment data, primarily derived from tweets related to the stocks, is analyzed by SentiGPT. This model, specifically trained to interpret sentiment data, generates predictions reflecting the potential impact of public sentiment on stock movements. Similar to TechGPT, SentiGPT also outputs rationales for each prediction, which detail how the sentiment data influences the predictive outcomes.

In the final step, the predictions and rationales generated by both TechGPT and SentiGPT are integrated using another specialized model, IntegraGPT. This model combines the insights from the technical and sentiment analyses to produce a unified prediction and a comprehensive rationale.

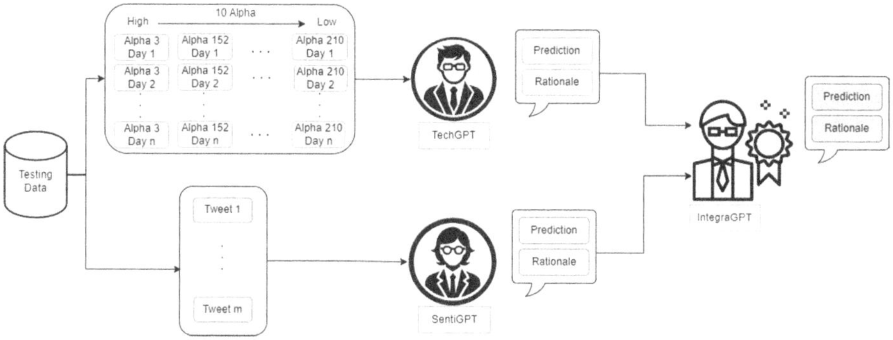


**Fig. 4.** Inference workflow with TechGPT, SentiGPT, and IntegraGPT

# 4 Experiment

The primary objective of the this chapter in this study is to evaluate the efficacy of the TechGPT, SentiGPT, and IntegraGPT models, each fine-tuned using the LoRA method. The models are assessed based on their ability to predict stock market movements accurately, leveraging both technical indicators and sentiment analysis derived from social media.

Our research is structured to explore the following questions:

1. **RQ1**: How do the rationales generated by IntegraGPT compare in performance with those produced by current LLMs?
2. **RQ2**: How does TechGPT, SentiGPT, and IntegraGPT's performance compare to that of existing LLM-based and traditional prediction models?
3. **RQ3**: What are the effects on the performance of TechGPT, SentiGPT, and IntegraGPT when they are trained without including rationale generation in their tasks?

## 4.1 Problem Formulation

The classification policy is predicated on the comparison between the adjusted closing price of the subsequent period and that of the current period, specifically whether the future adjusted closing price exceeds the present one:

$$y = \begin{cases} up & \text{if } adjclose_j > adjclose_i, \\ down & \text{if } adjclose_j \leq adjclose_i, \end{cases} \tag{1}$$

where $adjclose_i$ and $adjclose_j$ represent the adjusted closing prices at times $i$ and $j$ respectively.

## 4.2 RQ1: Rationale Performance

Building on the discussion of RQ1, where we evaluate the quality of rationales produced by various Large Language Models, Table 1 provides insights into each model's ability to generate coherent rationales using the BartScore metric.

IntegraGPT achieves the best score of −3.2534. This score not only outperforms the other LLMs but also highlights the effectiveness of IntegraGPT in synthesizing and contextualizing inputs to form more precise and relevant rationales.

**Table 1.** Rationale performance evaluation

| Model | BartScore |
|---|---|
| Meta-Llama-3-8B-Instruct | −3.5093 |
| Mistral-7B-Instruct-v0.2 | −2.4891 |
| Mistral-7B-Instruct-v0.3 | −2.526 |
| GPT-3.5-Turbo | −3.106 |
| IntegraGPT | **−2.4484** |

### 4.3 RQ2: Overall Performance

In our study, we assessed the performance of IntegraGPT against various baseline models including both traditional and LLM-based predictors. The results are presented in Table 2.

In analyzing the data from Table 2, which documents the accuracy and Matthew's Correlation Coefficient (MCC) of various models, we observe a notable trend: models that generate rationales, such as our IntegraGPT, tend to have lower accuracy compared to some models that do not focus on rationale production, like Ploutos. This pattern suggests that the task of generating rationales, while adding interpretative value, may indeed impact the model's accuracy negatively.

In our study, the accuracy of our models, specifically those designed to generate rationales, is observed to be lower compared to those in other published works. This phenomenon likely stems from the introduction of noise through the rationale generation process, which can complicate the training phase and consequently impact the model's overall predictive accuracy. Generating rationales inherently involves synthesizing complex data into interpretable outputs, which may divert the model's focus from achieving higher accuracy, thus necessitating a trade-off.

To substantiate the impact of rationale generation on model accuracy, we further analyze the evaluation loss of models with and without rationale production capabilities. Figure 5 illustrate the comparison of evaluation loss between TechGPT models that generate rationales and those that do not. These figures provide visual evidence supporting the notion that rationale production may indeed compromise the model's performance in terms of prediction accuracy.

Despite this apparent decrease in accuracy, the real value of generating rationales becomes evident in the decision-making process, especially when final judgments are rendered by humans. In contexts where model accuracies cluster around 60%, the substantive benefit of rationales lies not in statistical performance but in their utility as tools for enhancing human decision-making. Detailed rationales provide essential insights and context that can guide users in understanding model predictions and, more critically, in applying their judgment when automated decisions are ambiguous or suboptimal.

**Table 2.** Overall performance

| Model | Accuracy | MCC |
|---|---|---|
| *BaseLine Model* | | |
| ARIMA | 51.42 | −0.0210 |
| TimeGPT | 53.74 | 0.0662 |
| StockNet | 57.50 | 0.0810 |
| FinMA-7B | 51.00 | 0.0300 |
| Ploutos | **61.21** | **0.2050** |
| *LLMs* | | |
| gpt-3.5-turbo | 51.08 | −0.0060 |
| Meta-Llama-3-8B-Instruct | 51.73 | 0.0095 |
| Mistral-7B-Instruct-v0.2 | **52.10** | **0.0307** |
| Mistral-7B-Instruct-v0.3 | 50.49 | −0.0088 |
| *Ours* | | |
| TechGPT | 52.19 | 0.0130 |
| SentiGPT | 48.09 | −0.0181 |
| IntegraGPT | **52.29** | **0.0144** |

### 4.4 Ablation Study

The ablation study conducted examines the effects of including rationale generation in the training of the TechGPT, SentiGPT, and IntegraGPT models. The study compares performance metrics, Accuracy and Matthews Correlation Coefficient (MCC) between models trained with and without rationales. The results are summarized in Table 3.

The decrease in accuracy when TechGPT and SentiGPT generate rationales aligns with the expected trade-off between accuracy and the depth of explanation. However, the unique aspect of IntegraGPT's performance is particularly enlightening. Without rationales, IntegraGPT does not perform as well as it does with them, despite integrating the outputs of TechGPT and SentiGPT. This can be attributed to the lack of detailed contextual information that rationales provide, which are crucial for IntegraGPT's integrated approach.

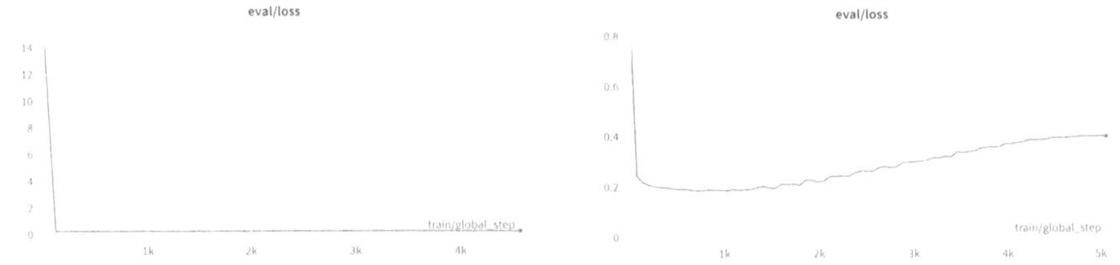


**Fig. 5.** On the left is the evaluation loss of TechGPT without generating rationales, while on the right is the evaluation loss of TechGPT with generating rationales. It can be observed that the evaluation loss of TechGPT generating rationales increases towards the end.

When rationales are generated, IntegraGPT can leverage the enriched contextual data, enhancing its decision-making process and ultimately improving its performance metrics. This suggests that IntegraGPT is specifically optimized to utilize the additional insights provided by rationales, without which it struggles to achieve competitive accuracy and MCC. This is a critical insight, as it underscores the importance of rationale generation not merely for transparency but for significantly contributing to the effectiveness of model predictions.

**Table 3.** Ablation study

| Model | Without Rationale | | With Rationale | |
|---|---|---|---|---|
| | Accuracy | MCC | Accuracy | MCC |
| TechGPT | **56.11** | **0.1194** | 52.19 | 0.013 |
| SentiGPT | 55.21 | 0.0918 | 48.09 | −0.0181 |
| IntegraGPT | 55.03 | 0.0565 | **52.29** | **0.0144** |

# 5 Analysis

## 5.1 Human Oversight in Model Predictions: The Case of Oversold Signal

As shown in Fig. 6, TechGPT predicts a downward movement for RDS-B stock based on multiple indicators, including the Decreasing indicator (DEC) and Vortex Negative Trend Indicator (VTXM), which suggest a bearish trend. However, the Ultimate Oscillator (UO) indicates an oversold condition with a value of 48.1, typically a buy signal in technical analysis. This presents a "Divergent Signals Dilemma," where different indicators provide conflicting signals.

This observation underlines a crucial aspect of predictive financial modeling: the role of human judgment in interpreting model-generated rationales. In this instance, TechGPT predicted a downward trend for RDS-B stock, despite clear indications from the Ultimate Oscillator (UO) of an oversold condition, which typically suggests potential for a price rebound. This oversold signal, evident in the model's rationale but overlooked in its final prediction, exemplifies a critical gap where model accuracy does not capture potentially lucrative trading signals.

This case illustrates the original purpose of generating rationales alongside predictions: to enhance the transparency and comprehensibility of model outputs for human analysts. By providing a rationale that includes a clear oversold signal, the model aids human analysts in making more informed decisions, especially in scenarios where the model's accuracy alone might be misleading.

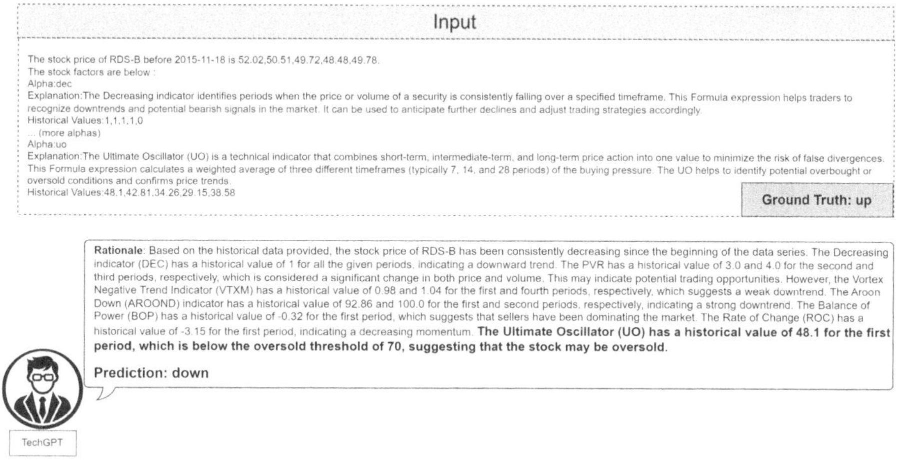


**Fig. 6.** The role of rationales in financial decision making

## 5.2 Comparative Analysis of Other LLMs and IntegraGPT

In the comparative analysis shown in Fig. 7 between Llama3 and the custom-trained IntegraGPT for stock market prediction, IntegraGPT not only provided more accurate predictions but also generated more detailed and contextually rich rationales.

While Llama3 referenced a non-existent 50-day moving average, indicating a tendency to generate hallucinated data, IntegraGPT's analysis was grounded in real and relevant market indicators. It meticulously detailed the reasons for a downward trend prediction through a comprehensive assessment involving multiple technical indicators such as the Decreasing indicator, PVR, and Vortex Negative Trend.

## 5.3 Case Study for Effectiveness of Integrated Prediction

In this case study shown in Fig. 8, we evaluate the effectiveness of IntegraGPT, a model that integrates insights from TechGPT and SentiGPT for stock movement

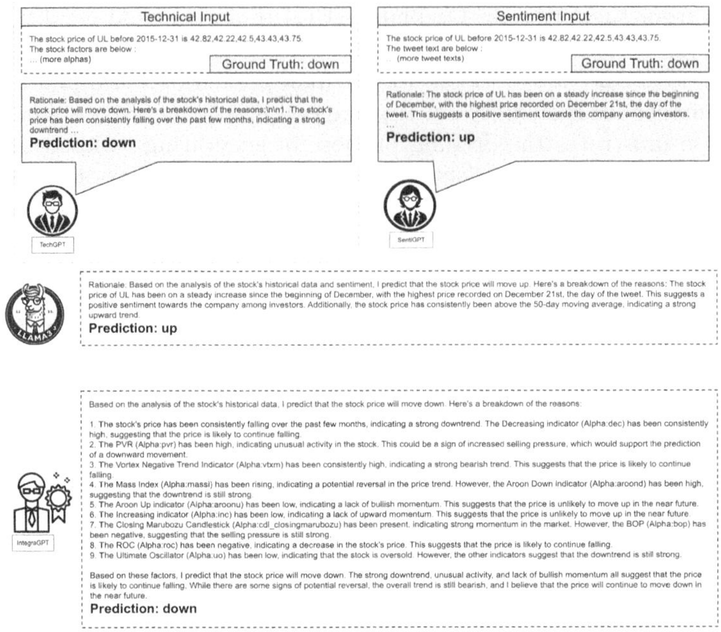


**Fig. 7.** Comparative analysis of Llama3 and IntegraGPT

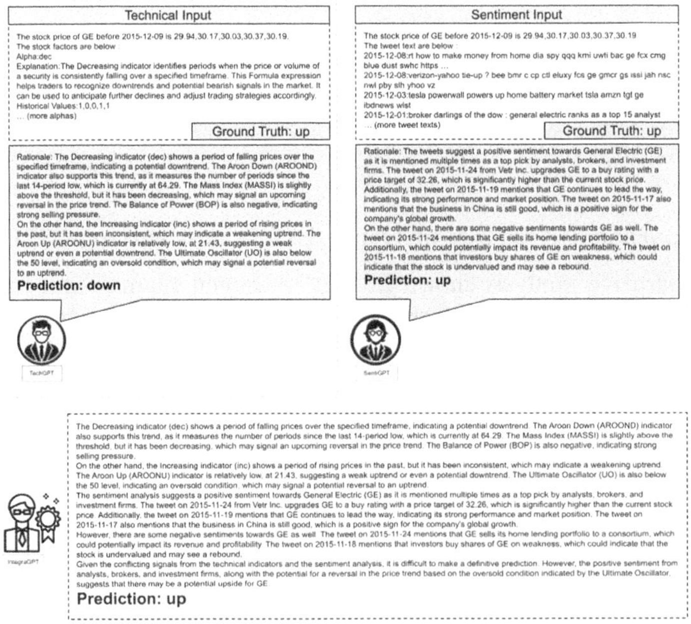


**Fig. 8.** Case study for effectiveness of integrated prediction

prediction. The example shows a conflict between the predictions of TechGPT and SentiGPT. TechGPT predicts a downturn based on technical indicators such as the decreasing indicator and the Aroon Down indicator. In contrast, SentiGPT predicts an upward trend due to positive market sentiment and favorable analyst opinions mentioned in tweets.

IntegraGPT successfully combines these insights, recognizing that while technical indicators suggest a downturn, the strong positive sentiment and favorable analyst opinions could outweigh these signals. As a result, IntegraGPT predicts an upward movement, aligning with the actual market outcome. This demonstrates the value of integrating diverse analytical perspectives to improve prediction accuracy.

## 6 Discussion and Conclusion

In this study, we introduced a novel framework that integrates multiple language models: TechGPT, SentiGPT, and IntegraGPT, each fine-tuned using the LoRA method to enhance the prediction of stock movements. Within this framework, TechGPT and SentiGPT are trained independently to analyze distinct types of market data. Their outputs are then combined and used as the training data for IntegraGPT. This approach not only leverages the strengths of individual models to enhance overall predictive accuracy but also provides a comprehensive view of market dynamics, which a single-model approach might fail to capture.

Although IntegraGPT did not consistently outperform all models across every metric, the integrated approach demonstrated potential in scenarios involving complex market dynamics. The findings suggest substantial benefits in using an ensemble of specialized models over single-model solutions, particularly in capturing the nuanced influences on stock price movements.

Furthermore, we explored the importance of generating rationales in large language models (LLMs) when predicting stock market trends. Firstly, the practice of generating rationales is crucial for understanding the basis of model predictions, especially when the model's highest accuracy is around 60%. The faithfulness and richness of the rationales become key indicators for evaluating model performance. This not only enhances the transparency of the model but also allows users to better trust the model's predictions because they can understand the reasons behind specific predictions. In the realm of financial investments, the utility of a predictive model often transcends its raw accuracy metrics. Investors and stakeholders typically value the insights and rationales provided by models, which help in understanding the model's thought process behind its predictions. This study considers the importance of rationale generation not merely as a feature of transparency but as a critical component for providing expert recommendations.

Additionally, we found that each LLM may have inherent biases, which could lead to the model favoring specific prediction outcomes, affecting the model's general applicability and reliability. To overcome these challenges, we adopted the stacked generalization method, effectively integrating the characteristics of various models and enhancing the model's ability to interpret complex market dynamics through ensemble learning.

Future research can explore further optimization of model structures and training processes to reduce biases and improve the quality of rationale generation, thereby maintaining or enhancing the interpretability of the model while improving its accuracy. Moreover, considering the current trade-off between interpretability and accuracy, developing new methods to better balance these two aspects will be an important direction for future research.

## References

1. Li, X., Li, Z., Shi, C., Xu, Y., Du, Q., Tan, M., Huang, J., Lin, W.: Alphafin: benchmarking financial analysis with retrieval-augmented stock-chain framework (2024). https://arxiv.org/abs/2403.12582
2. Lopez-Lira, A., Tang, Y.: Can chatGPT forecast stock price movements? return predictability and large language models (2023). https://arxiv.org/abs/2304.07619
3. Minaee, S., et al.: Large language models: a survey (2024). https://arxiv.org/abs/2402.06196
4. Tong, H., Li, J., Wu, N., Gong, M., Zhang, D., Zhang, Q.: Ploutos: towards interpretable stock movement prediction with financial large language model (2024). https://arxiv.org/abs/2403.00782
5. Wang, S., Yuan, H., Zhou, L., Ni, L.M., Shum, H.Y., Guo, J.: Alpha-GPT: human-AI interactive alpha mining for quantitative investment (2023). https://arxiv.org/abs/2308.00016
6. Xie, Q., et al.: Pixiu: a large language model, instruction data and evaluation benchmark for finance (2023). https://arxiv.org/abs/2306.05443
7. Xu, Y., Cohen, S.B.: Stock movement prediction from tweets and historical prices. In: Gurevych, I., Miyao, Y. (eds.) Proceedings of the 56th Annual Meeting of the Association for Computational Linguistics (Volume 1: Long Papers), pp. 1970–1979. Association for Computational Linguistics, Melbourne, Australia (2018). https://doi.org/10.18653/v1/P18-1183, https://aclanthology.org/P18-1183

# An Adaptive Sample Selection Approach for Learning with Noisy Labels

Jing-Yong Wang and Mei-Chen Yeh(✉)

Department of Computer Science and Information Engineering, National Taiwan Normal University, Taipei, Taiwan
myeh@ntnu.edu.tw

**Abstract.** To mitigate the costs of dataset construction and the challenges posed by mislabeled data during model training, learning with noisy labels (LNL) focuses on developing robust models in the presence of erroneous labels. The separation of clean and noisy samples, followed by a semi-supervised learning approach, has proven to be a vital solution to this problem. However, previous methods for selecting clean samples, such as Gaussian mixture models, have struggled to accurately identify clean samples. In this paper, we introduce a two-stage adaptive sample selection approach tailored for the LNL problem. By leveraging the disagreement between dual models, the stability of model predictions, and feature similarities, our method dynamically identifies clean samples more effectively. Experimental results demonstrate the robustness and effectiveness of our approach across various noise types and levels, confirming its superior performance.

**Keywords:** Deep learning · Image classification · Learning with noisy labels

## 1 Introduction

With the widespread adoption of deep learning technology, access to various open-source datasets for diverse downstream tasks has increased significantly. Despite this accessibility, the process of annotating data for these datasets often incurs substantial time and cost. Models trained using supervised learning require large and accurately labeled datasets for optimal performance. However, manual labeling, especially in complex and large datasets, is susceptible to annotation errors. Training models with these noisy samples (erroneously labeled samples) can inevitably harm the model, leading to a decline in performance [10,25]. The quantity of data and the cleanliness of labels in the dataset are crucial factors influencing model performance [23].

Learning with Noisy Labels (LNL) assumes that the label information provided in the training dataset may not be entirely correct. The challenge lies in the model not knowing whether it is learning from clean or noisy samples during

© The Author(s), under exclusive license to Springer Nature Singapore Pte Ltd. 2025
W.-T. Chu et al. (Eds.): TAAI 2024, CCIS 2414, pp. 139–153, 2025.
https://doi.org/10.1007/978-981-96-4589-3_10

training, and learning from noisy samples can decrease model performance. Distinguishing between clean and noisy samples is a challenging task that LNL aims to overcome. Another challenge is that, in the initial stages of training, without a reliable reference to differentiate between clean and noisy samples, the model may inadvertently learn from some noisy sample data. Thus, minimizing the impact of noisy samples on the model during training is also a critical issue.

To address these challenges, prevalent methodologies often resort to segregating the training dataset into distinct clean and noisy subsets. Following this, a common strategy is the adoption of semi-supervised learning approaches, where clean samples are employed for conventional supervised training, and noisy samples are utilized without corresponding ground-truth labels [10,15,25]. While these methods exhibit merit in handling label noise, they often grapple with the challenge of accurately distinguishing between clean and noisy samples during the early stages of training. However, in this semi-supervised learning framework, the quality is even more important than the quantity of pseudo labels. Using low-quality pseudo labels might hinder the model from effective classification [9].

Motivated by the importance of distinguishing clean and noisy samples in LNL, we propose a novel adaptive sample selection method in this work. In contrast to conventional approaches, our method adopts a more rigorous criterion for selecting clean samples, resulting in a more precise but smaller set of identified clean samples. By prioritizing sample quality over quantity, this strategy aims to mitigate the risk of propagating mislabeled data during model training. Subsequently, we harness the potential of the rigorously selected clean set by integrating it with a traditional machine learning approach—the $k$-nearest neighbor (kNN) algorithm. This synergy enables us to exploit the reliability of the selected clean samples for retrieving more clean samples from the training set. Leveraging the stability of model predictions and feature representations, our approach provides an effective mechanism for identifying and prioritizing clean samples throughout the training process.

We summarize the contributions of this paper as follows:

- We propose a rigorous sample selection criterion, utilizing the stability of model predictions, for selecting high-quality clean samples from the training set.
- We progressively extend the clean set by performing kNN classification on pre-filtered clean samples, maximizing the value of the clean set filtered in the previous stage.
- We conduct extensive experiments on several datasets, including CIFAR-10, CIFAR-100 [12], and WebVision [18]. The results demonstrate the superiority of our proposed method, showing comparable or even better performance than methods proposed in previous papers on these benchmarks.

In the following sections, we begin by reviewing related studies in Sect. 2. Section 3 outlines the main investigation method. Finally, experiments and results are discussed in Sect. 4, and the paper concludes in Sect. 5.

## 2 Related Work

In the past decade, supervised learning has demonstrated significant success across various domains [25]. However, these achievements are typically built on clean datasets. Real-world applications often introduce factors leading to a decline in model performance, such as human annotation errors or the long-tailed distribution of datasets. Overcoming the challenge of learning and achieving predictions close to supervised learning on datasets with label errors is the focus of our research. This paper specifically addresses this issue under the conditions of unknown noise types and noise rates.

Recent studies have predominantly employed a dual-model architecture developed based on the co-teaching concept [7,15,19,27]. In this architecture, two models jointly estimate the probability of a mislabeled sample being a correct sample, resulting in lower error prediction compared to using a single model. While utilizing a dual-model architecture demands more computational resources and time, it effectively distinguishes between clean and noisy samples by leveraging the predictions of both models.

In recent research, the classification of clean and noisy labels has been mainly tackled using the Gaussian Mixture Model (GMM). The approach involves calculating the loss between the current model's predictions and the labels of the validation dataset, using the size and distribution of the loss to predict which samples are clean and which are noisy [15]. The loss can be cross-entropy loss or other relevant loss functions.

In addition to methods for selecting clean samples, studies have proposed the use of relabeling techniques [3,6,13]. Relabeling involves modifying labels considered as noisy labels to correct labels and using them for training. This effectively introduces more samples to train a model. For instance, the k-nearest neighbor (kNN) algorithm is employed to predict which samples' features are most similar to the current sample's features, relabeling the sample with the class of the most similar features if both the kNN and model predictions exceed a certain threshold, treating it as a positive sample in subsequent training [6].

Another relabeling method is introduced in [13], where the best-performing model is saved when the model's performance reaches a plateau. During the relabeling phase, the saved model is used to modify labels considered errors by replacing them with pseudo-labels predicted by the model, and training restarts from scratch. [3] follows a similar approach but does not retrain the model. One notable drawback of these methods is that continuously training with incorrectly relabeled samples using the model's predictions can lead to worse results [6,13].

Finally, most papers, including ours, adopt semi-supervised methods to handle clean and noisy samples. Once samples can be separated into clean and noisy subsets, the problem of LNL can be transformed into a semi-supervised learning problem. Currently, a prevalent research direction in this field is the use of semi-supervised methods, often based on the design of DivideMix [15]. This involves employing an improved version of mixmatch [2], combining co-refinement and co-guessing. Co-refinement determines the labels of clean samples based on the probability predicted by the model for clean labels and the model's prediction results. Co-guessing determines the prediction of pseudo-labels by averaging the results of two model predictions. Our method also employs a semi-supervised approach to learn from noisy samples.

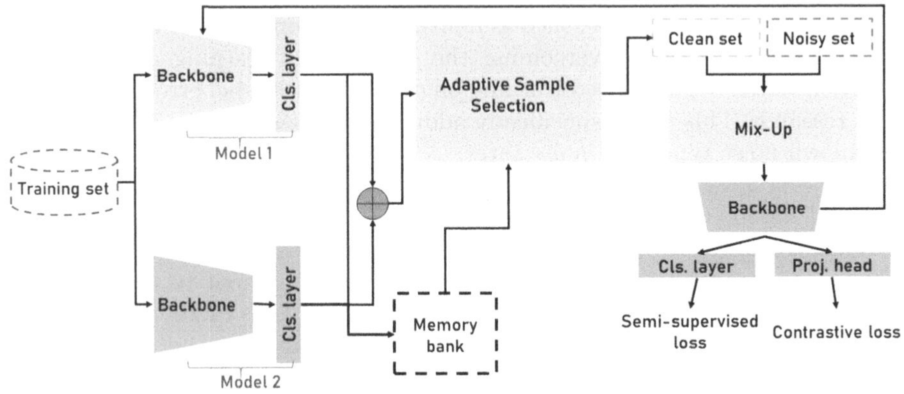


**Fig. 1.** Model architecture: The proposed adaptive sample selection scheme employs a memory bank to enhance clean sample selection, dynamically filtering samples based on model disagreement, recent prediction variations and training phase. This dual-model approach integrates semi-supervised learning, enhancing the robustness of the model against noisy labels. The adaptive selection approach ensures the precision and quality of the selected sample set for improved model training.

# 3 Method

In this section, we introduce the proposed method, particularly emphasizing the stability of model predictions in selecting clean samples and incorporating the use of the kNN algorithm to enhance the selection results.

## 3.1 Problem Statement

Let $D = \{X, Y\} = \{(x_1, y_1), (x_2, y_2), \ldots, (x_N, y_N)\}$ denote the training set, where $x_i$ is an image, $y_i$ is the corresponding ground-truth label, and $N$ is the total number of training samples. We instantiate the model with a feature extractor (Convolutional Neural Networks-based backbone), $f(\cdot; \theta)$, with parameters $\theta$ and a classification layer, $h(\cdot; \phi)$, with parameters $\phi$. For supervised training with ground-truth labels, we minimize the cross-entropy (CE) loss, $L_{CE}$, over the entire training set $D$:

$$\mathcal{L}_{CE} = -\frac{1}{N} \sum_{i=1}^{N} y_i^T \log \hat{y}_i, \tag{1}$$

where $\hat{y}_i = \text{softmax}(h(f(x_i;\theta);\phi))$ is the softmax probability score of the network prediction corresponding to $x_i$.

In this work, we consider the training set to be noisy, meaning that some images are incorrectly labeled. Because Deep Neural Networks (DNNs) learn simpler patterns before memorizing the noisy labels [1], several studies [7,15] attempt to separate clean samples from noisy ones at the early stage of training. This separation scheme partitions the dataset into a clean subset, $D_{\text{clean}}$, and a noisy subset, $D_{\text{noisy}} = D \setminus D_{\text{clean}}$. After that, $D_{\text{clean}}$ can be used for standard supervised training and $D_{\text{noisy}}$ can be used without the corresponding noisy ground-truth labels. This training is generally performed in a semi-supervised manner, where pseudo-labels are generated for the samples in $D_{\text{noisy}}$.

### 3.2 Method Overview

Our approach draws inspiration from UNICON [10], introducing modifications such as a sample selection mechanism, a memory bank, and the integration of the kNN algorithm for sample selection. Figure 1 illustrates the model architecture. Each model in this dual-model setup includes a backbone, a classification layer for clean/noisy sample classification, and a projection head for contrastive learning. The training alternates between the two models in each epoch: after filtering and training model 1, we re-filter and train model 2, and vice versa. The semi-supervised and contrastive loss functions are utilized to train the backbone's feature extraction and the classification layer's predictive capability.

### 3.3 Adaptive Sample Selection

Given a dataset $D$, we train two models with parameters $(\theta^{(1)}, \phi^{(1)})$ and $(\theta^{(2)}, \phi^{(2)})$. For an input sample $x_i$, we denote the average prediction probabilities from both models by $\mathbf{p}_i = [p_i^1, p_i^2, \ldots, p_i^C]$, and the ground-truth label by $\mathbf{y}_i = [y_i^1, y_i^2, \ldots, y_i^C]$, in which $C$ represents the number of classes. The disagreement between ground-truth labels and predicted probabilities is measured using Jensen-Shannon divergence (JSD), denoted as $d_i$. The JSD is defined as,

$$
\begin{aligned}
d_i &= \text{JSD}(\mathbf{y}_i, \mathbf{p}_i) \\
&= \frac{1}{2}\text{KLD}(\mathbf{y}_i || \frac{\mathbf{y}_i + \mathbf{p}_i}{2}) + \frac{1}{2}\text{KLD}(\mathbf{p}_i || \frac{\mathbf{y}_i + \mathbf{p}_i}{2}),
\end{aligned} \tag{2}
$$

where $\text{KLD}(\cdot)$ is the Kullback-Leibler divergence function. JSD values range from 0 to 1 and are symmetrically designed, similar to the results of GMM models fitted with cross-entropy loss distributions, without the need to build a GMM model. If the computed value is large, we consider the sample to be likely a noisy or difficult sample.

Despite that clean and noisy samples can be roughly distinguished based on the disagreement measurement, the quality is not sufficiently satisfactory. To enhance clean sample selection, we introduce a consistency-based sample selection criterion. A memory bank is introduced to store JSD values for each sample at different training epochs. We compute the average $d_i$ over the recent five epochs, denoted as $s_i$. We compute $d_{avg}$ and $s_{avg}$ as the average of all samples, $\{d_i : i \in (1, \ldots, N)\}$ and $\{s_i : i \in (1, \ldots, N)\}$, respectively. In this first-stage selection process, a sample is considered as a clean sample only if it satisfies both of the following conditions:

$$\begin{aligned} d_i &\leq d_{\text{avg}}, \\ s_i &\leq s_{\text{avg}} + s_{\text{avg}} \times (1 - d_{\text{avg}}) \times (1 - \frac{t}{T}), \end{aligned} \tag{3}$$

where $t$ is the index of current epoch and $T$ denotes the number of total epochs. The selection process dynamically incorporates multiple factors, including disagreement measurements, recent prediction variations, and the training phase. Our criterion for identifying clean samples is more rigorous compared to that used in [10]. In our approach, a sample is classified as clean only if it not only exhibits a small disagreement but also consistently maintains this small discrepancy in recent predictions. Additionally, the term $1 - d_{\text{avg}}$ is inversely proportional to the noise rate in $D$, thereby promoting a conservative selection of clean samples, particularly in scenarios with a high noise rate. Furthermore, the cutoff threshold decreases with more training iterations, contributing to a refined and adaptive selection mechanism.

In the second stage, a $k$-nearest neighbors search retrieves additional clean samples, leveraging the rigorously selected clean set from the first stage. The dynamic determination of the $k$ value is expressed as follows:

$$k = \sqrt{|D_{\text{clean}}|} \times \alpha_k, \tag{4}$$

where $\alpha_k$ is a scaling factor (set to 0.9 in our experiments), ensuring proportionality to the size of the clean set. This design would allow our approach to balance the trade-off between generalization (for large datasets) and local sensitivity (for small datasets) to optimize performance. However, if the kNN prediction of a previously identified clean sample contradicts the ground truth label, we evaluate further whether this sample should remain in the clean set. The sample is removed from $D_{\text{clean}}$ if it satisfies the following condition:

$$s_i \geq \left(s_{\text{avg}} + s_{\text{avg}} \times (1 - d_{\text{avg}})\right) \times \left(1 - \frac{t}{T}\right). \tag{5}$$

Notably, the threshold (right-hand side in Eq. 5) is lower than that in Eq. 3 because $s_i$ is now multiplied with $1 - \frac{t}{T}$ (lower than one). This selection is particularly effective when the noise rate is high. Similar to [10], we employ uniform selection to ensure an equal number of samples per class. Algorithm 1 summarizes our sample selection scheme.

Our work is similar to [14,27] in that the predictive reliability of a candidate sample is re-estimated by contrasting it against its feature-space nearest neighbors. However, there are notable differences in our approach. While other methods typically discard data points to clean the dataset, our approach with kNN not only removes less reliable data but also selectively incorporates what we

**Algorithm 1.** Adaptive Sample Selection

**Input:**
Training set $D = \{X, Y\}$;
A scaling factor $\alpha_k$;
**Output:**
Clean sample subset $D_{\text{clean}}$;
Initialize $D_{\text{clean}} \leftarrow \emptyset$;
**for** $x_i \in D$ **do**
  Calculate $d_i$ and $s_i$;
  **if** $d_i \leq d_{\text{avg}}$ **and** $s_i \leq s_{\text{avg}} + s_{\text{avg}} \times (1 - d_{\text{avg}}) \times (1 - \frac{t}{T})$ **then**
    $D_{\text{clean}} \leftarrow x_i$;
  **end if**
**end for**
Determine $k = \sqrt{|D_{\text{clean}}|} \times \alpha_k$;
**for** $x_i \in D$ **do**
  Perform k-NN label classification using $D_{\text{clean}}$
  **if** k-NN prediction equals ground-truth **then**
    $D_{\text{clean}} \leftarrow D_{\text{clean}} \cup \{x_i\}$
  **else**
    **if** $x_i \in D_{\text{clean}}$ **and** Equ. 5 holds **then**
      $D_{\text{clean}} \leftarrow D_{\text{clean}} \setminus \{x_i\}$;
    **end if**
  **end if**
**end for**
Perform Uniform Selection;
**return** $D_{\text{clean}}$;

deem as clean data into a refined training dataset. This dual strategy contributes significantly to our superior performance, especially in environments with high noise rates. Our experiments revealed that the initial kNN predictions were not very effective, leading us to adopt a more conservative approach early in training, with a larger threshold value. This threshold is not static but adjusts based on the training epochs and the model's prediction stability, as indicated by the average Jensen-Shannon divergence.

### 3.4 Semi-supervised Learning

Our semi-supervised learning strategy follows the approach introduced by UNICON [10], building upon the principles of FixMatch [24]. We perform semi-supervised learning with the samples from $D_{\text{noisy}}$. We generate two copies of each sample, applying weak and strong augmentations. Weak augmentation is a standard flip-and-shift augmentation strategy, and strong augmentation is based on AutoAugment [5]. Pseudo-labels are generated from the weakly augmented copy of the data and used to compute the semi-supervised loss, $L_{\text{semi}}$, on the strongly augmented copy. MixUp [28] augmentation is applied between samples from $D_{\text{clean}}$ and $D_{\text{noisy}}$. For the latter, we use pseudo-labels obtained from the weakly augmented copy.

In particular, contrastive learning (CL) [4] is used into the semi-supervised learning pipeline, facilitating feature learning without relying on pseudo-labels. This unsupervised feature learning scheme mitigates the risk of noisy label memorization since it does not depend on the imperfect separation of clean and noisy samples or incorrect pseudo-labels generated during semi-supervised training.

In our work, we employ contrastive loss only for the samples in the noisy sample set, $D_{\text{noisy}}$. The total loss we minimize is a combination of the semi-supervised and the contrastive loss values.

## 4 Experiments

In this section, we provide detailed descriptions of the datasets used, experimental setups, and the results of experiments, including ablation studies.

### 4.1 Datasets

We evaluated the proposed method using several benchmark datasets, including CIFAR-10 [12], CIFAR-100 [12], and WebVision [18].

CIFAR-10 and CIFAR-100 consist of 50,000 training images and 10,000 test images [12]. We introduced various levels of noisy labels and different types of noise. The noise types include symmetric noise, where all samples have an equal probability of being mislabeled, and asymmetric noise. Asymmetric noise is designed to simulate real-world error structures [16], mimicking human labeling errors.

WebVision is a large-scale dataset, containing over 2.4 million images collected from Flickr and Google Image Search [18]. The dataset's classification categories align with the 1,000 categories of the ILSVRC12 dataset. Following previous research [10,15,19,21,27], we utilized the first 50 classes of the Google resized image subset for training, and evaluated the trained networks on the same 50 classes of the WebVision and ILSVRC12 validation sets.

The evaluation of experiments involved calculating the accuracy, a common metric in single-label classification. This metric represents the proportion of correctly predicted samples among the test samples.

### 4.2 Implementation Details

In the utilization of backbone models, we employed the ResNet18 model [8] for the CIFAR-10 and CIFAR-100 datasets. For the WebVision experiment, the InceptionResNetV2 model [26] was used. The selection and configuration of these models followed previous works in the literature [15], ensuring fair comparisons with other methods.

For the CIFAR-10 and CIFAR-100 experiments, a warm-up period of 10 and 30 epochs, respectively, was applied. Each network underwent approximately 300 epochs of training, with a batch size of 64. The initial learning rate was set to 0.02, weight decay to 5e-4, and momentum to 0.9. For the WebVision dataset, a 2-epoch warm-up period was set. Each network underwent approximately 100 epochs of training, with a batch size of 32. The initial learning rate was set to 0.01, weight decay to 1e-4.

### 4.3 Experimental Results

We present the performance of the proposed method under different label noise scenarios. In particular, symmetric noise treats all errors equally, while asymmetric noise reflects a more realistic, biased pattern of label corruption. Following previous works [10, 15], we consider symmetric noise rates of 20%, 50%, 80%, and 90%, and asymmetric noise rates of 10%, 30%, and 40%.

Tables 1 and 2 present the results for CIFAR-10 and CIFAR-100 experiments, using symmetric and asymmetric noise rates, respectively. In most cases of symmetric noise (Table 1), our method outperforms previous methods, especially at higher noise rates. Similar results are observed in the case of asymmetric noise (Table 2).

**Table 1.** Experimental results on CIFAR-10 and CIFAR-100 with symmetric noise. Our method improves performance at almost every noise level.

| Method | CIFAR-10 | | | | CIFAR-100 | | | |
|---|---|---|---|---|---|---|---|---|
| | 20% | 50% | 80% | 90% | 20% | 50% | 80% | 90% |
| DMix [15] (*ICLR*'20) | 96.1 | 94.6 | 92.9 | 76.0 | 77.3 | 74.6 | 60.2 | 31.5 |
| ELR [20] (*NeurIPS*'20) | 95.8 | 94.8 | 93.3 | 78.7 | 77.6 | 73.6 | 60.8 | 33.4 |
| JPL [11] (*CVPR*'21) | 93.5 | 90.2 | 35.7 | 23.4 | 70.9 | 67.7 | 17.8 | 12.8 |
| MOIT [22] (*CVPR*'21) | 94.1 | 91.1 | 75.8 | 70.1 | 75.9 | 70.1 | 51.4 | 24.5 |
| UNICON [10] (*CVPR*'22) | 96.0 | 95.6 | 93.9 | 90.8 | 78.9 | 77.6 | 63.9 | 44.8 |
| Sel-CL+ [17] (*CVPR*'22) | 95.5 | 93.9 | 89.2 | 81.9 | 76.5 | 72.4 | 59.6 | 48.8 |
| DISC [19] (*CVPR*'23) | **96.5** | – | – | – | 80.1 | – | – | – |
| DivideMix+ [27] (*ICCV*'23) | 96.2 | 94.7 | 93.1 | - | 77.5 | 74.7 | 60.4 | – |
| Ours | 95.4 | **95.9** | **95.1** | **93.7** | **81.2** | **77.8** | **66.9** | **51.7** |

For CIFAR-10, in the low noise rate scenario (20%), although the accuracy is above 95%, it is slightly lower compared to other methods. Interestingly, in the CIFAR-10 symmetric noise setting, the performance at 20% noise rate is worse than at 50%. We carefully examined the set of clean samples selected during training and, in the case of CIFAR-10 symmetric noise at 20% and 50%, confirmed that the clean samples selected at 20% noise rate are indeed more numerous and cleaner. The lower accuracy at 20% compared to 50% is perhaps attributed to the use of a semi-supervised approach in training. In scenarios with high accuracy, the number of unlabeled data images is lower, leading to comparatively poorer performance.

**Table 2.** Experimental results on CIFAR-10 and CIFAR-100 with asymmetric noise. Our method consistently outperforms existing approaches across nearly all noise levels. Note that experimental results in this context are not provided in recent studies [19] and [27].

| Method | CIFAR-10 | | | CIFAR-100 | | |
|---|---|---|---|---|---|---|
| | 10% | 30% | 40% | 10% | 30% | 40% |
| DMix [15] (*ICLR*'20) | 93.8 | 92.5 | 91.7 | 71.6 | 69.5 | 55.1 |
| ELR [20] (*NeurIPS*'20) | <u>95.4</u> | 94.7 | 93.0 | 77.3 | 74.6 | 73.2 |
| JPL [11] (*CVPR*'21) | 94.2 | 92.5 | 90.7 | 72.0 | 68.1 | 59.5 |
| MOIT [22] (*CVPR*'21) | 94.2 | 94.1 | 93.2 | 77.4 | 75.1 | 74.0 |
| UNICON [10] (*CVPR*'22) | 95.3 | <u>94.8</u> | <u>94.1</u> | 78.2 | 75.6 | <u>74.8</u> |
| Sel-CL+ [17] (*CVPR*'22) | **95.6** | 94.5 | 93.4 | <u>78.7</u> | <u>76.4</u> | 74.2 |
| Ours | 95.1 | **95.0** | **94.3** | **81.5** | **80.0** | **78.1** |

**Table 3.** Experimental results on real noisy datasets. All methods are trained on the WebVision while evaluated on both WebVision and ILSVRC12 validation set. The best result and second best result in each case are highlighted in bold and underline respectively.

| Method | WebVision | | ILSVRC12 | |
|---|---|---|---|---|
| | Top-1 | Top-5 | Top-1 | Top-5 |
| DMix [15] (*ICLR*'20) | 77.32 | 91.64 | 75.20 | 90.84 |
| ELR [20] (*NeurIPS*'20) | 77.78 | 91.68 | 70.29 | 89.72 |
| MOIT [22] (*CVPR*'21) | 78.76 | – | – | – |
| UNICON [10] (*CVPR*'22) | 77.60 | **93.44** | 75.29 | **93.72** |
| DISC [19] (*CVPR*'23) | <u>80.28</u> | 92.28 | **77.44** | 92.28 |
| DivideMix+ [27] (*ICCV*'23) | 77.51 | 91.95 | 75.51 | 91.58 |
| Ours | **80.40** | <u>92.72</u> | <u>75.80</u> | <u>92.68</u> |

Table 3 presents the experimental results using WebVision, demonstrating the effectiveness of our method in handling real noisy datasets. Our approach performs the best or second best in top-1 accuracy compared to state-of-the-art methods. However, in terms of top-5 accuracy, it falls short of UNICON [10]. This discrepancy may be due to the long-tail distribution inherent in the dataset. Our method does not consistently achieve high accuracy across all categories; some categories exhibit accuracy above 95%, while others fall below 50%. We believe this variability in prediction performance across categories contributes to the lower top-5 accuracy relative to UNICON [10] (Table 4).

**Table 4.** Ablation on key components. Both consistency-based sample selection and kNN affect the performance especially for high/or low noise rates.

| Consistency-based selection | kNN | CIFAR-100 (sym) | | | |
|---|---|---|---|---|---|
| | | 20% | 50% | 80% | 90% |
| ✗ | ✗ | 79.2 | 77.7 | 65.8 | 45.2 |
| ✓ | ✗ | 77.9 | 75.7 | 66.3 | 45.9 |
| ✗ | ✓ | 80.7 | 77.2 | 66.8 | 51.3 |
| ✓ | ✓ | **81.2** | **77.8** | **66.9** | **51.7** |

### 4.4 Analyses and Discussions

To gain a deeper understanding of the proposed method, we conducted ablation studies focusing on the impact of key components in the proposed sample selection scheme, including consistency-based selection (first-stage filtering) and kNN (second-stage filtering). These experiments used the CIFAR-100 dataset with symmetric noise rates. In the cases of disabling the proposed consistency-based selection method, we used the disagreement/divergence between the ground-truth labels and the predicted probabilities as the clean sample measurement, identical to that in UNICON [10].

In the experiments where kNN is disabled (first two rows), it is observed that there is a slight improvement in high noise rates, while the performance significantly declines at low noise rates. This discrepancy is expected, as compared to UNICON [10], our method filters out more samples and retain fewer, but cleaner samples. The results indicate that our method, with the ability to filter more accurate clean samples, synergizes well with the kNN algorithm, leading to improved overall performance.

Figure 2 illustrates the ability of our method to filter clean samples. While the number of clean samples is slightly reduced compared to UNICON [10], there is a substantial reduction in the number of noisy samples. Previous experiments also show that our accuracy in the CIFAR-10 setting with a 90% noise rate surpasses that of UNICON [10]. The impact of noisy labels gradually increases with training epochs, and the model tends to fit these erroneous labels over time. Therefore, effectively selection clean samples in the early stages of training to reduce the presence of noisy samples significantly influences the final model's performance.

Figure 3 illustrates the differences in sample selection between our method and UNICON [10] across various noise rates in CIFAR-100. Under a 20% noise rate, we can filter in more clean samples than UNICON [10]. Despite fewer filtered clean samples at high noise rates, the reduction in noisy samples is substantial. Regarding the proportion of correctly labeled clean samples, we outperform UNICON [10], contributing to the higher accuracy of our trained model.

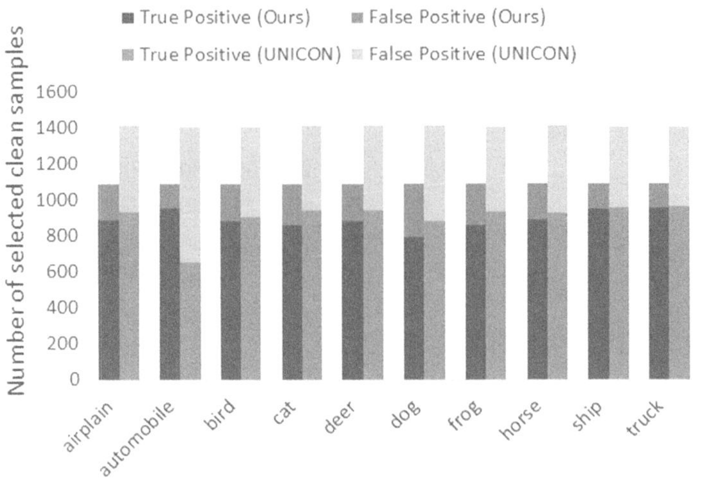


**Fig. 2.** Selecting clean sample sets for different classes after training for 100 epochs on CIFAR-10 with a 90% noise rate.

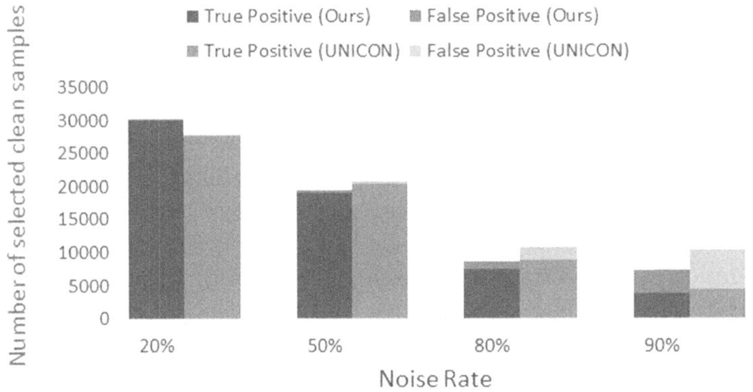


**Fig. 3.** Selecting clean sample sets after training for 100 epochs on CIFAR-100 under varying noise rates.

### 4.5 Limitations

A potential limitation of this study is the focus on image classification tasks with artificially introduced label noise. While the proposed method demonstrates strong performance on benchmark datasets like CIFAR-10, CIFAR-100, and WebVision, its effectiveness on other computer vision tasks or real-world noisy label scenarios may require further investigation. Additionally, the method's performance in less noisy settings (e.g., 20% on CIFAR-10) was slightly lower than some existing approaches, suggesting there may be room for improvement in such scenarios. The computational cost of the dual-model architecture and the kNN algorithm for sample selection could also be a limitation for large-scale applications. Finally, while the method shows promising results on long-tailed datasets like WebVision, the discrepancy between top-1 and top-5 accuracy improvements indicates that performance may vary across different categories.

## 5 Conclusion

In this paper, we introduced a novel sample selection method that considers the stability of model predictions, leveraging the differences in prediction stability between noisy and clean samples. This approach enhances the selection of clean samples by exploiting the distinctiveness in model predictions. Additionally, we employed the kNN algorithm alongside high-quality clean samples, enabling the selection of more clean samples. Through our dynamically designed selection approach, we effectively reduced the occurrence of noisy samples within the clean sample set.

Extensive experimental results showcase the feasibility of our proposed method, demonstrating its robust performance across various noise scenarios. By dynamically adapting to different noise levels, our approach consistently delivers promising results. The experiments conducted on CIFAR-10, CIFAR-100, and WebVision datasets illustrate the effectiveness of our method in handling label noise and enhancing model training.

Future work could explore several directions to extend this study. For example, applying our adaptive sample selection approach to other computer vision tasks like object detection or semantic segmentation could broaden its applicability. This method could be more robust by enhancing performance in low noise scenarios and adapting the method to handle more diverse types of label noise. We also consider optimizing computational efficiency for larger datasets and improving performance balance across categories in long-tailed distributions. Finally, integrating the proposed method with advanced semi-supervised or self-supervised learning techniques could lead to further improvements in learning from noisy labels.

**Acknowledgments.** This work was supported by the National Science and Technology Council of Taiwan (113-2221-E-003-016, 111-2221-E-003-016-MY2, 110-2634-F-002-050).

## References

1. Arpit, D., et al.: A closer look at memorization in deep networks. In: International Conference on Machine Learning (2017)
2. Berthelot, D., Carlini, N., Goodfellow, I., Oliver, A., Papernot, N., Raffel, C.: Mixmatch: a holistic approach to semi-supervised learning. In: Neural Information Processing Systems (2019)
3. Chen, D., Yu, Z., Bowman, S.R.: Clean or annotate: How to spend a limited data collection budget. In: NAACL Workshop (2021)

4. Chen, T., Kornblith, S., Norouzi, M., Hinton, G.: A simple framework for contrastive learning of visual representations. In: International Conference on Machine Learning (2020)
5. Cubuk, E.D., Zoph, B., Mane, D., Vasudevan, V., Le, Q.V.: Autoaugment: learning augmentation strategies from data. In: IEEE International Conference on Computer Vision and Pattern Recognition (2019)
6. Feng, C., Tzimiropoulos, G., Patras, I.: SSR: an efficient and robust framework for learning with unknown label noise. In: British Machine Vision Conference (2021)
7. Han, B., et al.: Co-teaching: robust training of deep neural networks with extremely noisy labels. In: Neural Information Processing Systems (2018)
8. He, K., Zhang, X., Ren, S., Sun, J.: Deep residual learning for image recognition. In: IEEE International Conference on Computer Vision and Pattern Recognition (2016)
9. Huang, Z.T., Chen, Y.H., Yeh, M.C.: Weakly- and semi-supervised object localization. In: IEEE International Conference on Acoustics, Speech, and Signal Processing (2023)
10. Karim, N., Rizve, M.N., Rahnavard, N., Mian, A., Shah, M.: UniCon: combating label noise through uniform selection and contrastive learning. In: IEEE International Conference on Computer Vision and Pattern Recognition (2022)
11. Kim, Y., Yun, J., Shon, H., Kim, J.: Joint negative and positive learning for noisy labels. In: IEEE International Conference on Computer Vision and Pattern Recognition (2021)
12. Krizhevsky, A., Hinton, G.: Learning multiple layers of features from tiny images. Master's thesis, Department of Computer Science, University of Toronto (2009)
13. Köhler, J.M., Autenrieth, M., Beluch, W.H.: Uncertainty based detection and relabeling of noisy image labels. In: CVPR Workshop (2019)
14. Li, J., Li, G., Liu, F., Yu, Y.: Neighborhood collective estimation for noisy label identification and correction. In: European Conference on Computer Vision (2022)
15. Li, J., Socher, R., Hoi, S.C.H.: Dividemix: learning with noisy labels as semi-supervised learning. In: International Conference on Learning Representations (2020)
16. Li, J., Wong, Y., Zhao, Q., Kankanhalli, M.S.: Learning to learn from noisy labeled data. In: IEEE International Conference on Computer Vision and Pattern Recognition (2019)
17. Li, S., Xia, X., Ge, S., Liu, T.: Selective-supervised contrastive learning with noisy labels. In: IEEE International Conference on Computer Vision and Pattern Recognition (2022)
18. Li, W., Wang, L., Li, W., Agustsson, E., Gool, L.V.: Webvision database: visual learning and understanding from web data. CoRR abs/1708.02862 (2017)
19. Li, Y., Han, H., Shan, S., Chen, X.: Disc: Learning from noisy labels via dynamic instance-specific selection and correction. In: IEEE International Conference on Computer Vision and Pattern Recognition (2023)
20. Liu, S., Niles-Weed, J., Razavian, N., Fernandez-Granda, C.: Early-learning regularization prevents memorization of noisy labels. In: Neural Information Processing Systems (2020)
21. Nishi, K., Ding, Y., Rich, A., Höllerer, T.: Augmentation strategies for learning with noisy labels. In: IEEE International Conference on Computer Vision and Pattern Recognition (2021)
22. Ortego, D., Arazo, E., Albert, P., OConnor, N.E., McGuinness, K.: Multi-objective interpolation training for robustness to label noise. In: IEEE International Conference on Computer Vision and Pattern Recognition (2021)

23. Radford, A., et al.: Learning transferable visual models from natural language supervision. In: International Conference on Machine Learning (2021)
24. Sohn, K., et al.: Fixmatch: simplifying semisupervised learning with consistency and confidence. In: Neural Information Processing Systems (2020)
25. Song, H., Kim, M., Park, D., Shin, Y., Lee, J.G.: Learning from noisy labels with deep neural networks: a survey. IEEE Trans. Neural Networks Learn. Syst. **34**, 8135–8153 (2023)
26. Szegedy, C., Ioffe, S., Vanhoucke, V., Alemi, A.A.: Inception-v4, inception-resnet and the impact of residual connections on learning. In: AAAI Conference on Artificial Intelligence (2017)
27. Xia, X., et al.: Combating noisy labels with sample selection by mining high-discrepancy examples. In: IEEE International Conference on Computer Vision (2023)
28. Zhang, H., Cisse, M., Dauphin, Y.N., Lopez-Paz, D.: mixup: beyond empirical risk minimization. In: International Conference on Machine Learning (2018)

# Games

# R-CoT: Reinforcement Chain of Thought Prompting for Task Specific Training

Hsu-Chih Chiu, Iuan-Kai Fang, and Che-Rung Lee(✉)

National Tsing Hua University, HsinChu 300044, Taiwan
cherung@cs.nthu.edu.tw

**Abstract.** The large language models (LLMs) have shown their superiority in solving various natural language processing tasks. However, owing to the lack of knowledge of specific domains, LLMs often perform poorly for applications of expert systems. In this paper, we introduce a new prompt engineering technique, called Reinforcement Chain of Thought (R-CoT), which incorporates the critical feedback and interactive steps to improve the Chain of Thought (CoT). By leveraging the automation advantages of large language models (LLMs), this technique reduces the need for extensive manual data annotation, and can be effectively applied in expert systems for specific domains. We have conducted experiments for the GSM8K math problem-solving dataset, the CSQA commonsense understanding dataset, and tasks from the Super- NaturalInstructions V2 benchmark using ChatGPT. Experimental results show that the accuracy of R-CoT achieves an accuracy of 80.7% on the CSQA dataset and 45.6% on the GSM8K dataset, which outperforms related methods.

**Keywords:** Prompt Engineering · Reinforcement Chain of Thought (R-CoT) · Expert System

## 1 Introduction

Although the rapid advancement of generative AI has enabled computers to handle increasingly complex tasks in various areas [5]. The current machine learning (ML) models still lack the basic understanding of the real world or the domain knowledge, which influences the generation of reasonable content [20]. To bridge the gap between human experts and the ML models, training ML models to comprehend the real world or domain intelligence is necessary. As mentioned in Fei-Fei Li'talk [8], the full potential of artificial intelligence will not be fully realized until humans impart spatial intelligence to AI.

One of the methods to impart domain intelligence to AI models is through prompt engineering for Large Language Models (LLMs), such as ChatGPT [1]. Unlike the traditional approach of fine-tuning with specific annotated datasets, GPT employs Model-Agnostic Meta Learning as its training foundation, with

© The Author(s), under exclusive license to Springer Nature Singapore Pte Ltd. 2025
W.-T. Chu et al. (Eds.): TAAI 2024, CCIS 2414, pp. 157–167, 2025.
https://doi.org/10.1007/978-981-96-4589-3_11

in-context learning. After the model is built, prompt engineering is used to provide input prompts requested by users, enabling the system to perform tasks or provide responses based on user prompts.

Many techniques for prompt engineering have been proposed [10]. Chain-of-Thought (CoT) Prompting [16] guides LLMs' reasoning process through a step-by-step approach. Graph-of-Thought (GoT) Prompting [18] proposes a graph-based framework that mimics human nonlinear thinking. Chain of Table Prompting [15] utilizes step-by-step tabular reasoning to dynamically generate table content. Tree-of-Thoughts (ToT) Prompting [17] represents the reasoning process in a tree structure, with each node representing a different reasoning step. Chain-of-Symbol (CoS) Prompting [4] uses a chain of symbols to represent the entire reasoning process, with each symbol representing a step and state of reasoning. Self-Consistency [13] involves generating multiple answers to the same question and selecting the most consistent one to reduce the likelihood of random errors. Thread of Thought (ThoT) Prompting [21] emphasizes a linear thought process, ensuring high coherence, making it suitable for text generation and logical reasoning, thereby reducing the chances of scattered and interrupted results.

However, prompting methods that use reasoning and logic, such as Chain of Thought (CoT) [16], Zero-Shot Chain-of-Thought (Zero-Shot-CoT) [7], and Automatic Chain-of-Thought (Auto-CoT) [19], only focus on whether the overall problem-solving context is correct, and neglect whether the meanings of nouns in different sentences or scenarios meet the user's needs. When setting up customized systems, these methods cannot produce satisfactory results for experts with varying understandings of different concepts. A recent paper [20] proposes the SELF-GUIDE method, which synthesizes task-specific input-output pairs from the student LLM, then uses these input-output pairs to finetune the student LLM itself. However, when the number of synthesized data increases, the potential errors could be accumulated.

In this work, we designed a novel prompt engineering method, called Reinforcement Chain-of-Thought (R-CoT), to address the need of expert systems. Based on Chain-of-Thought (CoT) [16], R-CoT systematically incorporates expert knowledge into large language models in a reasoning way. We enhanced the understanding of specific terms within the input problems or documents and include manual correction steps while guiding LLMs to solve problems. The goal is to make large language models having long-term memory for dialogue with model adjustment engineers to optimize and customize the model step by step, and use interactive input methods such as prompt words and generated result adjustments to enhance their memory reinforcement and error correction for the specifications, similar to reinforcement learning (RL) [6] where the relationship between the system, environment, and environmental feedback is used. By outputting and refining the language model's understanding of object nouns and overall comprehension of input documents, the model can better align with human needs in expert systems.

We have evaluated the proposed method by comparing R-CoT with three different training methods: Chain-of-Thought (CoT) [16], Zero-Shot Chain of

Thought (Zero-Shot-CoT) [7], and Automatic Chain of Thought (Auto-CoT) [19]. The evaluation was conducted using two types of datasets: the GSM8K math problem-solving dataset, and the CSQA commonsense understanding dataset. In addition, we also compared R-CoT with SELF-GUIDE [20] using the Super-NaturalInstructions V2 benchmark [14], which is a metadataset consisting of a variety of NLP tasks and instructions that describe them in plain language. The results show that the proposed R-CoT method is more effective in training large language models with expert knowledge and is also applicable to general problem datasets.

The major contributions of this work are summarized as follows:

- Propose an effective prompting technique to systematically incorporate expert knowledge into large language models.
- Utilize large language models in the system to automatically annotate files, saving time and human resources.
- Refine and feedback the large language model'understanding of object nouns and the content of automatically annotated files to optimize the language model, making it more aligned with human needs.

The rest of this paper is organized as follows: In Sect. 2, we give the related work on prompting engineering in recent years. In Sect. 3, we present the proposed Reinforcement Chain of Thought (R-CoT) technique and the adjustments and design of the furniture description file generation system. Section 4 compares the R-CoT method with three different training methods: Chain-of-Thought (CoT) [16], Zero-Shot Chain of Thought (Zero-Shot-CoT) [7], and Automatic Chain of Thought (Auto-CoT) [19]. In the last section, we summarize our work and outline the future work directions.

## 2 Related Work

The survey by Pranab Sahoo et al., 2024 [10], provides a comprehensive overview of various prompting techniques, categorizing them into 12 types based on their functionality, such as Reasoning and Logic, Code Generation and Execution, Fine-Tuning and Optimization, User Interaction.

Next, we will discuss the features of Chain of Thought (CoT) [16], Zero-Shot Chain of Thought (Zero-Shot-CoT) prompting [7], and Automatic Chain of Thought (Auto-CoT) [19].

### 2.1 Chain of Thought (CoT)

When dealing with tasks that involve more than one step, it often requires large language models (LLMs) to complete more than a single task. To improve their reasoning capabilities and ability to handle complex tasks, the paper proposes the Chain of Thought (CoT) technique [16]. Traditional prompting, which directly asks for results, can lead to large language models generating subpar outcomes due to the lack of reliable guidance. The CoT [16] technique offers a decision-making process similar to human thought, breaking down a complex task into multiple simpler tasks. This allows the large language model to complete a series of simpler tasks first, ensuring the overall direction of execution is correct.

Figure 1 shows an example of CoT [16]. When solving a math problem, we first need to provide a similar example and a manually written solution. This problem and the solution are input together into the LLM as reference data. Then, the actual question we want the system to answer is input.

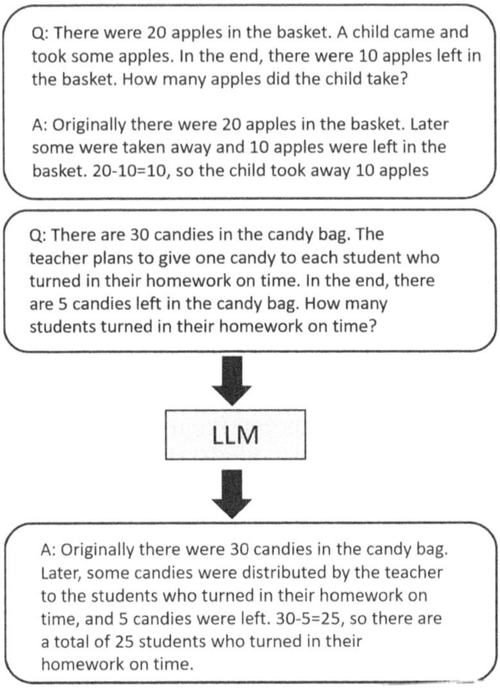


**Fig. 1.** An Example of Chain of Thought [16]. The blue and red words represent the problem we want to solve and the manually entered prompt respectively. (Color figure online)

## 2.2 Zero-Shot Chain of Thought Prompting

Zero-Shot Chain of Thought (Zero-Shot-CoT) prompting [7] refers to the technique where users provide the model with an input prompt without any task-specific examples, pre-labeled data answers, or fine-tuning from the model trainers. This prompt must be designed by the user in a step-by-step manner to guide the model in executing the task. This method effectively eliminates the language model's dependency on thousands of training data, making training more convenient and efficient while saving significant time and resources. However, since the model is not fine-tuned for specific tasks, the results produced by Zero-Shot-CoT prompting [7] may not be as effective as those from a model fine-tuned for particular tasks.

Figure 2 shows an example of Zero-Shot-CoT [7]. When encountering a math problem, we need to append a prompting request at the end of the problem, asking the LLM to "think step by step." The model will generate an orderly solution process. Then, the problem and the generated solution process are input together into the large language model again to obtain the desired answer.

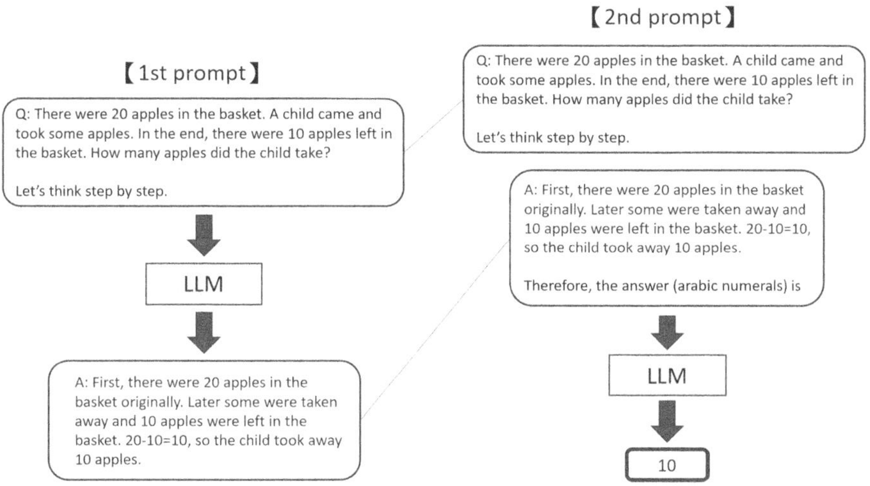


**Fig. 2.** A Simple Example of Zero-Shot-CoT Prompting [7]. The blue and red words represent the problem we want to solve and the manually entered prompt respectively. (Color figure online)

### 2.3 Automatic Chain of Thought (Auto-CoT) Prompting

The Automatic Chain of Thought (Auto-CoT) Prompting [19] improves upon the CoT [16] concept and Zero-Shot CoT [7] approach as a foundational model by incorporating a series of automatically generated reasoning steps to guide large language models in solving problems. Figure 3 demonstrates the operation steps of Auto-CoT. In the Clustering section, the questions are classified using the Sentence-BERT (SBERT) [9] technique. Then, the same with Zero-Shot-CoT [7] prompt is automatically applied to all questions. After obtaining the generation results from the LLM. Specific questions after clustering and the results generated by the LLM will be input into the LLM along with the new questions.

## 3 Reinforcement Chain of Thought (R-CoT) Prompting

The Reinforcement Chain of Thought (R-CoT) prompting method is based on the Chain of Thought (CoT) [16] prompting [10] and incorporates adjustments in

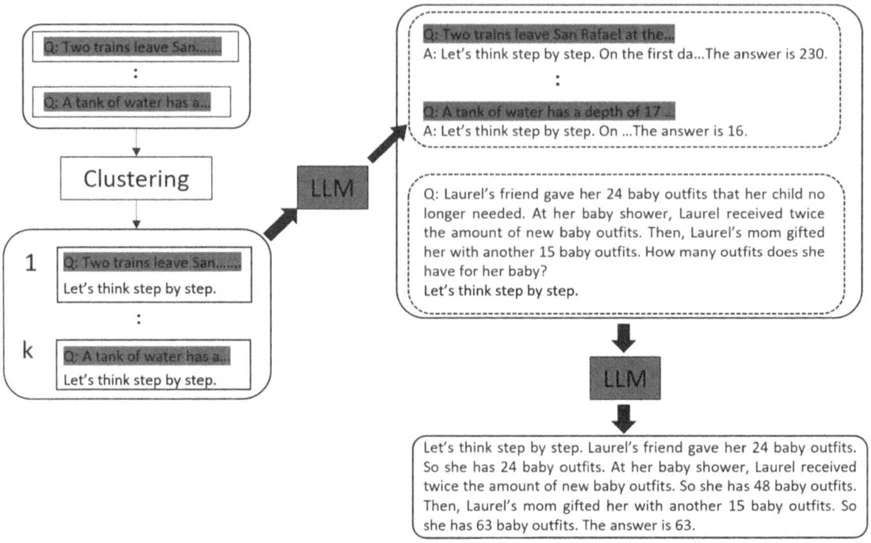


**Fig. 3.** An example of Auto-CoT [19]. The green parts are questions from the dataset, the red text is the manually entered prompts, and the blue text is the problem. (Color figure online)

the feedback process. R-CoT continues the CoT [16] method of breaking down problem solutions into orderly steps. However, when LLMs generate answers, their extensive databases often contain multiple instances of the same nouns or abbreviations with significantly different meanings. This can be useful in a broadly applicable conversational system, but can cause significant deviations in a system designed for specific functionalities.

As shown in Fig. 1, CoT [16] requires inputting a similar type of problem and a manually written text as a basis for generating results before solving the problem. The drawback is that it is quite labor-intensive when dealing with a large number of problems, as it relies on manually written step-by-step texts.

While humans can quickly understand the context of an abbreviation within a conversation, LLMs are prone to confusing similar terms, leading to completely different answers. To address this issue, we introduce four steps with humans in the loop to guide LLMs in solving problems rationally and orderly. The following four steps outline the R-CoT prompting operation process:

1. First, users need LLMs to analyze the specialized terms in the question and list corresponding explanations.
2. Users then modify these explanations and input them back into the customized LLMs database.
3. Next, users input a prompt to instruct the LLM to annotate the entire question.
4. After that, users fine-tune the annotations and input them again into the customized LLMs database. Meanwhile, users can also input the domain knowledge into the LLM to constrain the possible outputs.

These steps help ensure that the large language model generates answers that meet the requirements without significant discrepancies. Unlike CoT [16], R-CoT reduces the need for entirely manually written step-by-step text and instead uses the LLM to generate key noun explanations and annotations. Therefore, as shown in the experiment time in Fig. 4, R-CoT is more time-efficient compared to CoT [16]. R-COT repeatedly feedback on annotations and key term explanations can enhance LLMs' understanding of the subject and the scope of user requirements.

The R-CoT method can be applied in specific professional domain LLM systems, allowing experts to fine-tune specialized terms to ensure LLMs generate results that meet their requirements and constraints. Figure 4 shows an example to demonstrate the R-CoT and CoT prompting [16] process; the blue and red words represent the problem we want to solve and the manually entered prompt respectively. Since this problem is relatively simple, there is no need to modify the LLM's generated results.

From this example, we can observe the differences between R-CoT and CoT [16]. First, R-CoT does not require manually providing a similar example and a step-by-step solution beforehand when solving problems. Instead, it directly uses the LLM to analyze the mathematical methods needed for the problem. Then, it involves manually checking whether the results meet the problem requirements and storing the results in the database. Subsequently, the LLM generates the meaning of each sentence in the context and the corresponding mathematical formulas to obtain the answer. After the manual verification, the results are stored in the database. This way, when encountering similar problem types in the future, the LLM can refer to the previously stored content in the database.

### 3.1 Assessment on the Mode Collapse Problems

A recent paper [11] investigates the mode collapse problem when the LLM is trained by the model-generated content recursively. The mode collapse problems mean the generated contents show less and less variety or the original content distribution disappear. For instance, Zero-shot CoT and Auto-CoT all have the mode collapse problems.

Although our method also utilizes the model generated data for training, our method emphasizes the correct definition of the tasks, and it also has the human in loop to fine-tune the results, so that the errors cannot be accumulated and cause the mode collapse problems.

## 4 Experiments

### 4.1 Benchmark Tasks

To evaluate the general applicability of R-CoT, we selected the arithmetic question-answering dataset GSM8K [2] and the commonsense question-answering dataset CSQA [12]. The GSM8K [2] dataset includes 8,500 grade school-level math word problems (average words: 46.9), while the CSQA [12]

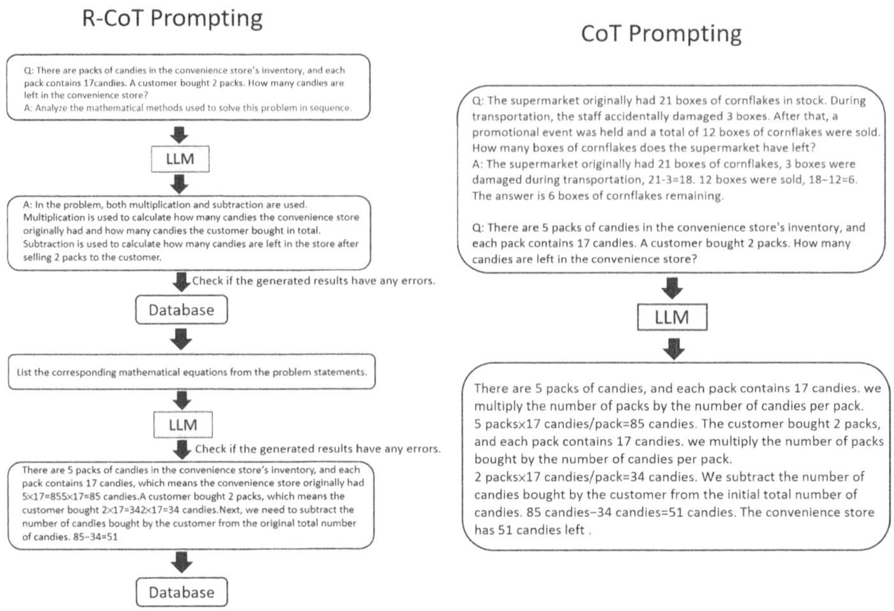


**Fig. 4.** A Simple example of R-CoT and CoT prompting [16]. The blue and red words represent the problem we want to solve and the manually entered prompt respectively. (Color figure online)

dataset consists of everyday common-sense questions with five answer choices (average words: 27.8).

As shown in Table 1, R-CoT(unclassified) achieved better accuracy in the CSQA [12] dataset compared to other prompting methods, due to the feedback from definitions that helped with certain questions. However, the accuracy of R-CoT (unclassified) in solving the GSM8K dataset problems (45.6%) is lower than that of Auto-CoT (47.3%). Therefore, we classified the dataset before inputting the corresponding R-CoT prompts, resulting in R-CoT (classified) achieving score gains from 45.6% to 50.2% on GSM8K and from 80.7% to 82.5% on CSQA.

### 4.2 Domain Specific Tasks

We also compare R-CoT with the SELF-GUIDE method [20]. The evaluation tasks are from the Super-NaturalInstructions V2 benchmark [14], which is a metadataset consisting of a variety of NLP tasks and instructions that describe them in plain language. All tasks have the same format, including definition, positive examples, negative examples, and instances.

We selected four classification tasks and four generation tasks. The evaluation metrics are described as follows

- Exact Match (classification task): which is the number of exact string match between the predicted and ground truth labels.

**Table 1.** We compared R-CoT(unclassified version and classified version) with Zero-Shot [1], Few-Shot [1], Auto-CoT [19], Zero-Shot CoT [7] and CoT [16], and observed the accuracy of these methods on the GSM8K [2] and CSQA [12] datasets.

| Model | GSM8K | CSQA |
|---|---|---|
| Zero-Shot | 23.1 | 71.3 |
| Few-Shot | 34.8 | 76.2 |
| Auto-CoT | 47.3 | 75.2 |
| Zero-Shot-CoT | 41.1 | 69.2 |
| CoT | 46.5 | 78.3 |
| R-CoT (unclassified) | 45.6 | 80.7 |
| R-CoT (classified) | **50.2** | **82.5** |

- ROUGE-L (generation tasks): which computes the longest common subsequence between the generated and reference texts.

For both metrics, the larger the better.

**Table 2.** We compared R-CoT with SELF-GUIDE method [20] for four classification tasks and four generation tasks.

| Task ID | R-CoT | SELF-GUIDE |
|---|---|---|
| Classification Tasks: | | |
| task1612 | 25.8 | 33.3 |
| task284 | 83.1 | 82.2 |
| task346 | 62.4 | 50.7 |
| task1529 | 48.3 | 54.5 |
| Avg | 54.9 | 55.2 |
| Generation Tasks: | | |
| task1345 | 63.2 | 50.5 |
| task281 | 51.3 | 49.3 |
| task1562 | 62.7 | 59.3 |
| task1622 | 86.1 | 78.5 |
| Avg | 65.8 | 59.4 |

The results are shown in Table 2. For the classification tasks, SELF-GUIDE is slightly better than R-CoT in terms of average, which are 54.9 and 55.2 for R-CoT and SELF-GUIDE respectively. If checking the results for each task, one can see that R-CoT wins two cases, task 284 and task 346, and SELF-GUIDE wins the rest. For task 1612 and task 346, their differences are significant; but for the other two they have similar performance.

In generation tasks, R-CoT significantly outperforms SELF-GUIDE. The substantial difference in average performance (65.8 vs. 59.4) indicates that R-CoT's reinforcement learning component is more effective at correcting errors during the generation process, which is particularly crucial for tasks that require precise content generation. Although SELF-GUIDE is also effective, it tends to overlook accumulated errors, resulting in poorer performance in tasks that demand high accuracy and consistency. The performance gap is especially pronounced in tasks such as task1345 and task1622. This is due to R-CoT's systematic feedback mechanism, which iteratively refines the generated output to better align with task requirements. SELF-GUIDE relies more on initial instructions and misses the opportunity for such iterative improvements, especially in tasks that require complex generation processes.

## 5 Conclusion and Future Work

Using the R-CoT prompting method, large language models (LLMs) achieve superior results in various tasks due to the inclusion of part definition feedback and overall feedback steps. The R-CoT method outperforms Auto-CoT [19] , Zero-Shot CoT [7], CoT [16], and SELF-GUIDE [20] prompting methods. This process not only improves the accuracy of special domain tasks, but also saves considerable human labor and time, as only corrections to errors are needed. This step is significantly beneficial for building expert systems in specific domains using LLMs and also aids in handling extensive datasets that require noun definitions.

There are several future directions to explore. First, R-CoT prompting is a training method designed to enhance expert knowledge, which can be applied to the training prompts to other tasks. Due to the specificity of its guiding steps, it is more suitable for homogeneous problem-solving that requires expert knowledge. Few-Shot Classification of InteractADL [3] introduces the InteractADL dataset, which primarily aims to provide complex ADLs (Activities of Daily Living) data in home environments. The dataset includes multi-view scenes of interactions between people, and between people and objects. Second, R-CoT can also be applied to the description of complex indoor scenes, defining the characteristics of different people and objects, and combining with image generation models to produce corresponding scenes. This approach aims to compensate for LLMs' lack of understanding of spatial concepts.

## References

1. Brown, T., et al.: Language models are few-shot learners. Adv. Neural. Inf. Process. Syst. **33**, 1877–1901 (2020)
2. Cobbe, K., et al.: Training verifiers to solve math word problems. arXiv preprint arXiv:2110.14168 (2021)
3. Durante, Z., et al.: Few-shot classification of interactive activities of daily living (interactadl). arXiv preprint arXiv:2406.01662 (2024)

4. Hu, H., Lu, H., Zhang, H., Song, Y.Z., Lam, W., Zhang, Y.: Chain-of-symbol prompting elicits planning in large language models. arXiv preprint arXiv:2305.10276 (2023)
5. Humble, N., Mozelius, P.: The threat, hype, and promise of artificial intelligence in education. Discover Artif. Intell. **2**(1), 22 (2022)
6. Kaelbling, L.P., Littman, M.L., Moore, A.W.: Reinforcement learning: a survey. J. Artif. Intell. Res. **4**, 237–285 (1996)
7. Kojima, T., Gu, S.S., Reid, M., Matsuo, Y., Iwasawa, Y.: Large language models are zero-shot reasoners. Adv. Neural. Inf. Process. Syst. **35**, 22199–22213 (2022)
8. Li, F.F.: With spatial intelligence, with spatial intelligence, AI will understand the real world [ted talk] (2024). https://youtu.be/y8NtMZ7VGmU?si=e18PxQKMD6_XqF-e
9. Reimers, N., Gurevych, I.: Sentence-Bert: sentence embeddings using SIAMESE BERT-networks. arXiv preprint arXiv:1908.10084 (2019)
10. Sahoo, P., Singh, A.K., Saha, S., Jain, V., Mondal, S., Chadha, A.: A systematic survey of prompt engineering in large language models: techniques and applications. arXiv preprint arXiv:2402.07927 (2024)
11. Shumailov, I., Shumaylov, Z., Zhao, Y., Papernot, N., Anderson, R., Gal, Y.: AI models collapse when trained on recursively generated data. Nature **631**, 755–759 (2024). this paper is dedicated to the memory of Professor Ross J. Anderson, our colleague and friend, who contributed much to this and other works we have produced over the years. We thank A. Thudi, D. Glukhov, P. Zaika, and D. Barak for useful discussions and feedback
12. Talmor, A., Herzig, J., Lourie, N., Berant, J.: CommonsenseQA: a question answering challenge targeting commonsense knowledge. arXiv preprint arXiv:1811.00937 (2018)
13. Wang, X., et al.: Self-consistency improves chain of thought reasoning in language models. arXiv preprint arXiv:2203.11171 (2022)
14. Wang, Y., et al.: Super-NaturalInstructions: generalization via declarative instructions on 1600+ NLP tasks. In: Goldberg, Y., Kozareva, Z., Zhang, Y. (eds.) Proceedings of the 2022 Conference on Empirical Methods in Natural Language Processing, Abu Dhabi, United Arab Emirates, pp. 5085–5109. Association for Computational Linguistics (2022)
15. Wang, Z., et al.: Chain-of-table: evolving tables in the reasoning chain for table understanding. arXiv preprint arXiv:2401.04398 (2024)
16. Wei, J., et al.: Chain-of-thought prompting elicits reasoning in large language models. Adv. Neural. Inf. Process. Syst. **35**, 24824–24837 (2022)
17. Yao, S., et al.: Tree of thoughts: deliberate problem solving with large language models. arXiv preprint arXiv:2305.10601 (2023)
18. Yao, Y., Li, Z., Zhao, H.: Beyond chain-of-thought, effective graph-of-thought reasoning in language models. arXiv preprint arXiv:2305.16582 (2023)
19. Zhang, Z., Zhang, A., Li, M., Smola, A.: Automatic chain of thought prompting in large language models. arXiv preprint arXiv:2210.03493 (2022)
20. Zhao, C., Jia, X., Viswanathan, V., Neubig, G., Wu, T.: Self-guide: better task-specific instruction following via self-synthetic finetuning. In: First Conference on Language Modeling (2024)
21. Zhou, Y., et al.: Thread of thought unraveling chaotic contexts. arXiv preprint arXiv:2311.08734 (2023)

# A Lookup Table for Deficiency Number Calculation in Mahjong

Shih-Chieh Tang[1], Jr-Chang Chen[2](✉), and I-Chen Wu[1,3]

[1] Department of Computer Science, National Yang Ming Chiao Tung University, Hsinchu, Taiwan
sctang0386033@gmail.com, icwu@csie.nctu.edu.tw

[2] Department of Computer Science and Information Engineering, National Taipei University, New Taipei City, Taiwan
jcchen@mail.ntpu.edu.tw

[3] Research Center for Information Technology Innovation, Academia Sinica, Taipei, Taiwan

**Abstract.** In the game of Mahjong, the deficiency number is an important metric to judge the quality of a given hand. Calculating this number on-the-fly using traditional methods, such as depth-first search, is time consuming. In this paper, we propose a formula for the deficiency number and design a greedy method to build a lookup table in advance, allowing for more efficient calculations. While using these tables, we introduce two methods to handle some special cases, named hidden tiles and pseudo-meld prioritization. By applying these methods, we ensure the correctness when using these tables. The experimental results show a speedup of 121.2 times compared to VeryLongCat and 6868.9 times compared to Botzone.

**Keywords:** Mahjong · Deficiency Number · Lookup Table

## 1 Introduction

Mahjong is a popular game in eastern Asia. It is a four-player imperfect information stochastic game. The complexity of Mahjong was estimated to be $4.3 \times 10^{185}$ [2], which is higher than that of Go [5]. There are various rules in different regions, such as Taiwanese Mahjong, Chinese Standard Mahjong, and Japanese Riichi Mahjong.

The *deficiency number* (a.k.a. *shanten number* in Chinese Standard Mahjong) is a concept used to measure how close a hand is to being complete. It represents the minimum number of tiles needed to achieve a winning hand. Given a hand, players often aim to reduce the deficiency number of their hands as soon as possible to increase the chances to win. This concept was used in many game-playing programs to enhance the performance, such as VeryLongCat [4] and SeoFon [7].

In this paper, we propose a method to build lookup tables and an algorithm to use them to efficiently calculate the deficiency number. To ensure accuracy, we

© The Author(s), under exclusive license to Springer Nature Singapore Pte Ltd. 2025
W.-T. Chu et al. (Eds.): TAAI 2024, CCIS 2414, pp. 168–177, 2025.
https://doi.org/10.1007/978-981-96-4589-3_12

also propose two methods to deal with some specific tile arrangements in hand. The experimental results show that the speedup reaches 121.2 times faster than VeryLongCat and 6868.9 times faster than Botzone [9].

## 2 Background

In this section, we briefly review the general rules of Mahjong in Subsect. 2.1 and related works of Mahjong in Subsect. 2.2.

### 2.1 Rules of Mahjong

We introduce the rules and terms of Taiwanese Mahjong with a mention of Chinese Standard Mahjong. Mahjong uses 144 tiles, divided into four *types* and 34 *patterns*, and flowers.[1] These types comprises three *suits* and an *honor*. The suits includes 1 to 9 *Character* (or *Man*, denoted by $C_1$ to $C_9$), 1 to 9 *Dot* (or *Pin*, denoted by $D_1$ to $D_9$), 1 to 9 *Bamboo* (or *Sou*, denoted by $B_1$ to $B_9$). An honor includes four *Winds* (East, South, West, and North) and three *Dragons* (White, Green, and Red). Each pattern has four identical tiles.

Each player starts with 16 tiles (or 13 tiles in Chinese Standard Mahjong) as his/her *hand*. The goal is to form a *winning hand*, which consists of five *melds* (or four melds in Chinese Standard Mahjong) and one *head*. In this paper, the definition of winning hands commonly used in most Mahjong rules is adopted. Melds can be either a *sequence* (three consecutive tiles of the same suit), a *triplet* (three identical tiles), or a *quadruplet* (four identical tiles). The head should be a *pair* (two identical tiles). Players take turns drawing a tile from the *wall* (like a deck shared with all players in card games) or taking a tile discarded from another player to accomplish their winning hand. A player wins the round when he/she accomplishes their winning hand; otherwise he/she must discard a tile from his/her hand. Refer to [1] for more information.

We introduce some additional Mahjong terms that are used in this paper as follows. An *incomplete sequence* consists of two tiles and needs one more tile to form a sequence, such as $\{C_5C_6\}$ and $\{C_5C_7\}$. A *pseudo-meld* is either a pair or an incomplete sequence. The deficiency number of a hand is the number of tiles that a player needs to change to accomplish a winning hand. A *pure hand* is a hand that contains tiles of only one suit or one honor.

### 2.2 Previous Works on Mahjong Agents

In research on calculating deficiency numbers, Wang [8] developed a method to compute the deficiency number of 14-tile hands without honor tiles in Chinese Standard Mahjong. The deficiency number is calculated by breaking down the hand and applying specific rules. Botzone [9] is a competitive platform for game AI education and research. It also provides a platform for the Chinese Standard

[1] Flower tiles are excluded in this paper.

Mahjong competition and includes codes to calculate the deficiency number for players.

In research on Taiwanese Mahjong game-playing programs, the program VERYLONGCAT [4] uses an expectimax tree to calculate the win rate of a given hand and applies a pruning method based on the deficiency number to reduce the number of nodes that need to be searched [6]. The program SEOFON [7] uses the deficiency number to split the hand and develops some ideas to improve the program, mainly in defense. The program SIMCAT [3] utilizes Monte Carlo sampling to calculate win rates after applying legal actions to a given hand. It also calculates the deficiency number to ensure that the program functions correctly.

# 3 Our Methods

In this section, we describe the formula to calculate the deficiency number of a given hand in Subsect. 3.1. Then, we propose a greedy method to build lookup tables, which can be accessed given a pure hand in Subsect. 3.2. When we calculate the deficiency number using lookup tables, we found that the results are incorrect in some cases, which are illustrated in Subsect. 3.3. To deal with them, we propose two methods in Subsect. 3.4. Finally, the procedure to calculate the deficiency number is described in Subsect. 3.5.

## 3.1 The Formula for the Deficiency Number

The main goal of this paper is to build a lookup table that allows a quick calculation of the deficiency number $dfcy$ of a hand. The formula shown in Eq. 1 is to calculate $dfcy$ based on the number of melds $n$ in a winning hand, along with the number of melds $n_m$, the number of pairs $n_p$ and the number of incomplete sequences $n_{is}$ in the current hand.

$$dfcy = \begin{cases} (n - n_m) \times 2 - \min(n - n_m, n_p - 1 + n_{is}) & \text{if } n_p > 0 \\ (n - n_m) \times 2 + 1 - \min(n - n_m, n_{is}) & \text{if } n_p = 0 \end{cases} \quad (1)$$

A winning hand requires $n$ melds and one head. We begin by assuming that the melds and the head are formed from individual tiles. Given a tile, forming a meld requires two additional tiles, and forming the head requires one additional tile. So, the initial $dfcy$ is set to $n \times 2 + 1$. If the current hand has already contained $n_m$ melds, we can save the tiles needed to create these melds, reducing $dfcy$ by $n_m \times 2$. Next, we form the remaining $n - n_m$ melds using pseudo-melds in the hand. It saves an additional tile compared to forming a meld from a single tile. More specifically, if the hand contains at least one pair, one of these pairs is selected as the head. It saves an additional tile needed to create the head from a single tile. The remaining pseudo-melds are then used to form at most $n - n_m$ melds. In this case, $dfcy$ is reduced by a total of $r_{head} = n_m \times 2 + \min(n - n_m, n_p - 1 + n_{is}) + 1$. Thus, $dfcy = (n \times 2 + 1) - r_{head}$, which is the case when $n_p > 0$ in Eq. 1. On the other hand, if the hand has no pair, a tile needed to create the head cannot be saved, so $dfcy$ is simply reduced by the number of tiles saved from using incomplete sequences to form melds, resulting in a total reduction of $r_{no\_head} = n_m \times 2 + \min(n - n_m, n_{is})$ tiles. Thus, $dfcy = (n \times 2 + 1) - r_{no\_head}$, which is the case when $n_p = 0$ in Eq. 1.

To calculate $n_m$, $n_p$ and $n_{is}$, we treat the tiles in each of the four types in the hand as separate pure hands, and then individually look them up in the lookup table. The table allows us to access the values of $n_m^t$, $n_p^t$, and $n_{is}^t$ for a pure hand $t$. By combining the results of the four types, we can calculate $dfcy$ by $n_m$, $n_p$, and $n_{is}$.

### 3.2 The Greedy Method for Building Lookup Tables

We design two tables, one for suits and the other for an honor. Each table is a one-dimensional array. The data of the element mainly include $n_m^t$, $n_p^t$, and $n_{is}^t$. The indices of the tables are generated by encoding pure hands as follows. A pure hand representing suits is encoded as a nine-digit base-5 number since there are four tiles in each of the nine patterns. Similarly, a pure hand representing honors is encoded as a seven-digit base-5 number. For example, the pure hand $t = \{C_1C_1C_2C_3C_4\}$ is encoded as $000001112_5$. Thus, there are $5^9 = 1,953,125$ entries in the lookup table for suits and $5^7 = 78,125$ entries for honors.

In practice, the table is built from the lowest encoding $000000000_5$ to the highest encoding $444444444_5$. Thus, we ensure that all pure sub-hands after some tiles are extracted have already been analyzed and their data have been stored in the lookup tables, since their encodings must be lower than the original pure hand. An illegal pure hand is skipped if its number of tiles exceeds 17 (for Taiwanese Mahjong) or 14 (for Chinese Standard Mahjong). Thus, 886,400 entries for suits and 64,200 entries for honors are actually used in the tables for Taiwanese Mahjong.

The analysis method to build lookup tables employs a greedy algorithm. First, we use the depth-first search (abbr. DFS) to determine the maximum number of melds $n_m^t$ that can be extracted from the pure hand $t$, and the remaining pure sub-hand $rt$. Next, if $n_m^t > 0$, it indicates that $rt$ has been analyzed. We can access the entry of $rt$ in the lookup table and assign $n_m^{rt} + 1$, $n_p^{rt}$ and $n_{is}^{rt}$ to $n_m^t$, $n_p^t$ and $n_{is}^t$, respectively. Otherwise, we use DFS to find the combination of $n_p^t$ and $n_{is}^t$ that can be extracted from $t$. We select the combination that maximizes $n_p^t + n_{is}^t$. For example, we prefer to divide the pure hand $t = \{C_2C_3C_3C_5\}$ into two incomplete sequences $\{C_2C_3, C_3C_5\}$ ($n_p^t + n_{is}^t = 2$), rather than one pair and two single tiles $\{C_2, C_3C_3, C_5\}$ ($n_p^t + n_{is}^t = 1$). If multiple combinations satisfy this condition, we select the one with the highest $n_p^t$.

Note that for honor tiles, correct values can be obtained by using DFS, but less efficiently. Since honor tiles cannot form sequences, we can directly count the number of identical tiles and then set its $n_m^t$ and $n_p^t$.

### 3.3 Problems in the Greedy Method

Building the lookup tables by the greedy method is efficient since the method reuses the results of pure sub-hands. However, simply summing the $n_m^t$, $n_p^t$, and $n_{is}^t$ of the four types and assigning the totals to $n_m$, $n_p$, and $n_{is}$ sometimes results in an incorrect deficiency number. This is illustrated by the following two cases.

The first case is called *hidden pairs*. We define a hidden pair as a pair that can be formed by breaking apart two incomplete sequences. For example, $\{C_3C_3\}$ is formed by breaking apart $\{C_2C_3\}$ and $\{C_3C_5\}$. Incorrectness occurs when a hand does not have a pair to serve as the head and the total number of incomplete sequences is greater than or equal to $n - n_m + 2$. This indicates that at least two of the identified incomplete sequences are redundant and not necessary to form a winning hand. If any two of the redundant incomplete sequences can generate a hidden pair, then we have the head, and there are still enough incomplete sequences to form a winning hand. Hence, the deficiency number obtained using the greedy method is further reduced by one.

The second case is called *pseudo-meld prioritization*. In the greedy method, we first extract the maximum number of melds. However, for some hands, only extracting three pseudo-melds can derive the correct deficiency number, and is better than extracting a meld by the greedy method. For example, given a hand with the tile arrangement $\{C_1C_3C_4C_4C_5C_7\}$, these tiles can form a meld and three single tiles $\{C_3C_4C_5, C_1, C_4, C_7\}$, or form three pseudo-melds $\{C_1C_3, C_4C_4, C_5C_7\}$. Using the values $n_m, n_p$ and $n_{is}$ calculated by the greedy method, if $n - n_m > n_p + n_{is}$, the current number of pseudo-melds, $n_p + n_{is}$, is not enough to complete all remaining melds $n - n_m$. In this case, forming a meld decreases the deficiency number by two, but forming three pseudo-melds may decrease the deficiency number by three. Hence, the deficiency number obtained using the greedy method is further reduced by one. In this case, we refer to these pseudo-melds as *hidden pseudo-melds*.

### 3.4 Handling Hidden Pairs and Pseudo-meld Prioritization

We design two methods to address hidden pairs and pseudo-meld prioritization. The methods are executed after the greedy method finishes.

In the first method, we determine whether a pure hand $t$ contains hidden pairs by the calculated values of $n_m^t$, $n_p^t$, and $n_{is}^t$. The process includes four steps. First, let $rt$ be the remaining pure hand after $n_m^t$ melds are extracted from $t$. Second, we extract the most pairs from $rt$, whose number is denoted by $n_{mp}^{rt}$, and let $rt2$ be the remaining pure hand after these pairs are extracted. Third, we use DFS to calculate the maximum number of incomplete sequences from $rt2$, denoted by $n_{is}^{rt2}$. Finally, a hidden pair exists if $n_{mp}^{rt} > n_p^t$ and $n_{is}^{rt2} < n_{is}^t$. The first condition means that at least one hidden pair is not counted in $n_p^t$ because it prevents $n_p^t + n_{is}^t$ from reaching the maximum value. The second condition means there are $n_{is}^t - n_{is}^{rt2}$ incomplete sequences that can be used to form a hidden pair. Let a boolean variable $hp$ denote whether there are any hidden pairs.

Note that using this method to generate a pair does not guarantee that the deficiency number will decrease. For example, there exists another pair that can serve as the head, or there are not enough incomplete sequences to form melds such that the winning hand is accomplished. Note that we only need to generate a pair to serve as the head.

In the second method, we determine whether a given pure hand $t$ has pseudo-meld prioritization. To extract the three hidden pseudo-melds, we check the following. First, we sequentially extract a pair $\{C_iC_i\}$ if it exists in $t$, where $i = 1, 2, \ldots, 9$, and let $rt$ denote the remaining pure hand. Second, since $rt$ is a sub-hand of $t$, it has been analyzed by the greedy method. We directly access the entry of $rt$ in the lookup table and obtain $n_m^{rt}$, $n_p^{rt}$, and $n_{is}^{rt}$. Third, three hidden pseudo-melds exist if $n_m^{rt} = n_m^t - 1$ and $(n_p^{rt} + 1) + n_{is}^{rt} \geq n_p^t + n_{is}^t + 3$. We set three separate variables to store $n_m^{t\,\prime} = n_m^{rt}$, $n_p^{t\,\prime} = n_p^{rt} + 1$, and $n_{is}^{t\,\prime} = n_{is}^{rt}$. Note that forming three hidden pseudo-melds does not guarantee that the deficiency number will decrease. For example, there are enough pseudo-melds to form melds such that the winning hand is accomplished. These variables will be used in the calculation of the deficiency number in Sect. 3.5.

Algorithm 1 shows the pseudo code to build the lookup table.

---

**Algorithm 1.** Analyze a pure hand

**Input:** $t$: a pure hand

$entry \leftarrow encode(t)$

$table[entry].n_m, rt \leftarrow$ ExtractMelds($t$) ▷ return # of melds & remaining pure hand

**if** $table[entry].n_m > 0$ **then**

  $entry2 \leftarrow encode(rt)$

  $table[entry].n_p, table[entry].n_{is} \leftarrow table[entry2].n_p, table[entry2].n_{is}$

**else**

  $table[entry].n_p, table[entry].n_{is} \leftarrow$ ExtractPairAndIncompleteSeq($rt$)

**end if**

$table[entry].hp \leftarrow$ FindHiddenPair($rt$) ▷ hidden pair

$table[entry].pp \leftarrow$ FindPseudomeldPrioritization($t$) ▷ pseudo-meld prioritization

---

### 3.5 Calculation of the Deficiency Number

After building the lookup table and completing the correction methods, we can calculate the deficiency number. The process includes the following steps and is shown in Algorithm 2.

First, sum the values of $n_m^t$, $n_p^t$, and $n_{is}^t$ for all types $t$ to obtain the overall $n_m$, $n_p$, and $n_{is}$, respectively. That is, $n_m = \sum_t n_m^t$, $n_p = \sum_t n_p^t$, and $n_{is} = \sum_t n_{is}^t$. Second, if there is no head, then we try to generate the head as follows. If

$n_{is} - (n - n_m) \geq 2$, there are at least two extra incomplete sequences. Then, we check whether there exists at least one hidden pair in any of the suits, that is, check whether $hp$ is true. If a hidden pair exists, $n_{is}$ is decreased by two and $n_p$ is increased by one. Third, if the number of pseudo-melds, $n_p + n_{is}$, is not enough to complete the remaining $n - n_m$ melds, then check each type to determine whether there has pseudo-meld prioritization to generate more pseudo-melds. Therefore, for a possible increase of $n_p + n_{is}$, we check ${n_m^t}'$, ${n_p^t}'$, ${n_{is}^t}'$ for each suit $t$ if available. If ${n_m^t}'$, ${n_p^t}'$, ${n_{is}^t}'$ are available, add ${n_m^t}' - n_m^t$, ${n_p^t}' - n_p^t$, and ${n_{is}^t}' - n_{is}^t$ to $n_m$, $n_p$, and $n_{is}$, respectively. Repeat this step until $n - n_m \leq n_p + n_{is}$ or all available ${n_m^t}'$, ${n_p^t}'$, ${n_{is}^t}'$ are used. Finally, we calculate the deficiency number according to Eq. 1.

**Algorithm 2.** Calculate the deficiency number

**Input:** $h$: the hand, $n$: the number of melds required
**Output:** $dfcy \geq 0$

$t_s[0:2], t_h \leftarrow \text{DivideHand}(h)$
$entry_s[0:2], entry_h \leftarrow encode(t_s[0:2]), encode(t_h)$
$n_m, n_p, n_{is} \leftarrow table[entry_h].n_m, table[entry_h].n_p, 0$
**for** each suit $i$ **do**
  $n_m \leftarrow n_m + table[entry_s[i]].n_m$
  $n_p \leftarrow n_p + table[entry_s[i]].n_p$
  $n_{is} \leftarrow n_{is} + table[entry_s[i]].n_{is}$
**end for**
**if** $n_{is} \geq n - n_m + 2$ **then**
  **for** each suit $i$ **do** ▷ hidden pair
    **if** $table[entry_s[i]].hp$ **then**
      $n_p, n_{is} \leftarrow n_p + 1, n_{is} - 2$
      **break**
    **end if**
  **end for**
**end if**
**for** each suit $i$ **do** ▷ pseudo-meld prioritization
  **if** $n_p + n_{is} < n - n_m$ **and** $table[entry_s[i]].pp \neq NULL$ **then**
    $n \leftarrow n + table[entry_s[i]].pp.{n_m^t}' - table[entry_s[i]].n_m^t$
    $n_p \leftarrow n_p + table[entry_s[i]].pp.{n_p^t}' - table[entry_s[i]].n_p^t$
    $n_{is} \leftarrow n_{is} + table[entry_s[i]].pp.{n_{is}^t}' - table[entry_s[i]].n_{is}^t$
  **end if**
**end for**
**if** $n_p > 0$ **then**
  $dfcy \leftarrow (n - n_m) \times 2 - \min(n - n_m, n_p - 1 + n_{is})$
**else**
  $dfcy \leftarrow (n - n_m) \times 2 + 1 - \min(n - n_m, n_{is})$
**end if**
**return** $dfcy$

## 4 Experiments

We conducted experiments by comparing our proposed method with the methods used in VeryLongCat [4], Botzone [9] and Wang [8]. VeryLongCat uses a lookup table, while Botzone and Wang do not. Using these programs, we calculated the deficiency number of hands and recorded the time taken for each calculation.

The experiments were done on a computer equipped with an AMD Ryzen 5 2600 6-Core processor and 32GB of memory.

### 4.1 The Datasets

The experiments were carried out with three datasets. The number of tiles in each hand is set to 14, as both Botzone and Wang were designed only for Chinese Standard Mahjong. Note that our method and VeryLongCat can be used for both 14 and 17 tiles in one hand. The first two datasets, Dataset_10k and Dataset_1M, contain 10,000 random hands and 1,000,000 random hands, respectively. The third dataset, Dataset_Pure, contains all combinations of a suit, amounting to a total of 118,800.[2] A dataset is classified into eight categories based on deficiency numbers, as shown in Table 1.

**Table 1.** The numbers of hands for different deficiency numbers

| Deficiency number | 0 | 1 | 2 | 3 | 4 | 5 | 6 | $\geq 7$ | Total |
|---|---|---|---|---|---|---|---|---|---|
| Dataset_10k | 0 | 3 | 202 | 1643 | 4130 | 2932 | 969 | 121 | 10000 |
| Dataset_1M | 0 | 611 | 19891 | 166334 | 408049 | 298575 | 94101 | 12439 | 1000000 |
| Dataset_Pure | 13259 | 91153 | 14298 | 90 | n.a. | n.a. | n.a. | n.a. | 118800 |

### 4.2 Time for Building and Loading Lookup Tables

We compare the time spent on building and loading the lookup tables in our method and VeryLongCat. The results are shown in Table 2. Although our method spent more time than VeryLongCat when building the tables, the time to load the tables from file to memory is close. When calculating the deficiency number, we do not need to spend time on building the tables again, but directly access them from the file.

[2] The total number of pure hands is the same as that mentioned in [8]. However, some pure hands were classified to different categories since the deficiency number for a quadruplet can reasonably be considered as either 1 or 2. For example, the *dfcy* of $\{C_1C_1C_1C_1\}$ is 1 in our method, although there are no more $C_1$ to form the winning hand.

**Table 2.** Comparison of the time spent on building and loading lookup tables.

| Methods | Build | Load |
|---|---|---|
| VeryLongCat | 0.24 s | 0.09 s |
| Our method | 10.24 s | 0.10 s |

### 4.3 Time for Calculating Deficiency Numbers

We compare the time spent on calculating deficiency numbers. In Botzone, we test the calculation of the deficiency numbers for the common winning hands mentioned in Subsect. 2.1, and skip the calculation for special winning hands in Chinese Standard Mahjong.

The results are shown in Table 3. The row for Wang is based on the average time mentioned in [8]. Our method performs better than all of the three programs. For VeryLongCat which also uses lookup tables, the speedup reaches 121.2 (= 4449.5/36.7) times in Dataset_1M and 81.19 times in Dataset_Pure. For Botzone and Wang that do not use lookup tables, the speedup is higher, reaching 6868.9 times and 8147.1 times in Dataset_1M, respectively, and 151652.97 times and 31854.98 times in Dataset_Pure, respectively. Note that the speedup tested in Dataset_10k is similar to that tested in Dataset_1M. The size of our lookup table is approximately 52 MB.

**Table 3.** Comparison on the time spent on calculating deficiency numbers

| Methods | Dataset_10k | Dataset_1M | Dataset_Pure |
|---|---|---|---|
| Botzone | 2656.75 ms | 252089.8 ms | 652107.8 ms [a] |
| Wang | 2990.00 ms | 299000.0 ms | 136976.4 ms |
| VeryLongCat | 44.13 ms | 4449.5 ms | 349.1 ms |
| Our method | 0.37 ms | 36.7 ms | 4.3 ms |

[a] An assert() in the code of Botzone was triggered when we tested with Dataset_Pure, so we disabled the assertion to complete the experiment. As a result, we cannot guarantee that Botzone functions correctly with this dataset.

## 5 Conclusion

In this paper, we propose a formula to calculate the deficiency number. To enhance efficiency, we design a greedy method to build lookup tables with a size of 52MB. Then, to handle two special cases, hidden pairs and pseudo-meld prioritization, we propose two methods to address them.

Our experimental results demonstrate that our method significantly accelerates the calculation of the deficiency number, achieving a speedup of 121.2

times compared to VeryLongCat and 6868.9 times compared to Botzone. Moreover, the concepts of handling hidden pairs and pseudo-meld prioritization offer an effective playing strategy for completing a winning hand, avoiding the need to wait for a single tile at the end.

**Acknowledgments.** This research was partially supported by National Science and Technology Council (NSTC) of Taiwan under grant numbers 113-2221-E-305-004-MY3, 113-2221-E-A49-127-. Thank Fong-Sheng Liao for the discussions that inspired us to design the methods.

## References

1. Mahjong competition rules. http://mahjong-europe.org/
2. Math of mahjong. http://www10.plala.or.jp/rascalhp/mjmath.htm/
3. Chen, J.C., Tang, S.C., Wu, IC.: Monte-Carlo simulation for mahjong. J. Inf. Sci. Eng. **38**(4) (2022)
4. Chuang, L.K., Wu, IC.: A Study of Mahjong Program Design. Master's thesis, National Chiao Tung University, Taiwan (2015)
5. van den Herik, H.J., Uiterwijk, J.W., van Rijswijck, J.: Games solved: now and in the future. Artif. Intell. **134**(1–2), 277–311 (2002)
6. Lin, C.H., Lin, C.C., Wu, IC.: The Study of Artificial Intelligence Program for Mahjong. Master's thesis, National Chiao Tung University, Taiwan (2010)
7. Lin, Z.H., Lin, S.S.: Using the Enhancement Strategy from Discarded-Tiles Information to Improve Mahjong Program. Master's thesis, National Taiwan Normal University, Taiwan (2021)
8. Wang, Q., Zhou, Y., Zhu, D., Li, Y.: A new approach to compute deficiency number of mahjong configurations. Entertainment Comput. **43**, 100509 (2022)
9. Zhou, H., Zhang, H., Zhou, Y., Wang, X., Li, W.: Botzone: an online multi-agent competitive platform for AI education. In: Proceedings of the 23rd Annual ACM Conference on Innovation and Technology in Computer Science Education, pp. 33–38 (2018)

# Player Models of Go Historical Master Figures

Kai-Sheng Huang, Yi-Yun Lee, Tong-Yuan Tu, and Shi-Jim Yen(✉)

National Dong Hwa University, Hualien, Taiwan
411021251@gms.ndhu.edu.tw, sjyen@mail.ndhu.edu.tw

**Abstract.** The objective of this research is to enable machines to simulate the gameplay of specific Go players and to obtain additional information during matches with opponents through AI recognition of Go move styles. To achieve this, two models were trained separately: a specific move policy model and a playing style recognition model. The specific player move policy model is designed to mimic the playing moves of a particular Go player. Since the game records of specific players usually consist of only a few hundred to a few thousand games, which is insufficient for training directly, we used transfer learning to train this model to solve this problem. Meanwhile, the playing style recognition model can identify the style of each move, categorizing it as fighting, balanced, or field type. We included the surrounding board conditions of the move in a $3 \times 3$ to $7 \times 7$ area as a feature map, achieving an accuracy of 83.2%. Then, these two models are combined to create an interface that allows players to choose and play against a specific Go player. Finally, this research recreates the style of historical Go masters, allowing current users to play Go against these historical figures.

**Keywords:** Deep learning · Go · historical figures · playing style · move policy

## 1 Introduction

Go is extremely complex and is even considered the most complex of all board games. This complexity comes from the size of the board, the possibilities created by each move, and the variety of variations in the game. The board has a $19 \times 19$ grid structure. Moves can be made at each intersection, and each move will greatly affect the progress of the entire game, making the situation of Go rich and varied. Therefore, in past research, it was almost impossible to use brute force search methods to handle Go [1–3]. This research will use deep learning methods to establish a Go player model and a Go playing style recognition model. We hope to use the training model to imitate the Go styles of different historical masters, so that players can freely choose to play against different opponents, improve their own skills, and increase the fun of the game.

This paper also studies the style and characteristics of a specific Go player. We use the results of this research to build a player model, play with a specific player and extend the game record that the player has not played before, so as to know the player's characteristics. Thought patterns and behaviors. At the same time, by establishing a playing style recognition model (including fighting, balance, and field type), we can

© The Author(s), under exclusive license to Springer Nature Singapore Pte Ltd. 2025
W.-T. Chu et al. (Eds.): TAAI 2024, CCIS 2414, pp. 178–189, 2025.
https://doi.org/10.1007/978-981-96-4589-3_13

display the opponent's playing style, so that players can understand whether the opponent will usually play fight, balance, or field moves in this board state. The user can even understand whether his moves are offensive or defensive, thus improving his learning effect.

Our team ranked sixth in the country in the AI Cup Go move imitation (*move policy*) and playing style recognition [4]. Based on this result, this research established a feature map and model that meet the characteristics required for Go playing style, and successfully improved the accuracy of the playing style recognition model with 82% accuracy. And a move policy model with a one-dan Go rank was trained, with an accuracy rate of 54%. In this research, we will continue to use the playing style recognition model and adjust the move policy model to the player model to conduct this research. However, the records left by historical master Go players in public are only a few thousand records. How to achieve a certain accuracy in the model of moves and styles of specific Go players in the absence of insufficient data is also an issue explored in this study.

## 2 Related Works

Deep learning has become the mainstream for developing computer Go. CNN (Convolutional Neural Networks) and ResNet (Residual Networks) are commonly used architectures and can be applied to feature extraction and strategy networks. Feature extraction is to extract spatial features from grid-like data such as the Go board, such as the shape and positional relationship of Go stones. These features are crucial for evaluating positions and predicting the next move. The move policy network can predict the next move position. By analyzing the characteristics on the board, the policy network can output the probability distribution of each position to guide the AI to make decisions [5–14].

Maddison et al. (2015) introduced a groundbreaking approach to Go move evaluation using deep convolutional neural networks (DCNNs). Their model, trained on a large dataset of professional games, achieved a remarkable 55% accuracy in predicting expert moves, comparable to a 6-dan human player. Without any search, it outperformed the traditional program GnuGo and matched the performance of a state-of-the-art Monte Carlo Tree Search. This work demonstrated the potential of deep learning in handling Go's complexity and laid a crucial foundation for the development of AlphaGo, which later achieved a historic victory against a world champion [7].

Cazenave (2016) investigates the application of ResNets, a deep learning architecture known for its success in image recognition, to the challenging domain of computer Go. The author proposes using ResNets to train a policy network for Go, which predicts the next move given the current board state [8]. AlphaGo Zero's deep learning framework centers around a single, powerful CNN with residual connections. The network's architecture leverages convolutional layers to capture spatial patterns on the Go board, and residual connections enable efficient training of deeper networks. The entire system is trained end-to-end through self-play and reinforcement learning, allowing it to learn directly from experience without relying on human data or expert knowledge [9].

Katago's deep learning framework is built on a CNN architecture. The architecture incorporates techniques like residual connections and batch normalization to enhance training efficiency and performance. Notably, Katago's network is trained on a massive dataset of self-play games using reinforcement learning, enabling it to learn powerful strategies and patterns without relying on human knowledge or expert data [10].

## 3 Move Policy Model

The source of the data set is game records from Japan's NIHON KIIN's competition website and Internet collection. Set each move of the player to be imitated as *y*, and use the board before the current move as *x*, and let the model learn where to place this board. Go is a two-dimensional game board. By converting the two-dimensional board into one dimension, 19×19 (361) classification problems are obtained. Table 1 gives the features of the move policy model.

**Table 1.** Features of the move policy model

| No. | features |
|---|---|
| 0 | Our moves |
| 1 | Opponent's moves |
| 2–5 | Liberties of our moves (1, 2, 3, >= 4) |
| 6–9 | Liberties of opponent's moves (1, 2, 3, >= 4) |
| 10 | Empty location |
| 11–18 | Last eight moves |

The model architecture is Resnet v2 [6]. There are two basic blocks that stack this model. One is Convolution Block: Bottleneck with Projection Shortcut, and the other is Identity Block: Bottleneck with Identity Shortcut. The model architecture diagram is as the left of Fig. 1. The original ResNet was designed to handle image classification problems, where the role of the pooling layer is to reduce the number of parameters and extract more important features. However, in the case of Go, the board only contains 19×19 information. If pooling is applied to the game board, it may cause distortion of the game board information. Therefore, we decided to remove the pooling layer of the original ResNet structure.

The model of the original Resnet v2 is a model built for image recognition, and the number of filters in the original Resnet gradually increases according to the depth, because the deeper the model for identifying images, the more filters are needed to find features. For example, deep filters represent comparisons. Abstract patterns (such as cats, dogs), and shallow filters represent more basic patterns (colors, etc.), but for Go, there is no need to continuously increase the number of filters (according to tests, the accuracy has no impact, but adding a lot of training time), and the number of shallow filters in the original version was set to 64, which was not enough to cope with the complexity of Go. According to the test, changing the number of shallow filters to 256 can increase the accuracy.

Considering that there are few game records of specific players, using these data alone to train the model may lead to insufficient data, thereby affecting the generalization

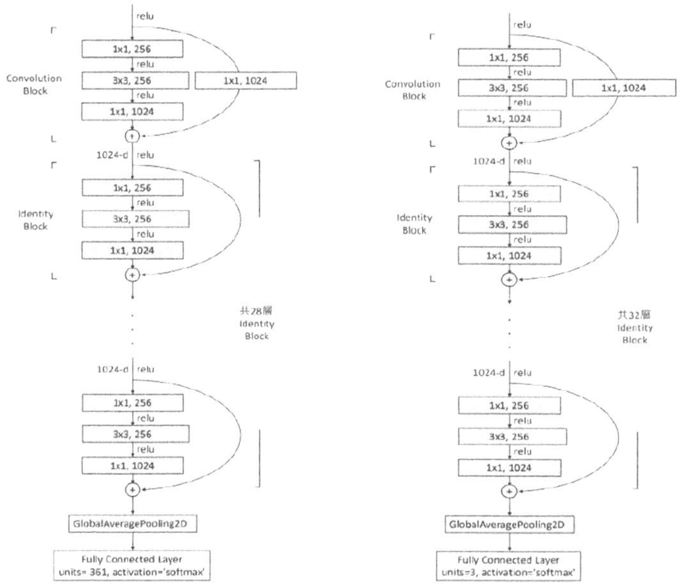


**Fig. 1.** The architecture of the move policy (left) and playing style recognition (right) model.

ability of the model. Therefore, we adopted the transfer learning method, first using a large number of data sets equivalent to the specific player's strength to train the basic model, and then using the specific player's game records for transfer learning to develop it into a specific player model. Through transfer learning, we can let the model focus on learning the playing style of a specific player, while also saving training time. In addition, we will also use data augmentation to amplify a single player's game record to eight times the original data to solve the problem of insufficient data sets.

This research develops an augmentation method inspired by the self-training concept. The specific process is shown in Fig. 2. First, we train a general model (Model 0) whose Go strength meet specific requirements. Then, we use the specific player's game records to fine-tune it and optimize the model to obtain an optimized model for that player.

We then use this model (Model 1) to predict positions $x$ that have similar strengths but that the model has not yet seen. Based on the predicted actions $y$, we merge $x$ and $y$ to generate a new data set. This new data set is merged with the original player-specific records and trained again using Model 0. Our goal is to test whether this method can produce superior results than the original method.

# 4 Playing Style Recognition Model

The playing style dataset was sourced from the 2023 AI Cup [15]. Each move in the dataset was labeled by two Go teachers independently. If both teachers assigned the same playing style label to a move, that move and its label were included in the final dataset. A total of 26,000 moves were labeled, each categorized as one of three playing styles: fighting, balanced, or field-oriented.

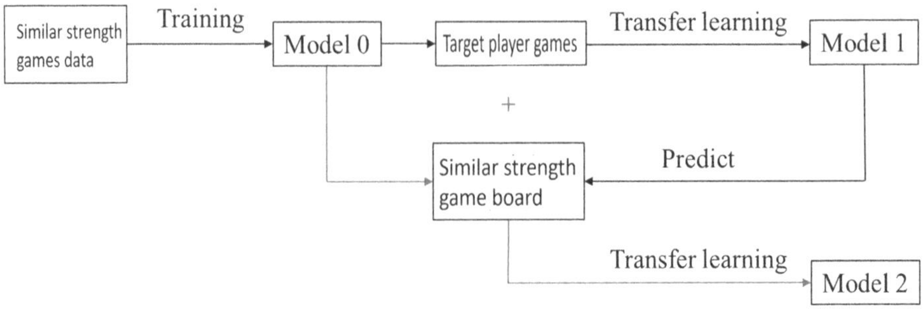


**Fig. 2.** Flowchart of the training process for the specific Go player model.

Because the training set style only has more than 26,000 labeled moves, which may cause the model to underfitting, so we rotated and mirrored the board to 8 times the original size (original board, rotated 90°, rotated 180°, rotate 270°, mirror horizontally, mirror horizontally and then rotate 90° counterclockwise, mirror vertically, mirror vertically and then rotate 90° counterclockwise). Color flipping (conversion of Black and White) can amplify the original 8-fold data to 16-fold. However, because the features are extracted separately by players and opponents, the same features will be obtained after color flipping, so the data amplification can only reach 8 times.

We believe that playing style is often judged by the condition of the board around the moves. Therefore, we will add 3×3, 5×5, and 7×7 boards around the hand as features. When judging the board situation, we extracted the liberties number of each stone on the board (one liberty, two liberties, three liberties, four or more liberties). If there is a stone with zero liberty, it means that the stone at this position has been captured, we will update the board situation in real time so that the model can better understand the situation of the board. The features are as in Table 2. The model framework is similar to that of move policy as in the right of Fig. 1. There are 32 Identity Block. The units of the Fully Connected Layer are 3.

**Table 2.** The features for the playing style model.

| No. | Features |
|---|---|
| 0 | Our moves |
| 1 | opponent's moves |
| 2–5 | Liberties of our moves (1, 2, 3, >= 4) |
| 6–9 | Liberties of opponent's moves (1, 2, 3, >= 4) |
| 10 | Empty location |
| 11–18 | Last eight moves |
| 19–21 | 7×7 board around the last move (ours, opponent's, empty) |
| 22–24 | 5×5 board around the last move (ours, opponent's, empty) |
| 25–27 | 3×3 board around the last move (ours, opponent's, empty) |

# 5 Experimental Results

## 5.1 Move Policy Model with Transfer Learning

This section analyzes and discusses the move policy models developed for kyu, dan, and professional Go players. The study investigates the impact of transfer learning across these skill levels. Twenty models were trained for each of the kyu and dan levels, using data from 20 ten-kyu and 20 one-dan players, respectively. Additionally, 18 models were trained for professional players, utilizing data from 18 professionals, including several renowned Go masters.

Figure 3 compares the accuracy of kyu move policy models. The green bars represent original models trained using each player's own game records (each kyu player has approximately 3,000 to 5,000 game records), while the blue bars represent models generated through the transfer learning method. The results show that the accuracy improved by at least 3.88% and up to 10.91%, with an average improvement of 6.44%. For the dan move policy models' results shown in Fig. 4, excluding "dansora" player (with 25,450 game records), the dataset sizes range from 1,000 to 2,700. The minimum improvement in accuracy was 2.68%, the maximum was 8.90%, and the average improvement was 5.37%. Based on these results, we can infer that for dan and kyu player models with over 1,000 game records in their datasets, an improvement in accuracy can generally be observed.

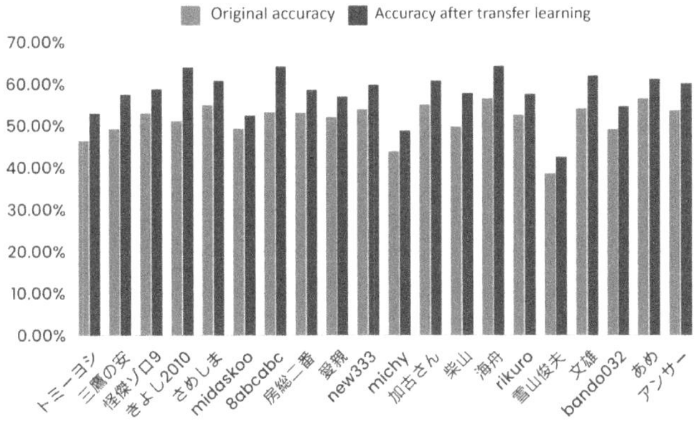


**Fig. 3.** Comparison of the accuracy of kyu move policy models

For professional players (Fig. 5), the dataset sizes range from 100 to 700 games. 阪田栄男 (363 games) and 劉昌赫 (443 games) showed significant improvements of 8.75% and 7.30%, respectively, which are notably higher compared to other professional players.

Based on the experimental results mentioned above, we observed that when there's a sufficient number of game records, the accuracy of specific player models can generally be improved. However, in the case of professional players with only a few hundred game records, transfer learning didn't lead to a significant improvement in accuracy. Despite this, two professional players did show a notable increase in accuracy after applying

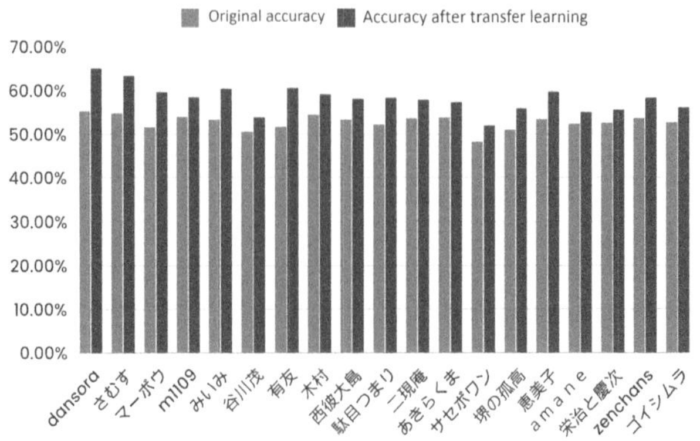


**Fig. 4.** Comparison of the accuracy of dan move policy models

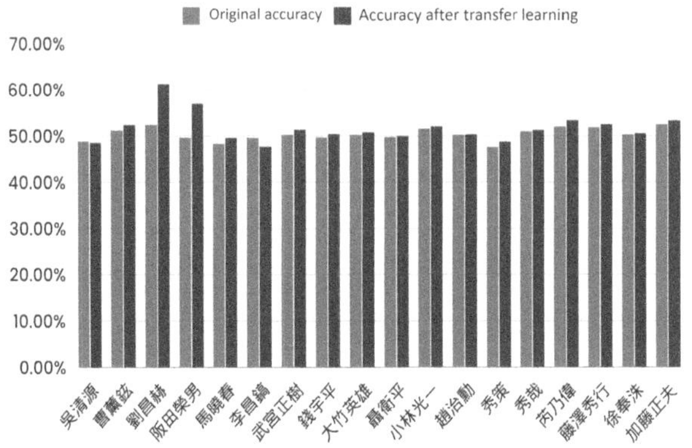


**Fig. 5.** Comparison of the accuracy of professional players move policy models

transfer learning. Therefore, we wanted to ascertain whether these results were due to biases caused by insufficient dataset size.

To further confirm this, we utilized three different random seeds to re-partition the training and validation sets for cross-validation. According to the results in Table 3 and Table 4, we can conclude that even with different validation set partitioning methods, the accuracy of these two players still showed a significant improvement compared to other professional players. Based on these findings, we speculate that if a player's playing style is relatively consistent, even with a smaller dataset, using transfer learning can still lead to an improvement in accuracy.

## 5.2 Move Policy Model with Augmentation

In this section, we will analyze and discuss the augmentation in Fig. 2. As we are uncertain about the optimal amount of new data to incorporate for the best results, we will first conduct tests using the "samusu" (さむす) player model. We will attempt to add 0.5, 1, 2, and 3 times the original training set size to the model training. From Table 5,

**Table 3.** 劉昌赫

| random seed | Original accuracy | After transfer learning | improvement |
|---|---|---|---|
| 300 | 52.38% | 61.13% | 8.75% |
| 400 | 52.82% | 60.60% | 7.78% |
| 500 | 52.24% | 64.55% | 12.31% |

**Table 4.** 坂田栄男

| random seed | Original accuracy | After transfer learning | improvement |
|---|---|---|---|
| 300 | 49.61% | 56.91% | 7.30% |
| 400 | 50.78% | 56.97% | 6.19% |
| 500 | 49.41% | 53.73% | 4.32% |

we can observe that the improvement across all four models is not significant, but the models with 1 times and 2 times additional data show relatively larger improvements compared to the other two cases. Considering the time cost of training, we will similarly mix 1 times the original training set size into the original dataset for other player models.

After testing, Table 6 shows that the accuracy after augmentation has improved, but the improvement is not substantial. We speculate that this method might have limited effectiveness for highly complex problems like Go.

**Table 5.** さむす models result

| Rate | Original accuracy | Use augmentation | Improvement |
|---|---|---|---|
| 0.5 | 63.33% | 63.64% | 0.31% |
| 1 | 63.33% | 63.78% | 0.45% |
| 2 | 63.33% | 63.74% | 0.41% |
| 3 | 63.33% | 63.49% | 0.16% |

**Table 6.** Augmentation experiment

| Player | Original accuracy | Use augmentation | Improvement |
|---|---|---|---|
| dansora | 65.05% | 65.35% | 0.30% |
| さむす | 63.33% | 63.78% | 0.45% |
| マーボウ | 59.50% | 60.20% | 0.70% |

### 5.3 Playing Style Experiment

Tables 7, 8 and 9 are the experimental results of the playing style models for three Go master players. Only predictions with a probability higher than 0.9 will be added to the following table. Playstyle 1 represents a fighting style; Playstyle 2 represents a balanced style; Playstyle 3 represents a field style.

We can observe that Playstyle 1 (fighting style) has a high proportion for all three players. This is because during battles, there's often only one optimal move, leaving the player no choice but to make a fighting move. Therefore, on average, fighting-style moves tend to be more frequent. Overall, Sakata Eio (坂田栄男) leans towards a fighting style, Kobayashi Koichi (小林光一) has more field-oriented moves, and Wu Qingyuan (呉清源) is more balanced, which aligns with the general understanding of these master players in Go literature.

**Table 7.** 呉清源 playing style analysis

| | Player | Playstyle 1 | Playstyle 2 | Playstyle 3 | |
|---|---|---|---|---|---|
| Black | 呉清源 | Sum: 3542 | Sum: 2157 | Sum: 1193 | Total: 6892 |
| | | Percentage: 51.39% | Percentage: 31.30% | Percentage: 17.31% | |
| | | Average: 4.83 | Average: 2.94 | Average: 1.63 | |
| White | | Sum: 4759 | Sum: 2936 | Sum: 1542 | Total: 9237 |
| | | Percentage: 51.52% | Percentage: 31.79% | Percentage: 16.69% | |
| | | Average: 6.48 | Average: 4.00 | Average: 2.10 | |

**Table 8.** 小林光一 playing style analysis

| | Player | Playstyle 1 | Playstyle 2 | Playstyle 3 | |
|---|---|---|---|---|---|
| Black | 小林光一 | Sum: 1198 | Sum: 807 | Sum: 472 | Total: 2477 |
| | | Percentage: 48.36% | Percentage: 32.58% | Percentage: 19.06% | |
| | | Average: 5.26 | Average: 3.55 | Average: 2.07 | |
| White | | Sum: 1166 | Sum: 880 | Sum: 500 | Total: 2546 |
| | | Percentage: 45.80% | Percentage: 34.56% | Percentage: 19.64% | |
| | | Average: 5.12 | Average: 3.87 | Average: 2.20 | |

**Table 9.** 表9. 坂田栄男 playing style analysis

| | Player | Playstyle 1 | Playstyle 2 | Playstyle 3 | |
|---|---|---|---|---|---|
| Black | 坂田栄男 | Sum: 2568 | Sum: 1355 | Sum: 812 | Total: 4735 |
| | | Percentage: 54.23% | Percentage: 28.62% | Percentage: 17.15% | |
| | | Average: 6.43 | Average: 3.39 | Average: 2.03 | |
| White | | Sum: 2278 | Sum: 1315 | Sum: 730 | Total: 4323 |
| | | Percentage: 52.69% | Percentage: 30.42% | Percentage: 16.89% | |
| | | Average: 5.71 | Average: 3.29 | Average: 1.83 | |

## 6 User Interface for the Player Models

We develop a Go engine that complies with the Go Text Protocol and support the use of GTP-enabled Go interfaces such as Sabaki. In order to provide a more convenient user experience, we have designed the opponent selection part into a graphical interface, allowing users to select opponents by clicking on the screen. Before the game starts, the system will display the left side of Fig. 6, which contains three options for opponent positions, divided into kyu level, dan level and professional level. Then, according to the user's selection, a list of opponents matching the rank will be displayed, as shown on the right side of Fig. 6. This list will display the names of qualified players, and the user can select a Go player from this list as an opponent for the game.

During the playing process, the window in the lower right corner will provide the following five pieces of information (Fig. 7): the current opponent, the five most probable moves as predicted by the model, the style classification of the most recent moves for both black and white, the cumulative frequency of each style employed by both players, and a button to facilitate the selection of an alternative opponent.

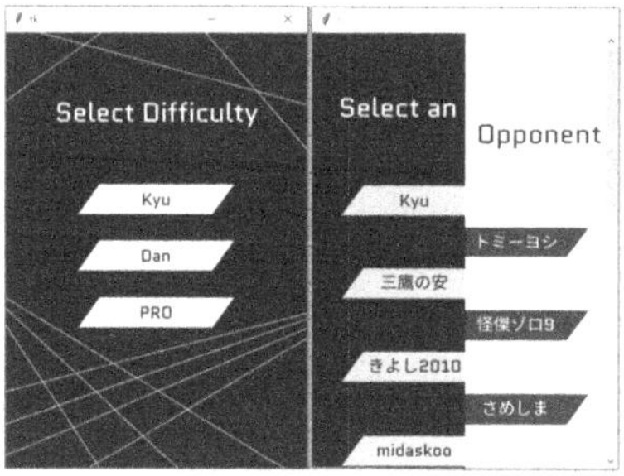


**Fig. 6.** The menu

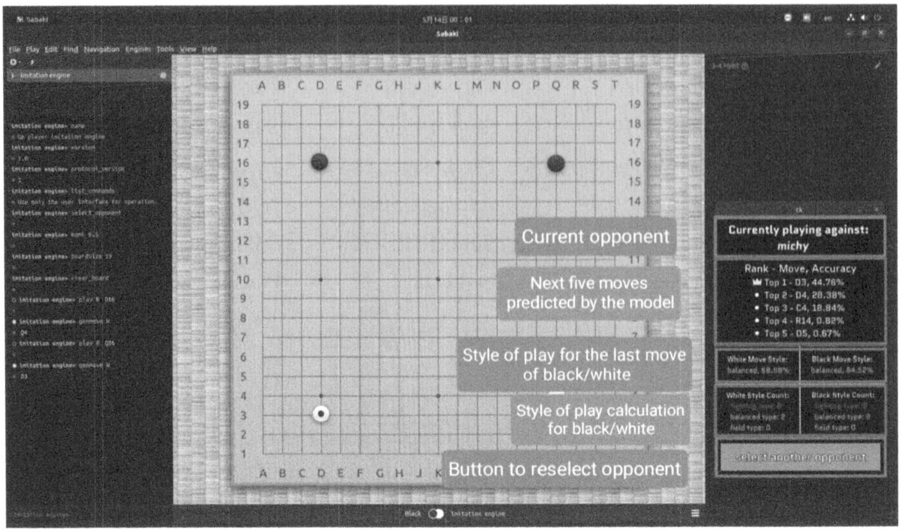


**Fig. 7.** User interface

# 7 Conclusion and Future Works

This study trained a move policy model and a playing style recognition model, which can imitate the moves of a specific Go player and identify whether the playing style of the move is offensive, defensive or balanced. In terms of the playing style recognition model, we tested a variety of feature map combinations. It was observed that adding $7\times 7$ around the move had the best effect, so we finally decided to add the board state within the surrounding $7\times 7$, and the model accuracy reached 83%.

As for the move policy model, after training a large number of game records with similar strength to a specific player to establish a basic model, the specific player's game records are then used for transfer learning. This method significantly improved the accuracy of the kyu level and dan level models, but due to the small data set, there was no significant improvement in the professional-level model. Finally, we tried augmentation, but the progress was limited.

In view of the problem that the professional history master imitation model cannot achieve significant progress due to too few data sets, in the future, we can try to merge the game records of professional players with similar playing styles and increase the amount of training set data to solve the problem of insufficient game records of a single Go player. We hope to achieve better results.

**Acknowledgments.** The authors would like to thank anonymous referees for their valuable comments in improving the overall quality of this paper. This work was supported in part by the National Science and Technology Council under the contract NSC 113-2813-C-259-008-E, NSC 113-2221-E-259-018-MY3, NSC 110-2221-E-259-007-MY3.

**Disclosure of Interests.** The authors declare that they have no known competing financial interests or personal relationships that could have appeared to influence the work reported in this paper.

## References


1. Silver, D., et al.: Mastering the game of Go with deep neural networks and tree search. Nature **529**(7587), 484–489 (2016)
2. Rimmel, A., Teytaud, O., Lee, C.S., Yen, S.J., Wang, M.H., Tsai, S.R.: Current Frontiers in Computer Go. IEEE Transactions on Computational Intelligence and AI in Games **2**(4), 229–238 (2010)
3. Lee, C.-S., et al.: Human vs. computer go: review and prospect. IEEE Computational Intelligence Magazine **11**(3), 13–24 (2016)
4. Huang, K.-S., Lee, Y.-Y.: AI-CUP-Tram_3839, 6$^{th}$, Dec., 2023. Github: yiyunrin/ AI-CUP-Team_3839
5. Clark, C., Storkey, A.: Playing Go without Game Tree Search using Convolutional Neural Networks. arXiv preprint arXiv:1907.04658 (2019)
6. He, K., Zhang, X., Ren, S., Sun, J.: Deep residual learning for image recognition. Proceedings of the IEEE Conference on Computer Vision and Pattern Recognition (CVPR), pp. 770–778 (2016)
7. Maddison, C.J., Huang, A., Sutskever, I., Silver, D.: Move Evaluation in Go using Deep Convolutional Neural Networks. arXiv preprint arXiv:1412.6564 (2015)
8. Cazenave, T.: Residual networks for computer Go. IEEE Transactions on Games **9**(3), 226–233 (2016)
9. Silver, D., Schrittwieser, J., Simonyan, K., et al.: Mastering the game of Go without human knowledge. Nature **550**, 354–359 (2017)
10. Wu, D.J.: Accelerating Self-Play Learning in Go. ArXiv abs/1902.10565 (2019)
11. Soemers, D.J.N.J., Mella, V., Piette, E., Stephenson, M., Browne, C., Teytaud, O.: Transfer of Fully Convolutional Policy-Value Networks between Games and Game Variants. arXiv preprint arXiv:2102.12375 (2021)
12. Zhu, Z., Lin, K., Jain, A.K., Zhou, J.: Transfer Learning in Deep Reinforcement Learning: A Survey. arXiv preprint arXiv:2009.07888 (2023)
13. Jie, W.-Z.: Investigating Reinforcement Learning and Transfer Learning in Hex Game (2023). https://hdl.handle.net/11296/hgh735
14. Pumperla, M., Ferguson, K.: Deep learning and the game of Go. Manning Publications (2019)
15. AI CUP. Go Strength Imitation and Go Style Recognition Competition (2023). https://tbrain.trendmicro.com.tw/Competitions/Details/29

# Machine Learning and Applications

# An Intrusion Detection System for Heterogeneous OT-Enabled Networks Using Hybrid Deep Learning Model

Chia-Mei Chen[1(✉)], Zheng-Xun Cai[1], Gu-hsin Lai[2], and Ya-Hui Ou[3]

[1] National Sun Yat-sen University, Kaohsiung, Taiwan
a84888888@ids.mis.nsysu.edu.tw
[2] Taiwan Police College, Taipei, Taiwan
[3] National Penghu University of Science and Technology, Penghu, Taiwan

**Abstract.** The Industrial Internet of Things (IIoT) is crucial for smart manufacturing and automation but is highly vulnerable to cyber-attacks due to inadequate security mechanisms and diverse communication protocols. Attackers can exploit weak IIoT devices to infiltrate entire networks, posing significant challenges in detecting malicious traffic within heterogeneous IIoT environments.

This study introduces a hybrid model, composed of BERT and LSTM network for anomaly detection in IIoT networks. Given that the effectiveness of such models depends on the quality of the training data, this research investigates the effects of data imbalance and granularity, offering solutions to these issues.

Experimental results show that the proposed method effectively identifies malicious traffic and outperforms other reference models in detection efficiency.

**Keywords:** Industrial Internet of Things · hybrid deep learning · industrial Control System

## 1 First Section

Information technologies have drastically improved industrial development across various domains, including Operation Technology (OT) networks. Particularly, Industry 4.0 has enhanced product quality and streamlined the manufacturing process by the implementation of the Industrial Internet of Things (IIoTs), expediting manufacturing processes and the reduction of operational costs. That the IIoT market is anticipated to attain a value of $197 billion by 2023, with an annual growth rate of 7.5% [1].

IIoT devices were initially designed for the isolated networks, which usually lacks security measures against cybercriminals; however, these devices are now integrated with IT networks. Despite this interconnectivity, many IIoT devices are constrained by computational limitations that hinder their ability to maintain robust and comprehensive defensive mechanisms [2]. Additionally, the majority of OT traffic is transmitted in plaintext, which, while advantageous for operational efficiency, exposes the network to vulnerabilities that can be exploited by malicious actors for cyberattacks. Consequently,

© The Author(s), under exclusive license to Springer Nature Singapore Pte Ltd. 2025
W.-T. Chu et al. (Eds.): TAAI 2024, CCIS 2414, pp. 193–206, 2025.
https://doi.org/10.1007/978-981-96-4589-3_14

OT networks have become primary targets for cyberattacks due to their critical role in business operations and national security.

Cyberattacks on OT networks have led to substantial damage and financial losses. The Stuxnet attack is one of the most infamous incidents and compromised over two hundred devices in nuclear power plants, which severely disrupted the operation of IIoT devices. The Stuxnet attack necessitates a complete shutdown of the plants to prevent further nuclear disasters. Another cyberattacks affected the largest oil pipeline supply system, and this incident resulted in a severe oil shortage along the east coast of the United States [1]. As the deployment of IIoT devices in critical infrastructures increases, the threat of OT cyberattacks has become a global concern. The Cybersecurity and Infrastructure Security Agency has issued warnings regarding the capability of cyber actors to compromise critical infrastructure across both IT and OT networks [3].

Industrial control systems (ICS) exposed to the internet are extremely susceptible to cyberattacks, with at least one-third of such systems having been compromised. The risk scenario for Operational Technology (OT) networks is further worsened by the proliferation of IIoT devices. Consequently, it is significant to develop robust defense mechanisms to protect IIoT devices from cyber threats.

Traditional intrusion detection systems (IDS) designed for IT networks are inadequate for OT environments due to fundamental differences in traffic patterns. IIoT devices typically generate regular communication as they execute programmed tasks, whereas traffic in IT networks may include malicious botnet activities reporting to command-and-control servers. These discrepancies in traffic patterns between IT and OT networks undermine the efficacy of conventional IDS in detecting anomalies.

In IT networks, hosts intercommunicate among nodes with a uniform set of network protocols. In contrast, OT environments are characterized by a diverse spectrum of communication protocols, as IIoT devices from different manufacturers may employ varying protocols to engage data exchange with other devices. In addition, IT hosts generally have sufficient computational resources to support fully-fledged defense mechanisms. In contrast, IIoT devices often have limited computing power and storage, which constrains their ability to implement robust security measures. The constraints on resources, coupled with the heterogeneity of devices and the extensive real-time data generated by IIoT systems, contribute to the dynamic nature of OT networks, rendering existing security solutions insufficient for effective threat detection in these environments [5].

Machine learning has witnessed significant advancements over recent decades, with several techniques proving effective for analyzing time-series data. Recurrent Neural Networks (RNNs) and their enhanced variant, Long Short-Term Memory (LSTM) networks, are employed in previous studies for malicious traffic classification. The literature states that LSTM networks are particularly bespoke for anomaly detection. However, existing research seldom explored the integration of LSTM with other DL techniques to address the challenge posed by limited minority samples.

To address the above challenges, this study applies three deep learning techniques to devise a novel anomaly detection method for heterogeneous IIoT environments. The proposed solution develops two-stage classification models to identify anomalies in various communication protocols in IIoT networks as well as improve detection performance.

The LSTM architecture is adopted for attack detection as it learns sequences of time-series events and is an optimal approach in the cybersecurity domain. To overcome the data imbalance issue, this study applied the transfer learning technique which applies a pre-trained model on another ML task. The state-of-the-art pre-trained model BERT (Bidirectional Encoder Representations from Transformers) is adopted to embed key traffic features from a small amount of training data. Furthermore, this study employs the genetic algorithm (GA) to automatically find an optimal hyperparameter setting of the proposed ML models. The main contributions of this work are summarized below.

- This work devises a two-stage classification approach to improve the detection performance in heterogeneous IIoT networks, where the first stage categorizes the communication protocol and the second stage identifies anomalies of the given protocol.
- This work employs a transfer learning approach to resolve the data imbalance issue and adopts the pre-trained model BERT to encode features where similar features are close together and different ones have large discrepancies.
- This work applies GA to construct optimal DL models for the proposed solution.
- Extensive experiments are conducted to evaluate the proposed solution on multiple real-world datasets. The results demonstrate that the proposed solution with the combined DL techniques outperforms the baseline approaches.

The remainder of this article is organized as follows. Section 2 briefly reviews the previous related research. Section 3 presents the proposed detection method, followed by the performance evaluation in Sect. 4. The last section draws the conclusion remark and the future directions of this study.

## 2 Related Work

Intrusion detection approaches can be categorized into two primary classes: signature-based detection and anomaly detection. Signatures define patterns corresponding to known attacks and anomaly detection identifies suspicious activities based on a detection model learned from the historical data. The literature review [1, 2] highlighted the better effectiveness and fewer false positives of DL techniques for anomaly detection when compared to conventional ML approaches. The LSTM architecture is an ideal solution in the security domain as it can deal with time series data. Furthermore, most conventional ML techniques are not inherently efficient and scalable enough to manage IoT data and thus require considerable adjustments [3].

Hindy et al. [4, 5] presented an ML-based detection model and evaluated several traditional ML techniques. Their evaluation concluded that the robustness of the detection model improves as the training data contains more attack samples. Additionally, Angseus and Ekbom [6] observed the static nature of OT networks since IIoT devices are programmed to perform specific tasks periodically. They investigated Modbus traffic and designed an anomaly score of a network flow regarding the discrepancies with the bytes per packet and the inter-arrival time of a flow record relative to the historical flow records.

Liu et al. [5] highlighted the issue that edge device failures have a significant impact on the production of industrial goods on IIoT networks. They proposed an anomaly detection framework based on the federated learning technique to enable decentralized edge devices to collaboratively train an anomaly detection model. Their evaluation demonstrated that the LSTM model can accurately detect anomalies. Based on the observation that advanced persistent threat (APT) attacks from IT to OT networks consist of several attack stages, Yu et al. [7] applied BERT to detect the attack sequences. They defined the actions of each attack stage and assumed that the evidence of each attack stage can be captured, which might not be applicable in real-world scenarios. In order to encode features with BERT, the training data requires manually labeling the characteristic information of the APT attack and the APT category to which the attack belongs.

Guo and Shen [8] presented a real-time monitoring system for IIoT environments. They applied the Bayesian algorithm to examine the quantities of vibration signals and LSTM to detect anomalies. Their anomalies are based on the logic of the P-F curve, where P represents a behavior profile of a device in normal operations and F in anomalies. Low-level signals from IIoT devices were collected so that point anomalies with sharp increases or decreases can be identified. Wu et al. [9] reviewed graphic neural networks on IIoT anomaly detection and illustrated three case studies in smart transportation, smart energy, and smart factory, respectively.

Sankaran and Kim [10] proposed an IIoT cloud framework, where IIoT data points are stored and transmitted securely in the cloud, and adopted a CNN-based classification model to detect outliers (anomalies) in IIoTs. Yazdinejad et al. [11] combined the LSTM and AE (Auto-Encoder) algorithms to identify suspicious activities in IIoT networks, where LSTM recognizes normal patterns and AE reduces feature dimension. Their evaluation demonstrated that LSTM outperforms conventional ML classifiers.

Most studies on anomaly detection applied supervised learning techniques, but few employed unsupervised learning techniques. Hore and Wakde [12] adopted the clustering technique to group sensed data under different working circumstances and then evaluated if new inspections fall into any of these clusters. The evaluation was conducted in a simulated network of two nodes. Huang et al. [13] presented an unsupervised anomaly detection framework for IIoT which applies an AE to detect anomalies through the reconstruction error.

Previous work has presented ML-based approaches to feature selection in order to improve the model performance. Park and Lee [14] proposed a process by applying a data envelopment analysis (DEA) model to identify key features for anomaly detection, where the process was borrowed from game bot detection. The DEA assesses the effectiveness of a system by measuring the ratio of the weighted sum of the outputs to that of the inputs. The evaluation of the effectiveness of the selected features is conducted with several conventional classification models, where random forest yields the best performance.

Neural Network (NN) has become one of the most adopted machine learning algorithms in recent years, and much research procured the effectual detection model with neural networks. Detection model applied Recurrent Neural Network (RNN) can represent sequences of communications on the network and discover anomalous traffic flows [15]. Prasse et al. [16] developed an LSTM-based detection model to unearth potential threats in HTTPS network flows and extracted features from domain name by natural language model. The experiments prove the effectiveness of the LSTM classification model and evince their superiority over the model trained with Random Forest. Research [17] attempted to accomplish significant enhancement in their detection model via implementation of hybrid model, taking advantage of CNN and LSTM model to extract spatial features and temporal characteristics respectively.

A study [18] managed IDS alerts via semantic analysis as well as ontology engineering techniques to transform multiple unprocessed IDS alerts into one summarized meta-alert. Bidirectional Encoder Representations from Transformers (BERT) is a transformer model proposed by Devlin et.al and a robust language presentation model that is designed to pretrain bidirectional representations from unlabeled text by jointly conditioning on both right and left context in all layers. The salient performance in modeling sequential data inspires much research on detection systems.

Research [19] deployed BERT in their log analysis system to learn the contextual relations among log key in a sequence and determine the existence of anomaly in the ocean of logs. Research [7] discovered the capabilities of BERT in detecting APT attacking sequences, and the experiments evinced the superior performance of BERT comparing with CNN, LSTM and Perception.

## 3 Proposed Method

This study employs several open datasets sourced from IIoT devices within OT networks. These datasets, originally consisting of raw packet data, are not directly compatible with the DL model. Consequently, this study first transforms the raw data into traffic vectors for BERT processing. The datasets are heterogeneous, possessing multiple communication protocols such as DNP3 and Modbus. The elevated level of complexity of traffic flows across these protocols can potentially lead to model confusion and degrade the performance of the detection model.

To address this issue, the study performs protocol categorization. Since BERT is a semantic analysis model designed to process word vectors, it necessitates the conversion of traffic flows into time-series word vectors. This conversion is essential for BERT to understand contextual relationships effectively. The study leverages the BERT encoder for feature extraction, taking advantages of BERT's capability to capture bidirectional correlations. The features extracted by BERT are then utilized as inputs for an LSTM model, which serves as the classification component of the system (Fig. 1).

### 3.1 Traffic Aggregation

This study leverages traffic aggregation by composing individual packets into traffic flows. A traffic flow, which consists of multiple packets, contains substantially more information than a single packet. Utilizing traffic flows for model training, as opposed to individual packets, can enhance the performance of the detection model by increasing the informational content of the training data, which is crucial for model efficacy.

The proposed approach involves reassigning labels to aggregated traffic flows, as the original datasets provide labels based on individual packets. By transitioning to flow-based labels, this method reduces the number of benign labels, thereby addressing issues

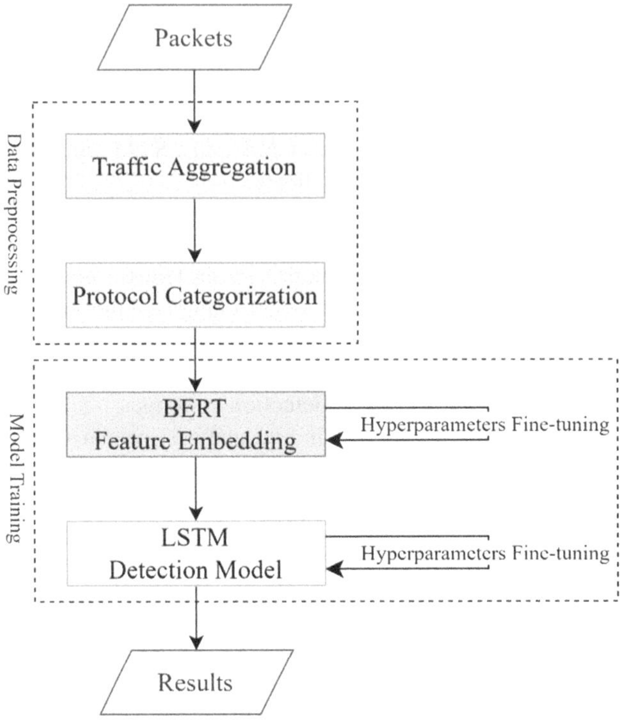


**Fig. 1.** System architecture.

related to data imbalance. Additionally, the proposed system assigns timestamps to each traffic flow in a chronological manner to preserve the time-series characteristics essential for accurate modeling.

### 3.2 Protocol Identification

This study operates under the assumption that the communication protocols within each network adhere to well-defined standards. Therefore, the proposed system is designed to identify communication protocols by examining multiple packet structures as specified in protocol documentation. The fundamental approach of the proposed protocol categorization involves identifying potential protocols by comparing the given packet with the data structures outlined for known communication protocols.

The system identifies the protocol by comparing the assumed packet length, derived from the intervals defined in the protocol documents, with the actual length of the packet. Specifically, for a set of known communication protocols $S = \{s_1, s_2, \ldots, s_x\}$ in OT environments such as Modbus and DNP3, the proposed system performs the following steps. Initially, It searches for the location of the fields that specify packet lengths within the protocol definitions in set $S$. These lengths are stored in a set $F = \{f_1, f_2, \ldots, f_x\}$, where each $f$ represents an interval with a beginning byte and an ending byte, denoted as $f_n = (b_n, e_n)$. Secondly, for a given packet $p$, the proposed system calculates its actual length $p_{acutal}$, and retrieves the assumed length $p[b_n : e_n]$ by converting byte-like values within the specified interval $f_n$ into an integer. Thirdly, If the assumed length matches the difference between the actual packet length and the preceding length $e_n$, the system identifies the protocol $s_n$ as the communication protocol used for the given packet $p$. Finally, the system asserts: If $p[b_n : e_n]$ is equal to $p_{actual} - e_n$, then protocol $s_n$ is the communicating protocol of the given packet.

### 3.3 BERT: Feature Embedding

The collected data consist of raw packets that are not directly suitable for machine learning modeling. To address that issue, this research attempts to extract traffic flows from these packet files and converting them into tabular data. Subsequently, the system transforms this tabular data into sentence representations, as illustrated in Table 1. The proposed system translates the bytecode in the packets into meaningful values based on the data structures defined by the protocols identified by the system.

**Table 1.** An example of converting tabular data into sentence

| Sequence | Src. IP | Dest. IP | Payload | Attacks |
|---|---|---|---|---|
| 10 | 10.10.10.10 | 10.10.10.11 | 0x123456 | MITM |
| Seq 10 is from 10.10.10.10 to 10.10.10.11 with payload 0x123456 and is MITM | | | | |

The translated packets are sequentially appended, starting with a timing feature labeled [CLASS (CLS)]. BERT is designed to handle sentences with varying lengths up to a maximum of 512 tokens, due to its positional embedding layer configuration of (512, 768). This configuration limits the number of tokens, including special tokens like [CLS] and [SEP], to 512. This study identifies that a few traffic flows may exceed this token limit. To address this issue, several methods, supported by the literature, can be employed:

1. Truncate the texts after 512 tokens: The BERT implementation automatically truncates contexts exceeding 512 tokens. While this feature may potentially lose a certain amount of information available, it is generally adequate in most scenarios.
2. Summarization: Summarize the sentence to reduce its length, thereby fitting it within the token limit.
3. Segmentation: Divide the context into smaller subtexts, classify each subtext separately, and then aggregate the results. Alternatively, the output tokens for each subtext can be processed by another network.

These strategies are designed to handle the limitations imposed by BERT's positional embedding layer while ensuring the effectiveness of the model in processing traffic flows.

There are multiple models of BERT, such as BERT-base and BERT-large, which have 110 million parameters and 345 million parameters respectively. The proposed system chooses BERT-base feature engineering model since BERT-large exhausts much computation and BERT-base is sufficient enough in most cases. BERT model can attain critical characteristics in an unknown varying length for time-series data. The proposed system will send the tokenized traffic flows to BERT internal transformer coding network composed of a multitude of transformer encoders. Each value in header is considered as token and the positional encoding will assign to them. After that, the data are now sent to Multi-Head Attention structure.

Attention function is similar to the function that maps a query and a set of key-value pair to an output, where the query, keys, values, and output are all vectors. Given there are $n$ embeddings in traffic flow $x$ and $x_1$ denotes the first token in $x$, so a set of the traffic flow $X$ can be defined as $X = \{ x_1, x_2, x_3 \ldots, x_n \}$. Three matrices will be initialized randomly while training the model, namely $W^Q$, $W^K$, and $W^V$ and each embedding is split into three vectors ($q_i$, $k_i$, and $v_i$) which are the product of the aforementioned matrices and embedding itself. Therefore, three sets are calculated, namely $Q = \{q_1, q_2, \ldots, q_n\}$, $K = \{k_1, k_2, \ldots, k_n\}$, and $V = \{v_1, v_2, \ldots, v_n\}$. To get the output of embedding $x_i$, the scores ($S$) calculation is performed by dot product of $q_i$ and the set of $K$ divided by the square root of the dimension of the key vector ($\sqrt{d(k_i)}$). After that, the sequence of the weight ($W$) via *Softmax* function is attained. Finally, the output the embedding $x_i$ ($z_i$) is the summation of the value vector set multiplied with weight ($z_i = \sum_{p=1}^{n} w_p \times v_p$). The formula of Attention is shown below.

$$Z = Attention(Q, K, V) = Softmax(\frac{Q \times K^T}{\sqrt{d_k}}) \times V \tag{1}$$

BERT learns multiple attention mechanisms, called heads, which operate in parallel to one another. The parameters of heads ($Z$) are independent from each other, and each head can learn its unique patterns. The BERT-base contains 12 layers and 12 heads, 144 special attention mechanisms in total. The $H$ concatenates all attention heads (h) together. The BERT generates random matrix $W^O$ while training and finally attains the Multi-Head Attention by the product of H and $W^O$. The formula of Multi-Head Attention is illustrated below.

$$MultiHead(Q, K, V) = H \times W^O \tag{2}$$

$$H = Concat\left(h_1, h_2 \cdots, h_j\right) \text{for } j = 12 \text{ in BERT-base} \tag{3}$$

$$\text{where } h_i = Attention(QW_i^Q, KW_i^K, VW_i^V) \tag{4}$$

The output of BERT will be sent to LSTM model, which is suitable for learning time series and periodic patterns according to the literature review. The LSTM model receives encoded vectors from BERT model and learn the patterns by the features extracted from Multi-Heads Attention. The chronological feature is also preserved because of the Positional Encoding in BERT before Attention.

### 3.4 LSTM: Detection Model

Devices within OT networks typically execute periodic tasks, unlike those in IT networks. IIoT devices in OT networks generate traffic flows that are more regular and consistent. Network traffic represents a form of time-series data characterized by temporal hierarchies, with information distributed across various time scales. To accurately identify malicious behaviors in network traffic, detection models are required to be capable of discerning traffic patterns from such time-series data. Prior performance analyses [20] suggest that hierarchical Recurrent Neural Networks (RNNs) are more effective for complex temporal tasks, as they capture a greater amount of time-series information compared to single-layer models. This effectiveness is attributed to each layer of the hierarchical RNN being a recurrent network that receives the hidden state of the previous layer as input.

Long Short-Term Memory (LSTM) networks, an advanced variant of RNNs, address several issues inherent to traditional RNN models, such as long-term dependency problems, vanishing gradients, and exploding gradients. LSTM networks leverage gates and cell states to manage these issues. The cell state in LSTM networks is capable of retaining time-series patterns from input sequences, while the gates determine whether to retain or discard information.

LSTM networks employ three types of gates: the input gate, the forget gate, and the output gate. The input gate regulates whether new information extracted from the input should be retained, the forget gate decides which information to discard, and the output gate computes the final output of the cell. Specifically, the gates in LSTM networks use the Sigmoid activation function, which outputs values typically between 0 and 1. This characteristic of the Sigmoid function facilitates the gates in making decisions about which information to keep or discard.

Firstly, the new input traffic flow at timestamp $t$, denoted as $x_t$, is fed into forget gate ($f_t$). Forget gate considers the information in previous shadow state ($h_{t-1}$) and the input ($x_t$), and activation function ($\sigma$) determines to keep or discard the information in previous state. The input gate ($i_t$) also compares the previous shadow state and new-coming input value, and the activation function also decides to hold or ignore the new information from the input. In the meantime, a memory cell candidate ($\tilde{c}_t$) is created and a old cell state ($c_{t-1}$) will be updated by Hadamard product of forget gate value and previous cell state plus Hadamard product of input gate value and memory state candidate. Last, the output is the shadow version of the new cell state, denoted as ($h_t$), which is decided by the output gate ($o_t$). The output ($y_t$) is exactly the same as the shadow state

$$f_t = \sigma\left(W_f \times x_t + U_f \times h_{t-1} + b_f\right) \tag{5}$$

$$i_t = \sigma(W_i \times x_t + U_i \times h_{t-1} + b_i) \tag{6}$$

$$\tilde{c}_t = tanh(W \times x_t + U \times h_{t-1} + b) \tag{7}$$

$$c_t = f_t \cdot c_{t-1} + i_t \cdot \tilde{c}_t \tag{8}$$

$$o_t = \sigma(W_o \times x_t + U_o \times h_{t-1} + b_o) \tag{9}$$

$$h_t = o_t \cdot tanh(ct) \tag{10}$$

$$y_t = h_t \tag{11}$$

Thereby, LSTM can keep the useful features and discard less important information during training by gates, where it helps the model to learn complex patterns in traffic flows.

### 3.5 Hyperparameter Fine-Tuning

Hyperparameters are essential in deep learning modeling, as they profoundly influence the model's learning behavior. Proper tuning of these hyperparameters is important, as inadequate tuning can lead to suboptimal performance by causing the model to converge to local minima rather than effectively minimizing the loss function. Hyperparameters are instrumental in determining the optimal values for model parameters, thereby enabling the model to assign appropriate weights to critical features. The process of hyperparameter tuning involves identifying the optimal set of hyperparameter values to enhance the model's ability to learn from a given dataset.

Genetic Algorithm (GA) is a search heuristic inspired by the principles of natural evolution. It selects the fittest individuals for reproduction to generate descendants for subsequent generations. The fitness function within GA evaluates the performance of each individual, assigning fitness scores to determine which individuals are most likely to contribute advantageous genes to the next generation.

This study employs GA to optimize hyperparameters. In this context, each chromosome in GA corresponds to a hyperparameter, and the value of each chromosome represents the hyperparameter itself, which is subject to updates throughout the evolutionary simulation. GA assesses the results of the loss function during model training and determines whether the current generation's genes are the fittest. This evaluation guides whether the genes should be propagated to future generations or eliminated. Consequently, GA can identify optimal hyperparameters more efficiently compared to manual adjustment methods.

## 4 System Evaluation

This study designed the following experiments to evaluate the effectiveness, performance, and robustness of the proposed system. Those experiments adopt confusion matrix as performance measurement, namely accuracy, precision, recall and F1 score.

1. Experiment 1 investigates the impact of the training and testing set ratio.
2. Experiment 2 measures the effectiveness of adopting Genetic Algorithm to adjust the hyperparameters of neural networks models.

### 4.1 Dataset

Real-life OT-enabled networks exhibit a broader range of traffic types compared to simulated environments, including cyberattacks, regular transmissions, and system faults. Previous research rarely pay attention to the dataset diversity when developing anomaly detection systems for OT-enabled networks. In practical settings, IIoT devices may experience operational faults and generate noise, complicating anomaly detection.

This study evaluates the efficacy of the proposed detection model in OT networks using multiple open datasets to account for the diverse nature of real-life IIoT environments, which involve varied communication protocols. The Morris dataset includes various traffic types such as OT cyberattacks, routine transmissions, and system faults, providing a comprehensive basis for the detection model to handle complex patterns in heterogeneous OT networks. The 4SICS dataset comprises data from servers, industrial network equipment (e.g., switches, firewalls), and diverse IIoT and IoT devices (e.g., PLCs, MTUs, network cameras), simulating a complex IIoT network environment with multiple communication protocols. The CSET dataset features both benign traffic—such as regular polling and manual operations—and malicious traffic, including remote exploits and command-and-control server connections, reflecting real-world attack scenarios where compromised devices are used to further infiltrate the network.

### 4.2 Experiment 1: Impact of Data Split Ratio

The amount of training data would have great impact on the performance of the detection model and training time. If the training data is not sufficient, the detection model will suffer from underfitting, where the model cannot recognize the difference between benign and malicious traffic; the excessive amount of training data would negatively influence the performance of the detection model since the model might overfit the patterns. So, this experiment evaluated the impact of the different portion of training and testing on the performance of the multiple deep learning model.

Table 2 illustrates the results of different ratio with various deep learning model. The 8:2 yields the best performance in each deep learning model and BERT + LSTM model outperform other models. The deep learning models need more data to learn the attack patterns due to the imbalanced portion of benign and attacks data, where most traffic flows are benign. Despite that the training time sky-rocketed with the increasement of training data, the performance of detection also grows substantially.

**Table 2.** The impact of different portion of training and testing data

| | LSTM | | | Stacked LSTM | | | BERT + LSTM | | |
|---|---|---|---|---|---|---|---|---|---|
| | 8:2 | 5:5 | 2:8 | 8:2 | 5:5 | 2:8 | 8:2 | 5:5 | 2:8 |
| Acc. | 97.06 | 94.18 | 92.94 | 98.87 | 95.64 | 93.22 | 98.15 | 97.94 | 97.05 |
| PPV | 94.85 | 94.01 | 92.58 | 96.81 | 95.33 | 93.48 | 97.19 | 97.05 | 96.41 |
| Rec. | 97.42 | 96.15 | 95.22 | 98.01 | 96.18 | 95.31 | 98.74 | 98.45 | 97.87 |
| F1 | 96.12 | 95.07 | 93.88 | 97.82 | 95.75 | 94.38 | 97.95 | 97.75 | 97.13 |

### 4.3 Experiment 2: Model Comparison

A multitude of deep learning algorithms are designed for time-series data, and LSTM is the well-known and famous deep learning model that is capable of memorizing patterns in time-series data. Different combinations of neural layers will produce different LSTM model, which is suitable for different area. This study selects three combinations of LSTM model. Vanilla LSTM is included in this experiment as the baseline model; stacked LSTM is an improved version of vanilla LSTM by stacking multiple LSTM cell together; BERT + LSTM is a common hybrid model in NLP, but it can be applied to other areas with the help of transfer learning. In proposed system, BERT is used as feature embedding that selects features for the LSTM model.

In this experiment, this research trained three different LSTM models 5 times and calculated the standard deviation for each model to determine the best combination and the stableness of each detection model. The results demonstrate BERT + LSTM outperforms other deep learning in all aspects except the average accuracy. However, the hybrid model fluctuates less than other two model do, meaning that the deviation of each training will be minimal in three of them (Table 3).

**Table 3.** The performance of different neural networks model

| | GA-LSTM | GA-Stacked LSTM | GA-BERT + GA-LSTM |
|---|---|---|---|
| Acc. | 97.48 ± 0.0211 | 98.95 ± 0.0143 | 0.9815 ± 0.0058 |
| PPV | 95.01 ± 0.0193 | 96.91 ± 0.0211 | 0.9719 ± 0.0049 |
| Rec. | 98.22 ± 0.0311 | 98.33 ± 0.0195 | 0.9874 ± 0.0064 |
| F1 | 0.9659 | 0.9761 | 0.9795 |

## 5 Conclusion

This article proposes a hybrid BERT + LSTM classification model for detecting malicious traffic flows in heterogeneous OT network environments, complemented by Genetic Algorithm (GA) for automatic hyperparameter optimization. A novel two-stage approach is introduced to manage data complexity: initially, traffic flows are categorized by their communication protocols before being input into the model for training, and subsequently, the model determines whether the traffic is malicious.

The study emphasizes the crucial role of hyperparameters in the detection model, as they influence the model's ability to learn from the data effectively and identify attack patterns with precision. Additionally, the proposed model is trained on multiple real-life datasets gathered from diverse sources and networks. These datasets, which include varied communication protocols, offer a realistic representation of OT networks and contribute to the model's robustness in detecting anomalies across different scenarios.

## References

1. Hussain, F., Hussain, R., Hassan, S.A., Hossain, E.: Machine learning in IoT security: current solutions and future challenges. IEEE Communications Surveys & Tutorials (2020)
2. Al Jallad, K., Aljnidi, M., Desouki, M.S.: Anomaly detection optimization using big data and deep learning to reduce false-positive. J. Big Data **7**(1), pp. 1–12 (2020)
3. Qiu, J., Wu, Q., Ding, G., Xu, Y., Feng, S.: A survey of machine learning for big data processing. EURASIP Journal on Advances in Signal Processing **2016**, 1–16 (2016)
4. Hindy, H., Brosset, D., Bayne, E., Seeam, A., Bellekens, X.: Improving SIEM for critical SCADA water infrastructures using machine learning. In: Computer Security: Springer, pp. 3–19 (2018)
5. Hindy, H., Brosset, D., Bayne, E., Seeam, A., Bellekens, X.: Improving SIEM for critical SCADA water infrastructures using machine learning. In: Computer Security: ESORICS 2018 International Workshops, CyberICPS 2018 and SECPRE 2018, Barcelona, Spain, September 6–7, 2018, Revised Selected Papers 2, pp. 3–19. Springer (2019)
6. Johan Angséus, R.E.: Network-based Intrusion detectionsystems for industrial control systems. Master, Computer Systems and Networks, University of Gothenburg (2017)
7. Yu, K., et al.: Securing critical infrastructures: deep-learning-based threat detection in IIoT. IEEE Commun. Mag. **59**(10), 76–82 (2021)
8. Guo, J., Shen, Y.: Online anomaly detection of industrial IoT based on hybrid machine learning architecture. Computational Intelligence and Neuroscience, 2022, p. 8568917, 2022/04/30 (2022). https://doi.org/10.1155/2022/8568917
9. Wu, Y., Dai, H.-N., Tang, H.: Graph neural networks for anomaly detection in industrial internet of things. IEEE Internet Things J. **9**(12), 9214–9231 (2021)
10. Sakthidasan Sankaran, K., Kim, B.-H.: Deep learning based energy efficient optimal RMC-CNN model for secured data transmission and anomaly detection in industrial IOT. Sustainable Energy Technologies and Assessments, vol. 56, p. 102983, 2023/03/01/ (2023). https://doi.org/10.1016/j.seta.2022.102983
11. Yazdinejad, A., Kazemi, M., Parizi, R.M., Dehghantanha, A., Karimipour, H.: An ensemble deep learning model for cyber threat hunting in industrial internet of things. Digital Communications and Networks, 2022/09/28/ (2022). https://doi.org/10.1016/j.dcan.2022.09.008
12. Hore, U.W., Wakde, D.: An effective approach of IIoT for anomaly detection using unsupervised machine learning approach. J. IoT Soc. Mob. Anal. Cloud **4**, 184–197 (2022)
13. Huang, Z., Wu, Y., Tempini, N., Lin, H., Yin, H.: An energy-efficient and trustworthy unsupervised anomaly detection framework (EATU) for IIoT. ACM Transactions on Sensor Networks **18**(4), 1–18 (2022)
14. Park, S., Lee, K.: Improved mitigation of cyber threats in IIoT for Smart Cities: a new-era approach and scheme. Sensors **21**(6), 1976 (2021)
15. Radford, B.J., Apolonio, L.M., Trias, A.J., Simpson, J.A.: Network Traffic Anomaly Detection using Recurrent Neural Networks. arXiv preprint arXiv:1803.10769 (2018)
16. Prasse, P., Machlica, L., Pevný, T., Havelka, J., Scheffer, T.: Malware detection by analysing network traffic with neural networks. In: 2017 IEEE Security and Privacy Workshops (SPW), IEEE, pp. 205–210 (2017)
17. Kim, T.-Y., Cho, S.-B.: Web traffic anomaly detection using C-LSTM neural networks. Expert Systems with Applications, pp. 66–76 (2018)

18. Saad, S., Traore, I.: A semantic analysis approach to manage IDS alerts flooding. In: 2011 7th International Conference on Information Assurance and Security (IAS), 5–8 Dec. 2011, pp. 156–161 (2011). https://doi.org/10.1109/ISIAS.2011.6122812
19. Guo, H., Yuan, S., Wu, X.: Logbert: log anomaly detection via bert. In: 2021 International Joint Conference on Neural Networks (IJCNN), IEEE, pp. 1–8 (2021)
20. Hermans, M., Schrauwen, B.: Training and analysing deep recurrent neural networks. Adv. Neural. Inf. Process. Syst. **26**, 190–198 (2013)

# Ranking Comments for Bug Reports Using Deep Learning

Ching-Hsiang Chang, Liang-Chen Lu, and Cheng-Zen Yang(✉)

Department of Computer Science and Engineering, Yuan Ze University, Taoyuan, Taiwan
{chc20,lcl23,czyang}@syslab.cse.yzu.edu.tw

**Abstract.** Important bug report comments can help developers efficiently fix bugs. This paper proposes a bug report comment ranking model called BRCR based on deep learning models. This paper also proposes a pseudo-labeling approach to address the few-shot problem. In the experiments, bug reports of three GitHub software projects are used to evaluate the proposed BRCR ranking model. The experimental results show that BRCR with LSTM and pseudo-labeled data can effectively outperform other ranking models.

**Keywords:** Bug Report · Comment Ranking · Deep Learning · Pseudo-labeling

## 1 Introduction

In the process of software development and maintenance, the effectiveness of processing software defects influences software quality. To efficiently address software defect problems, developers generally communicate with each other by providing comments in bug reports. Recently, various analytic issues on bug reports have been discussed, such as bug categorization [1,2], bug prioritization [1,21,22], and severity prediction [7,22]. Figure 1 shows a typical bug report extracted from the KDE software project. In this bug report, developers can find a summary title for the report, a description of the bug, and other related information for the management of the report. Historical bug reports will also be referenced because their comments can contain important information such as methods for resolving defects or steps to reproduce defects [25]. However, reading comments of historical bug reports is generally a tedious process because the number of comments can be large and they are not listed according to their importance.

To relief the tedious reading work, several unsupervised comment ranking models that can help developers to find important comments have been proposed [8]. Various ranking models are discussed, such as PageRank [4] and Louvain community detection algorithm [3], to decide the importance of each comment with respect to the title and the description of the report. However, these unsupervised models only take advantage of limited similarity or network properties among the texts.

© The Author(s), under exclusive license to Springer Nature Singapore Pte Ltd. 2025
W.-T. Chu et al. (Eds.): TAAI 2024, CCIS 2414, pp. 207–219, 2025.
https://doi.org/10.1007/978-981-96-4589-3_15

Bug 188311 - The applet panel should not overlap applets

Status: RESOLVED FIXED
Alias: None
Product: amarok
Component: Context View (show other bugs)
Version: unspecified
Platform: Compiled Sources Linux
Importance: NOR wishlist (vote)
Target Milestone: ---
Assignee: Amarok Developers
URL:
Keywords:
Duplicates (1): 174221 (view as bug list)
Depends on:
Blocks:

Reported: 2009-03-28 11:35 UTC by mangus
Modified: 2009-06-02 10:45 UTC (History)
CC List: 4 users (show)
See Also:
Latest Commit:
Version Fixed In:

mangus 2009-03-28 11:35:10 UTC Description

Version: svn (using Devel)
OS: Linux
Installed from: Compiled sources

In amarok2-svn I like the the new contextview , but I found the new bottom bar for managing applets annoying , as it covers parts of other applets sometimes , like lyrics one , so that you miss a part of it. Could be handy to have it appear and desappear onmouseover.
thanks

Dan Meltzer 2009-03-28 14:53:55 UTC Comment 1

The real solution is to make it not cover applets, not make it appear/disappear on mouse over.

**Fig. 1.** Bug report #188311 for the KDE project and its discussion thread.

In this paper, we propose a supervised learning model called BRCR (Bug Report Comment Ranking) using the deep learning techniques to harvest historical bug reports. In addition, we further propose a pseudo-labeling technique to tackle a few-shot problem [24] encountered in this work because the number of the labeled bug reports is not large enough to build deep learning models. The pseudo-labeling technique takes unsupervised models as pseudo-annotators to extend the training data set by labeling more bug reports. Although the unsupervised pseudo-labeling models provide moderate ranking performance, pseudo-labeling improves the ranking performance of BRCR.

To explore the effectiveness of the proposed BRCR model, we have conducted experiments using the data sets used in [8]. We further studied two implementations of BRCR using LSTM (Long-Short Term Memory) [10] and GRU (Gate Recurrent Unit) [6] in the experiments. The results show that BRCR outperforms previous unsupervised ranking models. BRCR achieves on average 0.57 in terms of $F1@10$, 0.8622 in terms of MRR (Mean Reciprocal Rank), and 0.6365 in terms of MAP (Mean Average Precision) [5].

The rest of the paper is organized as follows. Section 2 presents related work. Section 3 describes the proposed BRCR model. Section 4 presents the experiments. Section 5 discusses threats to validity of this work. Finally, Sect. 6 concludes the paper.

## 2 Related Work

To extract important information from bug reports for developers, past studies focus on devising methods to generate summaries for bug reports [13,16,19,25,26,28]. However, as pointed by [8,15], sentence-based summaries only provide condensed views of bug reports. Due to the restricted views, developers may still need to read the original comments.

The comment ranking problem is originated for an issue of how to generate comment-based summaries [8]. Therefore, developers can perceive a complete view of each important comment. In [8], four unsupervised techniques are discussed to construct ranking models: Cosine Similarity [17], Euclidean Distance [17], PageRank [4], and the Louvain community detection algorithm [3]. In the Cosine Similarity and Euclidean Distance ranking models, these two functions are separately used as the similarity function to calculate the similarity between each comment and the title/description of the report. Comments are then ranked according to their similarity scores. In PageRank, the probability of how often a developer stays on a comment is calculated from a relationship network graph, i.e., the importance score of the comment. In the Louvain algorithm, comments are firstly clustered. Then, the eigenvector centrality of each cluster is calculated to find the most important comment. Of the four ranking models, PageRank outperforms the others on average.

The comment ranking problem is also studied in various domains [9,11,27]. For example, a ranking method SWCP (Social Web Comment Prediction) is proposed in [11] to rank comments of Digg social networking messages. SWCP extracts 20 features from Digg reviews and uses the SVR (Support Vector Regression) model to rank comments based on the extracted features. Wei et al. studied the effectiveness of various features of Reddit forum data to rank argumentative comments using pair-wise learning-to-rank (LTR) models [27]. Besides five surface text features, six social interaction features and five argumentation features are discussed. Their experimental results show that the argumentation related features can have the best performance. However, these approaches cannot be directly applied to the problem of ranking comments of bug reports because they either consider more community-related features, such as the community rating score and the number of friends of the commenter, or tackle the ranking problem from different aspects. From a constructive perspective, Fujita et al. proposed an ensemble model HPA (a Hybrid method using the Pseudo Answer) that uses an unsupervised approach to integrate RankNet models for comment ranking [9]. Their experiments show that HPA outperformed other ranking models in terms of most metrics by integrating 100 randomly initialized RankNet models.

# 3 Comment Ranking Model

In this section, the proposed BRCR comment ranking model as shown in Fig. 2 will be elaborated. In BRCR, there are two phases: training and ranking. These two phases of BRCR are described in detail below.

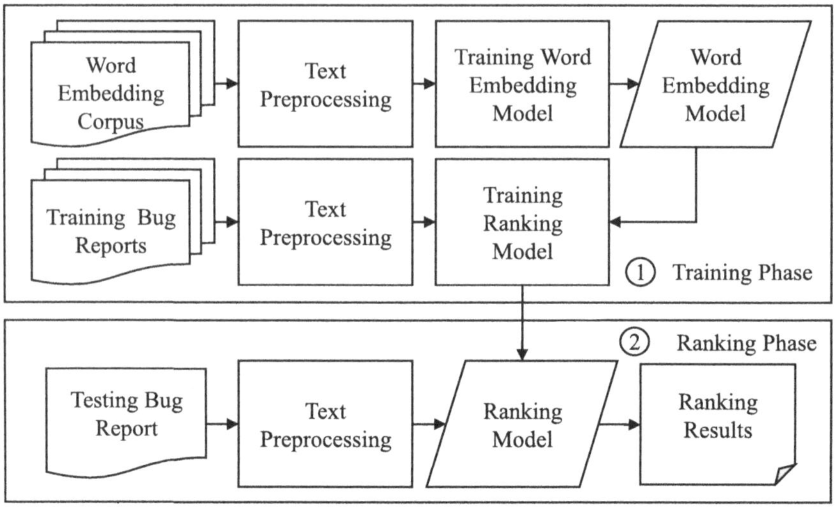


**Fig. 2.** Comment ranking process in BRCR.

## 3.1 Text Preprocessing

The title field of a bug report is a summary of the report. The description field of a bug report provides more information about the bug. These two fields and comments are described using unstructured sentences. BRCR performs the following steps to process the text before training and testing.

Firstly, sentences are segmented and the words are tokenized using NLTK [14]. In the tokenization step, punctuation marks and special symbols such as "," and "$" are removed. For URLs, "http" and "https" are reserved and others are removed. For stemming, each extracted word is converted to its root form using the Snowball stemmer [23]. After these text preprocessing steps, the title and the description are merged as the report body. The comments of the report are separated from the bug report. These text segments are used as input to the ranking model.

## 3.2 Ranking Approach

Figure 3 depicts the model architecture of BRCR. The BRCR model is developed based on the architecture of SummaRuNNer [20]. The first layer of BRCR is the word embedding layer. In the BRCR model, the words in the text segments are firstly converted into word embedding form. In this work, the CBOW (Continuous Bag-Of-Words) approach of Word2Vec [18] is used to derive word embeddings of words. The pre-trained word embeddings are used for both training and testing.

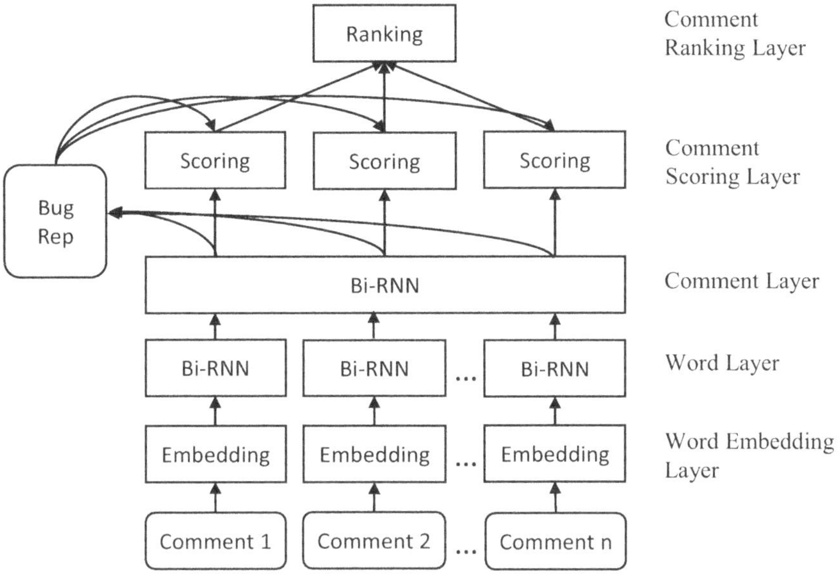


**Fig. 3.** BRCR ranking model.

The second layer is the word layer constructed by a bi-directional RNN (Recurrent Neural Network) network to sequentially process the input words. In this work, LSTM (Long-Short Term Memory) [10] and GRU (Gate Recurrent Unit) [6] are separately used to implement the word layer. The word layer derives the vectors of the comments.

The third layer is the comment layer that is also a Bi-RNN network to consider the relationships among these comments. Then the comment scoring layer calculates the importance of each comment to the entire bug report. For importance calculation, BRCR calculates the vector of the bug report $d$ represented as the Bug Rep data in Fig. 3. The vector calculation of $d$ is as follows:

$$d = \tanh\left(W_{\mathrm{d}} \frac{1}{N_{\mathrm{d}}} \sum_{j=1}^{N_{\mathrm{d}}} [h_j^{\mathrm{f}}, h_j^{\mathrm{b}}] + b\right), \quad (1)$$

where $h_j^{\mathrm{f}}$ and $h_j^{\mathrm{b}}$ are respectively the forward and backward vectors of the corresponding the $j$-th comment in the hidden layer of the comment layer, $N_{\mathrm{d}}$ is the number of the comments in the entire bug report, and [ ] represents the concatenating operation of vectors. The vector of the bug report and the comment vectors are used to calculate the importance scores of the comments as follows:

$$P(y_j = 1 \mid h_j, c_j, d) = \sigma(W_c h_j + h_j^{\intercal} W_s d - h_j^{\intercal} W_r \tanh(c_j) + W_{ap} p_j^a + W_{rp} p_j^r + b), \tag{2}$$

where $P(y_j = 1)$ is the probability to consider the $j$-th comment as an important comment, $h_j$ is the bidirectional concatenating hidden layer vector of the $j$-th comment, $c_j$ is the comment importance state to the $j$-th comment. $W$s are the weights, and $b$ is the bias.

In Eq. (2), $W_c h_j$ represents the content of the comment. $h_j^T W_s d$ is the degree to which the $j$-th comment covers the information in the entire error report. $h_j^T W_r tanh(c_j)$ calculates the degree of redundancy of information provided in the comments. $W_{ap} p_j^a$ and $W_{rp} p_j^r$ are respectively the absolute and relative position of the comment in the bug report. The comment importance state $c_j$ is calculated as follows:

$$c_j = \sum_{i=1}^{j-1} h_j P(y_i = 1 \mid h_j, c_j, d) \tag{3}$$

After the comment scoring layer calculates the importance of each comment, the comment ranking layer derives the comment ranking result. The scores are ranked in descending order. The larger the score, the higher the importance.

### 3.3 Pseudo-labeling

In this work, a few-shot problem [24] is encountered because the number of the labeled bug reports is not large enough to build deep learning models. To tackle this small data problem, we propose a pseudo-labeling technique to take unsupervised models as pseudo-annotators. With these pseudo-annotators, more training data can be labeled. The label quality is a major concern for pseudo labels. Although the pseudo-annotators individually provide moderate ranking performance, the experimental results show that the ensemble pseudo-labeling model improves the ranking performance of BRCR.

In this work, four unsupervised models studied by Ferreira et al. [8] are used as the pseudo-annotators: Cosine Similarity, Euclidean Distance, PageRank, and the Louvain model. In addition to these four unsupervised ranking models, an ensemble model of these four unsupervised models is also studied using linear combination. For a comment $cm_i$, its pseudo-labeled comment rank value $r_i^{\mathrm{En}}$ is decided as follows:

$$r_i^{\mathrm{En}} = r_i^{\mathrm{Co}} + r_i^{\mathrm{Eu}} + r_i^{\mathrm{Pg}} + r_i^{\mathrm{Lv}} \tag{4}$$

where $r_i^{\mathrm{Co}}$ is the pseudo-rank value of Cosine Similarity, $r_i^{\mathrm{Eu}}$ is the pseudo-rank value of Euclidean Distance, $r_i^{\mathrm{Pg}}$ is the pseudo-rank value of PageRank, and $r_i^{\mathrm{Lv}}$ is the pseudo-rank value of the Louvain model. Since the rank list of the Louvain model does not have all comments, the pseudo-rank of a comment $cm_j$ that is not in the list will be given $r_j^{\mathrm{Lv}} = max(r_i^{\mathrm{Lv}}) + 1$.

# 4 Experiments

## 4.1 Experimental Setup

In the experiments, this work uses TensorFlow to implement the BRCR model running with an NVIDIA RTX 2080 GPU. The experiments was conducted using the dataset[1] from [8] denoted as the ABJ dataset in this paper. The ABJ dataset has 15 bug reports with 519 comments collected from three open-source software projects on GitHub: AngularJS, Bootstrap, and jQuery. Since the original ABJ dataset has some inconsistencies such as text missing when we checked the original bug reports, these inconsistencies were corrected in the experiments. In this work, we collected bug reports of three projects to train the word embeddings. Table 1 shows the average numbers of comments, sentences, and words in the experimental ABJ dataset and the number of bug reports used for word embeddings training.

**Table 1.** The details of the ABJ dataset and the word embeddings training corpus.

| Project | # of comments | # of sentences | # of words | # of BR for Word2Vec |
|---|---|---|---|---|
| AngularJS | 37.2 | 118.8 | 2133.0 | 8,983 |
| Bootstrap | 35.8 | 86.0 | 1168.6 | 19,173 |
| jQuery | 30.8 | 93.0 | 1603.0 | 1,978 |

In the experiments, we also created a pseudo-labeled dataset PABJ by following the labeling method of [8] to select bug reports whose status is *Closed* and whose number of comments $m$ is $20 \leq m \leq 45$. from the same word embeddings corpus. In PABJ, the bug reports of the ABJ dataset are excluded. Therefore, there are 204 AngularJS reports, 184 Bootstrap reports, and 40 jQuery reports in PABJ.

We use Gensim for Word2Vec word embeddings training with the following configuration ($vector\_size$, $window$, $min\_count$, $sg$) $= (100, 5, 1, 0)$ to use the CBOW model. To train the BRCR ranking model, the batch size is 4; the number of the word layer units is 10; the number of the comment layer units is 10; the early-stopping patience is 2; the word length padding is 500; the comment length padding is 45. The word layer and the comment layer are all constructed with 10 bidirectional recurrent neurons. The early-stopping mechanism is used to monitor the changes of the validation loss such that the training can be stopped early. In the experiments, BRCR were executed 10 times and the results were averaged.

[1] https://github.com/isabellavieira57/bug-report-summarization, accessed on 9/1/2024.

### 4.2 Performance Metrics

To measure the performance of the proposed ranking model, *Precision@n*, *Recall@n* and *F1@n* are used as the performance metrics. They are defined as follows:

$$Precision@n = \frac{\#hits@n}{\#ranking} \tag{5}$$

$$Recall@n = \frac{\#hits@n}{\#oracle} \tag{6}$$

$$F1@n = 2 \cdot \frac{Precision@n \cdot Recall@n}{Precision@n + Recall@n} \tag{7}$$

where $\#ranking$ is the length of the predicted rank list, $\#oracle$ is the length of the gold standard list, and $\#hits@n$ is the number of correctly predicted comments in the top-$n$ ranked comments. In the ABJ dataset, the number of $\#oracle$ comments labeled in each bug report is 10.

This work also uses the mean reciprocal rank (MRR) and the mean average precision (MAP) [5] to measure the performance of each ranking model. MRR is calculated as follows:

$$\text{MRR} = \frac{1}{|B|} \sum_{b \in B} \frac{1}{k_b} \tag{8}$$

where $B$ represents the set of all bug reports, $k_b$ refers to the rank of the first gold standard comment for the bug report $b$. MAP is defined as follows:

$$\text{MAP} = \frac{1}{|B|} \sum_{b \in B} \frac{\sum_{n=1}^{N} P(n) \times ora(n)}{\#oracle} \tag{9}$$

where $N$ represents the total number of comments of bug report $b$, and $P(n)$ is the $Precision@n$. The function $ora(n)$ is used to determine whether the $n$-th comment of the predicted rank list is in $\#oracle$. If the $n$-th comment is in $\#oracle$, $ora(n)$ returns 1. Otherwise, $ora(n)$ returns 0.

### 4.3 Experimental Results

For the proposed BRCR ranking model, the following two research questions are investigated:

- RQ1: Can pseudo labeling be beneficial on the ranking performance of BRCR?
- RQ2: How effective is BRCR in comment ranking?

**RQ1: Effectiveness of Pseudo-labeling.** Because we use pseudo labeling to extend the number of the training data for BRCR, the quality of the pseudo-labeled data is a major concern. In the experiments, we implemented two kinds of the BRCR model: BRCR with only golden standard labels called BRCR-GS and BRCR with golden standard labels and pseudo-labels called BRCR-PL. Since the work [8] indicates that PageRank (PR) and Cosine Similarity (CS) are two promising unsupervised ranking models, we use these models as the pseudo-annotators. We further implemented the ensemble approach (EN) for pseudo-labeling. Because BRCR is further implemented with either GRU or LSTM, we further have four models: BRCR-GRU-PL-CS, BRCR-GRU-PL-PR, BRCR-GRU-PL-EN BRCR-LSTM-PL-CS, BRCR-LSTM-PL-PR, and BRCR-LSTM-PL-EN.

In the experiments, the performance was measured using a leave-one-out method, i.e., one bug report of the ABJ dataset was used as the testing report and other reports of the ABJ dataset were used as the training reports. For the simplicity sake, this paper presents the $F1@10$ performance of all implementations on three projects. Table 2 shows the performance of BRCR with different pseudo-labeling implementations.

**Table 2.** $F1@10$ performance of BRCR with different pseudo-labeling implementations.

| Model | AngularJS | Bootstrap | jQuery | Average |
|---|---|---|---|---|
| BRCR-GRU-GS | 0.4760 | 0.3000 | 0.5220 | 0.4327 |
| BRCR-GRU-PL-CS | 0.5860 | 0.5180 | 0.5860 | 0.5633 |
| BRCR-GRU-PL-PR | 0.5500 | 0.4460 | 0.6100 | 0.5353 |
| BRCR-GRU-PL-EN | 0.5600 | 0.5120 | **0.6160** | 0.5627 |
| BRCR-LSTM-GS | 0.4240 | 0.2900 | 0.4300 | 0.3813 |
| BRCR-LSTM-PL-CS | **0.5940** | 0.5340 | 0.5680 | 0.5653 |
| BRCR-LSTM-PL-PR | 0.5400 | 0.4400 | **0.6160** | 0.5320 |
| BRCR-LSTM-PL-EN | 0.5700 | **0.5360** | 0.6040 | **0.5700** |

From the table, we can find that the performance of BRCR using only golden standard labels as the training data is poor. BRCR-LSTM-GS has the lowest $F1@10$ performance. However, the performance is consistently improved for all BRCR models using pseudo labels. Among these eight models, BRCR-LSTM-PL-EN outperforms other models on average. Therefore, we take BRCR-LSTM-PL-EN as the representative for the next research question. The results show that pseudo-labeling can effectively improve the ranking performance.

**RQ2: Effectiveness of BRCR.** To investigate the effectiveness of BRCR, we measured the following performance metrics: $F1@1$, $F1@3$, $F1@5$, $F1@10$,

MRR, and MAP. BRCR-LSTM-PL-EN is compared with other five unsupervised ranking models. Table 3 shows the performance of various ranking models.

**Table 3.** Ranking performance of various ranking models.

| Model | $F1@1$ | $F1@3$ | $F1@5$ | $F1@10$ | MRR | MAP |
|---|---|---|---|---|---|---|
| Cosine Similarity | 0.1091 | 0.2462 | 0.3378 | 0.4333 | 0.7467 | 0.5247 |
| Euclidean Distance | 0.0848 | 0.1744 | 0.2667 | 0.3600 | 0.6033 | 0.3975 |
| Louvain | 0.0848 | 0.2359 | 0.2870 | 0.3225 | 0.6000 | 0.2823 |
| PageRank | 0.1091 | 0.2154 | 0.2756 | 0.4400 | 0.7578 | 0.4861 |
| Ensemble | 0.0970 | 0.1845 | 0.3250 | 0.4467 | 0.6844 | 0.4881 |
| BRCR-LSTM-PL-EN | **0.1358** | **0.3292** | **0.4382** | **0.5700** | **0.8622** | **0.6365** |

From the table, we can find that BRCR-LSTM-PL-EN outperforms other five ranking models. BRCR-LSTM-PL-EN achieves on average 0.57 in terms of $F1@10$, 0.8622 in terms of MRR, and 0.6365 in terms of MAP.

## 5 Threats to Validity

One of possible threats to construct validity relates to the validity of the performance evaluation metrics because $F1@n$, MRR, and MAP can only show a partial view of the performance of ranking models. Since these metrics have been used in many ranking problems such as [8,12,29], they are still suitable for performance evaluation. Another threat relates to hyperparameter optimization of the proposed BRCR deep learning model. In the experiments, this issue was not addressed. However, this threat does not hinder the validity of the ranking performance of BRCR.

There is a threat to internal validity because the implementations of the unsupervised ranking models are based on the work of [8]. There are differences between the performance of our implementations and the performance of the implementations of [8]. However, the differences have limited influences because we use our implemented unsupervised ranking models as the pseudo-annotators to construct BRCR. Another threat refers to the implementation of the text preprocessing steps that affects the performance results of the experiments. Since BRCR uses the same text preprocessing methods, this validity threat is also limited.

One of the possible threats to external validity refers to the experimental dataset. In the experiments, only three open-source software projects, AngularJS, Bootstrap, and jQuery, were studied. In addition, the ABJ dataset is constructed using heuristic filtering rules. Therefore, the external validity would be threatened and the experimental results may not be generalizable to other projects or other bug report tracking systems. However, since BRCR considers only text descriptions of the report content in stead of other meta data, this generalization problem is mitigated.

## 6 Conclusions

Because comments of historical bug reports contain abundant information to help developers process incoming bugs, important comments need to be ranked first for developers to read. This paper proposes a deep learning model BRCR to tackle the comment ranking problem. To mitigate the few-shot problem of the small dataset, BRCR uses pseudo-labeling to improve the ranking performance.

The experimental results show that pseudo-labeling can effectively enhance the ranking performance of the deep learning model. Using the LSTM implementation and the ensemble pseudo-labeled training data, BRCR achieves on average 0.57 in terms of $F1@10$, 0.8622 in terms of MRR, and 0.6365 in terms of MAP.

There are several issues in our future research plan. First, enhanced pseudo-labeling methods will be studied and investigated to improve the accuracy performance of pseudo-labels. The advanced pseudo-labeling methods may further improve the performance of the ranking model. Second, advanced deep learning techniques will be investigated to construct a more effective ranking model. These recent deep learning techniques are more powerful in many artificial intelligence tasks. The effectiveness of these techniques may highly improve the ranking performance. Finally, other features will be considered in the future research according to the past experiences on social networking. Although these features may be project-specific or BTS-specific, a modularized design in feature processing can improve the generalizability of the ranking model.

**Acknowledgments.** This work is supported in part by National Science and Technology Council, Taiwan under Grant NSTC 113-2221-E-155-048-MY2.

## References

1. Ahmed, H.A., Bawany, N.Z., Shamsi, J.A.: CaPBug-a framework for automatic bug categorization and prioritization using nlp and machine learning algorithms. IEEE Access **9**, 50496–50512 (2021). https://doi.org/10.1109/ACCESS.2021.3069248
2. Alsaedi, S.A., Noaman, A.Y., Gad-Elrab, A.A.A., Eassa, F.E.: Nature-based prediction model of bug reports based on ensemble machine learning model. IEEE Access **11**, 63916–63931 (2023). https://doi.org/10.1109/ACCESS.2023.3288156
3. Blondel, V.D., Guillaume, J.L., Lambiotte, R., Lefebvre, E.: Fast unfolding of communities in large networks. J. Stat. Mech: Theory Exp. **2008**(10), P10008 (2008). https://doi.org/10.1088/1742-5468/2008/10/P10008
4. Brin, S., Page, L.: The anatomy of a large-scale hypertextual web search engine. Comput. Netw. ISDN Syst. **30**(1–7), 107–117 (1998). https://doi.org/10.1016/S0169-7552(98)00110-X
5. Buckley, C., Voorhees, E.: Retrieval system evaluation. In: Voorhees, E., Harman, D. (eds.) TREC: Experiment and Evaluation in Information Retrieval, chap. 3. MIT Press (Jan 2005)
6. Chung, J., Gülçehre, Ç., Cho, K., Bengio, Y.: Empirical evaluation of gated recurrent neural networks on sequence modeling. CoRR arXiv: 1412.3555 (2014)

7. Dao, A.H., Yang, C.Z.: Automated priority prediction for bug reports using comment intensiveness features and SMOTE data balancing. Int. J. Software Eng. Knowl. Eng. **33**(3), 415–433 (2023). https://doi.org/10.1142/S021819402350002X
8. Ferreira, I., Cirilo, E., Vieira, V., Mourão, F.: Bug report summarization: an evaluation of ranking techniques. In: Proceedings of the 2016 X Brazilian Symposium on Software Components, Architectures and Reuse (SBCARS 2016), pp. 101–110 (2016). https://doi.org/10.1109/SBCARS.2016.17
9. Fujita, S., Kobayashi, H., Okumura, M.: Unsupervised ensemble of ranking models for news comments using pseudo answers. In: Jose, J.M., et al. (eds.) ECIR 2020. LNCS, vol. 12036, pp. 133–140. Springer, Cham (2020). https://doi.org/10.1007/978-3-030-45442-5_17
10. Hochreiter, S., Schmidhuber, J.: Long short-term memory. Neural Comput. **9**(8), 1735–1780 (Nov 1999). https://doi.org/10.1162/neco.1997.9.8.1735
11. Hsu, C.F., Khabiri, E., Caverlee, J.: Ranking comments on the social web. In: Proceedings of the 12th International Conference on Computational Science and Engineering (CSE 2009), pp. 90–97 (2009). https://doi.org/10.1109/CSE.2009.109
12. Huang, Q., Xia, X., Xing, Z., Lo, D., Wang, X.: API method recommendation without worrying about the task-API knowledge gap. In: Proceedings of the 33rd ACM/IEEE International Conference on Automated Software Engineering (ASE 2018), pp. 293–304 (2018). https://doi.org/10.1145/3238147.3238191
13. Liu, H., Yu, Y., Li, S., Guo, Y., Wang, D., Mao, X.: BugSum: deep context understanding for bug report summarization. In: Proceedings of the 28th International Conference on Program Comprehension (ICPC 2020). pp. 94–105 (2020). https://doi.org/10.1145/3387904.3389272
14. Loper, E., Bird, S.: NLTK: the natural language toolkit. In: Proceedings of the ACL-02 Workshop on Effective Tools and Methodologies for Teaching Natural Language Processing and Computational Linguistics (ETMTNLP 2002), pp. 63–70 (2002). https://doi.org/10.3115/1118108.1118117
15. Lotufo, R., Malik, Z., Czarnecki, K.: Modelling the 'Hurried' bug report reading process to summarize bug reports. Empir. Softw. Eng. **20**(2), 516–548 (2015). https://doi.org/10.1007/s10664-014-9311-2
16. Mani, S., Catherine, R., Sinha, V.S., Dubey, A.: AUSUM: approach for unsupervised bug report summarization. In: Proceedings of the ACM SIGSOFT 20th International Symposium on the Foundations of Software Engineering (FSE 2012), pp. 11:1–11:11 (2012). https://doi.org/10.1145/2393596.2393607
17. Manning, C.D., Raghavan, P., Schütze, H.: Introduction to Information Retrieval. Cambridge University Press (2008)
18. Mikolov, T., Chen, K., Corrado, G., Dean, J.: Efficient estimation of word representations in vector space. In: Proceedings of the 1st International Conference on Learning Representations (ICLR 2013) (2013)
19. Mukhtar, S., Lee, S., Heo, J.: A multidocument summarization technique for informative bug summaries. IEEE Access **12**, 158908–158926 (2024). https://doi.org/10.1109/ACCESS.2024.3487443
20. Nallapati, R., Zhai, F., Zhou, B.: SummaRuNNer: a recurrent neural network based sequence model for extractive summarization of documents. In: Proceedings of the 31st AAAI Conference on Artificial Intelligence (AAAI 2017), pp. 3075–3081 (2017). https://doi.org/10.1609/aaai.v31i1.10958
21. Panda, R.R., Nagwani, N.K.: Software bug priority prediction technique based on intuitionistic fuzzy representation and class imbalance learning. Knowl. Inf. Syst. **66**(3), 2135–2164 (2024). https://doi.org/10.1007/s10115-023-02000-7

22. Panda, R.R., Nagwani, N.K.: Software bug severity and priority prediction using smote and intuitionistic fuzzy similarity measure. Appli. Soft Comput. **150**, 111048 (2024). https://doi.org/10.1016/j.asoc.2023.111048
23. Porter, M.F.: Snowball: A Language for Stemming Algorithms. http://snowball.tartarus.org/texts/introduction.html (Oct 2001)
24. Qi, G.J., Luo, J.: Small data challenges in big data era: a survey of recent progress on unsupervised and semi-supervised methods. IEEE Trans. Pattern Analy. Mach. Intell., 1–20 (2020). https://doi.org/10.1109/TPAMI.2020.3031898
25. Rastkar, S., Murphy, G.C., Murray, G.: Summarizing software artifacts: a case study of bug reports. In: Proceedings of the 32nd ACM/IEEE International Conference on Software Engineering (ICSE 2010), pp. 505–514 (2010). https://doi.org/10.1145/1806799.1806872
26. Rastkar, S., Murphy, G.C., Murray, G.: Automatic summarization of bug reports. IEEE Trans. Software Eng. **40**(4), 366–380 (2014). https://doi.org/10.1109/TSE.2013.2297712
27. Wei, Z., Liu, Y., Li, Y.: Is this post persuasive? ranking argumentative comments in online forum. In: Proceedings of the 54th Annual Meeting of the Association for Computational Linguistics, pp. 195–200 (2016)
28. Yang, C.Z., Ao, C.M., Chung, Y.H.: Towards an improvement of bug report summarization using two-layer semantic information. IEICE Trans. Inform. Syst. **E101-D**(7), 1743–1750 (2018). https://doi.org/10.1587/transinf.2017KBP0016
29. Zanjani, M.B., Kagdi, H., Bird, C.: Automatically recommending peer reviewers in modern code review. IEEE Trans. Softw. Eng. **42**(6), 530–543 (2016). https://doi.org/10.1109/TSE.2015.2500238

# Hand Gesture Recognition from sEMG Signals Through Quantum Support Vector Machine

Giovanni Acampora and Autilia Vitiello(✉)

Department of Physics "Ettore Pancini", University of Naples Federico II, via Cintia 21, 80126 Naples, Italy
{giovanni.acampora,autilia.vitiello}@unina.it

**Abstract.** Hand gesture recognition is an essential task in the developing of upper limb prosthesis control systems. This task is typically addressed by classifying surface electromyography (sEMG) signals, i.e. electrical signals generated by muscle activity. Unfortunately, hand gesture recognition results in a very challenging task for several reasons such as signal variability, electrical noise, and the high-dimensionality of sEMG signals. In particular, the high-dimensionality of data makes machine learning models computationally expensive. In this scenario, quantum-powered machine learning models such as the Quantum-enhanced Support Vector Machine (QSVM) may help thanks to their inherently ability to work with large spaces due to the principle of quantum superposition. Starting from this consideration, this paper presents, for the first time, the application of QSVM to classify sEMG signals so as to predict hand gestures. As shown by results, QSVM is a suitable approach to face the hand gesture recognition task.

**Keywords:** Hand gesture recognition · Quantum computing · Quantum-enhanced support vector machine · Quantum artificial intelligence · Surface electromyography

## 1 Introduction

Hand amputees experience a significant decline in their quality of daily life compared to what it was before the amputation [7]. Indeed, all the routine activities can become challenging impacting on individual independence. However, the quality of life of hand amputees can be improved thanks to the use of a dexterous, self-powered hand prosthesis. This represents an advanced artificial hand designed to closely mimic natural hand movements and thanks to its own power source, enhance the user's independence and capability in daily activities. Among the different kinds of hand prostheses, myoelectric hand ones offer numerous advantages including improved dexterity and control and a more natural and intuitive operation. In this scenario, patients control the prosthesis via surface electromyography (sEMG) signals, i.e. electrical signals generated

© The Author(s), under exclusive license to Springer Nature Singapore Pte Ltd. 2025
W.-T. Chu et al. (Eds.): TAAI 2024, CCIS 2414, pp. 220–232, 2025.
https://doi.org/10.1007/978-981-96-4589-3_16

by muscle activity that are detected using electrodes placed on the surface of the skin. Indeed, hand movements are the result of the central nervous system driving different upper limb muscles. In detail, sEMG signals reflect the intensity of the muscle contraction that can be recorded in a non-intrusive fashion using surface electrodes [17]. To meet the hand-machine interaction function, the dexterous hands need to have good recognition and processing capabilities for sEMG signals in order to identify the hand movement to be performed [9]. Hence, hand movement recognition represents a crucial role in the developing of upper limb prosthesis control systems.

Hand gesture recognition based on sEMG can be naturally framed as a pattern classification problem in which a classifier is usually trained through supervised learning [10]. In literature, several machine learning techniques such as Support Vector Machine [8,14,16] and Neural Networks [5,13,15] have been already used to classifying sEMG signals and so as to predict hand gestures. However, hand gesture recognition is a challenging task due to different reasons. Firstly, sEMG signals are characterized by both intra-subject and inter-subject variability. Indeed, sEMG signals from the same person can vary due to factors like fatigue or emotional state, whereas, different individuals can produce significantly different sEMG signals, even when performing the same movement, due to differences in muscle mass and skin thickness. Moreover, sEMG can be affected by motion artifacts due to the movement of the electrodes or electrical noise due to external sources of interference. In addition, another important issue is the high-dimensionality of sEMG signals due to the fact that data can be collected from multiple electrodes placed on different muscle groups. In particular, this last issue is very critical for machine learning techniques because it leads to computationally expensive models as the data dimensionality grows.

In this scenario, quantum computers can help thanks to their inherently ability to work with large, high-dimensional spaces due to the principle of quantum superposition. This fundamental quantum principle refers to the fact that a quantum system can assume multiple states at the same time. Thanks to this principle, the so-called Quantum-enhanced Support Vector Machine (QSVM) allows processing high-dimensional feature spaces more efficiently than the classical counterpart. In detail, QSVM is a quantum-powered algorithm since it replaces the use of a classical kernel function with a quantum kernel. This quantum component enables the computation of inner products of data in exponentially large feature spaces more efficiently. Hence, QSVM could be a promising classifier for addressing the hand gesture recognition task.

Starting from this consideration, this paper presents, for the first time, the application of QSVM to classify sEMG signals so as to predict hand gestures. The suitability of this quantum-powered algorithm is shown in an experimental session involving the well-known Ninapro dataset [7]. Due to the difficulty of accessing real quantum computers that are only provided by international companies such as IBM via the cloud[1] after long queues, the experimental session involves the use of a simulator of a quantum computer. Since the simulator runs

[1] https://quantum.ibm.com/.

on classical computer, it limits the possibility of using high-dimensional datasets. Hence, the experimental session will involve the reduction of data by means of the application of the well-known Principal Component Analysis (PCA). In spite of this limitation, the results of the experimental session show that QSVM is suitable for addressing hand gesture recognition task.

## 2 Background Knowledge: Quantum Computing and Quantum Machine Learning

This section is devoted to describing the building blocks of the quantum computing, in the first part, and the basic notions of quantum machine learning, in the second part.

### 2.1 Quantum Computing: Basic Concepts

The basic unit to represent information in quantum computing is the so-called *qubit*. A qubit can be defined by a linear superposition of two *basis states*, $|0\rangle$ and $|1\rangle$. Only when measured, a qubit collapses into one of these two states [3]. Formally, a qubit, denoted as $|\psi\rangle$, is a unit vector in a two-dimensional Hilbert vector space as follows:

$$|\psi\rangle = \alpha|0\rangle + \beta|1\rangle$$

where $\alpha$ and $\beta$ are complex numbers, known as *amplitudes*, such that $|\alpha|^2 + |\beta|^2 = 1$, and $|\alpha|^2$ and $|\beta|^2$ are the probabilities that $|\psi\rangle$ will collapse, respectively, to $|0\rangle$ or $|1\rangle$, when measured. It is worth noting that each of these complex numbers, $\alpha$ and $\beta$, can be written in polar form as follows:

$$\alpha = |\alpha|e^{i\phi_0}, \quad \beta = |\beta|e^{i\phi_1}$$

where $|\alpha|$ and $|\beta|$ represent the magnitudes and $\phi_0$ and $\phi_1$ the phases of the quantum states $|0\rangle$ and $|1\rangle$, respectively.

An alternative visualization of a qubit, useful to better understand some quantum concepts, is the so-called *Bloch sphere*. This allows representing a qubit in a three-dimensional space using the following formula [12]:

$$|\psi\rangle = \cos\left(\frac{\theta}{2}\right)|0\rangle + e^{i\varphi}\sin\left(\frac{\theta}{2}\right)|1\rangle$$

In this representation, the computational basis states are located at opposite points on $z$-axis of the sphere, as shown in Fig. 1.

A set of qubits compose a *quantum register*. It is important to say that an $n$-qubit quantum register can be found in a superposition of all the $2^n$ computational basis states, as follows:

$$|\psi_n\rangle = \gamma_1|0\dots00\rangle + \gamma_2|0\dots10\rangle + \dots + \gamma_{2^n}|1\dots11\rangle$$

where $|\gamma_i|^2$, with $i = 1, \dots, 2^n$, is the probability that $|\psi_n\rangle$ will collapse to the $i$-th $n$-bit binary string, when measured [2].

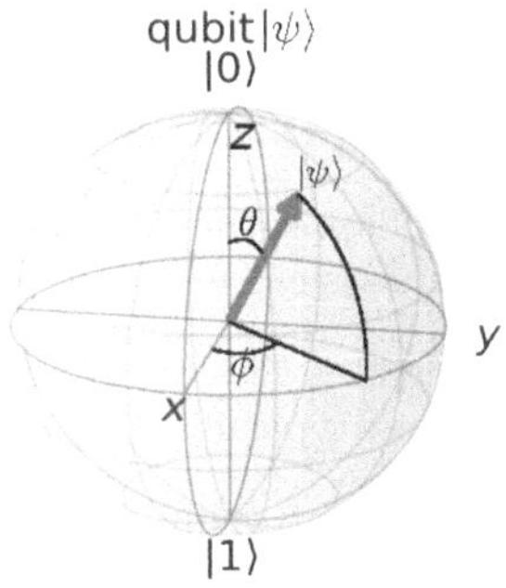


**Fig. 1.** Bloch sphere [4]

As for classical computation, *quantum algorithms* evolve quantum registers so as to transform, step by step, an input quantum state to an output quantum state, which will be conveniently measured and collapsed into a classical state [3]. Quantum algorithms are modelled by means of so-called *quantum circuits* composed of sequences of so-called *quantum gates*, i.e., reversible transformations on $n$-qubit registers. Precisely, a quantum gate is a *unitary operator* $U$ which operates on qubits as follows:

$$U|\psi\rangle = U[\alpha|0\rangle + \beta|1\rangle] = \alpha U|0\rangle + \beta U|1\rangle$$

A remarkable gate is surely the Hadamard gate ($H$). It is used to create a superposition of quantum states, each one characterized by the same probability to be measured. Together with superposition, entanglement is another quantum property useful for improving the performance of computing devices [4]. It is possible to create an entanglement between two qubits, $q_0$ and $q_1$, by applying a $CNOT$ gate (see Table 1) and considering $q_0$ as control bit and $q_1$ as a target bit. The behaviour is as follows: if $q_0$ takes value $|1\rangle$, then a bit flip is applied to $q_1$. Finally, another group of important gates are the so-called Pauli gates. In particular, Pauli-Z gate, or simply Z gate, modifies only the state $|1\rangle$ as follows: $Z|1\rangle = e^{i\phi}|1\rangle$. Essentially rotates by $\phi$ radians around the $z$-axis of the Bloch sphere. The most typical value for $\phi$ is $\pi$, hence, $Z|1\rangle = -|1\rangle$. Another example is the ZZ gate that is a two-qubit gate that applies a phase flip based on the combined state of two qubits as follows:

$$ZZ(\theta) = e^{-i\frac{\theta}{2}Z_1 \otimes Z_2}$$

where $\theta$ is a parameter to be set and $\otimes$ is the tensor product operator. Formally, the phase flip multiplies the phase of the $|1\rangle$ component by $-1$, without affecting the magnitude.

## 2.2 An Introduction to Quantum Machine Learning

Quantum Machine Learning (QML) combines quantum computing with classical machine learning to potentially enhance computational capabilities in different

**Table 1.** Quantum Gates used in this work

| Symbol | Name | Description |
|---|---|---|
|  | Measurement | It collapses the quantum state of a qubit in one of the classical states. |
| $-\boxed{H}-$ | Hadamard $H$ | It creates a uniform superposition of the two basis states, typically $\|0\rangle$ and $\|1\rangle$. |
| 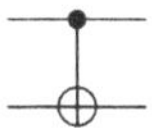 | CNOT | If the control qubit $c$ is in the state $\|1\rangle$ then apply the inversion operator on target qubit $t$. |
| $-\boxed{Z}-$ | Pauli $Z$ | It rotates the state about the $z$-axis of the Bloch sphere by $\pi$ radians. |
| $-\boxed{ZZ(\theta)}-$ | $ZZ$ gate | It is a two-qubit gate that introduces entanglement by applying a phase flip based on the combined state of two qubits. |

tasks such as classification, regression and clustering [1,6]. Our paper focuses on the classification and for this reason, also this section focuses on this topic. Traditional Machine Learning (ML) addresses classification tasks by learning mathematical models starting from labelled training data. Then, classification performance are evaluated by using testing data. Each instance of the datasets is composed of the vector of features and the output represented by categorical variables in the classification. These classical concepts continue to exist in QML since data are provided classically. On the contrary, in QML, the trained model is a quantum algorithm. Therefore, there is the need of encoding techniques capable of converting classical data in quantum states. Then, the operations represented by quantum gates in the quantum algorithm change the quantum states prepared with the encoded classical data in order to achieve the classification result.

## 3 Our Proposal

Our proposal is to apply, for the first time, QSVM for classifying sEMG signals in order to predict hand gestures (see Fig. 2). In detail, to capture sEMG signals, electrodes are placed on the skin to detect muscle activity, which is then amplified, filtered, converted to a digital format, and processed by a data acquisition system. Then, a feature extraction procedure is used to analyze and convert the raw sEMG signals into a set of meaningful numerical values, or features, that can be used for classification. At this point, QSVM is applied, after a training procedure, to predict hand movements. This prediction will be used to control the hand prosthesis. In the following of this section, details about the implemented QSVM are given.

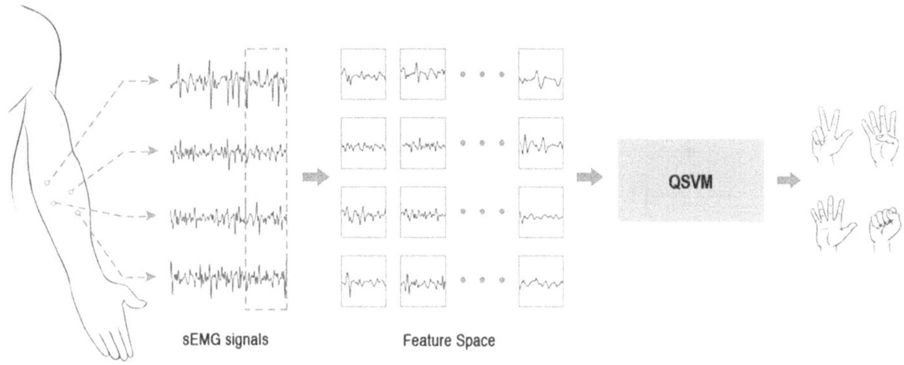


**Fig. 2.** The workflow of our proposal (image adapted from [10]).

### 3.1 Quantum-Enhanced Support Vector Machine

Quantum-enhanced Support Vector Machine (QSVM) was proposed by Havlicek et al. in [11] in order to improve the classical SVM in terms of efficiency. As described in [2], QSVM processes data provided purely classically and uses the quantum state space as the feature space. To covert classical data in quantum data, a so-called quantum feature map is exploited. In literature, there are different kinds of quantum feature map. In this work, the most common quantum feature map, namely the so-called ZZFeatureMap, is used. This choice is related to the fact that this feature map leverages entanglement, making it more expressive and suitable for a wide range of machine learning tasks. Precisely, the advantage of the entanglement is to enable to capture correlations between different features in the input data. Formally, the ZZFeatureMap converts a $n$-dimensional classical data $\boldsymbol{x}$ in a quantum state $|\Phi(\boldsymbol{x})\rangle$ on $n$-qubit register as follows:

$$|\phi(\boldsymbol{x})\rangle = U_{\Phi(\boldsymbol{x})} H^{\otimes n}$$

where $H$ denotes the conventional Hadamard gate and

$$U_{\Phi(\boldsymbol{x})} = \exp\left( i \sum_{S \subseteq [n]} \phi_S(\boldsymbol{x}) \prod_i Z_i \right)$$

where $Z_i$ is the Paul-Z gate (see Table 1) on the $i$-th qubit and $\phi_S$ is as follows:

$$\phi_S(\boldsymbol{x}) = \begin{cases} x_i & \text{if } S = \{i\} \\ (\pi - x_i)(\pi - x_j) & \text{if } S = \{i, j\} \end{cases}$$

with $|S| \leq 2$. It is important note that the $n$-qubit register is initialized to the state $|0\rangle^{\otimes n}$. In order to better understand, let us consider an example with a two-dimensional classical data (i.e., $n = 2$). In this case, it is as follows:

$$U_{\Phi(\boldsymbol{x})} = \exp\left( i x_0 Z_0 + i x_1 Z_1 + i(\pi - x_0)(\pi - x_1) Z_0 Z_1 \right).$$

From point of view of quantum circuits, $\exp(i\phi_i(\boldsymbol{x})Z_i)$ is given by the following circuit:

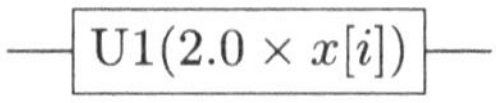


whereas, $\exp(i\phi_{\{i,j\}}(\boldsymbol{x})Z_iZ_j)$ is represented by the following circuit:

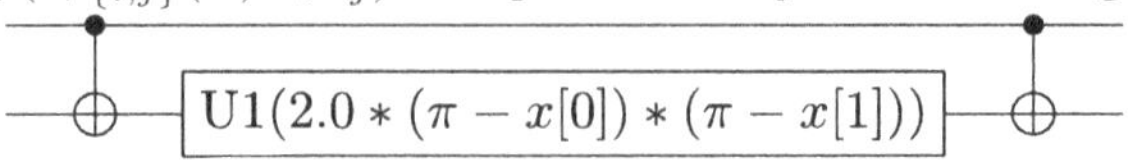


It worth noting that in the above quantum circuit, the two involved qubits are in entanglement due to the use of *CNOT* gate (see Table 1). By recalling our example on two-dimensional classical data $\boldsymbol{x}$, the whole quantum circuit to obtain $\phi(\boldsymbol{x})$ is given in Fig. 3. To summarize, the ZZFeatureMap consists of a sequence of single-qubit Z rotations applied to each qubit, followed by entangling two-qubit ZZ interactions between pairs of qubits. This pattern can be repeated. The number of times that this pattern is repeated is called *depth* of the ZZFeatureMap and it represents a hyperparameter. To conclude, the ZZFeatureMap is characterized by another hyperparameter named *entanglement type*. The entanglement type determines how qubits are connected and interact with each other through two-qubit entangling gates. For example, in the linear entanglement, qubits are entangled in a chain-like structure where each qubit interacts only with its nearest neighbor, whereas, in the full entanglement, all qubits are entangled with every other qubit. The depth and the entanglement type being hyperparameters will be adjusted for our application in the experimental session discussed in the next section.

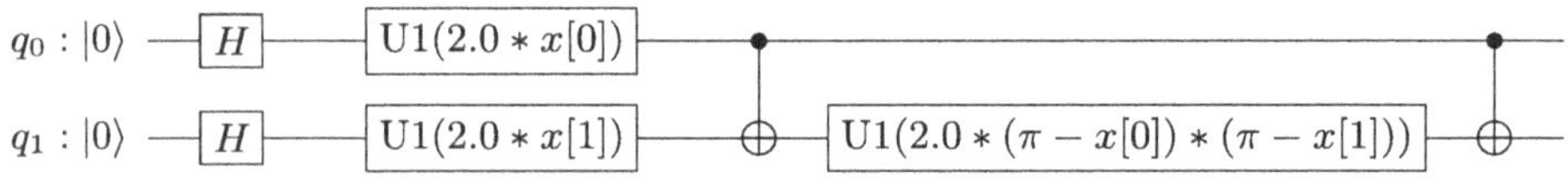


**Fig. 3.** Circuit for the quantum feature map of a two-dimensional classical data

# 4 Experiments and Results

This section is devoted to describing the experiments carried out to analyse the performance of QSVM for hand gesture recognition. Therefore, hereafter, the dataset used in the experiments, the setup of the experimental session and the obtained results are discussed.

## 4.1 Dataset

The experimental session involves a well-known database, named Ninapro[2], composed of several datasets. In our experimental session, we use the DB1 containing both sEMG and kinematic signals of the wrist and hand gathered from 27

[2] https://ninapro.hevs.ch/.

intact subjects performing 52 hand movements. However, in this paper, our focus is on sEMG signals, therefore, only these will represent our instance features. In detail, sEMG signals are captured using ten active double-differential Otto-Bock *MyoBock* 13200E sEMG electrodes which provide an amplified, bandpass-filtered, and Root Mean Square (RMS) rectified version of the raw sEMG signal [7]. Eight electrodes are uniformly placed around the forearm or stump using an elastic band, whereas, two additional electrodes are placed on the large flexor and extensor muscles of the forearm (see Fig. 4).

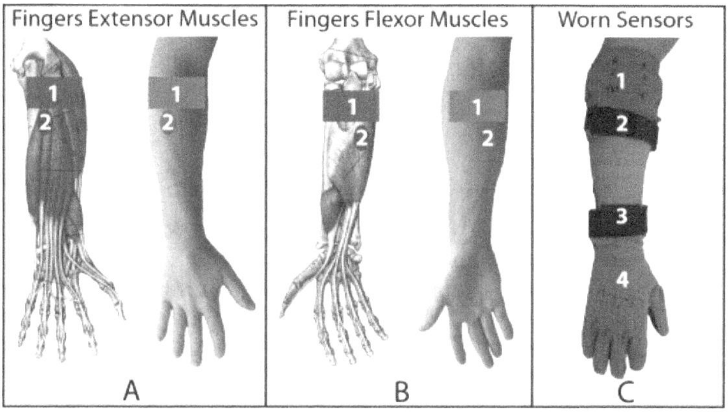


**Fig. 4.** Placement of the electrodes [7]: A.1, B.1 and C.1 show the eight equally spaced electrodes; A.2 and C.2 show the spare electrode on finger extensor muscles; B.2 shows the spare electrode placed on finger flexor muscles; C.3 shows the inclinometer and C.4 shows the Cyberglove used for kinematics data that are out of the focus of this paper.

The data acquisition is obtained by following this workflow. The subject sits on a chair, in front of a table with a large screen. The sEMG electrodes are worn on the right hand. The subject is presented with short movies appearing on the screen and is asked to simply replicate the movements depicted in the movies as accurately as possible. The dataset DB1 is obtained by asking to replicate 52 movements divided into four main classes. However, for our preliminary study, we have considered only three gestures belonging to the first class related to basic

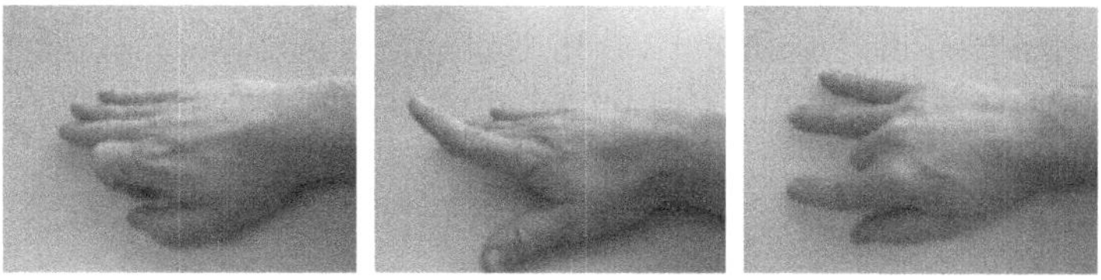

**Fig. 5.** Basic movements of the fingers [7] used in our paper as class labels.

movements of the fingers (flexions and extensions) reported in Fig. 5. Moreover, the experimental session involves the data related to 2 subjects out of 27: the first male (subject 1) and the first female (subject 6).

### 4.2 Experimental Setup

The experimental session involves the application of QSVM to solve the hand gesture recognition as binary and multi-class problem. In detail, the binary classification problem considers only the first two movements in Fig. 5, whereas, the multi-class one all the movements. In this paper, QSVM have been implemented using the Python library, provided by IBM, named Qiskit, and, in particular, the module related to quantum machine learning[3]. To run QSVM has been used an IBM simulator without noise that simulates quantum algorithms on a classical computer. This choice is due to the fact that IBM quantum real computers allow a free access only for few minutes by waiting long queue of jobs. These issues make difficult performing a complete experimentation on a real quantum computer. In order to apply QSVM, as aforementioned, it is necessary to perform a tuning procedure. Unfortunately, the use of a simulator makes the computation of experiments very expensive. For this reason, the tuning procedure is performed by considering only two values for depth and the entanglement type. In particular, $depth = 1, 3$ and $linear$ and $full$ for entanglement type. Moreover, only a reduced set of instances of the dataset are selected randomly to perform tuning procedure. In particular, 500 instances are used and split in training and test with a percentage 80%-20%. Then, 10% of the training is used for validation dataset in the tuning procedure. Finally, the Principal Component Analysis is applied to reduce the space of the features. In particular, the selected number of components are related to 95% of explained variance. The tuning procedure applies a Grid Search by considering the chosen values for the hyper-parameters and a ten-fold cross-validation in order to perform a tuning procedure independent from data. The best configuration obtained in the tuning procedure in terms of accuracy is used to predict the testing data.

The performance of QSVM are expressed in terms of standard evaluation metrics such as Accuracy, Precision, Recall, and F1 score. In detail, it is possible to compute a so-called confusion matrix by including the following information: True Positives (TP) represent positive instances that are correctly classified as positive; True Negatives (TN) represent negative instances that are correctly classified as negative; False Positives (FP) are negative instances that are incorrectly classified as positive, and False Negatives (FN) are positive instances that are incorrectly classified as negative. In the multi-class problem, each class is marked as positive to compute this information. Using these concepts, it is possible to compute the aforementioned evaluation metrics as follows:

[3] https://qiskit-community.github.io/qiskit-machine-learning/.

$$Accuracy = \frac{TP+TN}{TP+FP+TN+FN}$$
$$Precision = \frac{TP}{TP+FP}$$
$$Recall = \frac{TP}{TP+FN}$$
$$F1 - score = \frac{2 \times Precision \times Recall}{Precision + Recall}$$

### 4.3 Results

Figures 6 and 7 report the results of the tuning procedure for the male subject (subject 1) for the binary and multi-class problems, respectively. Instead, Figs. 8 and 9 report the same information for the female subject (subject 6). As shown in Fig. 6, the best configuration for the male subject in the binary problem is $depth = 3$ and linear entanglement in terms of the median accuracy, whereas, the best configuration for the multi-class problem is $depth = 3$ and full entanglement as shown in Fig. 7. As for the female subject, the best configuration in the binary problem is $depth = 3$ and full entanglement as shown in Fig. 8, whereas, the best configuration for the multi-class problem is $depth = 1$ and linear entanglement as shown in Fig. 9.

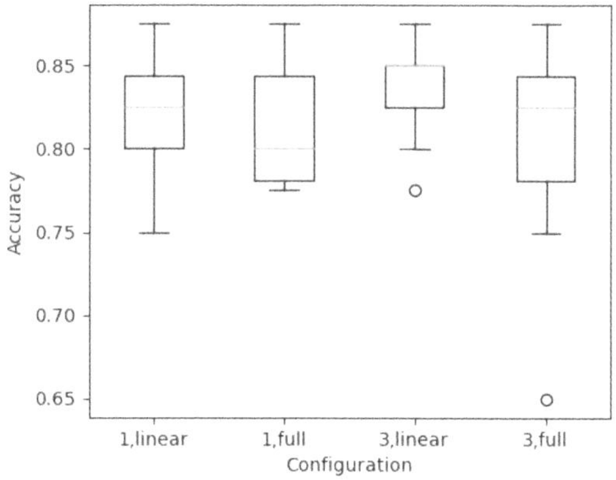


**Fig. 6.** Box plots for the tuning procedure of the male subject for binary problem

The best configurations are used to predict test data. The performance on testing data are reported in Table 2. As shown, QSVM achieves better performance for the male subject than female one. Moreover, QSVM outperforms better in binary problems than multi-class problems as predictable. However, in general, QSVM achieves good performance by achieving values for F1 score greater than 75% except for the multi-class problem of the female subject. By concluding, even if these results are preliminary due to the limitations for the expensive cost of the use of the quantum simulator, it is possible to say that QSVM can be applied to classify sEMG signals to predict hand movements.

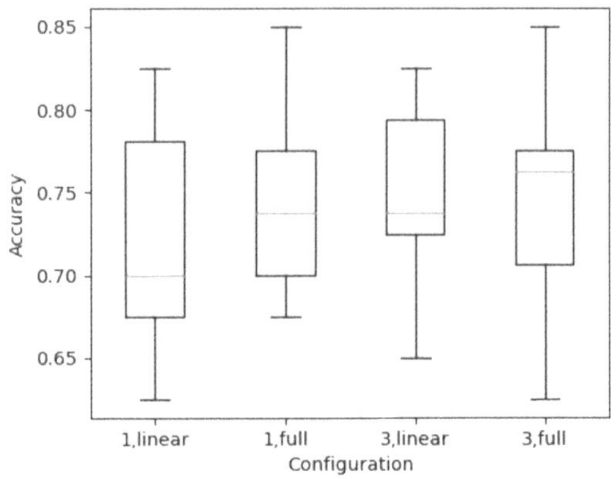


**Fig. 7.** Box plots for the tuning procedure of the male subject for multi-class problem

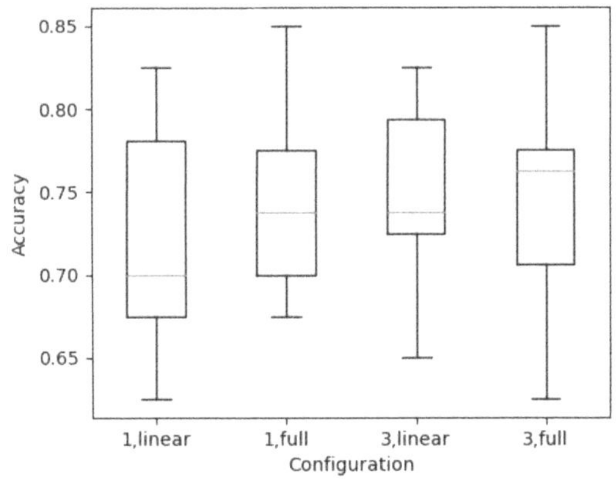


**Fig. 8.** Box plots for the tuning procedure of the female subject for binary problem

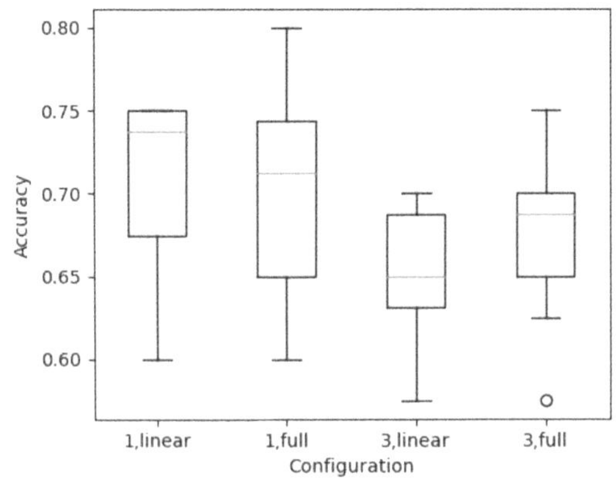


**Fig. 9.** Box plots for the tuning procedure of the female subject for multi-class problem

**Table 2.** Results of QSVM

| Problem | Accuracy | Precision | Recall | F1-score |
|---|---|---|---|---|
| Male subject - binary problem | 0.84 | 0.87 | 0.83 | 0.85 |
| Male subject - multi-class problem | 0.75 | 0.75 | 0.74 | 0.75 |
| Female subject - binary problem | 0.82 | 0.82 | 0.81 | 0.82 |
| Female subject - multi-class problem | 0.66 | 0.68 | 0.69 | 0.69 |

## 5 Conclusions

This paper presents the first application of QSVM to classify sEMG signals in order to predict hand movements. As shown by preliminary results, QSVM is suitable for this task. In the future, when there will be the possibility of accessing to the resources of real quantum computers, our proposal may be further validated by using large data and, in this way, by showing the true advantage of using quantum-powered algorithms for the classification of hand gestures.

**Acknowledgments.** This work was supported by the Italian Ministry of Research, under the complementary actions to the NRRP "Fit4MedRob - Fit for Medical Robotics" Grant (#PNC0000007).

**Disclosure of Interests.** The authors have no competing interests to declare that are relevant to the content of this article.

## References

1. Acampora, G.: Quantum machine intelligence. Quant. Mach. Intell. **1**(1), 1–3 (2019)
2. Acampora, G., Di Martino, F., Robertazzi, G.A., Vitiello, A.: A web application for running quantum-enhanced support vector machine. In: 2022 IEEE International Conference on Fuzzy Systems (FUZZ-IEEE), pp. 1–7. IEEE (2022)
3. Acampora, G., Vitiello, A.: Error mitigation in quantum measurement through fuzzy c-means clustering. In: 2021 IEEE International Conference on Fuzzy Systems (FUZZ-IEEE), pp. 1–6 (2021). https://doi.org/10.1109/FUZZ45933.2021.9494538
4. Acampora, G., Vitiello, A.: Implementing evolutionary optimization on actual quantum processors. Inf. Sci. **575**, 542–562 (2021)
5. Ahsan, M.R., Ibrahimy, M.I., Khalifa, O.O.: Electromygraphy (EMG) signal based hand gesture recognition using artificial neural network (ANN). In: 2011 4th International Conference on Mechatronics (ICOM), pp. 1–6. IEEE (2011)
6. Alchieri, L., Badalotti, D., Bonardi, P., Bianco, S.: An introduction to quantum machine learning: from quantum logic to quantum deep learning. Quant. Mach. Intell. **3**(2), 28 (2021). https://doi.org/10.1007/s42484-021-00056-8

7. Atzori, M., et al.: Building the ninapro database: a resource for the biorobotics community. In: 2012 4th IEEE RAS & EMBS International Conference on Biomedical Robotics and Biomechatronics (BioRob), pp. 1258–1265. IEEE (2012)
8. Chen, W., Zhang, Z.: Hand gesture recognition using SEMG signals based on support vector machine. In: 2019 IEEE 8th Joint International Information Technology and Artificial Intelligence Conference (ITAIC), pp. 230–234. IEEE (2019)
9. Cheng, Y., et al.: Gesture recognition based on surface electromyography-feature image. Concurren. Comput. Pract. Exp. **33**(6), e6051 (2021)
10. Geng, W., Du, Y., Jin, W., Wei, W., Hu, Y., Li, J.: Gesture recognition by instantaneous surface EMG images. Sci. Rep. **6**(1), 36571 (2016)
11. Havlíček, V., et al.: Supervised learning with quantum-enhanced feature spaces. Nature **567**(7747), 209–212 (2019)
12. Kaye, P., Laflamme, R., Mosca, M., et al.: An Introduction to Quantum computing. Oxford University Press (2007)
13. Mane, S., Kambli, R., Kazi, F., Singh, N.: Hand motion recognition from single channel surface EMG using wavelet & artificial neural network. Procedia Comput. Sci. **49**, 58–65 (2015)
14. Pomboza-Junez, G., Terriza, J.H.: Hand gesture recognition based on SEMG signals using support vector machines. In: 2016 IEEE 6th International Conference on Consumer Electronics-Berlin (ICCE-Berlin), pp. 174–178. IEEE (2016)
15. Simão, M., Neto, P., Gibaru, O.: EMG-based online classification of gestures with recurrent neural networks. Pattern Recogn. Lett. **128**, 45–51 (2019)
16. Toledo-Pérez, D.C., Rodríguez-Reséndiz, J., Gómez-Loenzo, R.A., Jauregui-Correa, J.: Support vector machine-based EMG signal classification techniques: a review. Appl. Sci. **9**(20), 4402 (2019)
17. Wang, X., Tang, L., Zheng, Q., Yang, X., Lu, Z.: IRDC-net: An inception network with a residual module and dilated convolution for sign language recognition based on surface electromyography. Sensors **23**(13), 5775 (2023)

# AI Studies

# Enhancing Literature Reviews in Human-Machine Collaboration: A Comparative Analysis of Topic Modeling Methods in Computer Science

Pei-Yi Chen[1], Yu-chen Hung[2(✉)], Jorng-Tzong Horng[1], and Li-Ching Wu[3]

[1] Department of Computer Science and Information Engineering, National Central University, Taoyuan, Taiwan
horng@db.csie.ncu.edu.tw

[2] School of Business, Singapore University of Social Sciences, Singapore, Singapore
ychung@suss.edu.sg

[3] Department of Biomedical Sciences and Engineering, National Central University, Taoyuan, Taiwan

**Abstract.** This study conducts a targeted literature review on human-machine collaboration (HMC) within computer science from 2019 to 2023, utilizing topic modeling to address challenges such as outdated research and manual curation costs. We compare Latent Dirichlet Allocation (LDA) and Non-Negative Matrix Factorization (NMF) to determine their effectiveness in analyzing HMC literature. Our results show that NMF, which leverages TF-IDF weighting, produces more distinct and interpretable topics compared to the overlapping clusters often generated by LDA. Specifically, NMF identifies four key themes in HMC: natural language processing applications, the integration of human strengths with algorithms, advancements in image-related tasks, and the application and evaluation of AI agents. These findings suggest that NMF is better suited for capturing nuanced research trends in HMC. This study provides valuable insights for improving literature review methodologies and advancing the understanding of human-machine collaboration in computer science.

**Keywords:** human-machine collaboration (HMC) · literature review · topic modeling

## 1 Introduction

With the rapid development and application of generative artificial intelligence (GAI), an algorithm trained on large datasets enables the creation of novel content, such as text, images, and audio [1]. The roles of humans in the workplace have evolved. The introduction of tools like ChatGPT, GitHub Copilot, and DALL-E has initiated widespread adoption across the industry to enhance productivity [2]. As a subset of AI agents, GAI is renowned for its ability to interact with human agents, understand human languages,

© The Author(s), under exclusive license to Springer Nature Singapore Pte Ltd. 2025
W.-T. Chu et al. (Eds.): TAAI 2024, CCIS 2414, pp. 235–246, 2025.
https://doi.org/10.1007/978-981-96-4589-3_17

and generate novel content [3]. Its application in creative tasks and various other fields presents an opportunity as well as challenges since humans are required to interact with GAI agents in tasks that are traditionally reserved for human agents, otherwise, they are at risk of being replaced [4]. An urgency to understand how to leverage human uniqueness and machine strength through HMC has emerged across disciplines.

An examination of publications on the topic of HMC across disciplines renders evidence of a rapid increase in scholarly interest over the past 5 years (see Table 2), where computer science shows the strongest growth. There is a need to overview the state of knowledge on human-machine interaction to assess the role that the academic communities play in informing the synthesis between human and machine strength.

Despite the rich literature on HMC, it remains limited for two reasons. Firstly, most existing systematic reviews focus on studies conducted before 2020, failing to adequately address the rapid developments in GAI and its implication on HMC in recent years. Secondly, most studies predominantly rely on manual curation for literature reviews. Manual curation is shown to be subject to constraints in subjective classification, managing the rapidly expanding volume of literature, and difficulties in maintaining up-to-date analyses [5, 6]. Due to these limitations, researchers have turned to topic modeling methods, where Latent Dirichlet Allocation (LDA) has been most widely adopted. However, LDA has the issue of generating overlapping topics due to its reliance on extracting topics based on raw word frequencies, which limits its ability to capture finer details within documents [7].

To address these limitations in pertinence and methods, we utilized web scraping techniques to collect articles related to HMC from prominent preprint servers, i.e., arXiv, by focusing on computer science research from 2019 to 2023. This process resulted in a research dataset comprising 2579 article abstracts. We then compared results from the two topic modeling methods, i.e., LDA and NMF, to analyze these abstracts. Unlike LDA, Non-Negative Matrix Factorization (NMF) depends on TF-IDF weighting, allowing it to capture subtle differences and specific content in the documents.

Our results show that the two methods suggest different optimum numbers of topics (LDA = 9 vs. NMF = 4) and high-frequency topic words (LDA model, system, user, learning vs. NMF = game, video, motion, action). The topic words are more specific in NMF, while LDA tends to offer generic terms. Overall, the NMF outputs offer more precise and interpretable results in terms of topics and numbers. The topics identified by NMF are human-machine collaboration in (1) the application of natural language processing (2) combining human strength with algorithms in bettering other techniques such as deep learning, (3) advancing image-related tasks such as medical image processing and game design, (4) the application of AI agents and the evaluation of their interpretability, such as AI systems capable of simulating human psychological states, exhibiting interpretable behaviors, and generating trust.

By incorporating updated research outputs and a comparison of topic modeling methods, this study provides a more comprehensive and in-depth understanding of HMC in the area of computer science. Our results contribute in two ways. Firstly, it suggests the 4 aspects of the CS community to address the synthesis of human and algorithm strength through HMC. Second, it compared the performance of two topic models for literature review, where NMF yielded more interpretable results diagnostic of the subfield in computer science.

## 2 Related Works

### 2.1 Human-Machine Collaboration (HMC)

**Concept.** HMC refers to the interaction and coordination behavior of humans and intelligent machines to achieve common goals jointly, focusing on the concept of "jointly" [8, 9]. For modern organizations, human-machine collaboration is of paramount importance, as it can integrate human expertise and the ability of machines to perform mundane and repetitive tasks, possessing the potential for hybrid intelligence that can contribute to enhancing work efficiency, performance, and decision-making within organizations [10, 11].

**Theories and Frameworks.** There are some research theories and frameworks for understanding HMC. The study by Li et al. [10] employed bibliometric analysis methods to systematically review the research landscape of human-machine collaboration at the organizational level. Based on the frequency and influence of publications, they synthesized the existing theories into four key dimensions: innovation skills, organizational performance, the impact of HMC on human resource management, and the role of HMC in the field of information technology. Akmeikina et al. [12] investigated AI-based HMC behaviors and categorized the literature by incorporating the notion of empowerment effects. They emphasized dividing hybrid intelligence behaviors into three categories: "human shaping machine behavior" through providing input data for AI to learn, "machine shaping human behavior" by utilizing machines as assistive tools, and "human-machine co-behavior" where machines enhance human work efficiency or substitute for humans.

**Techniques and Applications.** The technologies in computer science serve as the cornerstone of the flourishing development of HMC. Techniques like machine learning, natural language processing, and computer vision enable machines to perceive and learn, while human cognition excels in creativity and decision-making under uncertainty. This synergistic combination has inspired the development of intelligent assistants [13, 14], decision support systems [15], and other AI systems. Moreover, the use of HMC has become increasingly prevalent in the domains of electrical engineering, bioengineering, bioinformatics, and medicine.

**Concerns.** While HMC offers numerous potential benefits, it simultaneously raises a series of concerns worthy of deep reflection. Firstly, data privacy and security issues are particularly prominent. As machine learning algorithms continue to advance, the volume of data they process and analyze has increased dramatically, potentially elevating the risk of sensitive user information breaches [16]. Secondly, excessive reliance on machine assistance may reduce human cognitive autonomy and the emergence of automation bias, potentially resulting in erroneous decision-making by humans [17]. Lastly, in collaborative environments, human users continue to harbor doubts and distrust regarding machine performance, particularly in evaluating its accuracy and reliability [18, 19]. Therefore, while advancing HMC, these challenges must be carefully scrutinized to ensure the responsible development and application of HMC technologies.

### 2.2 Literature Review Methodologies

As mentioned above, previous studies have used systematic reviews to identify research focuses on HMC. These studies include the proposal of conceptual frameworks [10, 12] and the overview of technological advancements and research trends [20–23]. However, these studies may face the issue of high labor costs, subjectivity, and scalability. Therefore, we aim to achieve the same objective using automated topic modeling techniques.

Numerous prior studies have demonstrated that topic modeling assists in summarizing research trends across domains through literature analysis. For instance, in the field of bioinformatics, LDA highlighted key topics such as "Molecular Modeling," "Gene Expression," and "Immunoinformatics" exhibiting the interrelatedness of different research areas within the discipline [24]. LDA has also been applied to systematic literature reviews in industrial engineering and management, as well as social sciences and education [25, 26]. In addition, Grotheer et al. [27] organized scientific literature related to COVID-19 into a layer structure consisting of 8 main topics and 52 subtopics using hierarchical NMF. These examples highlight the practicality of topic modeling in discovering and understanding the evolving research trends across academic fields.

The study by Gurcan & Sevik [28] synthesizes the advantages we need to consider, such as the literature focusing on HMC and employing topic modeling methods to uncover latent topics. Nevertheless, the literature included in their analysis only extends up to 2018, which is insufficient to capture the rapid developments in the field of HMC in recent years. Additionally, given that the studies by Rizvi et al. [29] and Alnusyan et al. [30] indicate that LDA tends to generate more generic and irrelevant topics, we have incorporated NMF, which is also a traditional topic modeling method, into our study. We will compare the results of LDA and NMF. The comparison with the respective studies is shown in Table 1.

## 3 Materials and Methods

### 3.1 Data Collection

Firstly, we pre-defined a set of search terms: ("human-AI collaboration" OR "human-machine collaboration" OR "human in the loop" OR "human-machine co-creation" OR "human-AI teams" OR "human-robot collaboration"). Due to the advantages of preprints such as rapid academic circulation and open access [31], to keep up with the flourishing development of HMC research, we used a web crawler to obtain abstracts of HMC research published in Computer Science (CS) between 2019 and 2023 on arXiv, a well-known electronic preprint website. Ultimately, we created a research dataset containing 2579 article abstracts.

**Table 1.** The comparison between our study and others.

| Author (s) | Data size | Data period | HMC | Methodology |
|---|---|---|---|---|
| [12] | 38 | 2010 - 2021 | Yes | Manually |
| [20] | 32 | 2003 - 2009 | Yes | Manually |
| [21] | 337 | 1990 - 2002 | Yes | Manually |
| [22] | 45 | 2015 - 2020 | Yes | Manually |
| [23] | 758 | 1990 - 2008 | Yes | Manually |
| [10] | 111 | 1985 - 4 November 2022 | Yes | Bibliometric analysis |
| [27] | 25663 | - | No | NMF |
| [24] | 3875 | Until 9 March 2022 | No | LDA |
| [26] | 1185 | 1982 - 2021 | No | LDA |
| [25] | 45 | - | No | LDA |
| [28] | 33830 | 1998 - 2018 | Yes | LDA |
| Our work | 2579 | 2019 - 2023 | Yes | LDA, NMF |

At this stage, we conducted annual statistics on the total number of studies in computer science (*#All*) and the number of studies focusing on HMC (*#HMC*), and calculated its proportion (*HMC%*), as shown in Table 2. This growth trend indicates that over the past five years, HMC has received increasing attention in CS, further emphasizing the importance and potential applications of HMC.

**Table 2.** Descriptive statistics

| | 2019 | 2020 | 2021 | 2022 | 2023 |
|---|---|---|---|---|---|
| #HMC | 252 | 345 | 426 | 589 | 967 |
| #All | 47860 | 61984 | 71010 | 76555 | 98906 |
| HMC% | 0.5% | 0.6% | 0.6% | 0.8% | 1% |

### 3.2 Topic Modeling

Latent Dirichlet Allocation (LDA) and Non-Negative Matrix Factorization (NMF) are commonly used topic modeling methods, and both require text preprocessing, involving the following multiple steps to improve the quality of topic modeling results:

- Tokenization: Breaking the text into words or tokens, and converting all words to lowercase.
- Data Cleaning: Removing non-English characters, and punctuation.

- Stop Word Removal: Removing common words that carry little content-related meaning, such as "the", "a", "when", "is", etc. The pre-defined list of stop words can be excluded from the documents using NLTK in Python.
- Stemming and Lemmatization: Stemming involves removing suffixes from words to produce stems, while lemmatization is the process of mapping words to their base forms using a dictionary, helping to reduce the number of unique words in the data.
- Handling Bigrams and Trigrams: Bigrams and trigrams are combinations of two or three words that frequently appear together in text. Including these multi-word phrases can improve the model's ability to capture meaningful topics.

In addition to basic preprocessing, we also removed previously used search terms (i.e., "human-AI collaboration", "human-machine collaboration", "human in the loop", "human-machine co-creation", "human-AI teams", and "human-robot collaboration") and common abstract starters ("study", "research", "paper"). Since the search terms are known to be related to the search results, removing them might reveal different top words, thereby enhancing the distinctiveness of the topics.

After the text is pre-processed, it is input into the following two topic models:

- Latent Dirichlet Allocation (LDA): LDA is a generative probabilistic model used to uncover latent topics in a corpus [32]. As an unsupervised topic modeling algorithm, LDA reduces the need for manual annotation of data. It employs the "bag-of-words" concept, which calculates the frequency of words within each document; the higher the frequency of a word, the greater its relevance to a given topic [33].
- Non-Negative Matrix Factorization (NMF): Unlike LDA, NMF is not a probabilistic model but a linear algebra algorithm that utilizes matrix factorization [7]. It reveals latent topics by decomposing high-dimensional vectors into non-negative low-dimensional representations. Additionally, it takes a normalized TF-IDF matrix as input, allowing comparability between documents.

To evaluate the quality of topic modeling, topic coherence measures the degree of similarity among the top words within topics. We used the C_v measure to gauge the semantic coherence of the topics extracted by LDA and NMF [34]. C_v measure is an indirect confirmation measure that uses a one-set segmentation method and combines the cosine similarity with the normalized pointwise mutual information (NPMI) and the Boolean sliding window [35].

### 3.3 Topic Interpretation

After training and evaluating the topic model, we selected the hyperparameter settings with the highest coherence score. We then extracted the topic modeling results to gain a deeper understanding of the fundamental topics within the corpus. The process of interpreting the topics involved labeling based on themes with common or unique words and examining the articles containing these words. Through manual interpretation, we not only enhanced our understanding of the context but also ensured that the topics were meaningful.

# 4 Results

## 4.1 Selection of the Optimum Number of Topics

To determine the optimal number of topics, we sampled the highest coherence scores during parameter iterations. Figure 1 shows the coherence scores (*C_v*), along with the corresponding number of topics (*#topics*).

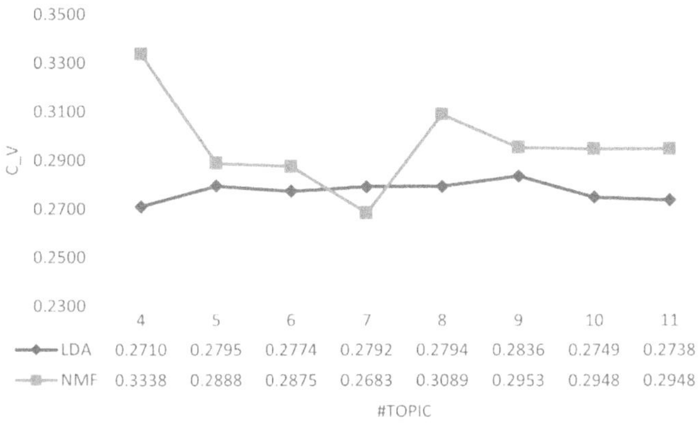


**Fig. 1.** Coherence scores and the corresponding number of topics.

Then, we apply LDA and NMF to extract latent topics from the abstracts, identifying the top 10 highest-weighted words within each topic. These words help label the topics and interpret the characteristics represented by each dimension.

Table 3 lists the dimensions extracted by the two topic models and their corresponding top words in CS.

**Natural Language Processing – LDA's Topic 1 and NMF's Topic 1.** It represents the technical support for HMC provided by natural language processing (NLP). For instance, Roth et al. [36] altered the tone of expressions in social robots to measure the impact on the strategies or emotions of human participants. Similarly, Domingo & Casacuberta [37] proposed a framework for scholars and machines to modernize historical documents together, generating new versions of these documents.

**Other Techniques – LDA's Topic 2 and NMF's Topic 2.** In addition to the support of NLP such as large language models (LLM), the importance of other techniques and algorithms in the field of computer science should not be underestimated. For example, Tjomsland et al. [38] used state-of-the-art deep learning methods to bring HMC closer to human-human collaboration. Klute et al. [39] suggested strategies that combine human strengths with algorithms to perform semi-automatic map labeling. Topic 2 from NMF illustrates applications of HMC based on reinforcement learning, such as robot-assisted dressing [40] and autonomous agents teaching complex skills to novice humans through communication and feedback [41].

**Table 3.** Topic modeling results for CS.

| LDA | | NMF | |
|---|---|---|---|
| Topic ID | Words | Topic ID | Words |
| 1 | model, system, task, data, learning, user, language, approach, work, llm | 1 | agent, data, llm, task, text, language, user, sensor, learning, behavior |
| 2 | model, method, learning, approach, task, using, data, system, object, algorithm | 2 | policy, control, action, rl, environment, reward, function, motion, learning, planning |
| 3 | model, design, approach, system, user,method, result, agent, different, show | 3 | object, video, task, action, 3d, ic, prediction, game, motion, pose |
| 4 | task, control, learning, user, performance, system, agent, model, approach, result | 4 | explanation, model, system, design, image, ml, trust, expert, data |
| 5 | learning, performance, dataset, data, model, system, method, task, datasets, language | | |
| 6 | task, system, safety, user, model, approach, method, work, learning, using | | |
| 7 | system, learning, model, task, user, analysis, present, framework, tool, decision | | |
| 8 | system, explanation, agent, learning, approach, design, user, data, work, model | | |
| 9 | learning, model, using, data, method, task, work, framework, agent, application | | |

**Imaging Task – NMF's Topic 3.** Advancements in HMC have contributed significantly to image-related tasks. For example, in medical image processing, Computer-Assisted Interventions (C4C) enhance the precision and reliability of clinical surgeries by integrating real-time sensory data with expert knowledge [42]. In the field of game design, HMC can be employed to train agents that mimic human interactions within environments, facilitating the creation of interactive Non-Player Characters [43].

**Application of AI Agents – LDA's Topics 3, 7, 8, 9 and NMF's Topic 4.** It discusses the application of AI agents and the evaluation of their interpretability. This includes AI systems capable of simulating human psychological states, exhibiting interpretable behaviors, and generating trust [44]. Debiasing these systems is also crucial [45]. Topic 4 from NMF can specifically correspond to Topic 8 from LDA. Although the combination of prominent words differs, there are key terms that can be identified as belonging to a similar cluster.

**Performance and Safety of HMC – LDA's Topics 4, 5, 6.** These studies show that collaboration between humans and AI can significantly enhance the performance of cybersecurity systems [46] and also impact performance in creative tasks [47].

## 4.2 Comparison of Word Clouds

In the next, based on the word clouds generated from the two topic models (see Figs. 2 and 3), clear differences between them can be observed. The topic words extracted by LDA for human-machine collaboration research are relatively uniform, with high-frequency general terms such as 'model' and 'system' being particularly prominent. In contrast, the topic words extracted by NMF are more diverse, and include more concrete terms related to application areas such as 'game' and 'video'.

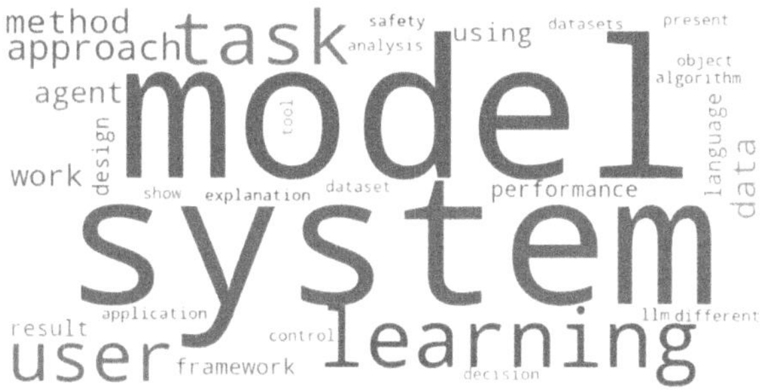


**Fig. 2.** Word clouds of top words extracted by LDA.

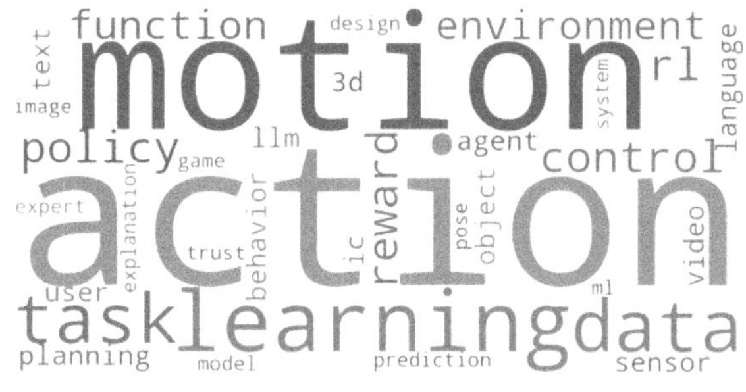


**Fig. 3.** Word clouds of top words extracted by NMF.

Overall, LDA produced clusters that were more general and subject to multiple interpretations, whereas NMF provided more diverse and specialized topic words [7], potentially aligning better with human judgment and expectations. This suggests that NMF may offer advantages over LDA in uncovering research trends and providing more refined topic interpretations, which is particularly important for further exploration of the development of human-machine collaboration in specific disciplines.

## 5 Discussions and Conclusions

Compared to previous studies that predominantly employed a single methodology, this research incorporates two distinct topic modeling techniques, LDA and NMF, providing a more diverse array of analytical results and insights. According to the study's findings, while LDA generates topics with broad coverage, it may fall short in terms of detail. In contrast, the topics produced by NMF are more granular, capturing subtle differences and specific content within the documents. This dual analytical approach not only enhances the accuracy and richness of topic modeling but also offers multi-faceted insights, aiding in a deeper understanding of the complexity and diversity of HMC.

Our work reviewed literature from the past five years to address the rapidly evolving field of HMC, revealing the current state of research in this domain. However, this study also has certain limitations. Firstly, although our dataset was drawn solely from computer science literature, HMC is also thriving in other fields, such as education, management, and finance. This means that our findings may not fully reflect the latest developments and characteristics of HMC in these excluded domains. Secondly, the test documents mainly collected from ArXiv also create another issue of missing regular research literature. Thirdly, we employed traditional topic modeling methods, LDA and NMF, in our research. In this era of continuous advancements in NLP technologies, novel topic modeling methods such as Top2Vec and BERTopic may offer richer analytical results and insights.

In conclusion, our study utilized LDA and NMF to extract latent topics in the field of HMC within computer science. We found that, in the performance of traditional topic models, NMF might be better suited than LDA for topic modeling on abstracts. Future research could not only expand the dataset to include more domains, make full use of regular research literature (such as journal articles), and adopt emerging research methods but also extend the time span to cover longer-term trends and changes, providing a more comprehensive perspective.

**Acknowledgments.** This work was supported by the National Science and Technology Council, Taiwan (NSTC113–2221-E-008–005).

## References

1. Feuerriegel, S., et al.: Generative ai. Bus. Inf. Syst. Eng. **66**(1), 111–126 (2024)
2. Cu, M.K., et al.: Humans+ AI: exploring the collaboration between AI and human labor in the workplace. In: 2023 9th International HCI and UX Conference in Indonesia (CHIuXiD). IEEE (2023)
3. Mahesh, A., et al.: GAI in healthcare system: transforming research in medicine and care for patients. In: Applied Data Science and Smart Systems, pp. 63–70. CRC Press (2025)
4. Xiao, L., Kumar, V.J.J.o.S.R.: Robotics for Customer Service: a Useful Complement or an Ultimate Substitute? **24**(1), 9–29 (2021)
5. Butcher, B., et al.: Optimising Human-Machine Collaboration for Efficient High-Precision Information Extraction from Text Documents **1**(2), 1–27 (2024)
6. Järvelin, K., Vakkari, P.: The evolution of library and information science 1965–1985: a content analysis of journal articles. Inf. Process. Manage. **29**(1), 129–144 (1993)

7. Egger, R., Yu, J.: A topic modeling comparison between lda, nmf, top2vec, and bertopic to demystify twitter posts. Front. Sociol. **7**, 886498 (2022)
8. Bauer, A., Wollherr, D., Buss, M.J.I.J.o.H.R.: Human–robot collaboration: a survey **5**(01), 47–66 (2008)
9. Grosz, B.J.: Collaborative systems (AAAI-94 presidential address). AI Mag. **17**(2), 67 (1996)
10. Li, J.-M., et al.: Systematic literature review of human–machine collaboration in organizations using bibliometric analysis. Manag. Decis. **61**(10), 2920–2944 (2023)
11. Castro, A., Silva, F., Santos, V.J.S.: Trends of Human-Robot Collaboration in Industry Contexts: Handover, Learning, and Metrics **21**(12), 4113 (2021)
12. Akmeikina, E., et al.: Empowerment Effects in Human-Machine Collaboration-a Systematic Literature Review and Directions on Hybrid Intelligence Behavior Patterns (2022)
13. Azvine, B., et al.: The Intelligent Assistant: An Overview, pp. 215–238 (2000)
14. Petricek, T., et al.: Ai assistants: A framework for semi-automated data wrangling **35**(9), 9295–9306 (2022)
15. Marois, A., et al.: Policy Capturing to Support Pilot Decision-Making (2023)
16. Mughal, A.A.J.J.o.A.I., Li, M.: Management, Artificial Intelligence in Information Security: Exploring the Advantages, Challenges, and Future Directions **2**(1), 22–34 (2018)
17. Goddard, K., Roudsari, A., Wyatt, J.C.: Automation bias: a systematic review of frequency, effect mediators, and mitigators. J. Am. Med. Inform. Assoc. **19**(1), 121–127 (2012)
18. Yan, L., et al.: Human-AI Collaboration in Thematic Analysis using ChatGPT: A User Study and Design Recommendations. in Extended Abstracts of the CHI Conference on Human Factors in Computing Systems (2024)
19. Brinkley, J., et al.: An Open Road Evaluation of a Self-Driving Vehicle Human–Machine Interface Designed for Visually Impaired Users **35**(11), 1018–1032 (2019)
20. Agrawal, A., Boese, M., Sarker, S.: A Review of the HCI Literature in IS: The Missing Links of Computer-Mediated Communication, Culture, and Interaction (2010)
21. Li, N.L., Zhang, P.: The intellectual development of human-computer interaction research: a critical assessment of the MIS literature (1990–2002). J. Assoc. Inf. Syst. **6**(11), 9 (2005)
22. Semeraro, F., et al.: Human–Robot Collaboration and Machine Learning: A Systematic Review of Recent Research **79**, 102432 (2023)
23. Zhang, P., et al.: The Intellectual Advancement of Human-Computer Interaction Research: A Critical Assessment of the MIS Literature (1990–2008) **1**(3), 55–107 (2009)
24. Ebrahimi, F., Dehghani, M., Makkizadeh, F.J.B.R.I.: Analysis of Persian Bioinformatics Research with Topic Modeling **2023**(1), 3728131 (2023)
25. Queiroz, G.A., Alves Junior, P.N., Costa Melo, I.J.S.: Digitalization as an Enabler to SMEs Implementing Lean-Green? A Systematic Review through the Topic Modelling Approach **14**(21), 14089 (2022)
26. Nylander, E., Tan, J.J.I.J.o.C.E.: Typifying Educational Research in Singapore and Sweden: a Comparative Bibliometric Approach Based on Topics 2000–2020 **24**(3/4), 125–143 (2022)
27. Grotheer, R., et al.: COVID-19 Literature Topic-Based Search via Hierarchical NMF (2020)
28. Gurcan, F., Sevik, S.: Human-computer interaction: a literature analysis from 1998 to 2018 using automated text mining. In: 2019 1st International Informatics and Software Engineering Conference (UBMYK). IEEE (2019)
29. Rizvi, R.F., et al.: Analyzing social media data to understand consumer information needs on dietary supplements. In: MEDINFO 2019: Health and Wellbeing e-Networks for All, pp. 323–327. IOS Press (2019)
30. Alnusyan, R., et al.: A semi-supervised approach for user reviews topic modeling and classification. In: 2020 International Conference on Computing and Information Technology (ICCIT-1441). IEEE (2020)
31. Smart, P.J.S.E.: The Evolution, Benefits, and Challenges of Preprints and their Interaction with Journals **9**(1), 79–84 (2022)

32. Blei, D.M., Ng, A.Y., Jordan, M.I.J.J.o.m.L.r.: Latent Dirichlet Allocation. **3**(Jan), 993–1022 (2003)
33. Asmussen, C.B., Møller, C.J.J.o.B.D.: Smart Literature Review: a Practical Topic Modelling Approach to Exploratory Literature Review **6**(1), 1–18 (2019)
34. M'sik, B., Casablanca, B.M.J.I.J.: Topic Modeling Coherence: A Comparative Study Between lda and nmf Models using Covid'19 Corpus **9**(4) (2020)
35. Röder, M., Both, A., Hinneburg, A.: Exploring the space of topic coherence measures. In: Proceedings of the Eighth ACM International Conference on Web Search and Data Mining (2015)
36. Roth, A.M., et al.: A robot's expressive language affects human strategy and perceptions in a competitive game. In: 2019 28th IEEE International Conference on Robot and Human Interactive Communication (RO-MAN). IEEE (2019)
37. Domingo, M., Casacuberta, F.J.a.p.a.: An Interactive Machine Translation Framework for Modernizing Historical Documents (2019)
38. Tjomsland, J., Shafti, A., Faisal, A.A.J.a.p.a.: Human-Robot Collaboration via Deep Reinforcement Learning of Real-World Interactions (2019)
39. Klute, F., et al.: Exploring semi-automatic map labeling. In: Proceedings of the 27th ACM SIGSPATIAL International Conference on Advances in Geographic Information Systems (2019)
40. Clegg, A., et al.: Learning to Collaborate from Simulation for Robot-Assisted Dressing **5**(2), 2746–2753 (2020)
41. Roy, S., et al.: Mutual Reinforcement Learning (2019)
42. Vercauteren, T., et al.: Cai4cai: the Rise of Contextual Artificial Intelligence in Computer-Assisted Interventions **108**(1), 198–214 (2019)
43. Borovikov, I., et al.: Towards interactive training of non-player characters in video games (2019)
44. Kambhampati, S.: Challenges of human-aware AI systems: AAAI presidential address. AI Mag. **41**(3), 3–17 (2020)
45. Mualla, Y., et al.: Towards Explainability for a Civilian UAV Fleet Management using an Agent-Based Approach (2019)
46. Alam, S.J.a.p.a.: Cybersecurity: Past, Present and Future (2022)
47. Shaikh, S.J., Cruz, I.J.a.p.a.: Alexa, Do You Know Anything? The Impact of an Intelligent Assistant on Team Interactions and Creative Performance Under Time Scarcity (2019)

# Metal Price Prediction by Encoding Daily Insights of Sparse Macroeconomic Factors and Integrating Dynamic Asset Correlations

Tzu-En Wu[1], Shiou-Chi Li[2], and Jen-Wei Huang[1(✉)]

[1] Department of Electrical Engineering, National Cheng Kung University, Tainan, Taiwan
n26102084@gs.ncku.edu.tw , jwhuang@mail.ncku.edu.tw
[2] Institute of Computer and Communication Engineering, Department of Electrical Engineering, National Cheng Kung University, Tainan, Taiwan

**Abstract.** The intrinsic value of metals provides a stable hedge against inflation; however, various macroeconomic factors, such as inflation, interest rates, and money supply, can have a profound impact on metal prices. This paper proposes a deep learning model to predict the prices of non-ferrous and precious metals, given their importance as components in investment portfolios. Positional encoding was applied to encode the daily insights of the sparse macroeconomic data, and a dynamic correlation encoder was used to model asset relationships without predefined information. In experiments, the proposed framework outperformed state-of-the-art methods in terms of Mean Absolute Error (MAE).

**Keywords:** Metal price prediction · Daily Insights of Macroeconomic indicators · Dynamic Asset Correlations

## 1 Introduction

In predicting metal prices, investors must contend with highly specific economic factors at the global scale. Metals have traditionally been a reliable hedge against inflation, due to a stable foundation provided by their intrinsic value. The ability to obtain reliable predictions of metal prices is crucial to investors and industry alike.

Time series prediction, commonly used to deal with financial data, has also been applied to the price of metals. Multivariate time series prediction [20,23] enhances model performance by incorporating cross-variate information and relative features. The FEDformer model [25] uses Transformer to enhance long-term forecasting by enabling trend decomposition. It is interesting to note that these complex models are often outperformed by simpler models [23] in which historical data are decomposed into trend and seasonal components. Nonetheless, this simpler approach often overlooks some fundamental aspects of financial markets,

© The Author(s), under exclusive license to Springer Nature Singapore Pte Ltd. 2025
W.-T. Chu et al. (Eds.): TAAI 2024, CCIS 2414, pp. 247–261, 2025.
https://doi.org/10.1007/978-981-96-4589-3_18

prompting research [3,13] into the relationships between different assets, sectors, or industries.

Similarities between the time series of stock prices and those of metals make it possible to transfer the methods used in stock price prediction to the prediction of metal prices. From the basic method, such as ARIMA-based [22] and SVR-based [2] models or conventional Recursive Neural Network-based machine learning methods [4,24] are employed, projecting time series in multidimensional space helps to obtain better representations and enhancing prediction performance. GNN-based methods [3,10,13] were developed with the aim of modeling multiple assets simultaneously and assessing the relationships among them.

However, metal prices are highly correlated with global economic trends and thus have different characteristics compared to stock price predictions. Stock price predictions are often influenced by specific financial performance, market sentiment, and short-term supply-demand fluctuations, while metal prices are more significantly affected by macroeconomic factors such as global economic conditions, geopolitical events, monetary policies, and inflation rates. Therefore, if methods designed specifically for stock market predictions are used to predict metal prices, they may not capture the impact of macroeconomic variables on metal prices, leading to limited predictive performance.

The interrelationship between metal prices and macroeconomic factors has been demonstrated in several studies [8,14,15,19]. Indicators such as inflation rates, interest rates, and money supply can have a profound impact on metal prices. For example, the fear of inflation typically drives up the prices of gold or other precious metals. The ability to obtain accurate predictions of metals prices depends on an understanding of the underlying influences and how to exploit them. Unfortunately, reports pertaining to macroeconomic indicators generally include only one value per month or season. The lack of research on the use of macroeconomic indicators to predict asset prices can largely be attributed to the sparsity of data, which makes it difficult to train predictive models. In this study, we sought to improve prediction capability by developing a module designed specifically to deal with sparse data. This module performs daily insight encoding, which is data extension method in conjunction with positional encoding [20] to enrich macroeconomic indicators, thus facilitating precise predictions using monthly data.

In some cases, metal prices might be used to predict macroeconomic indicators, or vice versa. However, such approaches typically require access to additional non-public data, such as trade agreements or tariff policies. If these types of data were accessible, they could potentially be used more directly to improve the prediction of metal prices.

Note that much of the research in this field relies on the training of predictive models using specific sets of data prepared in advance. This predefined information is crucial to the way that models learn patterns, relationships, and dependencies among multiple variables to make accurate predictions. Unfortunately, this kind of information, such as the relationships among different sectors, lacks dynamism and is not always available. To replace the predefined information, this work proposed the Dynamic Correlation Encoder to learn from the correlation between the assets. In addition, the relationship between the assets might be changed through time. The proposed module also learn the dynamic correlation between the assets.

We selected the average asset price in each of the following weeks as our prediction targets, considering the relative stability of metal prices and their unambiguous reaction to global economic trends. This approach differs from most previous work on stock predictions, which focus on prices for the next day. In experiments, the proposed framework outperformed state-of-the-art methods in terms of Mean Absolute Error (MAE).

The contributions of this study are summarized as follows:

- We considered macroeconomic indicators in our model to enhance the accuracy and reliability of metal price forecasts.
- We designed a module that enables the use of sparse data via daily insight encoding in monthly indicators.
- We used a Dynamic Correlation Encoder to consider the relationships among assets and in so doing capture the dynamic interactions required to enhance prediction performance.

## 2 Related Works

### 2.1 Interrelationships Among Metal Prices and Macroeconomic Factors

Researchers have demonstrated the predictability of precious metals prices and relationships among gold, silver, and platinum [8,15]. There also appears to be a strong correlation between copper prices and those of other metals [14]. Numerous researchers have discussed the influence of macroeconomic factors, such as the rate of inflation, unemployment rate, or consumer price index, on the price of metals [7,15,21].

### 2.2 Multivariate Time Series Prediction Methods

The performance of time series prediction models can be enhanced by incorporating cross-variate information. Transformer-based methods [8], such as FEDformer [25], integrate trend decomposition to improve long-term time series forecasting, such as exchange rate predictions. Nonetheless, researchers have demonstrated that the same prediction accuracy can be achieved using far simpler linear-based models [23]. In experiments on exchange rate prediction, the best overall performance was achieved using the relatively simple Decomposition Linear (DLinear) model, which decomposes historical data into trend and seasonal components [23]. StockMixer [9] employs a simple MLP-based architecture to analyze stock and market correlations, representing a state-of-the-art methodology in the field.

### 2.3 Machine Learning-Based Stock Price Prediction

Methods based on Recursive Neural Networks [4,24] are widely used to deal with the temporal patterns of stock prices, and methods based on Long Short-term Memory (LSTM) and Gated Recurrent Units (GRU) have greatly improved prediction performance. SFM model [24] has further improved LSTM by capturing trading frequencies in historical data. Researchers have recently begun exploring the relationships among stocks based on predefined information at the sector-level, industry-level, or investment interaction-level [3,10,13]. One approach involves modeling the relationships among listed companies using graph-based methods, such as Graph Convolutional Networks (GCN) and Temporal Graph Convolution Networks (TGCN), in conjunction with LSTM networks; however, a reliance on predefined information limits their applicability [3,10]. The FinGAT model uses Graph Attention Networks (GAT) to learn relationships among stocks and sectors without relying on predefined information [13].

### 2.4 Metal Price Prediction

Most of the work on predicting metal prices has focused on a single asset. In one study, LSTM and association rules were used to predict gold prices [1], while in another study, the researchers employed CNN-LSTM to predict both the price and movement of gold [18]. LSTM decomposition has also been used with Variational Mode Decomposition (VMD) to forecast the price of non-ferrous metals [17]. It is important to consider that focusing on a single asset makes it impossible to account for interactions among metals and the broader economic context.

## 3 Methodology

### 3.1 Metal Price Prediction Problem

The relative stability of commodities, compared to regular stocks, precludes the use of short-term trends in stocks to predict gold prices. Thus, this study focused on long-term trends to predict prices for periods lasting several weeks.

The features of $k$ asset at day $d$ of week $i$ is denoted as $v$. Each asset $v_{i,d} \in \mathbb{R}^{T\times F}$ contains historical data, where T indicates the length of the look-back window and F is the feature dimension in each timestep. The monthly macroeconomic indicator is denoted as indi. Given daily closing price C, the average closing price for week i can be derived as follows:

$$Y_i = \frac{\sum_{j=1}^{d} C_j}{d}$$

Our objective in this work was to predict the average closing price for the following $n$ weeks, based on given price features and monthly indicators. This involved bringing model output $\hat{Y}_i$ as close as possible to the actual value of $Y_i$.

### 3.2 Model Overview

As shown in Fig. 1, the proposed model comprises five components: (1) Learning From Assets, (2) Learning From Macroeconomic Factors, (3) Learning From Asset Correlation, (4) Fusion of Different Perspectives, and (5) Prediction. We first extract crucial features from time series sequences and consider interactions among assets. Then, we incorporate macroeconomic indicators into the model, fuse the learned embeddings together, and predict the target.

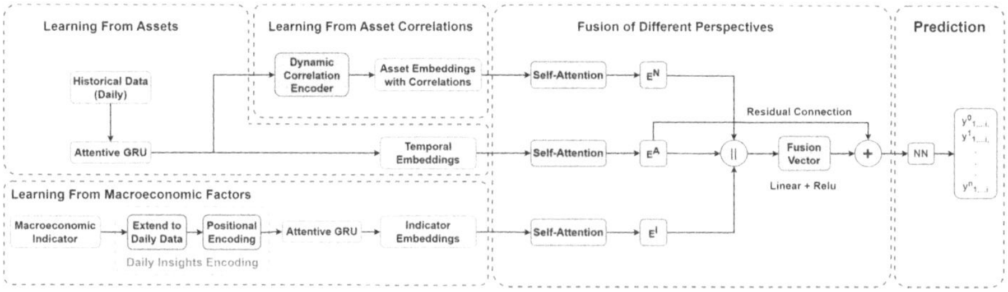


**Fig. 1.** Model Framework

### 3.3 Learning From Assets

This process involves the extraction of temporal information using GRU in order to encode daily sequential features that capture short-term representations. Attention mechanisms integrated into an attentive GRU model weigh the importance of the temporal features with the aim of generating embeddings that effectively represent the data. This attentive GRU structure is well-suited to recognizing important parts of a sequence of price data.

Let $h_{i,d}(\text{Asset})$ be the hidden state for each day $d$ in week $i$, where $v_{i,d}(\text{Asset})$ is the asset feature. The attention mechanism and GRU are incorporated by calculating the attention score using all hidden states $h_{i,d}$ in each week $i$. Finally, an *Temporal Embedding* $(A)$ is generated for each asset.

### 3.4 Learning From Macroeconomic Factors

Our objective in designing this part was to account for global economic influence in our predictions. Therefore, we added the macroeconomic indicators to the model as features. Note that the available monthly indicators and daily price features differ in terms of time scale, which means that they cannot be used together for training. Thus, this module is implemented in two stages. We first expand the monthly indicators into daily indicators via data alignment and positional encoding. We then sort the daily price features and corresponding monthly indicators week by week to give them a common shape amenable to model training. Finally, we perform sequential learning, as outlined in the Section on the Learning From Assets.

**Transforming Macroeconomic Indicators Into Daily Insights**

*Extending Indicators to Daily Data.* Macroeconomic data for monthly indicators include only one value per month. We set the indicators of month $m$ as $indi^m$, $indi^m \in \mathbb{R}^N$, where $N$ indicates the number of selected indicators. Note that instead of using the daily values directly, the same monthly value is used for all days within that month to prevent the model from having access to future information, thereby ensuring that predictions for any given day are based only on data available up to that day (i.e., not later in the month).

*Encoding Daily Insights via Positional Encoding.* Repeated indicator values indicate a lack of information, which could hinder training efficiency. To address this, we employed positional encoding using the Transformer architecture [20]. This makes it possible for the model to understand input relationships and generate unique embeddings for each value. Positional encoding is detailed in the following:

$$PE_{(pos,2i)} = \sin\left(\frac{pos}{10000^{\frac{2i}{d_{model}}}}\right) \tag{1}$$

$$PE_{(pos,2i+1)} = \cos\left(\frac{pos}{10000^{\frac{2i}{d_{model}}}}\right) \tag{2}$$

where $pos$ refers to the position (i.e., date of the current month), $i$ is an individual dimension within the positional encoding, and $d_{model}$ is the total number of dimensions in the model embedding vectors. We set the value of $d_{model}$ to match the number of indicators, $N$. Positional encoding is applied on a monthly basis, wherein the same encoding is assigned to every day within a given month. This facilitates the recognition of data positions, thereby improving information representations and increasing the training capacity for macroeconomic indicators.

The *Daily Insights of Macroeconomic Factors* (*DIMF*) is obtained by adding the indicator value (*indi*) to the positional encoding (*PE*) as follows:

$$DIMF = indi + PE$$

$$DIMF = \{DIMF_{1,1}, \ldots, DIMF_{i,d}\}$$

As in the previous definitions, it denotes $DIMF$ of day $d$ in week $i$.

**Short-Term Representation Learning of Macroeconomic Factors.** The final data preprocessing step involves deriving the *DIMF* value on a weekly basis to enable the alignment of time scale in the Learning From Assets. For instance, if we used an $n$-week lookback window, we would also aggregate the data on a monthly basis over a period of $n$ weeks. As with weekly sequential learning, the attentive GRU is used to extract crucial information from the temporal sequence to obtain *Indicator Embeddings* for each week $i$ given by $I = \{I_1, I_2, \ldots, I_i\}$.

### 3.5 Learning From Asset Correlations

The objective here is to learn the relationships between assets, based on the assumption that one asset can influence other assets within the same category. Instead of using predefined information, we use the Dynamic Correlation Encoder to dynamically learn latent relationships among assets.

*Dynamic Correlation Encoder.* We aim to consider the relationships between the assets. In this section, we use the Transformer encoder layer as our encoder [20]. This is because the Transformer encoder layer includes a multi-head self-attention mechanism and a position-wise feed-forward network, which helps each asset to observe the prices of other assets.

### 3.6 Fusion of Different Perspectives

After processing the Learning From Assets and Learning From Macroeconomic Factors, we obtain the *Temporal Embeddings with Correlations* $E^{TC}$ and *Temporal Embeddings* $E^A$ from the Learning From Assets and *Indicator Embeddings* $E^I$ from the Learning From Macroeconomic Factors. To aggregate these embeddings into long-term representations for the prediction of targets for the next $n$ weeks, we apply attention mechanisms to the weekly scale embeddings to weigh the importance of each week within our lookback window. Finally, we obtain the aggregated embeddings for each module, in the following form: $E^{TC}$, $E^A$, and $E^I$, representing by

$$
\begin{aligned}
E^{TC}(\text{Asset}) &= \text{Attention}(\text{TC}(\text{Asset})) \\
E^{A}(\text{Asset}) &= \text{Attention}(\text{A}(\text{Asset})) \\
E^{I} &= \text{Attention}(\text{I})
\end{aligned}
$$

Here, $E^{TC}$, $E^A$, and $E^I$ are the long-term representation vectors for *Asset with Correlation, Temporal*, and *Indicators*, respectively.

Prior to the prediction step, it is necessary to combine the embeddings by concatenating $E^R$ and $E^A$ into a new asset embedding $E$ for each asset.

$$E(\text{Asset}) = \left[E^R \parallel E^A\right]$$

We then concatenate $E^I$ with $E$ for each asset embedding as a monthly embedding $E^M$.

$$E^M(\text{Asset}) = \left[E(\text{Asset}) \parallel E^I\right]$$

Subsequntly, we aggregate the embeddings into the final feature vector, using ReLU as the activation function to introduce nonlinearity into the model. We obtain the final fusion vector via the fusion layer using the following formula:

$$E^F = \text{ReLU}(E^M(\text{Asset})W_f)$$

where $W_f$ is the learnable weight matrix.

Finally, we apply residual connection before the prediction. The concept of residual connection proposed by He et al. [11] can be used to preserve original information, prevent the problem of vanishing gradients, and allow learning in deeper networks. In time series prediction tasks, maintaining the original temporal features is crucial to the final output. Therefore, we integrated residual connections into our model, connecting long-term Temporal Embeddings $E^A$ with fusion vector $E^F$. The prediction output is given by:

$$\text{OutputVector} = E^F + E^A$$

### 3.7 Prediction

The final step involves learning to predict the target. The proposed model incorporates various features for use in predicting the average price during the following $n$ weeks. These features include *Asset Embeddings with Correlation* $E^{TC}$, *Temporal Embedding* $E^A$ for each asset, and *Indicator Embedding* $E^I$.

### 3.8 Loss Function

Our aim in designing the proposed framework was to predict the average prices for each of the following $n$ weeks. This regression task is performed using L1 Loss (Mean Absolute Error, MAE) as our loss function, while using the formula below to calculate the average absolute difference between the predicted and actual values:

$$L(Y_i, \hat{Y}_i) = \frac{1}{n} \sum_{i=1}^{n} \left| Y_i - \hat{Y}_i \right| \tag{3}$$

where $Y_i$ is the ground truth (average price of the actual asset in week $i$), $\hat{Y}_i$ is the predicted average price in week $i$, and $n$ is the total number of elements.

## 4 Experiments

### 4.1 Datasets

**Metal Assets.** This study focused on data pertaining to gold, silver, copper, zinc, palladium, and platinum collected from Yahoo Finance (yfinance)[1] for each trading day from 2015 to 2023 (2,262 d for each asset). The features of each asset included *Open, High, Low, Close, Adjusted Close, and Volume (OHLCV)*. We also calculated the moving averages($MAs$) over 5-day intervals as features. When using a 20-day window, we computed MAs for 5, 10, 15, and 20 d by averaging the closing prices. Moving averages were retained because they have a higher correlation with the prediction target, as both are focused on extracting longer-term features. The inclusion of MAs helps to smooth out price trends, thereby enhancing the model's ability to capture the underlying market dynamics over time. Finally, we concatenated these MAs with the initial feature vector $v$.

[1] https://finance.yahoo.com/.

**Macroeconomic Indicators.** We collected macroeconomic data from Federal Reserve Economic Data (FRED)[2] for each month from 2015 to 2023, resulting in 108 values for each indicator. Table 1 lists the classifications of the selected monthly indicators.

Below is a brief introduction to the selected indicators:

1. **M1SL (M1 Money Stock):** The total amount of M1 money stock in the economy. M1 is an indicator of the total available for spending and consumption in the economy.
2. **M2SL (M2 Money Stock):** The total amount of M2 money stock in the economy. M2 includes M1, and adds other types of deposits, which are relatively liquid and comprehensive.
3. **FF (Federal Funds Rate):** The interest rate at which banks charge each other for overnight loans of their reserves. It is the benchmark of short-term interest rates.
4. **CPIAUCSL (Consumer Price Index for All Urban Consumers):** The price index of a basket of goods and services purchased by urban consumers. Changes in percentage reflect inflation rates.
5. **CPIENGSL (Consumer Price Index for All Urban Consumers: Energy):** A subset of the CPI that tracks prices for energy-related goods and services. It measures the impact of energy prices on overall inflation.
6. **UNRATE (Unemployment Rate):** The percentage of the total number of unemployed individuals in the labor force who are actively seeking employment and willing to work.
7. **DTWEXBGS (Nominal Broad U.S. Dollar Index):** An index that measures the value of the U.S. dollar relative to other world currencies, adjusting for the level of trade activity with each country.
8. **POILBREUSDM (Global price of Brent Crude):** The global market price of Brent crude oil, quoted in U.S. dollars. It serves as a crucial indicator for energy markets and economic trends.
9. **GEPUCURRENT (Global Economic Policy Uncertainty Index: Current Price Adjusted GDP):** An index that measures the level of uncertainty in global economic policies, adjusted by current GDP prices, reflecting fluctuations in the worldwide economy.
10. **REAINTRATREARAT1YE (1-Year Real Interest Rate):** The Federal Reserve Bank of Cleveland estimates the expected inflation rate over the next 30 years, including inflation risk premiums, real risk premiums, and the real interest rate.

[2] https://fred.stlouisfed.org/.

**Table 1.** Classification of Economic Indicators

| Category | Indicators |
|---|---|
| Monetary and Interest Rates | M1SL (M1 Money Stock)<br>M2SL (M2 Money Stock)<br>FF (Federal Funds Rate)<br>REAINTRATREARAT1YE (1-Year Real Interest Rate) |
| Inflation and Price Indexes | CPIAUCSL (Consumer Price Index for All Urban Consumers)<br>CPIENGSL (Consumer Price Index for All Urban Consumers: Energy) |
| Labor Market | UNRATE (Unemployment Rate) |
| Market and Uncertainty | DTWEXBGS (Nominal Broad U.S. Dollar Inde)<br>POILBREUSDM (Global Price of Brent Crude)<br>GEPUCURRENT (Global Economic Policy Uncertainty Index) |

### 4.2 Models Included in the Comparisons

The proposed model was compared with baseline models, including Temporal Convolutional Network [16], LSTM [12], GRU [5], GRU with Attention [6], Decomposition Linear Model [23], VMD-LSTM [17], FinGAT [13], and StockMixer [9]. Note that the FinGAT model considers the relationships between stocks and sectors as well as relationships between sectors. Note also that the previous works conducted experiments in terms of rank and accuracy, while in the current study, we applied those methods to the prediction of accurate asset prices via regression.

### 4.3 Experiment Settings

The rolling window method was used to train and test the models. For each year from 2019 to 2023, we used data from the previous four years for training and data from the current year for testing. Table 2 shows the periods of the data set. This approach ensures that our training data always include a full five years, helping us capture important trends and patterns in the data. Every experiment was run ten times, and results were then averaged.

For training, we set a batch size of 128 with an embedding dimension of 64. We used the Adam optimizer with the learning rate set to 0.001 and the dropout rate set to 0.2. We also explored the effect of varying the number of training weeks 3, 4, 5, 6. In the following experiments, we set the number of training weeks (lookback window) to four. The results are presented as the average across all assets.

**Table 2.** The Period of Training and Testing Sets

| Year | Training Set | Testing Set |
|---|---|---|
| 2019 | 2015/01/01 - 2018/12/31 | 2019/01/01 - 2019/12/31 |
| 2020 | 2016/01/01 - 2019/12/31 | 2020/01/01 - 2020/12/31 |
| 2021 | 2017/01/01 - 2020/12/31 | 2021/01/01 - 2021/12/31 |
| 2022 | 2018/01/01 - 2021/12/31 | 2022/01/01 - 2022/12/31 |
| 2023 | 2019/01/01 - 2022/12/31 | 2023/01/01 - 2023/12/31 |

### 4.4 Evaluation Metrics

Model performance was assessed in terms of Mean Absolute Error (MAE), calculated using the following equation:

$$\mathrm{MAE} = \frac{1}{n}\sum_{i=1}^{n}\left|Y_i - \hat{Y}_i\right| \tag{4}$$

where $Y_i$ denotes the ground truth (i.e., the actual average price of the target week $i$), $\hat{Y}_i$ indicates the predicted average price for week $i$, and $n$ indicates the total number of elements.

### 4.5 Experiment Results

**Comparison of Baselines and Previous Works.** As shown in Fig. 2, the annual Mean Absolute Error (MAE) for each model from 2019 to 2023 indicate that our proposed framework delivers the best performance except 2021. We can observe that our proposed framework achieves the best performance for each year. FinGAT and StockMixer rank as the second-best model, further demonstrating the robustness of our approach compared to other methods. Although DLinear is effective for multivariate time series prediction, it relies on longer data to capture seasonal patterns and trends. Therefore, with a four-week lookback window in our experimental setup, it does not perform as effectively as the other models. Although the VMD-LSTM model is specifically designed for predicting metal prices, it does not effectively handle indicators and price features separately. As a result, its performance is inferior to that of other models.

**Lookback Window Analysis.** Here, we explore the influence of lookback window length. The MAE results from 2019 to 2023 with different week numbers are in Table 3. We can see that, except for 2022, a three-week lookback window performs less effectively in capturing long-term information. Specifically, a four-week lookback window proves to be the optimal choice each year.

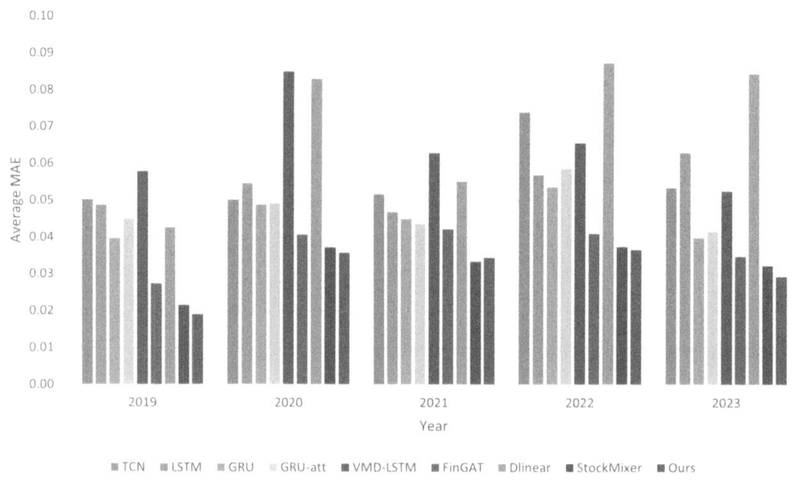


**Fig. 2.** Main Experimental Results of MAE from 2019 to 2023

## 4.6 Ablation Studies

In this section, we analyze the effect of each component in our framework through ablation studies conducted for the year 2023. As shown in Table 4, each component plays a crucial role in the overall performance of our model.

1. w/o Assets Correlation: without *Learning From Assets Correlation.*
2. w/o Positional Encoding: without *Positional Encoding* in *Learning From Macroeconomic Factors.* (i.e., Using repeated indicators only)
3. w/o Macro. Factors: without *Learning From Macroeconomic Factors*, which means only using the *Learning From Assets* and *Learning From Assets Correlation.*

Removing *Learning From Assets Correlation* (w/o Assets Correlation) increases the overall MAE to 0.0307. This indicates that it significantly contributes to reducing prediction errors, especially in the fourth week, where the MAE rises to 0.0376.

Excluding *Learning From Macroeconomic Factors* (w/o Macro. Factors) has a significant impact on the first and second weeks, with MAE values of 0.0259 and 0.0311, respectively. This suggests that *Learning From Macroeconomic Factors* is crucial to stabilizing performance in the early stages. The overall MAE without the *Learning From Macroeconomic Factors* is 0.0362.

When *Positional Encoding* (w/o Positional Encoding) is removed, the overall MAE is 0.0306. While the impact is lesser compared to the removal of *Learning From Assets Correlation* and *Learning From Macroeconomic Factors*, Positional Encoding still plays an essential role, particularly noticeable in the third week, where the MAE is 0.0333.

**Table 3.** Results from 2021 to 2023 with different weeks of lookback window

| Year | Week Num | First | Second | Third | Fourth | Average |
|---|---|---|---|---|---|---|
| 2021 | 3 | 0.0261 | 0.0332 | 0.0392 | 0.0434 | 0.0355 |
| | 4 | **0.0247** | **0.0319** | **0.0383** | 0.0427 | **0.0344** |
| | 5 | 0.0279 | 0.0339 | **0.0383** | 0.0413 | 0.0353 |
| | 6 | 0.0293 | 0.0355 | 0.0388 | **0.0412** | 0.0362 |
| 2022 | 3 | **0.0252** | **0.0339** | **0.0400** | **0.0452** | **0.0361** |
| | 4 | 0.0260 | 0.0343 | **0.0400** | 0.0458 | 0.0365 |
| | 5 | 0.0308 | 0.0371 | 0.0428 | 0.0486 | 0.0398 |
| | 6 | 0.0325 | 0.0387 | 0.0450 | 0.0515 | 0.0419 |
| 2023 | 3 | **0.0210** | 0.0287 | 0.0354 | 0.0407 | 0.0315 |
| | 4 | 0.0224 | **0.0275** | **0.0320** | **0.0354** | **0.0293** |
| | 5 | 0.0249 | 0.0300 | 0.0344 | 0.0386 | 0.0320 |
| | 6 | 0.0248 | 0.0294 | 0.0338 | 0.0377 | 0.0314 |

The *Full Model*, which incorporates all components, achieves the lowest MAE of 0.0293. This indicates that the integration of all parts optimizes the performance of the model in all weeks.

**Table 4.** The Average MAE in Ablation Studies for the Year 2023

| Model | First | Second | Third | Fourth | Average |
|---|---|---|---|---|---|
| w/o Assets Correlation | 0.0232 | 0.0287 | 0.0332 | 0.0376 | 0.0307 |
| w/o Macro. Factors | 0.0259 | 0.0311 | 0.0394 | 0.0484 | 0.0362 |
| w/o Positional Encoding | 0.0232 | 0.0286 | 0.0333 | 0.0371 | 0.0306 |
| Full Model | **0.0224** | **0.0275** | **0.0320** | **0.0354** | **0.0293** |

## 5 Conclusions

The intrinsic value of metals makes them an important component of investment portfolios, providing a stable hedge against inflation. Nonetheless, various macroeconomic factors can have a profound impact on metal prices. This paper proposes a deep learning model to predict the prices of precious metals. We applied positional encoding to encode the daily insights of monthly macroeconomic data. We also used a Dynamic Correlation Encoder to capture the dynamic asset correlations without the need for predefined information. In experiments, the proposed framework outperformed state-of-the-art methods in terms of Mean Absolute Error (MAE).

## References


1. Boongasame, L., Viriyaphol, P., Tassanavipas, K., Temdee, P.: Gold-price forecasting method using long short-term memory and the association rule. J. Mobile Multimedia, 165–186 (2023)
2. Cao, L.J., Tay, F.E.H.: Support vector machine with adaptive parameters in financial time series forecasting. IEEE Trans. Neural Netw. **14**(6), 1506–1518 (2003)
3. Chen, Y., Wei, Z., Huang, X.: Incorporating corporation relationship via graph convolutional neural networks for stock price prediction. In: Proceedings of the 27th ACM International Conference on Information and Knowledge Management, pp. 1655–1658 (2018)
4. Cheng, L.C., Huang, Y.H., Wu, M.E.: Applied attention-based lstm neural networks in stock prediction. In: 2018 IEEE International Conference on Big Data (Big Data), pp. 4716–4718 (2018). https://doi.org/10.1109/BigData.2018.8622541
5. Cho, K., et al.: Learning phrase representations using rnn encoder-decoder for statistical machine translation. arXiv preprint arXiv:1406.1078 (2014)
6. Dhingra, B., Liu, H., Yang, Z., Cohen, W.W., Salakhutdinov, R.: Gated-attention readers for text comprehension. arXiv preprint arXiv:1606.01549 (2016)
7. Erdoğdu, A.: The most significant factors influencing the price of gold: an empirical analysis of the us market. Economics **5**(5), 399–406 (2017)
8. Erkan, T.E., Karaçor, A.G.: On predictability of precious metals towards robust trading. Industry 4.0 **5**(2), 87–89 (2020)
9. Fan, J., Shen, Y.: Stockmixer: a simple yet strong mlp-based architecture for stock price forecasting. In: Proceedings of the AAAI Conference on Artificial Intelligence, vol. 38, pp. 8389–8397 (2024)
10. Feng, F., He, X., Wang, X., Luo, C., Liu, Y., Chua, T.S.: Temporal relational ranking for stock prediction. ACM Trans. Inform. Syst. (TOIS) **37**(2), 1–30 (2019)
11. He, K., Zhang, X., Ren, S., Sun, J.: Deep residual learning for image recognition. In: Proceedings of the IEEE Conference on Computer Vision and Pattern Recognition, pp. 770–778 (2016)
12. Hochreiter, S., Schmidhuber, J.: Long short-term memory. Neural Comput. **9**(8), 1735–1780 (1997)
13. Hsu, Y.L., Tsai, Y.C., Li, C.T.: Fingat: financial graph attention networks for recommending top-$k$ k profitable stocks. IEEE Trans. Knowl. Data Eng. **35**(1), 469–481 (2021)
14. Iwaszczuk, N., Wzorek, A., Łamasz, B.: Relationship between copper price and selected metals prices. In: Engineering and Technology on Non-Ferrous Metals. Key Engineering Materials, vol. 682, pp. 336–341. Trans Tech Publications Ltd (Mar 2016). https://doi.org/10.4028/www.scientific.net/KEM.682.336
15. Kucher, O., McCoskey, S.: The long-run relationship between precious metal prices and the business cycle. Q. Rev. Econ. Finance **65**, 263–275 (2017)
16. Lea, C., Flynn, M.D., Vidal, R., Reiter, A., Hager, G.D.: Temporal convolutional networks for action segmentation and detection. In: Proceedings of the IEEE Conference on Computer Vision and Pattern Recognition, pp. 156–165 (2017)
17. Liu, Y., Yang, C., Huang, K., Gui, W.: Non-ferrous metals price forecasting based on variational mode decomposition and lstm network. Knowl.-Based Syst. **188**, 105006 (2020)
18. Livieris, I.E., Pintelas, E., Pintelas, P.: A cnn-lstm model for gold price time-series forecasting. Neural Comput. Appl. **32**, 17351–17360 (2020)

19. Roberts, M.C.: Duration and characteristics of metal price cycles. Resour. Policy **34**(3), 87–102 (2009)
20. Vaswani, A., et al.: Attention is all you need. Adv. Neural Inform. Process. Syst. **30** (2017)
21. Vigne, S.A., Lucey, B.M., OConnor, F.A., Yarovaya, L.: The financial economics of white precious metals a survey. Inter. Rev. Financial Anal. **52**, 292–308 (2017). https://doi.org/10.1016/j.irfa.2017.04.006, https://www.sciencedirect.com/science/article/pii/S1057521917300480
22. Wang, J.H., Leu, J.Y.: Stock market trend prediction using arima-based neural networks. In: Proceedings of International Conference on Neural Networks (ICNN 1996), vol. 4, pp. 2160–2165. IEEE (1996)
23. Zeng, A., Chen, M., Zhang, L., Xu, Q.: Are Transformers Effective For Time Series Forecasting? In: Proceedings of the AAAI Conference on Artificial Intelligence, vol. 37, pp. 11121–11128 (2023)
24. Zhang, L., Aggarwal, C., Qi, G.J.: Stock price prediction via discovering multi-frequency trading patterns. In: Proceedings of the 23rd ACM SIGKDD International Conference on Knowledge Discovery and Data Mining, pp. 2141–2149 (2017)
25. Zhou, T., Ma, Z., Wen, Q., Wang, X., Sun, L., Jin, R.: Fedformer: frequency enhanced decomposed transformer for long-term series forecasting. In: International Conference on Machine Learning, pp. 27268–27286. PMLR (2022)

# Smart Lighting Control Built on AI Architecture

Song-Bor Chiang[1,2](✉) and Chung-Hao Tien[1]

[1] Department of Photonic, National Yang Ming Chiao Tung University, 1001 University Road, Hsinchu, Taiwan 300093, Republic of China
SBChiang@itri.org.tw

[2] Green Energy and Environment Research Laboratories, Industrial Technology Research Institute, 195, Sec. 4, Chung Hsing Road, Chutung, Hsinchu, Taiwan 310401, Republic of China

**Abstract.** This study explores the use of computer vision combined with AI algorithms as a potential replacement for traditional PIR and microwave sensors commonly used in lighting control systems. By implementing an AI-based Intelligent Lighting System in a library, we successfully extended the detection range to more than 20 m, several times greater than the previous sensor systems. The system was able to switch lights on or off within two seconds of detecting the presence or absence of an object, meeting the requirements for efficient smart control and energy savings. During the research, it was found that signal transmission across the network was a critical factor in the system's overall response time. In this study, the time from the PLC server to each lighting fixture accounted for approximately 40% of the total system response time. Additionally, significant variations in response time were observed during the power supply's activation, largely due to transient electrical responses in the components used to drive the lighting fixtures.

**Keywords:** Artificial Intelligent · Lighting · YOLO

## 1 Introduction

In the development of future Smart City systems, energy consumption monitoring and management across various life systems. Those are such as power supply, lighting, water supply, transportation, buildings, and oil and gas pipelines. By embedding sensors and integrating big data with multi-layered AI technologies, eventually leading to the control of a Main AI system, the integration of human society with physical systems can be achieved. This fosters the sustainable development of urban economies, society, and environmental resources, improving energy efficiency and coordination. The system could also be used for instant energy load distribution, enhancing national energy management.

For example, transitioning traditional lighting to LED systems can save approximately 50–70% in electricity consumption. Further, with the implementation of smart systems for automatic optimization and management, an additional 10–20% savings can be realized. This not only reduces energy consumption but also increases efficiency,

© The Author(s), under exclusive license to Springer Nature Singapore Pte Ltd. 2025
W.-T. Chu et al. (Eds.): TAAI 2024, CCIS 2414, pp. 262–275, 2025.
https://doi.org/10.1007/978-981-96-4589-3_19

prolongs the lifespan of lighting equipment by reducing long-term wear, and minimizes environmental pollution from equipment failures or damage.

According to the U.S. Department of Energy (DOE), LED lighting is 6–7 times more efficient than traditional lighting and has a lifespan over 25 times longer. Over the next 20 years, LED lighting is expected to save the U.S. $250 billion in energy costs, reduce lighting electricity consumption by nearly 50%, and cut carbon emissions by 18 million tons. When combined with smart energy management using ICT (Information and Communication Technology), it is estimated that energy consumption could be further reduced and efficiency increased by an additional 5–10%.

The demand for smart energy management spans a wide range of industries. In addition to indoor lighting, sectors with high energy consumption, such as industrial power and buildings, require smart energy management to achieve energy efficiency and conservation goals. The overall market potential for smart energy management is promising, attracting significant investment from related industries.

With the advent of the AI era, the demand for smart IoT systems and IoT-enabled lighting has become a pressing issue that manufacturers are eager to address. The quality of light sources in smart lighting systems is not only closely tied to fixture design but also fundamentally depends on the quality of the light source itself and the AI-powered human-centric control interface. Currently, various smart lighting technologies on the market are beginning to adopt wireless control technologies such as Bluetooth, Zigbee, and WiFi, along with relevant modules.

By integrating technologies across different fields: including collaboration between control system providers and traditional LED lighting manufacturers and incorporating IoT technology, these systems can be tailored to specific needs. Through the use of light environment sensing and dimming functions, they can meet the requirements of diverse application scenarios. Furthermore, smart control based on feedback from sensor signals can achieve optimized energy-saving effects.

## 2 Concept and Theory

With the advancement of smart lighting control systems, real-time management allows for the adjustment of lighting conditions based on different dates, times, and the operational status of specific functional areas. Using image recognition technology, lighting requirements for the entire or partial space can be controlled, reducing lighting output when areas are not in use. This significantly reduces energy consumption in spaces like indoor libraries, 24-h convenience stores, large retail stores, and parking lots, which require long-term lighting, and greatly contributes to energy-saving and carbon reduction efforts. The key components driving smart lighting systems are the sensors that detect the presence of people or objects.

Sensors play a critical role in shaping the Internet of Things (IoT) and are recognized as one of the essential components in this domain. Their core function is to collect a vast amount of data, making them applicable across various sectors, both commercial and consumer. Due to the broad range of applications for sensors and the growing demand for IoT solutions, the sensor market is expected to experience significant growth in the coming years.

According to a report by YOLE Development, the global sensor market was valued at $360 million in 2020, with projections to reach $460 million by 2025. Among the various sectors, the smart building segment (including smart homes and smart offices) is expected to see the highest growth [1].

In terms of smart lighting control, the most commonly used sensors for lighting detection are Passive Infrared (PIR) sensors and microwave sensors. The PIR sensor, short for Passive Infra-Red sensor, is also known as a Passive Infrared detector, often used in the security industry. The PIR sensor consists of an optical system, an infrared sensor, and electronic circuitry. It operates by detecting infrared radiation, typically from moving individuals, within a specific wavelength range, generating a signal based on the potential difference caused by the infrared energy emitted by the target [1]. However, PIR sensors often face challenges in terms of sensitivity to vehicles or human motion and limited detection range [2].

Microwave sensors, on the other hand, utilize the Doppler effect—an electromagnetic wave principle—to detect movement. These sensors emit radar signals, typically around 5.8 GHz, to scan the environment. When a moving object enters the radar's electromagnetic field, the antenna sends a signal back to the receiving circuit, triggering a change in the system's operation. Microwave sensors detect objects based on changes in the reflected wave, indicating whether an object is approaching or receding, and converting this change into an electrical signal. The detection range is typically between 5 to 9 m. However, objects within the detection range may not trigger the sensor if they remain stationary, which poses certain limitations in real-world applications.

Both PIR and microwave sensors have limitations in detection range—PIR sensors detect up to 5 m, while microwave sensors detect up to 8 m. These limitations, coupled with the high costs of deploying such systems for large-scale lighting detection, make them expensive solutions.

In contrast to traditional smart lighting detection technologies, this research proposes a new control mechanism based on image capture (Computer Vision), human recognition technology, and light environment sensing technology. This system offers features such as light environment monitoring and lighting adjustment control, presenting a novel approach to smart lighting management. In addition to integrating security monitoring with intelligent lighting control for energy savings, this system can significantly reduce the cost of using sensors like IR/PIR, providing a more cost-effective option for smart lighting providers.

## 3 Environmental and Experimental Setting

### 3.1 Computer Vision

Computer Vision systems refer to the use of computers to replicate human visual functions, enabling the recognition of the objective three-dimensional world. In current understanding, the human visual system's sensory component is the retina, functioning as a 3D sampling system. The visible part of a 3D object projects onto the retina, where humans interpret the object based on the two-dimensional image, allowing for three-dimensional understanding. This involves analyzing the shape, size, distance from the observation point, texture, and motion characteristics of the observed object.

Computer Vision systems are an integrated technology that combines optics, electronics, mechanics, and computer information systems. It empowers machines to process and analyze real-world images, converting them into data that the system can understand—serving as a key application of AI. By leveraging optical and non-contact sensing methods, computer Vision captures images and interprets them to extract specific information for controlling machinery or processes.

Key features of computer vision applications include:

- Safety
- Full inspection
- Reproducibility (minimizing human error)
- Cost reduction
- Speed improvement
- Enhanced precision and detail detection
- System simplification
- Object feature enhancement
- Increased signal-to-noise ratio
- Computer Vision in Inspection and Illumination Systems

As a detection technology, computer vision can replace human eyes, brain, and hand movements. When integrated with vision sensing devices, it detects product defects, selects and sorts products, and monitors illumination systems. By converting grayscale information into digital data, it measures the illuminance at target points within a space and links this information to control systems.

The rise of deep learning, particularly through convolutional neural networks (CNN), has enabled the completion of many such tasks, with classification being the most fundamental. Most applications now employ transfer learning, where CNNs are pre-trained on massive datasets like the 2012 ImageNet classification task, then adapted for specific tasks such as localization, detection, or segmentation. The deeper the base network in an object detection model, the higher the detection accuracy within certain limits, based on the transfer learning concept.

### 3.2 YOLO: A Breakthrough in Object Detection

The YOLO (You Only Look Once) series is a neural network algorithm specifically designed for object detection. Built with a compact Darknet framework, YOLO stands out for its lightweight, efficient design, making it highly valuable for industrial applications such as pedestrian detection and industrial image inspection [3].

For the image technology used in this research, focusing on object and personnel detection, two main detection methods can be employed: single-stage and two-stage. The former offers higher speed but lower accuracy, while the latter is slower but more precise. YOLO, as a single-stage model, frames object detection as a regression problem, using an end-to-end network to complete the input of raw images to the output of object locations and classes.

- YOLOv3: Advancements and Improvements

1. YOLOv3 has introduced several strategies to optimize its detection accuracy while maintaining the high speed that sets YOLO apart. Key improvements include: Better Pre-trained Model: YOLOv3 employs a new pre-trained network, Darknet-53, which integrates ideas from YOLOv2, Darknet-19, and ResNet [4]. It features 53 layers with a combination of 3x3 and 1x1 kernels and includes ResNet's shortcut connection. Darknet-53 offers comparable classification accuracy to ResNet-152 but with significantly fewer floating-point operations, making it faster and more efficient (Fig. 1).

| | Type | Filters | Size | Output |
|---|---|---|---|---|
| | Convolutional | 32 | 3 × 3 | 256 × 256 |
| | Convolutional | 64 | 3 × 3 / 2 | 128 × 128 |
| 1x | Convolutional | 32 | 1 × 1 | |
| | Convolutional | 64 | 3 × 3 | |
| | Residual | | | 128 × 128 |
| | Convolutional | 128 | 3 × 3 / 2 | 64 × 64 |
| 2x | Convolutional | 64 | 1 × 1 | |
| | Convolutional | 128 | 3 × 3 | |
| | Residual | | | 64 × 64 |
| | Convolutional | 256 | 3 × 3 / 2 | 32 × 32 |
| 8x | Convolutional | 128 | 1 × 1 | |
| | Convolutional | 256 | 3 × 3 | |
| | Residual | | | 32 × 32 |
| | Convolutional | 512 | 3 × 3 / 2 | 16 × 16 |
| 8x | Convolutional | 256 | 1 × 1 | |
| | Convolutional | 512 | 3 × 3 | |
| | Residual | | | 16 × 16 |
| | Convolutional | 1024 | 3 × 3 / 2 | 8 × 8 |
| 4x | Convolutional | 512 | 1 × 1 | |
| | Convolutional | 1024 | 3 × 3 | |
| | Residual | | | 8 × 8 |
| | Avgpool | | Global | |
| | Connected | | 1000 | |
| | Softmax | | | |

**Fig. 1.** Feature Extractor: Darknet-53

2. Classification in Detection: Unlike YOLOv1, which uses softmax for classification, YOLOv3 uses binary cross-entropy. This method allows YOLOv3 to handle more complex datasets, such as the Open Images Dataset [5], where multiple overlapping labels may exist in the same grid.
3. Multi-Scale Prediction: YOLOv3 predicts objects at three different scales within the network, allowing it to better handle small and large objects. The first detection module is located at the 82nd layer, predicting large objects. The subsequent detection modules at the 94th and 106th layers handle medium and small objects, respectively.
4. Performance in MSCOCO: In the MSCOCO dataset, YOLOv3 performs well, particularly in scenarios with a lower Intersection over Union (IoU) threshold. It is faster than RetinaNet [6], although its performance drops when higher IoU is required (Fig. 2 and Table 1).

**Table 1.** The comparisons among YOLOv3 and others

| | backbone | AP | $AP_{50}$ | $AP_{75}$ | $AP_S$ | $AP_M$ | $AP_L$ |
|---|---|---|---|---|---|---|---|
| *Two-stage methods* | | | | | | | |
| Faster R-CNN+++ [5] | ResNet-101-C4 | 34.9 | 55.7 | 37.4 | 15.6 | 38.7 | 50.9 |
| Faster R-CNN w FPN [8] | ResNet-101-FPN | 36.2 | 59.1 | 39.0 | 18.2 | 39.0 | 48.2 |
| Faster R-CNN by G-RMI [6] | Inception-ResNet-v2 [21] | 34.7 | 55.5 | 36.7 | 13.5 | 38.1 | 52.0 |
| Faster R-CNN w TDM [20] | Inception-ResNet-v2-TDM | 36.8 | 57.7 | 39.2 | 16.2 | 39.8 | **52.1** |
| *One-stage methods* | | | | | | | |
| YOLOv2 [15] | DarkNet-19 [15] | 21.6 | 44.0 | 19.2 | 5.0 | 22.4 | 35.5 |
| SSD513 [11, 3] | ResNet-101-SSD | 31.2 | 50.4 | 33.3 | 10.2 | 34.5 | 49.8 |
| DSSD513 [3] | ResNet-101-DSSD | 33.2 | 53.3 | 35.2 | 13.0 | 35.4 | 51.1 |
| RetinaNet [9] | ResNet-101-FPN | 39.1 | 59.1 | 42.3 | 21.8 | 42.7 | 50.2 |
| RetinaNet [9] | ResNeXt-101-FPN | **40.8** | **61.1** | **44.1** | **24.1** | **44.2** | 51.2 |
| YOLOv3 608 × 608 | Darknet-53 | 33.0 | 57.9 | 34.4 | 18.3 | 35.4 | 41.9 |

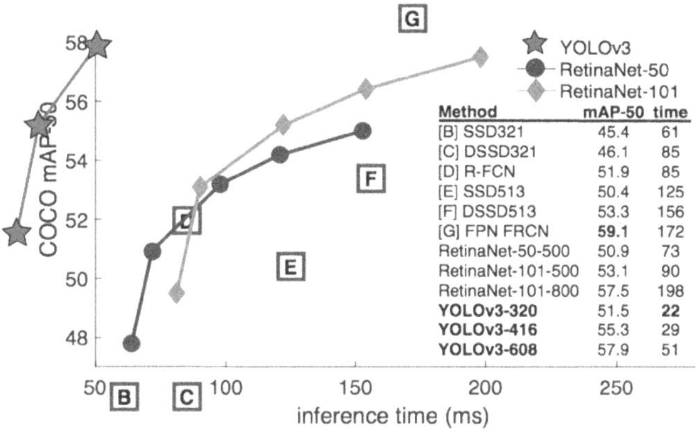


**Fig. 2.** YOLOv3 runs significantly faster than other detection methods with comparable performance.

## 3.3 AI-Driven Object Detection Framework for Lighting Systems

This project develops an AI-based object detection technology to drive lighting equipment. Using image monitoring technology, it detects objects in the environment and controls the lighting system based on the analysis of image data. This method replaces the traditional PIR and Microwave sensor detection methods, simplifying the control loop complexity.

A library was selected as the demonstration site for this research. After conducting on-site assessments and evaluations of 18 public libraries in Hsinchu County, including township libraries and the Cultural Affairs Bureau Library, the Baoshan Township Library was ultimately chosen for system implementation and technology demonstration. To enhance LED lighting quality, we first measured the library's internal dimensions and confirmed the building structure, establishing a 3D analytical model, as shown in Fig. 3. We performed lighting configuration and illuminance analysis using DIALux optical simulation software. The illuminance planning references the Illuminating Engineering Society of North America (IESNA) lighting design guide, which provides standards for reading environments. Through analyzing lighting quality and installing soft, evenly distributed, low-glare LED panel lights, we created an environment that meets the required lighting standards for reading.

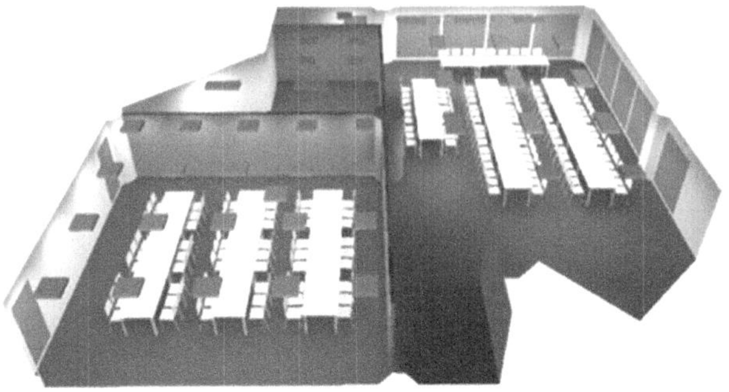

**Fig. 3.** The 3D model of Baoshan Township Library (2nd-floor)

For the indoor library lighting environment, the project adheres to the IESNA Lighting Handbook (9th edition) [7] standards (see Fig. 4). Not only is the brightness and distribution on the walkway floor or reading tables crucial, but the illuminance at the reading desk plane, which is 70–80 cm above the floor, must also be adequate. Thus, the focus of the lighting setup and analysis at Baoshan Township Library is based on the following parameters.

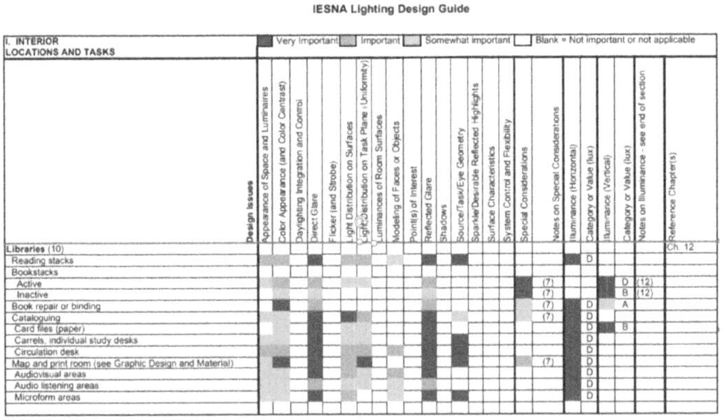


**Fig. 4.** IESNA lighting design guide for the libraries [7]

Illuminance, the primary indicator of lighting conditions, measures the luminous flux density on a surface per unit area ($lm/m^2$, lux). In general indoor public spaces, standard illuminance levels range from 75–300 lx for corridors, while the table illuminance in reading rooms must be between 500–750 lx. By reconstructing the library's 3D model in DIALux lighting simulation software, we assessed whether the illuminance on the walkways and multifunctional meeting room tables met Illuminating Engineers Society (IES) standards and design requirements (see Fig. 5). Adjustments to lighting placements were made to improve reading illumination quality.

| IES Illuminance Categories & Values | | |
|---|---|---|
| **Activity** | **LUX** | **Footcandles** |
| View CRT screen | 50 - 100 | 5 - 10 |
| Read standard document, photocopy or newspaper | 200 - 500 | 20 - 50 |
| View photo in moderate detail; reference phone book | 500 - 1000 | 50 - 100 |
| Perform visual task of low contrast or small size over prolonged periods of time | 2000 - 5000 | 200 - 500 |

**Fig. 5.** Illuminating Engineers Society recommended lighting levels for common office tasks [8]

After determining the specifications of the lighting fixtures, we evaluated the power configuration and installation. The installation process must comply with safety standards for lighting fixtures. The lights were tested in a laboratory accredited by TAF (Taiwan Accreditation Foundation), following the National Standards of the Republic of China, with tests covering basic electrical properties, luminous efficiency, power factor, waterproof/dustproof ratings (IP), and surge protection. The lighting system installation and control scope for spaces over 650 square meters required independent control of 99 lighting units, with eight subsystems for zoned control. Other system and communication specifications include:

1. Lighting system communication format and interface: Greater than 100 Mbit/s, with communication across subsystems using Modbus protocol and the 2.400 GHz ~ 2.497 GHz (2.4 GHz Band), supporting the number of lighting units.
2. Lighting control signal transmission speed: Bidirectional lighting control and signal feedback should be under 30 ms, with packet loss below 0.002%. The control modules and system architecture should simulate an industrial PLC architecture, with signal resolution exceeding 30,000 levels.
3. External I/O connections: RS232/RS485/TCP/IP, with individual control switches installed in each zone.
4. Real-time light environment energy consumption monitoring: A minimum of 24 groups, with monitoring and reporting of the eight control zones mentioned earlier. The system should provide a human-machine interface (HMI) with touchscreen control and connect to a PC via RS232/RS485/TCP/IP.
5. Customizable lighting settings: Lights can be configured for zoning, timing, or manual presets, with options to turn on/off or dim individual lights or zones based on PC signal input.

6. Component specifications: All components should comply with IEC or PROFINET communication standards for automated Ethernet networks. The system should allow control and configuration via mobile/tablet/PC with HMI.
7. Installation and specifications: The installation process must meet CNS, IEC, EN (12464–1:2011) standards for electrical and lighting construction. A timeline for sample installation and production must be provided, corresponding to the demonstration lighting area.

To achieve wide-area object movement detection that exceeds the limited range (8–9 m) of PIR and microwave sensors, this research aims to reach a detection range of 20 m. In the test environment, the camera equipment could detect objects at distances exceeding 20 m.

The system computing platform for this research used the PyTorch deep learning framework on Windows 10 [9], with a GPU powered by NVIDIA 1080 Ti. YOLOv3 achieved processing speeds of 20 frames per second (FPS) on this platform. In the test conducted at the Baoshan Township Library in Hsinchu County, multiple cameras (more than three cameras) shared one GPU. The system is able to meet the original design's expectation of detecting pedestrians and determining their posture under 2 s per camera as well as completes the triggered of the lighting system.

The system's recognition rate exceeded 70% in the well-known MOT17 Det dataset [10]. The test data came from the MOT17Det-Testing training dataset and the JTA dataset [11]. The actual detection results in the library are shown in Fig. 6.

**Fig. 6.** The test data came from the MOT17Det-Testing training dataset and the JTA dataset

### 3.4 The Closed-Loop of AI-Based Intelligent Lighting Systems

The AI-based intelligent detection closed-loop control system developed in this study is illustrated in Fig. 7. Images captured by POE digital cameras are processed by the AI computer, which analyzes them through image stitching techniques and the Yolov3 model to determine the presence of target objects (people) within the space. The detection information is then transmitted to the PLC lighting control module, establishing bidirectional communication with the lighting fixtures. This ensures that the fixtures receive the control signals and report their actual operating status, allowing the system to control the lighting: turning lights on or off as required. This process creates a closed-loop feedback control mechanism that continuously adjusts the lighting in response to the environment, achieving intelligent lighting detection and control.

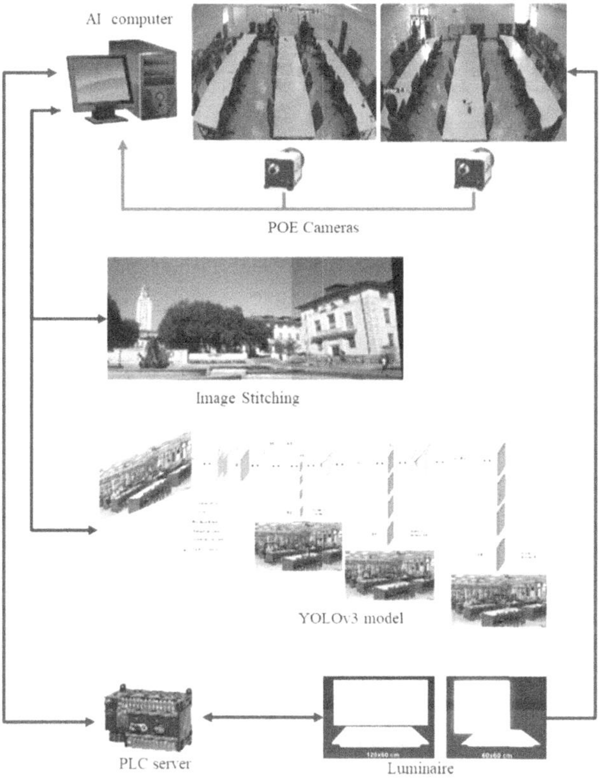


**Fig. 7.** The closed-loop control mechanism of AI-based Intelligent Lighting Systems

## 4 Results and Discussions

Based on the principles of YOLOv3 and its effectiveness in pedestrian detection, coupled with the use of the Open Images dataset to enhance accuracy in personnel detection, the AI computer achieves a detection speed of approximately 10 FPS. Using image recognition technology, response speed and detection distance tests were conducted in the demonstration area for the lighting system. The maximum detection distance of the camera installed in the 2nd-floor general reading room of the demonstration site was measured at 21.63 m, as shown in Fig. 8. This analytical distance closely matches the original completion drawings of the library, as depicted in Fig. 9.

Figure 10 presents data analyzed using the afore-mentioned camera system, grayscale image, and personnel recognition technology, with the control system interface based

**Fig. 8.** Measurement of the maximum image analysis range in the demonstration area

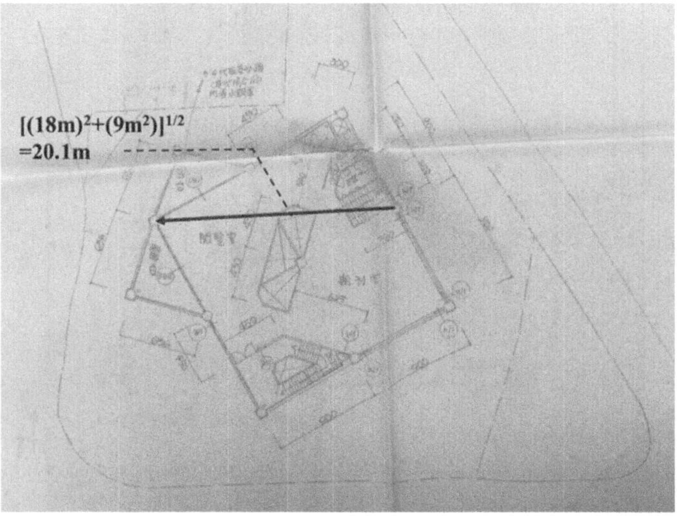


**Fig. 9.** Original 2nd-floor completion drawings of the demonstration site and estimation of the maximum measurable distance

on the system architecture shown in Fig. 7. Verification tests using continuous image-based lighting system control demonstrated that the system could detect the presence of personnel and activate the lighting within 1.5 to 1.8 s. When personnel exited the detection range, the system was able to turn off the lights within 1.4 to 1.9 s (Fig. 11).

The processing and analysis time required by the AI intelligent lighting system for each step is as follows:

- The time taken from the camera receiving the image to the AI computer is approximately 100–150 ms.
- YOLOv3 model calculation time is around 100 ms (processing rate: ~10 FPS).

**Fig. 10.** Central control system image analysis results of the 2nd-floor general reading room

**Fig. 11.** It shows the reliability of personnel detection using zoomed images from the camera.

- Signal transmission to the PLC server and subsequent signal reception takes about 300–400 ms.
- Sending signals to the PLC I/O module takes approximately 300 ms.
- Transmission to the lighting power drive modules takes about 300–500 ms, mainly due to varying distances between the main controller and the lighting circuits.
- The time for the lighting power supply driver to activate the lights is approximately 100–500 ms.

The variation in the lighting system's response time for turning lights on or off is primarily caused by differences in the response times of the power supply drivers used for each light, resulting in a delay of about 100–500 ms. This leads to variations in the overall lighting system's response. Several factors influence transient response performance in general lighting power supply control architectures. For instance, every component in the electronic circuit has a reaction time. After a load change, there is a minimal delay before the system reacts, as shown in Fig. 12.

Other factors that affect transient response include the compensation level of the internal error amplifier, which is used to regulate the Pulse Width Modulation (PWM). The PWM adjusts the transistor's conduction time to accommodate changes in output voltage. Additionally, the bandwidth of the control loop affects the regulation speed; a larger bandwidth allows faster adjustments to load changes.

Two external factors also influence transient response. The first is the output capacitor: larger capacitance can reduce sudden voltage changes but increases the response time. The second factor is the rate and amplitude of load current changes: the slower the rise or fall of the load current, the smaller the transient voltage peak. Conversely, a larger instantaneous change in load current causes more significant fluctuations in output voltage.

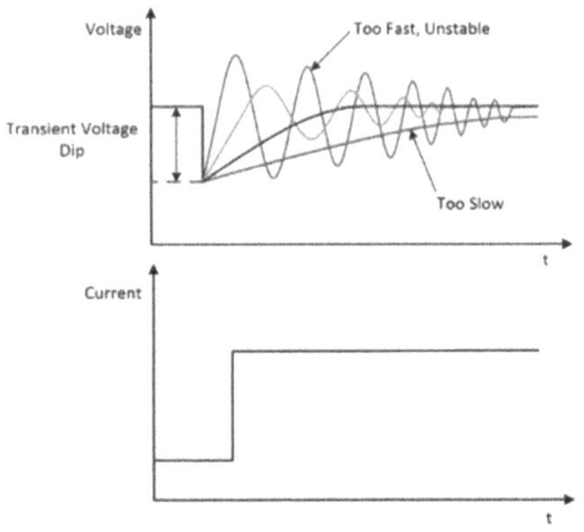


**Fig. 12.** Characteristics and variations in transient response within the power supply control architecture [12]

## 5 Conclusions

This study aims to introduce a novel detection technology to replace traditional PIR or microwave sensors used for object detection and lighting control. By integrating computer vision for image capture with AI-based algorithms, and utilizing the well-established YOLOv3 model, this research successfully achieved efficient lighting system control at detection distances exceeding 20 m, with a response time of under 2 s. The AI-based Intelligent Lighting System demonstrated activation times of 1.5 to 1.8 s for turning lights on, and 1.4 to 1.9 s for turning them off. Signal transmission accounted for the majority of the system's response time, with the total time from the PLC server to the individual lighting fixtures being approximately 600 to 800 ms, representing around 40% of the overall system response. Additionally, the variation in response time, particularly delays, was largely influenced by the transient response of the lighting power supply drivers, which took between 100 and 500 ms.

This AI-based intelligent lighting control technology has been successfully implemented and tested long-term at Baoshan Township Library. In addition to introducing advanced AI technology, it also provides significant benefits in terms of energy savings.

**Acknowledgments.** This work was financially supported by the Energy Fund of Energy Administration, Ministry of Economic Affairs of Taiwan government.

**Disclosure of Interests.** The authors have no competing interests to declare that are relevant to the content of this article.

## References

1. YOLE Homepage. https://www.yolegroup.com/product/report/thermal-imaging-and-sensing-2024/
2. OSLENS Homepage. https://www.oslens.com.tw/en/index.html
3. https://mropengate.blogspot.com/2018/06/YOLO-YOLOv3.html
4. Kaiming, H., Xiangyu, Z., Shaoqing, R., Jian, S.: Deep residual learning for image recognition. In CVPR (2016)
5. Alina, K., Hassan, R., Neil, A., Jasper, U., Ivan, K., et al.: Open- images: a public dataset for large-scale multi-label and multi-class image classification. Dataset Available from Openimages (2017)
6. Tsung-Yi, L., Priya, G., Ross, G., Kaiming, H., Piotr, D.: Focal loss for dense object detection. In ICCV (2017)
7. The IESNA LIGHTING HANDBOOK, Ninth Edition
8. CE Center - Task Lighting Solutions Homepage. https://continuingeducation.bnpmedia.com/courses/humanscale/task-lighting-solutions-their-economic-and-ergonomic-benefits/2/
9. Paszke, A., et al.: Pytorch.: Computer software. Vers. 0.31 (2017)
10. Milan, A., Leal-Taixé, L., Reid, I., Roth, S., et al.: MOT16: A Benchmark for Multi-Object Tracking. arXiv preprint arXiv:1603.00831 (2016)
11. Fabbri, M., Fabio, L., Simone, C., Andrea, P., Roberto, V., Rita, C.: Learning to detect and track visible and occluded body joints in a virtual world. In ECCV (2018)
12. https://www.ni.com/zh-tw/shop/electronic-test-instrumentation/power-supplies-and-loads/what-are-programmable-power-supplies/line-load-regulation-cascading.html

# Predicting 24-Hour Emergency Room Revisits: A Concept Bottleneck Approach

Yun-Chien Tseng[1], Cong-Tinh Dao[1], Chuan-Wei Kuo[1], Fang-Ming Hung[2], Chih-Chieh Hung[3(✉)], and Wen-Chih Peng[1(✉)]

[1] Department of Computer Science, National Yang Ming Chiao Tung University, Hsinchiu, Taiwan
{kt.yctseng.cs05,dcongtinh.ee13,auberonkuo.cs07,wcpengcs}@nycu.edu.tw

[2] Surgical Trauma Intensive Care Unit, Far Eastern Memorial Hospital, New Taipei City, Taiwan
philip@mail.femh.org.tw

[3] Department of Management Information Systems, National Chung Hsing University, Taichung, Taiwan
smalloshin@nchu.edu.tw

**Abstract.** Predicting emergency room revisits is a significant challenge due to data imbalance and the complexity of patient conditions. Traditional machine learning models have shown promise, but their lack of interpretability limits their practical use in clinical settings. In this paper, we present a novel framework for predicting emergency room revisits within 24 h. To address the challenge of model explainability, we incorporate a concept bottleneck layer. This layer allows the model to first predict a set of predefined, human-understandable concepts, enabling the integration of domain-specific knowledge from physicians into the prediction process. We consulted experienced emergency department physicians to identify the top 10 diseases most associated with revisits, such as unspecified abdominal pain, COVID-19 exposure, and chest pain. A key challenge in this approach is generating auxiliary labels for the concept layer, which we address by leveraging large language models (LLMs) to interpret patient electronic health records (EHRs) and generate patient-specific embeddings. These embeddings are then used to predict the likelihood of revisits based on their similarity to the top 10 diseases. Experimental results demonstrate the effectiveness of this approach, providing both high predictive performance and enhanced model interpretability.

**Keywords:** EHR · ED revisit prediction · Concept Embedding · Machine Learning · Healthcare

## 1 Introduction

The emergency room revisit problem occurs when patients return to the emergency department for additional care within a short period after their initial visit. This is a critical issue, as it may point to several underlying problems, such as insufficient initial treatment, unresolved health conditions, or complications stemming from the original diagnosis. With the widespread adoption of electronic

© The Author(s), under exclusive license to Springer Nature Singapore Pte Ltd. 2025
W.-T. Chu et al. (Eds.): TAAI 2024, CCIS 2414, pp. 276–290, 2025.
https://doi.org/10.1007/978-981-96-4589-3_20

health records (EHRs), predicting emergency room revisits has become increasingly feasible. EHRs provide a comprehensive and continuous record of a patient's medical history and treatment, enabling more accurate predictions over time.

Predicting emergency room revisits poses a significant challenge due to the highly imbalanced nature of the data. To address this, researchers have often focused on specific patient groups with particular diseases or behaviors to enhance the performance of machine learning models. For example, [Lee et al. (2023)] utilized logistic regression, random forest, XGBoost, and LightGBM to predict 30-day emergency room revisit risk for lung cancer patients at a hospital in Korea, achieving AUC scores around 0.70. Similarly, [Saggu et al. (2024)] focused on children aged 4–17 with mental health issues treated at McMaster Children's Hospital's Child and Youth Mental Health Program, applying Graph Neural Networks to predict revisits within 30 d. Additionally, [Heo et al. (2023)] investigated revisit rates among chemotherapy-induced febrile neutropenia patients, also using logistic regression. These studies underscore the continued popularity and acceptance of logistic regression, a statistical model, in emergency room revisit prediction.

Despite the promise of machine learning models in predicting emergency room revisits, they exhibit certain limitations. One of the key challenges is the lack of explainability inherent in many of these models. For medical professionals, understanding the factors driving these predictions is essential for refining clinical workflows and treatment strategies. Without clear interpretability, it becomes difficult for healthcare providers to trust and implement the insights from these models effectively. Another significant drawback is the difficulty in integrating the expert knowledge of medical professionals into the models. Physicians, drawing on years of experience, often identify important factors contributing to emergency revisits, many of which are complex and implicit. For instance, interactions between multiple comorbidities, such as diabetes, hypertension, and cardiovascular disease, can complicate a patient's prognosis. Physicians rely on clinical judgment to anticipate complications that may not be fully captured in the structured data used by machine learning models. This nuanced expertise is often difficult to incorporate into machine learning algorithms, limiting the models' ability to fully leverage the knowledge and experience of healthcare professionals.

In this paper, we introduce a framework for predicting emergency room revisits within the next 24 h. The framework is shown in Fig. 1. To tackle the challenge of model explainability, we incorporate a bottleneck layer inspired by the concept bottleneck model framework [Koh et al. (2020)]. Unlike conventional models that rely solely on raw input data for predictions, the concept bottleneck layer serves as an intermediate step where the model first predicts a set of predefined "concepts" before making the final prediction. These concepts represent human-understandable, domain-specific knowledge, which allows for the integration of physicians' expertise into the decision-making process. In this study, we consulted experienced emergency department physicians to identify the top 10 diseases most strongly associated with emergency revisits, such as unspecified abdominal pain, COVID-19 exposure, unspecified fever, and chest pain. One of the key challenges of this approach is generating auxiliary labels for the concept layer. While the top 10 diseases linked to revisits are identified, it is not straightforward to manually label each concept in the data. To address this, we propose generating concept labels by uncovering hidden risks within a patient's electronic health records (EHRs) that are related to these dominant diseases. For instance, patients with heart disease are frequently at risk of chest pain. In our framework, we leverage a large language model (LLM) to interpret doctors' notes and diagnoses in the patient's EHR and convert this information into an embedding of the patient's health profile. This embedding is then used to generate concept labels based on the similarity between the patient's profile and the embeddings of the top 10 diseases. Finally, a classifier utilizes these embeddings to predict whether a patient will revisit the emergency room within 24 h.

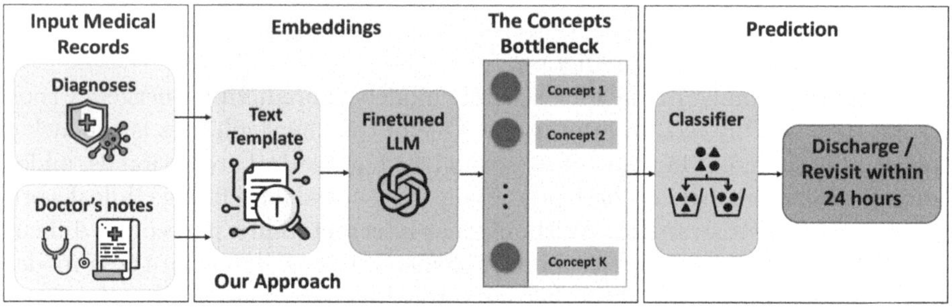


**Fig. 1.** The full structure of our proposal involves a text template provided by emergency physicians, closely resembling the format they use when writing clinical reports. We use a pre-trained LLM and a linear classifier.

The remainder of this paper is organized as follows: Sect. 2 provides a review of the relevant literature. Section 3 presents the technical details of the proposed model. Section 4 discusses the experimental results. Finally, Sect. 5 concludes the paper with a summary of key findings and future research directions.

## 2 Related Work

Predicting emergency room (ER) revisits is a complex task approached through various perspectives, primarily focusing on time intervals and specific medical conditions. First of all, the predicting emergency room revisits problem involves predicting patient returns within time periods ranging from 48 h to 30 d. For instance, [Pellerin et al. (2018)] employed logistic regression to assess revisit risk within 72 h, factoring in demographics, previous healthcare usage, and the initial diagnosis. Similarly, [Hong et al. (2019)] demonstrated the superiority of XGBoost [Chen and Guestrin (2016)] over logistic regression for predicting revisits within 72 h and 9 d. [Palungwachira et al. (2022)] focused on revisits within

48 h, using logistic regression for short-term prediction. Although machine learning techniques like XGBoost have shown better performance, logistic regression remains a widely used method due to its statistical transparency.

Given the inherent label imbalance in ER revisit prediction, some researchers concentrate on specific patient groups with particular conditions to improve model performance. For example, [Lee et al.(2023)] utilized logistic regression, random forest, XGBoost, and LightGBM [Ke et al. (2017)] to predict 30-day revisit risk for lung cancer patients, achieving an AUC score of 0.70. [Saggu et al. (2024)] applied Graph Neural Networks (GNNs) to predict revisits within 30 d for children with mental health issues. Additionally, [Heo et al. (2023)] explored chemotherapy-induced febrile neutropenia patient revisits, using logistic regression. Despite advances in machine learning, logistic regression continues to be widely adopted due to its interpretability in the medical domain.

# 3 Method

## 3.1 Problem Statement

The objective of this work is to address the problem of 24-hour emergency room revisits. A significant limitation of most existing studies is the underutilization of textual information within electronic health records (EHRs). Previous approaches, whether statistically based [Palungwachira et al. (2022)] [Pellerin et al. (2018)] or machine learning-based [Saggu et al. (2024)], primarily rely on non-textual data, such as patient age, Canadian Triage Acuity Scale (CTAS), visit disposition, diagnosis, and the type of services rendered during the visit. In our proposed framework, we enhance prediction accuracy by incorporating physician notes, which often contain critical information such as the patient's chief complaint, objective findings, diagnosis, treatment plan, and summaries. These notes, provided by experienced physicians, offer more valuable and direct insights compared to unsummarized tabular data. The problem we aim to solve is formally defined as follows:

**Problem** (24-Hour Emergency Room Revisit Prediction). *Given a patient's emergency room visit records $EHR_n$, which include both tabular health data and physician notes. The tabular health records capture the patient's historical information, such as diagnoses $d_1, \cdots, d_k$, gender $s$, and blood pressure $bp$. The physician notes consist of textual descriptions, including chief complaint $t_s$, objective findings $t_o$, diagnosis $t_a$, treatment plan $t_p$, and summary $t_{ab}$. The goal is to predict whether the patient will return to the emergency room within 24 h of discharge.*

## 3.2 Framework Overview

The figure presents an overview of the proposed framework for predicting emergency room revisits within 24 h using a concept bottleneck model and large language models (LLMs). The input of this framework includes structured and unstructured text data about patients, specifically diagnoses and physician's notes. These inputs contain valuable information about the patient's health status, which is crucial for making predictions. The output of this framework is a binary prediction of either patient discharge or a potential emergency room revisit within 24 h. The framework consists of the following components: 1) Text Template: The input medical records are processed and converted into a text template format. This step is essential for structuring the data, especially the physician's notes, so that it can be effectively utilized by the language model; 2) Finetuned LLM: The text template is passed through a finetuned large language model. The LLM generates embeddings from the input medical data, capturing complex and subtle relationships between the diagnoses, doctor's notes, and patient condition; 3) The Concepts Bottleneck: The generated embeddings are then passed through a concept bottleneck layer. This layer predicts a set of predefined concepts, which are ten diseases that are recognized as the most important related to returning to emergency room based on the learned embeddings; 4) Classifier: The predicted concepts are input into a classifier, which uses them to make the final prediction—whether the patient will be discharged or is likely to revisit the emergency room within the next 24 h.

This framework integrates physician expertise through concepts while leveraging the power of large language models to process medical records, offering both accurate predictions and enhanced model interpretability.

### 3.3 Text Template

Given an input electronic health record (EHR) denoted as $EHR_i = Tab_i, Text_i$, where $Tab_i$ represents the structured tabular data, including patient-specific details such as diagnoses $d_1^i, \ldots, d_k^i$, gender $s^i$, and blood pressure $bp^i$. The component $Text_i$ comprises the physician's unstructured medical notes corresponding to the $i^{th}$ patient, which include key textual descriptions such as the chief complaint $t_s^i$, objective findings $t_o^i$, diagnosis $t_a^i$, treatment plan $t_p^i$, and summary $t_{ab}^i$. The structured and unstructured data are combined into a single textual representation $T_i$ using a predefined template $T$[1], thereby synthesizing all relevant medical information for the input patient record.

### 3.4 Fine-Tuned LLM

Here, we leverage the capabilities of large language models (LLMs) to embed the information contained in the text template and the selected disease concepts. The choice of LLMs may include open-source models fine-tuned on medical data, such as Medical-Llama3-8b [Mavlanov(2024)], or powerful commercial models like GPT. These LLMs are capable of transforming the text data in $T_i$ into an embedding vector $\boldsymbol{tv}_{(i)} \in \mathbb{R}^n$. For simplicity, we denote this embedding

[1] The predefined template can take various forms, such as a structured table with predefined attributes or a simple concatenation of the structured and unstructured data into a continuous string.

as $\mathbf{v}$. To generate concept embeddings, the LLM also transforms each disease in the concept set into embeddings $c_1, \ldots, c_k$ using their disease names and corresponding ICD-10 codes. These embeddings are then utilized to compute the similarity between the patient's EHR and the disease concepts, determining how closely the patient's data aligns with each disease.

### 3.5 Concept Bottleneck Layer

This layer is inspired by Concept Bottleneck Models (CBMs) [Koh et al. (2020)]. Concepts are usually defined by key objective labels provided by domain experts. For example, in post-hoc CBMs [Yang et al. (2023)], images are used as input with labels such as color and shape, which are relatively objective. In emergency room cases, there are no objective labels for doctors to use when predicting whether a patient will be discharged or revisited. Hence, it will lead to a challenge to define concepts. The method we choose concepts will be discussed in Sect. 4.2.

For the formulation, given an embedding vector output from an LLM, $v = [v_1, \cdots, v_n]$ representing a patient, we aim to map $v$ into $\mathbb{R}^k$, the concept space, through the following mapping:

$$\mathbf{g}(\mathbf{v}) = \mathbf{e_c} = \mathbf{W}\mathbf{v} + \mathbf{b} \tag{1}$$

where $\mathbf{e_c} \in \mathbb{R}^k$ is the vector of concept representations, with each component $e_{ci}$ corresponding to a specific concept, $\mathbf{W} \in \mathbb{R}^{k\times n}$ is the weight matrix, where each row corresponds to a linear combination of the input features that define a concept and $\mathbf{b} \in \mathbb{R}^k$ is the bias vector, allowing for a shift in the concept space.

To find a suitable mapping function $g$, we consider the independent bottleneck case in [Koh et al. (2020)], we try to find a minimum

$$\hat{g} = \arg\min_{g} \sum_{i,j} L_{C_j}(g_j(x^{(i)}), c_j^{(i)}).$$

where $g_j : \mathbb{R}^n \rightarrow \mathbb{R}^k$ are similarity functions between vector, $L_{C_j} : \mathbb{R} \times \mathbb{R} \rightarrow \mathbb{R}^+$ is a loss function that measures the discrepancy between the predicted and true $j$-th concept. The true $j-th$ concept depends on whether the characteristic is mentioned in the diagnosed disease or clinical texts or on the closeness of the disease. For the loss function, we apply Cross-Entropy $= -\sum_{i=1}^{n}\sum_{c=1}^{C} y_{i,c}\log(\hat{y}_{i,c})$. Compared with the original concept bottleneck model, we handle function $\hat{f}$ to the classifier.

### 3.6 Classifier

In the final layer, a classifier is applied to the vectors output by the concept bottleneck. Let $\mathbf{e_c} = \mathbf{g}(\mathbf{v})$ be an embedded vector produced by the concept bottleneck layers, where $g : \mathbb{R}^n \rightarrow \mathbb{R}^k$ s a function that maps the LLM-represented vector $\mathbf{v}$ into concept space. $\mathbf{e_c}$ is a vector representing a patient's characteristics in the concept space.

The prediction $\hat{y}$ can be obtained by:

$$\hat{y} = f(\mathbf{e_c}) \tag{2}$$

where $f : \mathbb{R}^k \rightarrow \mathbb{R}$ is a function that maps the concept representations to the final output. We apply MSE as loss function: $\text{MSE} = \frac{1}{n}\sum_{i=1}^{n}(y_i - \hat{y}_i)^2$.

# 4 Experiment

## 4.1 Dataset

We evaluated our model on a real-world EHR dataset provided by Far Eastern Memorial Hospital (FEMH) in Taiwan. The FEMH Research Ethics Review Committee approved the study, and all data were de-identified. We used emergency room visit records, including emergency room visit time, discharge time, height, weight, blood pressure, pulse, ICD101, ICD102, ICD103, ICD104, ICD105, ICD106, chief complaint (S), objective (O), diagnosis (A), and plan (P), totaling 16 columns. In accordance with the policy, we only used data from patients aged 15 and older. Moreover, there were 848,965 emergency room visits from January 1, 2016, to December 31, 2023, of which 19,117 were revisits within 24 h. This corresponds to a 2.25% revisit rate in the dataset. We limited our data based on the revisit interval, dropping records where the revisit occurred more than 5 d apart. In the end, we retained 45,080 inputs. Figure 2 shows the process flow of how we obtain our input.

All of our input diseases are represented using the International Statistical Classification of Diseases and Related Health Problems, 10th Revision (ICD-10)[2]. All the disease codes mentioned in this paper are listed in Table 1.

## 4.2 Concepts Selecting

As for a concept bottleneck for our model, we do some observations to select some top diseases from the dataset as the concepts. The following Table 2 are the top 10 common diseases in both revisit cases and overall cases for emergency room visits.

The disease with the code R109 appears as the most common in both revisit cases and all ER cases, with a significantly higher proportion in revisit cases (8.38%) compared to all ER cases (2.80%). Another notable observation is that some diseases, like R1013, K2900, and K861, appear in the top 10 of cases that are revisited but not at the top of overall emergency room visit cases.

As for comparing to our dataset, each admission is recorded for at least six diseases. Hence, we choose the top six diseases in the revisit cases for the concept space. Note that we exclude Z20822, as it refers to "Contact with and (suspected) exposure to COVID-19", which does not represent a disease but rather factors influencing health status and contact with health services. Therefore, the six diseases in the concept space are R109, R509, K861, N390, R079, and R1013, which include two diseases that are not among the top 10 most common emergency room visit cases.

[2] https://www.cdc.gov/nchs/icd/icd-10/.

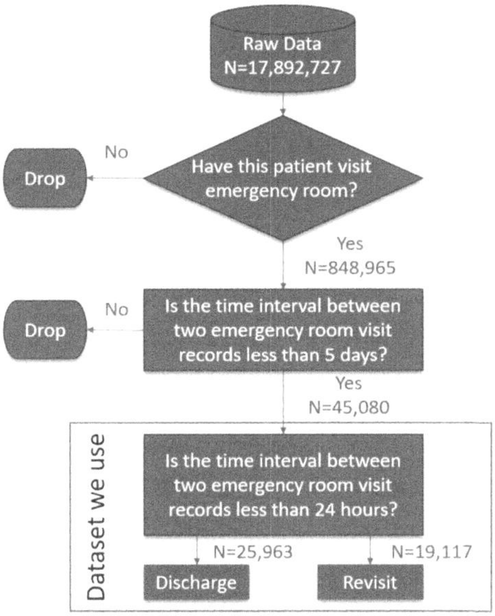


**Fig. 2.** Preprocessing flow for obtaining our input data.

**Table 1.** ICD-10 codes and their corresponding disease names. The disease ICD codes and names were referenced from https://www.icd10data.com/.

| ICD-10 Code | Disease Name |
|---|---|
| K2900 | Acute gastritis without bleeding |
| K861 | Other chronic pancreatitis |
| R109 | Unspecified abdominal pain |
| R509 | Fever, unspecified |
| N390 | Urinary tract infection, site not specified |
| R079 | Chest pain, unspecified |
| Z20822 | Contact with and (suspected) exposure to COVID-19 |
| R42 | Dizziness and giddiness |
| S0990XA | Unspecified injury of head, initial encounter |
| R1013 | Epigastric pain |
| K5289 | Other specified noninfective gastroenteritis and colitis |
| J189 | Pneumonia, unspecified organism |
| R6889 | Other specified general symptoms and signs |
| R0789 | Other chest pain |
| J180 | Bronchopneumonia, unspecified organism. |
| I110 | Hypertensive heart disease with heart failure |
| I509 | Heart failure, unspecified |
| N939 | Abnormal uterine and vaginal bleeding, unspecified |
| R103 | Pain localized to other parts of lower abdomen |

**Table 2.** The top 10 diseases in revisit cases and across all emergency room cases. There are a total of 30,001 diagnosed diseases in revisit cases and 1,069,763 diagnosed diseases in all emergency room visits.

| Rank | Disease (revisit) | Frequency | Ratio | Diseases (all) | Frequency | Ratio |
|---|---|---|---|---|---|---|
| 1 | R109 | 2517 | 0.0838 | R509 | 30037 | 0.0280 |
| 2 | Z20822 | 1528 | 0.0509 | N390 | 30001 | 0.0280 |
| 3 | R509 | 1058 | 0.0352 | R109 | 29472 | 0.0275 |
| 4 | K861 | 1020 | 0.0339 | R079 | 27355 | 0.0255 |
| 5 | N390 | 788 | 0.0262 | R42 | 24506 | 0.0229 |
| 6 | R079 | 641 | 0.0213 | S0990XA | 24087 | 0.0225 |
| 7 | R1013 | 532 | 0.0177 | Z20822 | 23556 | 0.0220 |
| 8 | K5289 | 473 | 0.0157 | K5289 | 22177 | 0.0207 |
| 9 | R42 | 467 | 0.0155 | J189 | 20492 | 0.0191 |
| 10 | K2900 | 464 | 0.0154 | R6889 | 19060 | 0.0178 |

### 4.3 Baselines

For the embedding layer, we chose **text-embedding-ada-002**[3], developed by OpenAI, as it is designed to generate dense vector embeddings for general text. This model also helps ease the computational load on our local computer, making it more manageable and cost-effective. Additionally, it excels at capturing the nuanced meanings of words and phrases within context, making it highly effective for tasks that require understanding the relationships between different pieces of text.

We implemented and evaluated several traditional machine learning models as baselines. These models were chosen due to their well-established performance in various classification tasks and their ability to handle different types of data.

- **Random Forest(RF)** [Breiman(2001)] is an ensemble learning method that constructs multiple decision trees during training and outputs the mode of the classes (classification) or mean prediction (regression) of the individual trees.
- **Adaptive Boosting (AdaBoost)** [Margineantu and Dietterich(1997)] is an ensemble learning technique that combines the predictions of several weak learners to create a strong classifier.
- **Support Vector Machine (SVM)** [Margineantu and Dietterich(1998)]is a supervised learning algorithm that finds the optimal hyperplane to separate data points of different classes in a feature space. It can handle high-dimensional spaces and works well for both linear and non-linear classification problems.
- **Light GBM (LGBM)** [Ke et al. (2017)] is a gradient-boosting framework that uses tree-based learning algorithms. It is designed to handle large

[3] https://platform.openai.com/docs/guides/embeddings.

datasets with faster training speeds and lower memory usage compared to other boosting methods while maintaining high accuracy.
- **XGBoost** [Chen and Guestrin(2016)] is an optimized gradient-boosting framework that uses decision trees. It is known for its performance and efficiency, offering features like regularization to reduce overfitting and handling sparse data effectively.
- **Multi-Layer Perceptron (MLP)** [Popescu et al. (2009)] is a class of feed-forward artificial neural networks composed of multiple layers of nodes. Each node in one layer connects to every node in the following layer with associated weights. MLPs are capable of learning complex patterns in data, making them useful for a variety of tasks such as classification, regression, and even complex function approximation.
- **Logistic regression** [Kleinbaum et al. (2002)] is a model commonly used in ED revisit problems. It is a linear model used for binary classification tasks, estimating the probability that a given input belongs to a particular class using a logistic function.

These traditional models were not only evaluated as standalone predictors but also integrated within our framework's classifier to establish a robust comparative baseline.

### 4.4 Results

In our experiment, we aim to discuss the following points: (1) The significance of text descriptions in EHRs for the ED revisit problem, (2) The benefits of our proposed structure, and (3) The most suitable machine learning model for EHR-related problems.

We discuss Table 3 different configurations and then give an overall conclusion.

**Without Text Input and Concept Embeddings.** In the first configuration, SVM and MLP demonstrate the strongest overall performance, with SVM achieving the highest scores in accuracy, recall, F1, and AUC. MLP follows closely, particularly in accuracy and precision. However, models like AdaBoost and Random Forest show relatively lower recall, which indicates that these models may struggle to correctly identify positive cases without the inclusion of additional information, such as text input and concept embeddings. The Random Forest model, while showing a competitive precision, falls behind in recall, which affects its F1 score.

**Without Concept Embedding.** When concept embeddings are removed but medical text inputs are included, we observe an overall improvement in model performance. The MLP model shows the best performance in accuracy, precision, and AUC, indicating that the inclusion of medical text significantly enhances the model's ability to distinguish between classes. SVM also performs well, especially

**Table 3.** We conducted all experiments using 10-fold cross-validation, so the results are presented as the mean (the humber before the brackets) and the standard deviation (the number in the brackets). The results shows the performance of seven machine learning models under three different configurations: without both medical text input and concept embeddings, without concept embedding layers, and using our proposed structure. Note that RF refers to Random Forest, Ada refers to AdaBoost, SVM refers to Support Vector Machine, LGBM refers to Light Gradient Boosting Machine, XGB refers to eXtreme Gradient Boosting, MLP refers to Multi-Layer Perceptron, and LR refers to Logistic Regression.

| Model | Accuracy | Precision | Recall | F1 | AUC |
|---|---|---|---|---|---|
| Without text input and concepts embedding | | | | | |
| RF | 0.5774(0.0041) | 0.5763(0.0082) | 0.4942(0.0134) | 0.5321(0.0066) | 0.5752(0.0043) |
| Ada | 0.5802(0.0056) | 0.6224(0.0204) | 0.3474(0.0267) | 0.4459(0.0071) | 0.5740(0.0050) |
| SVM | **0.5965(0.0045)** | 0.5844(0.0176) | **0.5887(0.0191)** | **0.5865(0.0073)** | **0.5963(0.0043)** |
| LGBM | 0.5746(0.0075) | 0.5881(0.0149) | 0.4172(0.0181) | 0.4881(0.0063) | 0.5703(0.0068) |
| XGB | 0.5753(0.0038) | 0.5734(0.0099) | 0.4942(0.0108) | 0.5308(0.0058) | 0.5731(0.0052) |
| MLP | **0.5965(0.0112)** | **0.5913(0.0554)** | 0.5509(0.1052) | 0.5704(0.0451) | 0.5952(0.0077) |
| LR | 0.5963(0.0035) | 0.5769(0.0137) | 0.5605(0.0151) | 0.5686(0.0074) | 0.5846(0.0078) |
| Without concepts embedding | | | | | |
| RF | 0.6138(0.0041) | 0.6252(0.0095) | 0.5614(0.0070) | 0.5915(0.0030) | 0.6136(0.0041) |
| Ada | 0.6349(0.0042) | 0.6532(0.0090) | 0.5694(0.0092) | 0.6083(0.0055) | 0.6347(0.0043) |
| SVM | 0.6419(0.0036) | 0.6590(0.0081) | **0.5826(0.0073)** | **0.6184(0.0044)** | 0.6417(0.0036) |
| LGBM | 0.6278(0.0087) | 0.6422(0.0242) | 0.5783(0.0597) | 0.6062(0.0254) | 0.6279(0.0089) |
| XGB | 0.6277(0.0050) | 0.6509(0.0081) | 0.5449(0.0121) | 0.5931(0.0073) | 0.6275(0.0049) |
| MLP | **0.6483(0.0040)** | **0.6800(0.0087)** | 0.5551(0.0081) | 0.6111(0.0051) | **0.6479(0.0039)** |
| LR | 0.6167(0.0046) | 0.6240(0.0093) | 0.5802(0.0076) | 0.6013(0.0047) | 0.6166(0.0047) |
| Our proposed structure | | | | | |
| RF | 0.5818(0.0069) | 0.6336(0.0148) | 0.3807(0.0223) | 0.4750(0.0127) | 0.5809(0.0049) |
| Ada | 0.5898(0.0078) | 0.6365(0.0080) | 0.4099(0.0138) | 0.4985(0.0105) | 0.5890(0.0062) |
| SVM | 0.5684(0.0059) | 0.5761(0.0113) | **0.5029(0.0093)** | 0.5369(0.0070) | 0.5681(0.0060) |
| LGBM | 0.5790(0.0107) | 0.6522(0.0595) | 0.3697(0.1073) | 0.4581(0.0647) | 0.5781(0.0088) |
| XGB | 0.5789(0.0047) | 0.5913(0.0051) | 0.4982(0.0133) | **0.5407(0.0069)** | 0.5786(0.0039) |
| MLP | **0.5922(0.0060)** | **0.6740(0.0120)** | 0.3501(0.0132) | 0.4606(0.0101) | **0.5911(0.0041)** |
| LR | 0.5810(0.0040) | 0.6038(0.0097) | 0.4603(0.0117) | 0.5222(0.0061) | 0.5806(0.0036) |

in recall and F1 score, suggesting its robustness across different metrics even without concept embeddings. The inclusion of text inputs alone improves recall across most models, showing that the text data provides valuable information that contributes to the model's ability to correctly identify positive cases.

**Our Proposed Structure.** In the final configuration, which uses our proposed structure, including both medical text inputs and concept embeddings, the results are mixed. While MLP achieves the highest accuracy, precision, and AUC, it suffers a significant drop in recall and F1 scores, which suggests a potential trade-off between precision and recall when both text and concept embeddings are included. SVM and XGB show balanced performance, with SVM excelling in recall and XGB in F1 score. AdaBoost also shows improved performance in accuracy and AUC, indicating that the integration of concept embeddings can help certain models, though it may not uniformly benefit all metrics. The LGBM model shows high variability, as indicated by the larger standard deviations, particularly in precision and recall, suggesting it might be more sensitive to the inclusion of concept embeddings compared to other models.

### 4.5 Discussion

Overall, the inclusion of medical text inputs generally improves the models' performance, particularly in recall, while the addition of concept embeddings offers varying benefits depending on the model. MLP and SVM are consistently strong performers across different configurations, though their strengths shift depending on the specific structure of the input data. The proposed structure appears to introduce trade-offs, enhancing precision and AUC but potentially at the cost of recall, depending on the model.

Our proposed framework does not show a significant improvement compared to methods without concept layers. However, embedding information into a lower dimension can result in some loss of information. On the other hand, in machine learning, lower dimensional leads to faster training times, saving both space and time. We chose $k = 6$, which is a very low dimension, yet the results still closely follow those of the models without concept layer embeddings. Most importantly, the concept layers provide domain experts with explanations for the prediction results, making the model's outcomes more acceptable to physicians.

### 4.6 Case Study

To give an example of the explainability of our framework, We explore two patients as a case study.

The first case is from 2022. Patient 1 is a 49-year-old male who was diagnosed with four diseases [R0789, J180, I110, I509] for one visit. For the configuration without the concept embedding, random forests, xgboost, and MLP predict that this patient will be revisited. However, without reviewing the clinical notes, we cannot determine the reason for revisiting the prediction, which is not persuadable to doctors. If we add a concept space [R109, R509, K861, N390, R079, R1013], only random forest predicts the patient will revisit the emergency room; other models predict that she will be discharged. The concept embedding vector is [0.4591, 0.5535, 0.4311, 0.4578, 0.6461, 0.3922], which represents the risk of having the diseases corresponding to the concept space [R109, R509, K861, N390, R079, R1013]. With the concept embedding, doctors can see the relations between his diagnosed disease R0789 and speculate he will be revisited due to R079 since it has a higher risk. It is very reasonable for doctors to predict the revisit of this patient due to R079 since we can find out in his notes that he has COVID-19.

The second case is from 2023. Patient 2 is a 30-year-old female who was diagnosed with N939 during her visit. In the configuration without the concept embedding, the random forest, XGBoost, and MLP models predicted that this patient would revisit the emergency room. However, when we added the concept embedding, random forest, SVM, LightGBM, XGBoost, and logistic regression models all predicted that she would revisit. Although N939 and the concept space [R109, R509, K861, N390, R079, R1013] do not seem directly related, Patient 2 revisited the emergency room within 24 h for N939 again. In detail, the embedded vector [0.4961, 0.4445, 0.4067, 0.5937, 0.4294, 0.4695] indicates the highest risk of return due to N390. In ICD-10, both N390 and N939 start with "N," signifying they are diseases related to the genitourinary system. Therefore, it is reasonable to consider that patient 2 is likely to revisit due to N390. However, the second highest risk corresponds to R109, which is indeed the reason for her revisit. The clinical notes mentioned: "... pain, dizziness, bleeding tendency", thus, the patient returned to the ER again, with the keyword "pain" being closely related to R109.

Although the prediction accuracy decreases after adding the concept layer, it provides a reasonable explanation that aligns with real-world scenarios, benefiting doctors by offering a quick review of the patient's situation. Moreover, the training was done in AMD Ryzen Threadripper 3960X, 256 GB RAM, Nvidia 3090 and CUDA 11.4. When using the LLM embedded results to train and predict a patient's label, the framework without concept layers takes 1,047 s, whereas the framework with concept layers takes only 84 s, making it significantly faster.

In both cases, we see that the concepts offer insights into the reasons for revisiting the emergency room, even if the prediction results do not always align perfectly with the actual outcomes [Zarlenga et al. (2022)]. This discrepancy highlights the challenge of selecting appropriate concepts, which remains an open problem and can be explored further in our future work.

## 5 Conclusion

In this study, we explored the integration of medical text descriptions and concept embeddings within machine learning models to predict revisiting outcomes in the emergency department (ED). While our proposed framework, which included concept embeddings, did not demonstrate a significant performance improvement over models without these layers, it provided valuable interpretability. The ability to embed complex medical information into lower-dimensional concept spaces offers the potential for faster training times and more efficient use of computational resources. Despite the trade-offs in predictive accuracy, the inclusion of concept layers makes the model's outcomes more understandable and acceptable to domain experts, particularly physicians, by providing clear explanations for the predictions. Moving forward, we aim to enhance the predictive capabilities of our model and refine the concept layers to improve both the accuracy and interpretability of predictions, making it a more powerful tool for clinical decision support.

For future work, we plan to expand our approach in two key directions. First, we aim to enhance our model's ability to predict future diagnostic outcomes, allowing for more proactive and informed medical decision-making. Second, we will continue working on refining and strengthening the concept layers in ED revisit problems to provide even more robust and insightful explanations, thereby improving the overall accuracy and interpretability of our model.

## References


Breiman, L.: Random forests. Mach. Learn. **45**(2001), 5–32 (2001)

Chen, T., Guestrinm C.: Xgboost: a scalable tree boosting system. In: Proceedings of the 22nd ACM SIGKDD International Conference on Knowledge Discovery and Data Mining, 785–794 (2016)

Hearst, M.A., Dumais, S.T., Osuna, E., Platt, J., Scholkopf, B.: Support vector machines. IEEE Intell. Syst. their Appli. **13**(4), 18–28 (1998)

Heo, S., et al.: Clinical factors predicting return emergency department visits in chemotherapy-induced febrile neutropenia patients. Am. J. Emerg. Med. **67**(2023), 90–96 (2023)

Hong, W.S., Haimovich, A.D., Taylor, R.A.: Predicting 72-hour and 9-day return to the emergency department using machine learning. JAMIA open **2**(3), 346–352 (2019)

Ke, G., et al.: Lightgbm: a highly efficient gradient boosting decision tree. Adv. Neural Inform. Process. Syst. **30** (2017)

Kleinbaum, D.G., Dietz, K., Gail, M., Klein, M., Klein, M.: Logistic regression. Springer (2002)

Koh, P., et al.: Concept bottleneck models. In: International Conference on Machine Learning, pp. 5338–5348. PMLR (2020)

Lee, A.R., Park, H., Yoo, A., Kim, S., Sunwoo, L., Yoo, S.: Risk prediction of emergency department visits in patients with lung cancer using machine learning: retrospective observational study. JMIR Med. Inform. **11**(2023), e53058 (2023)

Margineantu, D.D., Dietterich, T.G.: Pruning adaptive boosting. In ICML, vol. 97, pp. 211–218. Citeseer (1997)

Mavlanov, R.: Medical-Llama3-8B (2024). https://huggingface.co/ruslanmv/Medical-Llama3-8B Accessed 10 Sep 2024

Palungwachira, P., Montimanutt, G., Musikatavorn, K., Savatmongkorngul, S.: Reducing 48-h emergency department revisits and subsequent admissions: a retrospective study of increased emergency medicine resident floor coverage. Intern. J. Emergency Med. **15**(1), 66 (2022)

Pellerin, G., Gao, K., Kaminsky, L.: Predicting 72-hour emergency department revisits. Am. J. Emergency Med. **36**(3), 420–424 (2018)

Popescu, M.-C., Balas, V.E., Perescu- Popescu, L., Mastorakis, N.: Multilayer perceptron and neural networks. WSEAS Trans. Circ. Syst. **8**(7), 579–588 (2009)

Saggu, S., et al.: Prediction of emergency department revisits among child and youth mental health outpatients using deep learning techniques. BMC Med. Inform. Decision Making **24**(1), 42 (2024)

Yang, Y., Panagopoulou, A., Zhou, S., Jin, D., Callison-Burch, C., Yatskar, M.: Language in a bottle: language model guided concept bottlenecks for interpretable image classification. In Proceedings of the IEEE/CVF Conference on Computer Vision and Pattern Recognition, pp. 19187–19197 (2023)

Zarlenga, M.E., et al.: Concept embedding models: Beyond the accuracy-explainability trade-off. arXiv preprint arXiv:2209.09056 (2022)

# JSAI Special Session 1

# Proposal on Dashboard Generation Support Using Knowledge Graphs and Association Rules

Jin Taniguchi(✉), Hiroki Shibata, and Yasufumi Takama

Tokyo Metropolitan University, 1-1 Minami-Osawa, Hachioji, Japan
taniguchi-jin@ed.tmu.ac.jp, {hshibata,ytakama}@tmu.ac.jp

**Abstract.** This paper proposes a method for recommending views to be added to dashboards using Knowledge Graphs (KGs) and association rules. With the increasing importance of information visualization driven by digitalization, dashboards have become essential tools in various fields. However, creating dashboards remains a challenging task that requires experience and expertise. As a basic technology for supporting dashboard creation, this paper proposes a method to predict appropriate views to be added to a dashboard under creation. Three methods are proposed, based on knowledge graph embedding (KGE), association rules, and a combination of both, and evaluated with a dataset created from actual dashboard data.

**Keywords:** dashboard creaction · KGE · association rule

## 1 Introduction

This paper proposes a method to recommend views to be added to a dashboard using Knowledge Graphs (KGs) and association rules. A dashboard is a data visualization tool that consolidates graphs and charts to provide an at-a-glance understanding of data. With the increasing importance of data visualization driven by digital transformation, the role of dashboards has become more significant across various fields. One of the famous dashboards displays COVID-19 infection status, recovery rates, and mortality rates around the world[1]. Another example is a dashboard that tracks real-time inventory value and replenishment costs to support efficient inventory management[2].

Although the importance of dashboards is increasing, their creation requires complicated procedures, experience, and knowledge. To support dashboard creation, this study proposes a method to predict appropriate views to be added

[1] https://community.fabric.microsoft.com/t5/Data-Stories-Gallery/Global-Stock-Market-World-s-Top-200-Companies/td-p/1482649.

[2] https://community.fabric.microsoft.com/t5/Community-Blog/Inventory-Management-and-Analysis-Using-Power-BI/ba-p/930928.

© The Author(s), under exclusive license to Springer Nature Singapore Pte Ltd. 2025
W.-T. Chu et al. (Eds.): TAAI 2024, CCIS 2414, pp. 293–304, 2025.
https://doi.org/10.1007/978-981-96-4589-3_21

to a dashboard under creation based on association rules and KG constructed from actual dashboard data.

This paper also uses Knowledge Graph Embedding (KGE) to utilize KGs. KGE embeds a KG in a vector space. By embedding a KG into a vector space, logical reasoning such as a link prediction can be performed using vector operations. Sosa et al. utilized KGE to discover potentially effective drugs for disease treatment [10]. Drugs are designed to target specific diseases . However, many drugs are also effective for other disease. Discovering such drugs is challenging because it needs information from pharmacology, genetics, and pathology literature. They demonstrated that KGE, constructed from pharmaceutical literature and biomedical knowledge could be used to discover such drugs [10].

Association rules are feature patterns extracted by analyzing co-occurrence relationships among item sets. In the retail sector, basket analysis is used to discover combinations of frequently purchased items by analyzing customer purchase patterns. This helps identify opportunities for cross-selling and up-selling [8]. That is, association rules can be used for item recommendation. This paper realizes a view recommendation to support dashboard creation by combining the ability of association rules to find patterns with the logical inference using KGE.

The proposed method predicts appropriate views to be added to a dashboard based on both association rules and KGE. Apriori [2] is applied by treating views in a dashboard as items and a set of items within the same dashboard as a transaction. KGE model is obtained by treating dashboards and views as entities. Dashboards have themes and views have graph types and sizes as their attributes. These attributes are also regarded as entities. Triplets in KG are obtained by defining the relation between those entities. Furthermore, this paper also proposes to incorporate the extracted association rules into the KG by representing them as triplets. Experimental results show the effectiveness of the proposed methods. In particular, it is shown that incorporating association rules into KG improve a recommendation accuracy.

## 2 Related Work

### 2.1 Knowledge Graph and Its Applications

A knowledge graph (KG) describes real-world knowledge in a computationally accessible manner. It represents entities as nodes and their relationships as labeled, directed edges. A triplet $(h, r, t)$ represents a fact that head $(h)$ and tail $(t)$ entities have a relation $(r)$. A KG comprises a collection of such triplets. Although KG contains only explicitly stated triplets, it is impractical to describe all facts in a target domain as triplets. To address this issue, knowledge graph embedding (KGE) has been studied for automatically inferring missing triplets. KGE models are categorized into translation-based models, bilinear models, and neural network-based models. It is known that the performance of KGE models depends heavily on parameter tuning and training strategies. Actually, simple models sometimes outperform state-of-the art ones [11].

TransE [5] is the first translation-based model. It embeds triplets $(h, r, t)$ into Euclidean space, so that $\boldsymbol{h}+\boldsymbol{r}$ is close to $\boldsymbol{t}$, where $\boldsymbol{h}$, $\boldsymbol{r}$, and $\boldsymbol{t}$ are the embeddings of $h$, $r$, and $t$. The objective function $\mathcal{L}$ to be minimized is defined as Eq. (1).

$$\mathcal{L} = \sum_{(h,r,t)\in S} \sum_{(h',r,t')\in S'_{(h,r,t)}} \left[\gamma + d(\boldsymbol{h}+\boldsymbol{r},\boldsymbol{t}) - d\left(\boldsymbol{h}'+\boldsymbol{r},\boldsymbol{t}'\right)\right]_{+} \tag{1}$$

Here, notation $[x]_+$ denotes the positive part of $x$ and $\gamma$ represents a margin (hyperparameter). The distance function $d(\boldsymbol{x}, \boldsymbol{y})$ calculates the distance between vectors $\boldsymbol{x}$ and $\boldsymbol{y}$. $S$ denotes the training data, and $S'$ is the set of negative examples generated by randomly replacing either $h$ or $t$ in each triplet in $S$, which is defined as Eq. (2).

$$S'_{(h,r,t)} = \{(h', r, t) \mid h' \in E \wedge h' \neq h\} \cup \{(h, r, t') \mid t' \in E \wedge t' \neq t\} \tag{2}$$

Santos et al. constructed a Knowledge Graph (KG) about urban indicators and city data to support the automatic generation and data visualization of urban indicators in smart cities. They also proposed a Semantic BI (Business Intelligence) Generator to create dashboards from the constructed KG [9]. Using ontologies that define the classes about transportation infrastructures such as mobility history and bicycle-sharing systems, data acquisition activities, and urban entities, Semantic BI Generator discovers indicators about economy, environment and urban mobility, and extracts the necessary data from the KG using Protocol and RDF Query Language (SPARQL) [12]. It then automatically generates an interactive dashboard using the dashboard generation tool Qlik Sense[3]. The automatically generated dashboards can be used for decision-making without knowing how the original data was generated. This study demonstrates the effectiveness of KG in integrating different data sources and enhancing interoperability.

The KGE has been utilized in various fields and for different purposes to leverage knowledge graphs. For instance, Sosa et al. used KGE to discover drugs that may be effective in treating diseases [10]. While drugs are designed to work effectively against specific diseases, they may also be beneficial for treating other conditions. However, discovering such drugs is challenging due to the necessity of integrating information from pharmacology, genetics, and pathology literature. Sosa et al. demonstrated that by embedding a KG constructed from pharmaceutical literature and biomedical knowledge into vector space, it is possible to discover such drugs [10]. This study illustrates that KGE enables high-precision item recommendations by leveraging existing knowledge.

## 2.2 Data Mining and Association Rules

Data mining refers to the technology of extracting useful information and patterns from large datasets aiming at creating new knowledge. It does not only

[3] https://www.qlik.com/us/products/qlik-sense.

focus on mining algorithms but also includes preprocessing, post-processing, and feedback, forming a series of steps widely used to identify hidden patterns and correlations in large datasets and understand the data. As leveraging large amount of data is crucial nowadays, data mining has been utilized for various tasks such as market trend analysis and linguistic analysis [4].

Association rule mining is one of pattern discovery algorithms, which extracts co-occurrence relationships among items [1]. Within a transaction $T$, which is a subset of the set of all items $I$, the algorithm identifies an item set $B$ that frequently appears together with an item set $A$. When $A$ and $B$ co-occur in many transactions, such a relation is extracted as a rule in the form of $A \rightarrow B$ [1]. Common metrics used for extracting association rules are support and confidence. Support indicates the ratio of transactions that include all items in the union of $A$ and $B$ to all transactions. Confidence represents the ratio of transactions that include all items in the union of $A$ and $B$ to the transactions that include all items in $A$. Rules of which support and confidence exceed given thresholds are extracted. Apriori algorithm is one of the representative methods for mining association rules [2].

### 2.3 Dashboard

A dashboard is a data visualization method that aggregates graphs and charts to provide an at-a-glance understanding of data. By consolidating essential information onto a single screen, it helps users quickly understand the situation. It is also a powerful tool for information sharing and communication [7]. However, creating a useful dashboard requires efficiently organizing a large amount of information within a limited space and displaying it in an easy-to-understand manner [7].

Typical applications of dashboards target the COVID-19 infection status, recovery rates, and mortality rates across many countries[4]. During the early stages of the COVID-19 pandemic, Dong et al. also developed an online interactive dashboard to visualize reported cases of infection in real-time, which contributed to global sharing of infection data [6]. This dashboard is not only useful for researchers and public health professionals but also for the general public to track the spread of the infection from its early stages. Another example in the field of marketing is a dashboard designed to track a company's inventory value and replenishment costs in real-time, which supports efficient inventory management[5].

## 3 Proposed Method

This study proposes a method to predict the appropriate views to be added to a dashboard based on association rules and KGE. To construct a KG and extract association rules, target data are collected from the Microsoft PowerBI DataStoryGallery[4]. The proposed method involves scraping dashboard data, extracting

[4] Microsoft. https://community.fabric.microsoft.com/t5/Data-Stories-Gallery/bd-p/DataStoriesGallery, (Accessed: 2024/08/12).

co-occurrence between views within dashboards as association rules, and obtaining KGE model from a KG constructed from the collected data. Additionally, this paper also proposes to incorporate the extracted association rules into the KG.

### 3.1 Dashboard Data

Dashboard data are extracted from the Microsoft PowerBI DataStoryGallery[9] through web scraping. The URL (Uniform Resource Locator), title, and elements such as graphs in a dashboard are extracted from the page's HTML (Hyper text Markup Language) source file. Python[5] packages BeautifulSoup and Selenium are used for the data scraping. Figure 1 shows an example of a dashboard[6], and Fig. 2 shows a part of the corresponding HTML source file.

In Fig. 1, the title "Executive Insights by Decisive Data" at the top of the dashboard and each graph or table in the dashboard are collected by parsing the HTML source file. As shown in Fig. 2, title is written within a span tag, which is a child element of a h1 tag (Line 3). Views correspond to div tags that have a word "visual" in the class attribute. For example, Line 7 in Fig. 2 corresponds to the pie chart in the center-right of Fig. 1. The last element in the class attribute, visual-donutChart, is collected as a graph type. The size of the view is collected from the height and width attributes of the svg tag, which is a child element of the div tag corresponding to the view. For the above-mentioned pie chart, its height (about 220) and width (about 148) are collected from Line 9 in Fig. 2.

The area of each view is calculated from its height and width, and the proportion of the area in the dashboard is determined. Views in a dashboard are then sorted in ascending order of this proportion and the value of a size attribute is set to S (Small), M (Medium), or L (Large) so that the ratio of views with each value is approximately 1:1:1. We determine this value based on relative size rather than absolute area because the size of dashboards varies. If the height and width of a view cannot be obtained, it has NOSIZE as a size attribute.

Preprocessing is applied to the names of the graphs, including deletion and normalization. For instance, views with meaningless names, such as "visual-actionButton," or non-standard names created automatically by PowerBI, such as "visual-deneb7E15AEF80B9E4D4F8E12924291ECE89A," are deleted. Additionally, names that include numbers or alphabets due to PowerBI's specifications, such as "visual-Sunburst1445472000808" are normalized to "visual-Sunburst."

The theme of a dashboard represents its purpose and the genre of its target data. This paper classifies themes by giving a prompt to ChatGPT along with a CSV file containing the titles of 1000 collected dashboards. The prompt instructs to categorize the titles into 10 themes and output the CSV with the added theme column. Table 1 shows the theme names and the number of corresponding dashboards.

[5] https://www.python.org/.
[6] https://community.fabric.microsoft.com/t5/Data-Stories-Gallery/Executive-Insights-by-Decisive-Data/td-p/181742,(Accessed:2024/08/12).

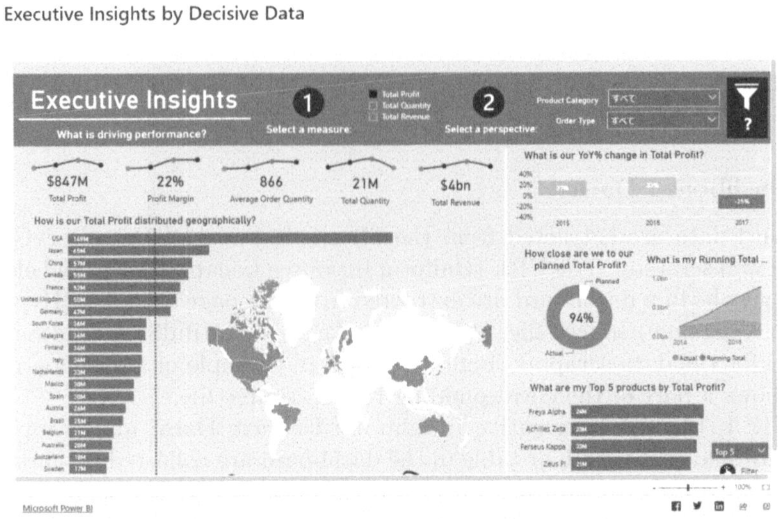


Fig. 1. Example of dashboard.

## 3.2 Recommendation with Association Rules

The co-occurrence relationship between views within a dashboard is extracted as association rules. An item is defined as the combination of the graph type and the size of a view, and a transaction is defined as the set of items contained within the same dashboard.

Evaluation procedure when using association rules consists of the following steps.

1. For each dashboard in the test data, randomly select one item from the set of items included in the dashboard and treat it as a correct item.
2. Use the remaining items as input (query) to select association rules.
3. For every subset ($s$) of the input, extract association rules of which antecedent is $s$.
4. For each $s$ in Step 3, select the top 5 association rules with the highest support.
5. Among all the association rules selected in Step 4, select the top $K$ association rules with the highest support.
6. Recommend items included in the consequent part of the association rules selected in Step. 5.
7. A recommendation is considered successful if the correct item selected in Step 1 is recommended in Step 6.

The above process is applied to all dashboards in the test data. The accuracy of the recommendation results is evaluated using Hits@$K$ [3], which represents the proportion of successful recommendation in the test data. The experimental details are described in Sect. 4.

```
<h1 class="PageTitle lia-component-common-widget-page-title">
    <span class="lia-link-navigation lia-link-disabled">
        Executive Insights by Decisive Data
    </span>
</h1>
...
<div ... class="visual customPadding allow-deferred-rendering
     visual-donutChart" ...>
    ...
    <svg ... width="220.0850546780073" height
    ="148.34750911300122" ...>
        ...
    </svg>
    ...
</div>
```

**Fig. 2.** HTML source file of Fig. 1. ... means that a portion of the text has been omitted.

### 3.3 Recommendation with KGE

The entities and relations defined in this paper are shown in Tables 2 and 3, respectively. Each dashboard is treated as an entry, which is related with views in it through HasView relation. It has a theme as an attribute, which is represented with Has Theme relation. Views are distinguished by their graph type and size: views of the same graph type and size are considered the same entity. The attributes of a view, size and graph type, are respectively specified with HasSize and HasType relations.

This paper constructs two types of Knowledge Graphs (KGs): one containing triplets representing association rules(KG with association rules) and one without (KG without those triplet related to association rules). The Knowledge Graph Embeddings (KGE) are learned from each of these KGs.

In the KG with association rules, entities for describing association rules are frequent itemsets ($s$), association rules ($r$), and graph types ($g$) as shown in Table 2. The relations used are MemberOf($g, s$) representing that $s$ contains $g$ as an item, and AntecedentsOf($s, r$) and ConsequentsOf($s, r$) are used to respectively specify the antecedent and consequent parts of $r$. As a dashboard is treated as a transaction, ConcludedIn($r, d$) is used to describe that $r$ is included in $d$. As described in Sect. 3.2, in the extraction of association rules, combinations of graph type and size were treated as items. However, in the construction of the KG, size is ignored, and only graph type is considered as an item.

Evaluation procedure when using KGE consists of the following steps.

1. For each dashboard in the test data, randomly select a triplet $x$ from the set of triplets with a dashboard (head entity) and HasView (relation).
2. Use the view (tail entity) of $x$ as the correct view.

**Table 1.** The summary of themes

| Name of theme | Number of dashboards |
|---|---|
| Miscellaneous | 566 |
| Sales, Marketing, and Retail | 146 |
| Technology, Innovation, and Digital Media | 137 |
| Global Issues and International Affairs | 37 |
| Human Resources and Employment | 30 |
| Specific Industries and Services | 19 |
| Public Sector, Government, and Policy | 18 |
| Financial and Economic Analysis | 16 |
| Corporate, Business, and Enterprise | 14 |
| Operations, Management, and Performance | 11 |
| Environmental, Energy, and Sustainability | 6 |
| Total | 1,000 |

**Table 2.** Overview of Defined Entities

| Symbol | Description | Example |
|---|---|---|
| $d$ | Dashboard | Revenue Dashboard |
| $t$ | Theme of the Dashboard | Technology and Digital Media |
| $v$ | View | donutChart_M |
| $g$ | Graph type of view | donutChart |
| $size$ | Size of view | M |
| $s$ | Frequent itemset (elements: $g$) | ['donutChart', 'map'] |
| $r$ | Association rule | ['donutChart', 'map']→['lineChart'] |

**Table 3.** Overview of Defined Relations

| Name | Description of relationship | Head | Tail |
|---|---|---|---|
| HasTheme | Dashboard and theme | $d$ | $t$ |
| HasSize | view and size | $v$ | $size$ |
| HasType | view and graph type | $v$ | $g$ |
| HasView | Dashboard and views it contains | $d$ | $v$ |
| MemberOf | frequent itemset and its element (graph type) | $g$ | $s$ |
| AntecedentsOf | association rule and its antecedents | $s$ | $r$ |
| ConsequentsOf | association rule and its consequents | $s$ | $r$ |
| ConcludedIn | association rule and Dashboard | $r$ | $d$ |

3. Use the dashboard (head entity) of $x$ as the input (query).
4. Predict the view (tail entity) that has HasView relation to the dashbaord (head entity) selected in Step 3 through link prediction.
5. Recommend the views with the top $K$ views with the highest score.
6. A recommendation is considered successful if the correct view selected in Step 2 is recommended in Step 5.

In step 5, the score of a view is calculated as the distance between the composite vector of a query view and HasView relation, and that of a predicted view in Euclidean space.

The above process is applied to all dashboards in the test data. The accuracy of the recommendation results is evaluated using Hits@$K$. The experimental details are described in Sect. 4.

# 4 Experiments

## 4.1 Overview of Experiments

Hits@$K$ [3] is used as an evaluation metric, which represents the proportion of times the correct answer is included in the top $K$ recommendations. It is defined as Eq. (3). Here, $q$ denotes the query, $Q_{\text{test}}$ is the test data, and rank($q$) is the rank of the correct answer in the recommendation list for $q$.

$$\text{Hits@}K = \frac{|\{q \in Q_{\text{test}} \mid \text{rank}(q) \leq K\}|}{|Q_{\text{test}}|} \tag{3}$$

In the case of the recommendation method using association rules, the dashboards, which are treated as transactions, are divided into training data and test data at a ratio of 9:1. Association rules are extracted from the training data. Association rules are extracted using the Apriori algorithm [2]. Frequent_patterns.apriori module in a Python library mlxtend (version 0.21.0)[7] is used. Regarding parameters, a minimum support of 0.002, a minimum confidence of 0.002 and a minimum lift of 0.01 are used. The low lift and confidence thresholds aim to exclude too rare rules only. Rules of which confidence equals 1.00 are not used, because too specific rules are not suitable for recommendation. When the confidence is equal to 1.00, it indicates that the pattern is not a general one but originates from a specific dashboard. As a result, 6647 rules were extracted.

In the case of the recommendation method using KGE, Table 4 shows the number of generated triplets for each relation. KGE is obtained using the TransE model. The 'pykeen' package[8], specifically 'pykeen.models.TransE'[9], is used with an embedding dimension of 50. For negative sampling,

[7] https://rasbt.github.io/mlxtend/.
[8] https://pykeen.readthedocs.io/en/stable/index.html.
[9] https://pykeen.readthedocs.io/en/stable/api/pykeen.models.TransE.html.

'pykeen.training.SLCWATrainingLoop'[10] is utilized with 100 epochs and a batch size of 256.

The learning process of KGE consists of the following steps.

1. The dashboards ($d$) are split into $\boldsymbol{d}_{train}$ and $\boldsymbol{d}_{test}$ at a ratio of 3:2
2. As noted in Sec. 3.3, one triplet with the HasView relation is randomly selected for each dashboard ($d$) in $\boldsymbol{d}_{test}$.
3. The remaining triplets are used for training KGE model.

Dashboards that have only one triplet are not used. Due to some troubles in the an experiment, a part of the triples in the test data was not used. As a result, 42,298 triplets were used for KGE training, and 94 triplets were used for evaluation.

**Table 4.** Number of Created Triplets

| Relation Name | Count |
|---|---|
| HasTheme | 968 |
| HasSize | 128 |
| HasType | 128 |
| HasView | 2084 |
| MemberOf | 2348 |
| AntecedentsOf | 6649 |
| ConsequentsOf | 6649 |
| ConcludedIn | 23533 |
| Total | 42487 |

### 4.2 Result

The experimental results of KGE with association rules, KGE without association rules, and association rules are shown in Table 5. The table shows that KGE with association rules achieves the highest Hits@$K$ values across all $K$. This indicates that combining knowledge graphs with association rules enables more accurate view recommendations than those using KGE and association rules alone.

Comparing KGE without association rules and using association rules alone, it is clear that KGE achieves higher accuracy. This result can be attributed to the fact that in KGE, views with the same graph type but different sizes share information through the entities of graph type in the learning process.

[10] https://pykeen.readthedocs.io/en/stable/api/pykeen.training.SLCWATrainingLoop.html.

In contrast, when using the association rule alone, such views are treated as different items, which is supposed to affect the recommendation accuracy. Additionally, KGE with association rules shows a larger difference between Hits@3 and Hits@5 compared to KGE without association rules. This suggests that combining association rules with KGE is effective for improving the accuracy of top recommendation results.

**Table 5.** Experimental Results

| | Hits@3 | Hits@5 | Hits@10 |
|---|---|---|---|
| KGE with association rules | 0.31 | 0.40 | 0.57 |
| KGE without association rules | 0.16 | 0.21 | 0.31 |
| Association Rules | 0.02 | 0.06 | 0.12 |

## 5 Conclusion

This paper proposed a method to recommend appropriate views to be added to a dashboard, aiming to support dashboard creation by leveraging association rules and KGE.

In the proposed method relationships between co-occurring views within a dashboard are extracted as association rules. In addition to those relationships, the relationships between dashboards and views are converted into triplets, from which KGE models are obtained. A KGE incorporating triples representing the extracted association rules was also constructed.

Experiments were conducted to evaluate the recommendation accuracy using the association rules, using KGE alone, and using KGE with association rules. The experimental results showed that KGE-based recommendations achieved higher accuracy than association rule-based recommendations. Furthermore, incorporating association rules into KGE improved recommendation accuracy, in particular the accuracy of top recommendation results.

Future works include the optimization of hyperparameters to achieve further accuracy. Realizing dashboard creation support system based on the proposed method is also one of the future works.

**Acknowledgments.** This work was partially supported by JSPS KAKENHI Grant Numbers JP22K19836, JP23K24953, and JP21H03553.

## References

1. Agrawal, R., Imieliński, T., Swami, A.N.: Mining association rules between sets of items in large databases. In: Proceedings of the 1993 ACM SIGMOD International Conference on Management of Data, **22**, 207–216 (1993)

2. Agrawal, R., Srikant, R.: Fast algorithms for mining association rules. In: Proc. 20th International Conference on Very Large Data Bases, pp. 487–499 (1994)
3. Ali, M., et al.: Bringing light into the dark: a large-scale evaluation of knowledge graph embedding models under a unified framework. IEEE Trans. Pattern Anal. Mach. Intell. **44**(12), 8825–8845 (2022). https://doi.org/10.1109/TPAMI.2021.3124805
4. Bharati, M.: Data mining techniques and applications. Indian J. Comput. Sci. Eng. **1**, 301–305 (2010)
5. Bordes, A., Usunier, N., Garcia-Duran, A., Weston, J., Yakhnenko, O.: Translating embeddings for modeling multi-relational data. Adv. Neural. Inf. Process. Syst. **26**, 2787–2795 (2013)
6. Dong, E., Du, H., Gardner, L.M.: An interactive web-based dashboard to track covid-19 in real time. Lancet. Infect. Dis **20**, 533–534 (2020)
7. Few, S.: Information dashboard design: The effective visual communication of data. O'reilly Sebastopol (2006)
8. Kaur, M., Kang, S.: Market basket analysis: Identify the changing trends of market data using association rule mining. Proc. Comput. Sci. **85**, 78–85 (2016). https://doi.org/10.1016/j.procs.2016.05.180
9. Santos, H., Dantas, V., Furtado, V., da Silva, P.P., McGuinness, D.L.: From data to city indicators: a knowledge graph for supporting automatic generation of dashboards. Extended Semantic Web Conference, pp. 94–108 (2017)
10. Sosa, D.N., Derry, A., Guo, M., Wei, E., Brinton, C., Altman, R.B.: A literature-based knowledge graph embedding method for identifying drug repurposing opportunities in rare diseases. Pac. Symp. Biocomput. **25**, 463–474 (2019)
11. Teach, Y.C., Ruffinelli, D., Broscheit, S., Gemulla, R.: You can teach an old dog new tricks! on training knowledge graph embeddings. In: International Conference on Learning Representations, p. 20 (2020)
12. W3C: Sparql 1.1 query language (2024). https://www.w3.org/TR/sparql11-query/

# Synthetic Data Generation for Book Recommendation Using Knowledge Graph Embedding

Shunji Suzuki(✉), Hiroki Shibata, and Yasufumi Takama

Tokyo Metropolitan University, 1-1 Minami-Osawa, Hachioji, Japan
suzuki-shunji@ed.tmu.ac.jp, {hshibata,ytakama}@tmu.ac.jp

**Abstract.** This paper proposes a method of generating synthetic data for book recommendation based on knowledge graph embedding (KGE). Collaborative filtering (CF) has been widely and commonly used in recommender systems, which determines items to recommend from a rating matrix. However, its performance significantly decreases when enough amount of rating data is unavailable. In addition, privacy concerns have become a major issue in recent years. To solve these problems, the approach of generating synthetic data based on the statistical characteristics of real data is attracting attention in the field of machine learning and recommendation. The proposed method constructs a knowledge graph from user's reading history and synthesizes a rating matrix by simulating the user's reading behavior based on the link prediction using KGE. The effectiveness of the proposed method is shown by comparing it with an actual rating matrix in terms of precision and recall in a book recommendation task.

**Keywords:** Synthetic data · Recommendation · Knowledge Graph Embedding

## 1 Introduction

This paper proposes a method for generating a synthetic rating matrix that can be used for book recommendations using collaborative filtering.

Recent advancements in information technology have enabled everyone to post and get large amounts of information. However, the abundance of information has made it difficult for us to obtain information that matches our preferences and purposes. To solve this issue, recommender systems have been studied for supporting users' information gathering and decision-making by identifying and presenting information that aligns with their preferences and purposes.

Collaborative filtering (CF) [3] is one of the common approaches used in recommender systems. It uses a rating matrix that consists of users' rating to items to determine items to recommend. However, there is a problem related to data quantity such as the cold-start problem, which is caused by the lack of

© The Author(s), under exclusive license to Springer Nature Singapore Pte Ltd. 2025
W.-T. Chu et al. (Eds.): TAAI 2024, CCIS 2414, pp. 305–318, 2025.
https://doi.org/10.1007/978-981-96-4589-3_22

ratings for new users to items. Furthermore, recent concerns about privacy protection makes it increasingly difficult to collect and utilize private information of users. As a means to prepare enough amount of data for machine learning, recommender systems, etc., an approach of extracting statistical features from real data and creating synthetic data with similar characteristics has been studied [10]. The use of synthetic data can lead to improve the accuracy of machine learning models by resolving data shortages. Additionally, it makes the publication and sharing of data easy, as it does not contain information about actual individuals.

The purpose of this paper is to create a synthetic rating matrix that can be used for book recommendations using CF. The proposed method generates a synthetic rating matrix by simulating users' reading behavior through link prediction using Knowledge Graph Embedding (KGE). KGE is a technology that treats knowledge by assigning vector representations to entities and relations, which are elements of a Knowledge Graph (KG). Previous studies have shown that KGE can be applied to information recommendations through link prediction by treating users and items as entities, and interactions between users and items as relations [1]. Moreover, KGE can simultaneously embed heterogeneous information such as user preference tendencies and book attributes, which affect users' reading behavior including selecting books to read and evaluating them. Therefore, KGE trained with such knowledge can be expected to be used for simulating users' reading behaviors.

The proposed method uses the books, their attributes, and the user's evaluation data for the books contained in the Goodreads dataset [12,13] to train KGE. TransE [1], which is one of the popular KGE models, is used in this paper. A synthetic rating matrix is generated based on the sequential book evaluation behaviour by simulated users.

In the experiment, precision and recall of the recommendation result using the synthetic rating matrix generated by the proposed method is compared with that using the actual rating matrix and the synthetic rating matrix when simulated users randomly select books to read. The experimental result shows the effectiveness of the proposed method and the validity of the assumed users' reading behavior.

## 2 Related Work

### 2.1 KGE Models

Knowledge Graph Embedding (KGE) is a technique that enables algebraic operations on a knowledge graph (KG) by embedding entities, which are elements of KGs, into a vector space. KGE models are classified into Distance-based Models and Semantic Matching Models [2].

TransE [1], which is one of the distance-based models, learns a $D$-dimensional vector for each entity and relation by minimizing a loss function defined as Equation (1), where $S$ is a set of triples $(h, r, t)$ indicating that there is a relation $r$ between entities $h$ and $t$, $[x]_+$ represents the positive part of $x$, and $\gamma$ is a hyperparameter representing the margin.

$$\mathcal{L} = \sum_{(h,r,t)\in S} \sum_{(h',r,t')\in S'_{(h,r,t)}} [\gamma + \mathrm{d}(h + r, t) - \mathrm{d}(h' + r, t')]_+ \tag{1}$$

A function $\mathrm{d}(x, y)$ represents a distance (L1 or L2 norm) between vectors corresponding to $x$ and $y$. $S'$ is a set of negative example triples, which are obtained by replacing either $h$ or $t$ of triples in $S$ with a randomly selected entity. It is defined as shown in Eq. (2).

$$S'_{(h,r,t)} = \{(h', r, t) \mid h' \in E\} \cup \{(h, r, t') \mid t' \in E\} \tag{2}$$

Other distance-based models are TransH [14], TransR [4], and RotatE [11]. Examples of semantic matching models are RESCAL [6] and DistMult [18].

## 2.2 Recommendation Using KG

KGs can manage various relationships between entities in a single data structure. By leveraging this characteristic, KG can be used for recommendation by treating user feedback on items as relationships between user entities and item entities [1]. Palumbo et al. demonstrated that KGE models such as TransE outperform collaborative filtering (CF) and popularity-based baseline methods in terms of recommendation accuracy for item recommendation tasks. They also showed that the embedding dimension of KGE affects recommendation accuracy, by optimizing which as a hyperparameter recommendation accuracy can be improved [7]. Zhang et al. proposed a recommendation framework called Collaborative Knowledge Base Embedding (CKBE) [19], which constructs a knowledge base consisting of three types of heterogeneous knowledge: structural knowledge about relationships between items and attributes, textual knowledge summarizing item content, and visual knowledge of item-related images. TransR [4] is trained using the structural knowledge [19].

Explainable recommendation has been proposed in recent years, which aims at improving transparency, persuasiveness, effectiveness, reliability, and satisfaction of recommender systems [20]. By using KGs, it is possible to manage not only user-item relationships but also attribute information of users and items in a single data structure. Therefore, it is possible to explain the reason for the recommendation by utilizing paths from user entities to item entities on a KG. Xie et al. proposed a framework that constructs KGs to obtain a set of items for which the reason for the recommendation is explainable and selects items to recommend from the set considering recommendation accuracy, diversity, and explainability using multi-objective optimization [16].

### 2.3 Synthetic Data

Synthetic data is artificially generated data that simulate the real data. The purposes of generating synthetic data include privacy protection and data augmentation.

Methods for generating synthetic data are classified into three types: A statistical-based approach generates data according to statistics obtained from real data, an agent-based approach generates data based on the behaviour of agents following predefined rules, and a machine learning-based approach generates data by models trained with real data.

As an example of the statistical-based approach, Pei et al. proposed a method to generate synthetic data for evaluating clustering algorithms and outlier detection algorithms. They applied linear transformations to basic datasets that are generated using uniform and normal distributions [8].

As an example of the agent-based approach, Weyland et al. generated synthetic data by simulating soldier movement paths and combat actions based on parameters such as enemy recognition ability, movement speed, and shooting success rate. The generated data was used for evaluating military operation decision support systems [15].

As an example of the machine learning-based approach, Xu et al. proposed Tabular GAN (TGAN), which is a kind of Generative Adversarial Network (GAN), for generating synthetic tabular data [17]. TGAN can generate synthetic data containing both discrete and continuous variables. The results of experiments on three different datasets have shown that it outperforms traditional statistical methods in terms of reproducing correlations between columns and scalability to the size of a dataset [17]. As a study aiming at generating synthetic data for recommendation, Moriyoshi et al. proposed a method for generating a rating matrix consisting of explicit feedback by defining rational rating behaviors of users who prefer popular or unpopular items [5]. They used only the popularity information calculated from a rating matrix, no attribute information about items. Furthermore, they did not consider the sequence of item selections by users.

Regarding the privacy protection, Slokom proposed SynRec, a data protection framework for publishing data to be used for recommendation. It employs a machine learning-based approach using CART (Classification And Regression Tree), a type of decision tree. It reduces the risk of data leakage by replacing sensitive values and key identifiers in the real data with multiple imputations [9].

## 3 Synthetic Data Generation for Book Recommendation

This section proposes a method for generating a synthetic rating matrix for book recommendation. The proposed method trains KGE model using a book dataset including users' evaluation history and simulates users' reading behavior using the resulting model.

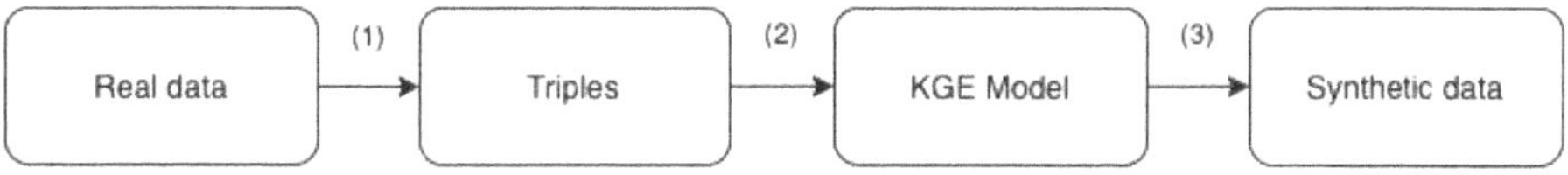


**Fig. 1.** Outline of the proposed method

Figure 1 shows the outline of the proposed method, which generates a synthetic rating matrix with the following procedures:

(1) Create triples related to book information and rating information from the book dataset.
(2) Train the KGE model.
(3) Generate synthetic data in the form of a rating matrix by simulating users' reading behavior using the KGE model.

### 3.1 Training KGE Model

This paper uses the Goodreads dataset[1] as a dataset. This dataset is composed of three parts: metadata of the books, interactions between users and books, and users' book reviews. The book metadata includes information such as the book title and authors, and the users' book reviews include ratings given by users to books and review texts. From this dataset, the proposed method creates triples about users' rating information and book attribute information.

Triples about the rating information describe a user's rating to a book. When a user $x$ gave a rating $r$ to a book $y$, a triple ($x$, likes, $y$) is created if $r \geq t_p$ ($t_p$ is a threshold), and ($x$, dislikes, $y$) is created if $r \leq t_n$ ($t_n$ is a threshold). This type of triple is created only for users with two or more rating histories.

The Goodreads dataset contains 29 types of attributes about books. However, it is supposed that some of these attributes do not affect users' book selection or evaluation. To create triples only about the attributes that affect users' reading behavior, attribute selection is performed as preprocessing. It is applied to book attributes that take discrete values. For an attribute $a$ of a book, if the books rated by a certain user have specific values for $a$, it is assumed that $a$ affects rating behavior of the user. Based on this assumption, this paper introduces the attribute value concentration and denotes it as $\rho(a)$. $\rho(a)$ is defined by Eq. (3). The meanings of the symbols used in the equation are shown in Table 1. Larger values of $\rho(a)$ indicate each user tends to select books with specific values for $a$.

$$\rho(a) = 1 - \frac{1}{|X|} \sum_{x \in X} \frac{|\bigcup_{y \in Y_x} V_a(y)|}{\sum_{y \in Y_x} |V_a(y)|} \tag{3}$$

To determine the attributes that affect users' reading behavior, we selected a set of users $X$ as following,

$$X = \{x; |\hat{Y}_x| \geq 2, \sum_{y \in Y_x} |V_a(y)| \geq t_v\}, \hat{Y}_x = \{y; y \in Y_x, r_{xy} \geq t_p \lor r_{xy} \leq t_n\},$$

[1] https://mengtingwan.github.io/data/goodreads.html.

**Table 1.** Symbols used in the proposed method and their meanings

| $X$ | User set |
|---|---|
| $Y$ | Item set |
| $Y_x$ | Set of items selected by user $x$ ($\in X$) |
| $A$ | Attribute set |
| $V_a$ | Set of attribute values that attribute $a$ ($\in A$) can take |
| $V_a(y)$ | Set of attribute values of attribute $a$ assigned to item $y$ ($\in Y$) |
| $\rho(a)$ | The attribute value concentration of $a$ |
| $n_p$ | The number of nearest neighbors of the user profile |
| $n_b$ | The number of nearest book vectors |
| $r_{x,i}$ | The rating of book $i$ by user $x$ |

where $r_{xy}$ is a rating of book $y$ by user $x$. Using the selected users $X$, $\rho(a)$ is calculated for two cases for each $a$ ($\in A$): when using their actual rating histories (actual data), and when assuming that they have read the same number of randomly selected books as the actual histories (random selection). For example, if the attribute "author" is selected, a triple ($y$, is_written_by, $u$) is created, where $u$ is the author of a book $y$. Selected attribute are shown in Table 5, which will be explained in Sect. 4.2.

The triples created as described above are divided into training and validation sets for tuning the hyperparameters of a KGE model. TransE [1] is used as the KGE model. The hyperparameters are dimension of the embedding space ($D$), margin ($\gamma$), learning rate, distance function d, number of epochs, and batch size. All triples are used for training a KGE model.

### 3.2 Synthetic Data Generation

Using the trained KGE model, a synthetic rating matrix is generated by simulating the behavior of users sequentially reading books that match their preferences. Specifically, the proposed method simulates the behaviors of evaluating books sequentially and searching for similar books when they find books they like.

Let $X'$ be a set of synthetic users, each element of $X'$ is randomly selected from real users, and the following process is performed for each $x'$ ($\in X'$). Letting $v_{x'}$ be the embedding vector of $x'$, $v_{\text{likes}}$ be the embedding of the relation of "likes," $p'_x = v_{x'} + v_{\text{likes}}$, $t$ be the step in a iteration, the algorithm of the proposed method is defined as following. Note that $\mathrm{d}(x, y)$ is the Euclidean distance between $x$ and $y$ here.

1. When $t=1$, randomly select a book entity $b_t$.
2. Let $S'_x$ be the $n_p$ nearest neighbors of $p'_x$, and repeat the following process until all books in $S'_x$ are rated.
   (a) Let $S_t$ be the $n_b$ nearest books of $b_t$ and determine $x'$'s rating $r_{x',i}$ for $b_i \in S_t$ that satisfies the condition in Table 2, where $d = \mathrm{d}(p'_x, b_i)$.

(b) If there exists books $b_i \in S_t, \mathrm{d}(p'_x, b_i) < \mathrm{d}(p'_x, b_t)$, choose the one with the smallest $\mathrm{d}(p'_x, b_i)$ and regard it as $b_{t+1}$. If not, randomly select an unrated book from $S'_x$ and regard it as $b_{t+1}$. Set $t \leftarrow t + 1$ and return to (a).

**Table 2.** Correspondence between Euclidean distance from user profile and rating

| Euclidean distance $d$ | Rating |
|---|---|
| $0 \leq d \leq 0.5$ | 5 |
| $0.5 < d \leq 0.7$ | 4 |
| $0.7 < d \leq 1.0$ | 3 |
| $1.0 < d \leq 1.5$ | 2 |
| $1.5 < d$ | 1 |

# 4 Experiments

## 4.1 Dataset

The experiments use books of the Comics&Graphics genre in the Goodreads dataset as target items. The book data contains attribute information for 89,411 books, and the rating data contains 542,338 6-level ratings (0 to 5) by 59,347 users. The distribution of ratings in the rating data is shown in Table 3.

**Table 3.** Distribution of ratings

| Rating | Count |
|---|---|
| 5 | 164,713 |
| 4 | 192,486 |
| 3 | 121,916 |
| 2 | 39,354 |
| 1 | 11,063 |
| 0 | 12,806 |

Ratings of 0 may include cases where users forgot to give a rating, and it is not appropriate to consider them as low ratings. Therefore, such data were excluded. As shown in Table 2, synthetic users described in Sect. 3.2 also does not give rating 0. The summary of the rating data after the removal is shown in Table 4.

**Table 4.** Summary of the rating data

| #users | #books | #ratings | Density |
|---|---|---|---|
| 58,111 | 88,356 | 529,532 | 0.00010 |

### 4.2 Creation of Triples

**Triples About Users' Rating Information.** In creating triples about users' rating information, the thresholds mentioned in Sect. 3.1 were set to $t_p = 5$ and $t_n = 2$. As shown in Table 3, the rating data contains many 4 or higher ratings. These thresholds are determined to minimize the difference between the number of high and low ratings as much as possible. As a result, 201,601 triples about users' rating information were generated (153,270 likes relations and 48,331 dislikes relations).

**Triples About Attribute Information.** Attributes to be used for creating triples are selected following the procedure described in Sect. 3.1. The same thresholds used for triples about users' rating information were used: $t_p$ =5 and $t_n$=2.

When $t_v$ is extremely small, the attribute value concentration (Equation (3)) tends to be low. It is also not suitable to include users with low $t_v$ in the calculation for understanding attributes about user rating behavior. On the other hand, if it is too large, the number of users satisfying the condition becomes small and does not reflect the trend of the dataset. Based on this consideration, the threshold $t_v$ was set to 10. The attribute value concentration for each attribute is shown in Table 5. To correctly handle books belonging to the same series, attribute "series_name" was added to the dataset. The attribute values for "series_name" are obtained from the title attribute of books using regular expressions.

**Table 5.** Attribute value concentration for each attribute

| Attribute | Actual data | Random selection |
|---|---|---|
| author | 0.256 | 0.011 |
| country_code | 0.944 | 0.944 |
| language_code | 0.864 | 0.609 |
| publisher | 0.474 | 0.109 |
| work_id | 0.001 | 0.000 |
| series_id | 0.001 | 0.001 |
| series_name | 0.423 | 0.032 |

It is shown that there is a difference in attribute value concentration between Actual data and random selection for the attributes "author", "language_code", "publisher", and "series_name". Therefore, triples about book attribute information were generated for these four attributes. The number of triples created for each attribute is shown in Table 6.

**Table 6.** Selected attributes and the number of generated triples

| Attribute | Relation | #triples |
|---|---|---|
| author | is_written_by | 113,528 |
| language_code | is_written_in | 59,797 |
| publisher | is_published_by | 69,986 |
| series_name | is_classified_as | 45,870 |

### 4.3 KGE Training

**Hyperparameter Tuning for TransE.** The triples created in Sect. 4.2 were randomly divided into 392,625 for training and 98,157 for validation, and the hyperparameters of TransE were tuned using Bayesian optimization with MRR (Mean reciprocal rank) as the embedding accuracy evaluation metric. The batch size was fixed at 8,192, and the hyperparameters were selected from the following ranges: dimension ($D$) $\in \{100, 200, 300\}$, margin ($\gamma$) $\in \{0, 0.5, 1, 1.5, 2\}$, learning rate $= \{0.0001, 0.001, 0.01\}$, distance function ($d$) $\in$ {L1, L2}. The highest accuracy was obtained in 100 trials when $D = 200, \gamma = 1$, the learning rate was 0.001, and $d = L2$. The highest MRR was obtained when the number of epochs was 70. We used these values as hyperparameters.

**Model Construction for Synthetic Data Generation.** About 80% of the users were randomly selected and used for training data, and the remaining users were used for test data. Users in the test data were selected from those with 10 or more ratings in the real data. The training data included 161,425 triples about users' rating information, consisting of 123,292 likes relations and 38,133 dislikes relations. The triples of book attribute information were also used to train the KGE model.

### 4.4 Synthetic Data Generation

Regarding the parameters mentioned in Sect. 3.2, $n_p = 100$, $n_b = 10$, and the number of synthetic users $|X'| = 1000$ were set, and 185,896 ratings were generated. The distribution of generated ratings is shown in Table 7.

Comparison between the generated synthetic rating matrix and real data (training data) is shown in Table 8.

From Table 8, it can be seen that the created synthetic data is smaller than the real data, but its density is considerably high. It is because each synthetic user made more than 100 ratings by setting $n_p$=100. In the real data when excluding rating 0, the average number of ratings per user was 9.112.

**Table 7.** Distribution of ratings in the generated synthetic data

| Rating | Count |
|---|---|
| 5 | 61,028 |
| 4 | 45,004 |
| 3 | 50,108 |
| 2 | 25,723 |
| 1 | 4,033 |

**Table 8.** Comparison of synthetic data and training data

| | #users | #books | #ratings | Density |
|---|---|---|---|---|
| Synthetic data | 1,000 | 12,937 | 185,896 | 0.01437 |
| Training data | 46,489 | 78,360 | 420,732 | 0.00012 |

## 5 Results

To evaluate the synthetic data generated by the proposed method, recommendation accuracy when synthetic data is used as training data is compared with that when real data is used as a training data. SVD (Singular Value Decomposition) in the Python library Surprise[2] was used as the recommendation algorithm. Evaluation is conducted in leave-one-out manner: for each user included in the test data, 80% of the ratings were added to the training data as rating history of test users should also be included in the training data. The prediction was evaluated by regarding the remaining ratings of that user as correct answers. This process was repeated for all users in the test data and the macro average for all users was obtained. As for correct answers, books with 4 or higher ratings were considered as positive. Table 9 shows precision@$k$ and recall@$k$ when using SVD trained with synthetic data, and Table 10 shows those when real data was used for training. To evaluate the validity of the users' reading behaviors assumed in the proposed method, we also created the synthetic rating matrix based on a random behavior: ratings were generated by 1000 synthetic users who randomly select and read 200 books each. The books to be evaluated were randomly selected following a uniform distribution, and the ratings were randomly determined following the actual distribution of ratings in the book rating data. Table 11 shows the result when using this synthetic data. Figures 2 and 3 respectively show the comparison of macro average precision@$k$ and recall@$k$ among those three cases.

The result shows that the precision and recall when recommending using SVD trained with synthetic data generated by the proposed method were lower than those trained with real data, but the difference was sufficiently small when $k \geq 10$. Furthermore, when comparing with results trained with synthetic data

[2] https://surpriselib.com/.

**Table 9.** Macro average precision@$k$ and recall@$k$ of recommendation results using SVD trained with synthetic data

| $k$ | 1 | 5 | 10 | 15 | 20 | 25 | 30 | 35 | 40 |
|---|---|---|---|---|---|---|---|---|---|
| precision@$k$ | 0.773 | 0.598 | 0.409 | 0.310 | 0.251 | 0.211 | 0.182 | 0.161 | 0.143 |
| recall@$k$ | 0.239 | 0.783 | 0.904 | 0.942 | 0.961 | 0.972 | 0.979 | 0.984 | 0.987 |

**Table 10.** Macro average precision@$k$ and recall@$k$ of recommendation results using SVD trained with real data

| $k$ | 1 | 5 | 10 | 15 | 20 | 25 | 30 | 35 | 40 |
|---|---|---|---|---|---|---|---|---|---|
| precision@$k$ | 0.832 | 0.616 | 0.414 | 0.315 | 0.254 | 0.213 | 0.184 | 0.162 | 0.144 |
| recall@$k$ | 0.260 | 0.797 | 0.908 | 0.946 | 0.964 | 0.974 | 0.981 | 0.985 | 0.988 |

**Table 11.** Macro average precision@$k$ and recall@$k$ of recommendation results using SVD trained with synthetic data based on random behavior

| $k$ | 1 | 5 | 10 | 15 | 20 | 25 | 30 | 35 | 40 |
|---|---|---|---|---|---|---|---|---|---|
| precision@$k$ | 0.715 | 0.577 | 0.398 | 0.305 | 0.247 | 0.209 | 0.180 | 0.159 | 0.142 |
| recall@$k$ | 0.217 | 0.772 | 0.896 | 0.938 | 0.959 | 0.971 | 0.978 | 0.983 | 0.986 |

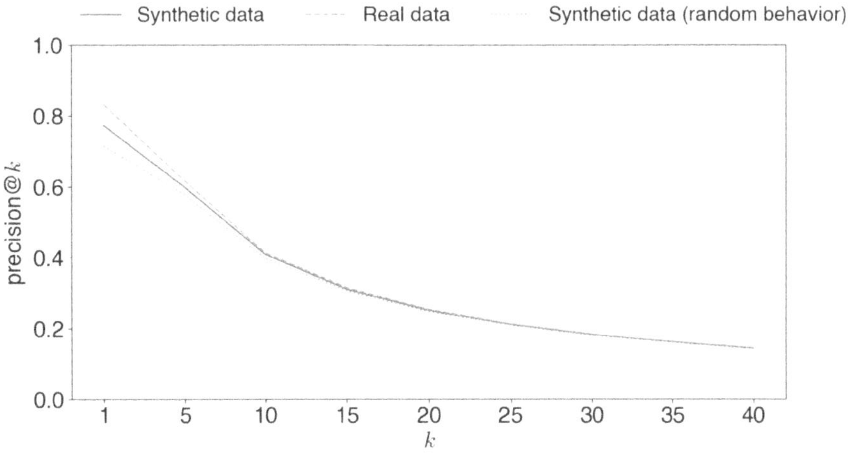


**Fig. 2.** Comparison of macro average precision@$k$

based on random behavior, using the data generated by the proposed method achieved higher precision and recall regardless of the value of $k$. These results indicate that the synthetic data potentially contains information effective for rating prediction, suggesting the validity of the proposed users reading behavior.

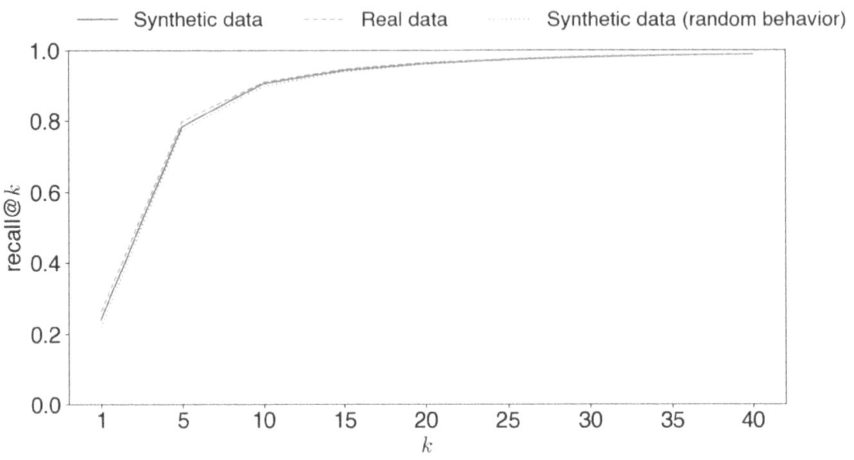


**Fig. 3.** Comparison of macro average recall@$k$

# 6 Conclusions

This paper proposed a method to generate a synthetic rating matrix for book recommendation that uses collaborative filtering. The proposed method creates triples about rating information and attribute information from a book dataset. The method then generates a synthetic rating matrix by simulating user book rating behavior using a TransE model trained with the created triples.

In the experiment, synthetic data was generated using the Goodreads dataset and the validity of the proposed method was evaluated by comparing macro average precision@$k$ and recall@$k$ of recommendation results using SVD (Singular Value Decomposition). The results showed that although macro average precision@$k$ and recall@$k$ using synthetic data were lower compared to real data, the difference was sufficiently small for values of $k \geq 10$. It was also shown that both metrics when using the synthetic data generated by the proposed method outperformed those using the synthetic data based on random behavior regardless of the values of $k$. This indicates that the synthetic data contains important information for rating prediction, supporting the validity of assumed users reading behavior. Specifically, it is considered that the strength of relationships between book attributes and the association rules regarding users' rating to books were reflected as Euclidean distance in the vector space. The preprocessing for attribute selection and hyperparameter tuning contributed to constructing a KGE model suitable for synthetic data generation.

Future works include considering alternative KGE (Knowledge Graph Embedding) models, adding more attributes, improving the simulation of user behavior in book selection, and experiments using other datasets.

**Acknowledgements.** This work was partially supported by JSPS KAKENHI Grant Numbers JP22K19836, JP23K24953, and JP21H03553.

## References


1. Bordes, A., Usunier, N., Garcia-Durán, A., Weston, J., Yakhnenko, O.: Translating embeddings for modeling multi-relational data. In: Proceedings of the 26th International Conference on Neural Information Processing Systems, NIPS 2013, vol. 2, pp. 2787–2795. Curran Associates Inc., Red Hook, NY, USA (2013)
2. Ge, X., Wang, Y.C., Wang, B., Kuo, C.C.J.: Knowledge graph embedding: An overview (2023). https://doi.org/10.48550/arXiv.2309.12501
3. Goldberg, D., Nichols, D., Oki, B.M., Terry, D.: Using collaborative filtering to weave an information tapestry. Commun. ACM **35**(12), 61–70 (1992). https://doi.org/10.1145/138859.138867
4. Lin, Y., Liu, Z., Sun, M., Liu, Y., Zhu, X.: Learning entity and relation embeddings for knowledge graph completion. In: Proceedings of the AAAI Conference on Artificial Intelligence. vol. 29. AAAI Press (2015). https://doi.org/10.1609/aaai.v29i1.9491
5. Moriyoshi, K., Shibata, H., Takama, Y.: Generation of rating matrix based on rational behaviors of users. J. Adv. Comput. Intell. Intell. Inform. **28**(1), 129–140 (2024). https://doi.org/10.20965/jaciii.2024.p0129
6. Nickel, M., Tresp, V., Kriegel, H.P.: A three-way model for collective learning on multi-relational data. In: Proceedings of the 28th International Conference on Machine Learning, ICML 2011, pp. 809–816. Omnipress, Madison, WI, USA (2011)
7. Palumbo, E., Rizzo, G., Troncy, R., Baralis, E., Osella, M., Ferro, E.: Translational models for item recommendation. In: Gangemi, A., Gentile, A.L., Nuzzolese, A.G., Rudolph, S., Maleshkova, M., Paulheim, H., Pan, J.Z., Alam, M. (eds.) The Semantic Web: ESWC 2018 Satellite Events. vol. 11155, pp. 478–490. Springer International Publishing, Cham (2018). https://doi.org/10.1007/978-3-319-98192-5_61
8. Pei, Y., Zaïane, O.: A synthetic data generator for clustering and outlier analysis (2006). https://doi.org/10.7939/R3B23S
9. Reiter, J.P.: Using cart to generate partially synthetic, public use microdata. J. Official Statist. **21**, 441–462 (2005)
10. Slokom, M.: Comparing recommender systems using synthetic data. In: Proceedings of the 12th ACM Conference on Recommender Systems, RecSys 2018. pp. 548–552. Association for Computing Machinery, New York (2018). https://doi.org/10.1145/3240323.3240325
11. Sun, Z., Deng, Z.H., Nie, J.Y., Tang, J.: Rotate: Knowledge graph embedding by relational rotation in complex space. In: International Conference on Learning Representations (2019)
12. Wan, M., McAuley, J.: Item recommendation on monotonic behavior chains. In: Proceedings of the 12th ACM Conference on Recommender Systems, pp. 86–94. ACM, Vancouver British Columbia Canada (2018). https://doi.org/10.1145/3240323.3240369
13. Wan, M., Misra, R., Nakashole, N., McAuley, J.: Fine-grained spoiler detection from large-scale review corpora. In: Proceedings of the 57th Annual Meeting of the Association for Computational Linguistics, pp. 2605–2610. Association for Computational Linguistics, Florence, Italy (2019). https://doi.org/10.18653/v1/P19-1248
14. Wang, Z., Zhang, J., Feng, J., Chen, Z.: Knowledge graph embedding by translating on hyperplanes. In: Proceedings of the AAAI Conference on Artificial Intelligence, vol. 28. AAAI Press (2014). https://doi.org/10.1609/aaai.v28i1.8870

15. Weyland, L.F., Schadd, M.P., Henderson, H.C.: Exploring the fidelity of synthetic data for decision support systems in military applications. In: 2024 International Conference on Military Communication and Information Systems (ICMCIS), pp. 1–8 (2024). https://doi.org/10.1109/ICMCIS61231.2024.10540934
16. Xie, L., Hu, Z., Cai, X., Zhang, W., Chen, J.: Explainable recommendation based on knowledge graph and multi-objective optimization. Complex Intell. Syst. **7**(3), 1241–1252 (2021). https://doi.org/10.1007/s40747-021-00315-y
17. Xu, L., Veeramachaneni, K.: Synthesizing tabular data using generative adversarial networks (2018). https://doi.org/10.48550/arXiv.1811.11264
18. Yang, B., Yih, W.t., He, X., Gao, J., Deng, L.: Embedding entities and relations for learning and inference in knowledge bases. In: International Conference on Learning Representations (2014)
19. Zhang, F., Yuan, N.J., Lian, D., Xie, X., Ma, W.Y.: Collaborative knowledge base embedding for recommender systems. In: Proceedings of the 22nd ACM SIGKDD International Conference on Knowledge Discovery and Data Mining, pp. 353–362. ACM, San Francisco California USA (2016). https://doi.org/10.1145/2939672.2939673
20. Zhang, Y., Chen, X.: Explainable recommendation: a survey and new perspectives. Foundations Trends® Inform. Retrieval **14**(1), 1–101 (2020). https://doi.org/10.1561/1500000066

# Proposal on Dashboard Creation for Understanding Users from Rating Matrix

Ryo Ishino(✉), Hiroki Shibata, and Yasufumi Takama

Tokyo Metropolitan University, 1-1 Minami-Osawa, Hachioji, Japan
ishino-ryo@ed.tmu.ac.jp, {hshibata,ytakama}@tmu.ac.jp

**Abstract.** This paper proposes a method for creating a dashboard, assuming the task of the visual analysis on rating matrices used for information recommendation. Recommender systems have been developed to help people find relevant information. One of the most representative recommendation algorithms is collaborative filtering (CF), which utilizes rating matrices consisting of user-item interactions. However, CF does not explicitly take into account the type of person interacting with items. The proposed dashboard is composed of information that is expected to be useful for understanding user profiles, which are extracted from a rating matrix. It includes visualizations such as heatmaps and histograms that display information about users and items. By using it, analysts can find trends of user preferences and identify users with distinctive preferences. Furthermore, the developers of recommendation services can obtain valuable information for generating recommendation explanations and considering new systems. To show the effectiveness of the proposed method, this paper describes a case study assuming the users using the proposed dashboard. One of the authors uses the dashboard as if he were the user of the given rating history, and tries to find those with similar preferences by examining highly/poorly rated items and evaluation strictness. The result shows that similar users can be found by using the proposed dashboard, which demonstrates the effectiveness of the proposed method.

**Keywords:** Information Recommendation · Rating Matrix · Information Visualization

## 1 Introduction

This paper proposes a method for creating a dashboard, assuming the visual analysis of rating matrices used for information recommendation. In recent years, science and technology continue to develop at a rapid pace and we are living in an advanced information society. Individuals can easily get data on a scale that was previously handled by governments and corporations. However, there is a limit to the amount of information that an individual can process, and it is

© The Author(s), under exclusive license to Springer Nature Singapore Pte Ltd. 2025
W.-T. Chu et al. (Eds.): TAAI 2024, CCIS 2414, pp. 319–331, 2025.
https://doi.org/10.1007/978-981-96-4589-3_23

extremely difficult for us to select the relevant information from a huge amount of information. Recommender systems have been developed to solve this problem.

Recommender systems collect and use the interaction history of users such as rating. One of the most representative recommender algorithms is collaborative filtering, which handles such interaction history in the format of a rating matrix [1]. Generally, a rating matrix consists of ratings users gave to items and are represented as a two-dimensional matrix of users and items. The derivative methods of CF recommend items to a target user based only on the ratings of users similar to the target user with respect to the rating patterns in a rating matrix. That is, the profile of such similar users are not explicitly considered in these methods. However, understanding the users behind the determination of items to recommend is expected to be beneficial for generating recommendation explanations and getting ideas for improving recommendation services.

This paper proposes to generate a dashboard by analyzing a rating matrix and extracting useful information for understanding user profiles. To the best of our knowledge, this is the first attempt to generate a dashboard targetting a rating matrix. The proposed dashboard consists of several views including a heatmap visualizing a rating matrix, histograms visualizing the distribution of the average rating of each user or movie, and detailed information on specific users or movies. Each view is coordinated together, which allows users to interactively analyze a rating matrix, such as by drilling down from an overview to details.

Based on the information presented in the dashboard, users can find rating trends common to the majority of users and distinctive users who have different taste from the majority. Additionally, by investigating the items preferred by users of interest, it is possible to study items favored by users with certain preferences.

When the users of some recommendation services use the proposed dashboard, they could find items of interest without providing the services with their personal information such as their behavioral history or preferences. Moreover, recommendation service operators and recommender system researchers could use the dashboard for generating recommendation explanations and considering new recommendation algorithms.

To show the effectiveness of the proposed method, this paper describes a case study assuming users of a recommendation service use the proposed dashboard. In the case study, one of the authors uses the dashboard as if the author was a user of the given rating history. The task is to find users who have similar preferences to the author by examining their highly/poorly rated items and evaluation strictness. The case study shows how the visualizations and interactions implemented in the proposed dashboard can be utilized in the analysis. Furthermore, the similarity between the user conducting the analysis and similar users the author found is evaluated based on the similarity of their ratings. The result shows the effectiveness of the dashboard for finding similar users.

# 2 Related Work

## 2.1 Information Recommendation

In recent years, the development of information technology has made it easier for anyone to distribute and access diverse and large volumes of information. Under such circumstances, it has become difficult for people to quickly and accurately obtain the information they need. One of the technologies that have gained importance in addressing this challenge is information recommendation. This section introduces studies on information recommendation, focusing on representative recommendation methods and methods of generating user profiles.

Selecting information that matches users' preferences or needs from large amounts of information is called information filtering. A recommender system is a kind of information filtering system, which selects and presents useful information or items to users [2]. Recommendation methods are divided into content-based filtering and collaborative filtering (CF) [3].

Content-based filtering recommends items by matching users' preferences with item features. In contrast, CF uses the interaction histories of users to recommend items that are preferred by users with similar tastes [4].

User profiles represent users' preference and interest. Methods of generating user profiles are categorized into explicit (direct) methods and implicit (indirect) methods [5], which are summarized as follows:

- Explicit (Direct) Methods:
  This method directly collects information about users' preferences and interests from the users. Examples include asking users to answer questions about their interests or having them rate the degree of interest in viewed information or items on a five-point scale.
- Implicit (Indirect) Methods:
  This method estimates users' interests based on their interaction histories such as buying items and clicking links in a web page. Clues such as browsing time and focus points are also used for estimation [6].

## 2.2 Information Visualization

In advanced information society, it is important to support individuals without sufficient computing skills to effectively utilize data [7]. Therefore, information visualization technology has been attracting attention in recent years.

The concept of visualization grammar has been proposed to reduce the cost of generating visualizations. It refers to the rules and principles for visually representing data. Vega[1] is one of the popular visualization grammars and Vega-Lite[2] is its simplified version [8]. The advantage of using visualization grammar is that it requires less programming skill from users than when using programming languages suited for computer graphics, such as Java[3] and Processing[4]. Although

[1] https://vega.github.io/vega/about/
[2] https://vega.github.io/vega-lite/
[3] https://www.java.com/ja/
[4] https://processing.org

Processing is also designed to implement visualization efficiently, it requires manual adjustments of axes, line lengths, and point sizes in a view depending on a dataset. On the other hand, Vega-Lite automatically configures these elements, making it easier to reuse the same source code to different datasets.

Dashboards, such as Microsoft Power BI[5] and Looker Studio[6], are tools for analyzing large amounts of data and visualizing them with the combination of various formats, such as tables and graphs. Unlike a single graph, a dashboard displays multiple visualizations at once and provides drill-down function, which allows users to dive into detailed information from an overview. It is useful for exploratory data analysis.

When creating dashboards, it is crucial how to design a user interface. Not only the screen that users see but also interactions such as buttons and transition between screens should be carefully designed. To design a user interface, Halasz et al. incorporated the concept of mental models [9]. A mental model refers to the operational image that is constructed by users to understand the behavior of the system they are interacting with. A well-constructed model allows users to operate the system accurately. Norman categorized user activities into seven stages for building user-friendly systems [10].

## 3 Proposed Method

This paper proposes a method for creating dashboards from a rating matrix to support users' data analysis such as the identification of users with distinctive preferences or those with similar tastes. The proposed dashboard also aims to provide valuable insights for developers of recommender systems and algorithms by supporting the analysis of rating matrices.

Figure 1 shows the dashboard created by the proposed method. Table 1 shows the elements of the dashboard, and Fig. 2 illustrates the coordination between the components.

The dashboard is controlled through operations on a terminal window. The process begins by grasping the overview of the dataset from one of the three components indicated in the "overview" section of Fig. 2. If analysts are interested in a specific movie or user, they can use the drill-down function in the "all-histogram" to visualize the detailed information about it within the components indicated in the "details" section.

Furthermore, they can access additional information, such as specific user details or movie jacket images, by reapplying the drill-down function. After checking the detailed information, analysts can re-enter the user/movie ID in the terminal window to analyze other users/items.

The "all-user attributes" shown in Fig. 3 is used to retrieve users by selecting age and occupation. The retrieval result includes a list of IDs and corresponding

[5] https://www.microsoft.com/ja-jp/power-platform/products/power-bi

[6] https://lookerstudio.google.com/u/0/navigation/reporting

**Fig. 1.** Dashboard created by the proposed method (Numbers in circles correspond to No. in Table 1.)

**Table 1.** Dashboard Components

| No. | Name | Description | Format |
|---|---|---|---|
| 1 | all-user attributes | Selection of user occupation/age | Dropdown |
| 2 | all-heatmap | Visualization of the entire rating matrix | Heatmap |
| 3 | all-histogram | Distribution of average ratings of users/movies | Histogram |
| 4 | det-rating information | Information such as average ratings and the number of ratings of specified users/movies | Text |
| 5 | det-rating counts (users) | Distribution of ratings of the specified user | Histogram |
| 6 | det-rating counts (movies) | Distribution of ratings of the specified movie | Histogram |
| 7 | det-list (users) | List of movies highly/poorly rated by the specified user | Text |
| 8 | det-list (movies) | List of users who highly/poorly rated the specified movie | Text |
| 9 | det-jacket | Cover image of the specified movie | Image |

attributes of users who match the selected criteria. When users of a recommendation service use the dashboard, they can use this component to discover users with similar attributes to themselves.

The "all-heat map" shown in Fig. 4 visualizes a rating matrix using a heat map. Users and items are respectively assigned to the rows and columns of the rating matrix in ascending order of IDs. The starting and ending IDs for users and items to be visualized on the heat map are specified from the terminal window. By checking the heat map, analysts can easily explore items that are rated by users who have rated the same items as themselves or items that have a lot of ratings. By assigning warm and cold colors to high and low ratings, analysts can easily explore popular or unpopular items.

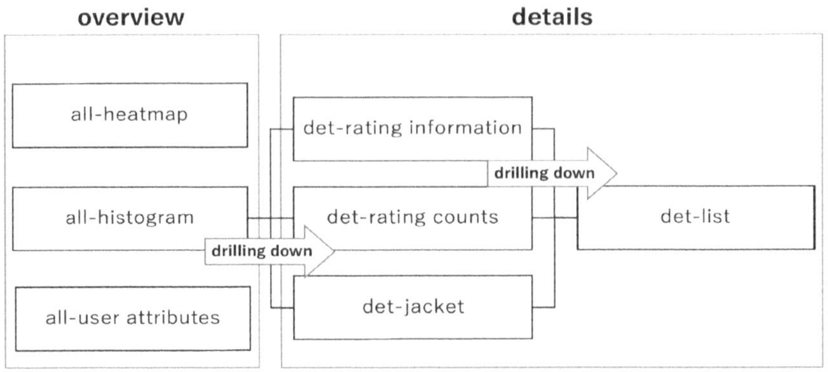


**Fig. 2.** Coordination relationships between components

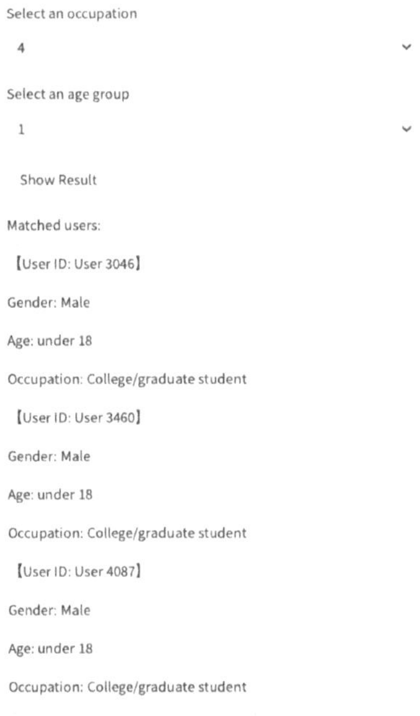


**Fig. 3.** all-user attributes

The "all-histogram" visualizes the distribution of average ratings of users or movies. Figure 5 shows an example of a histogram of movies. By specifying a movie (or user) ID from the terminal window, the position of its average rating is indicated by a red dotted line. This enables analysts to visually confirm the popularity of the specified movie in the dataset.

After confirming the overall visualizations described above, if analysts are interested in a particular user or movie, they can proceed to check detailed

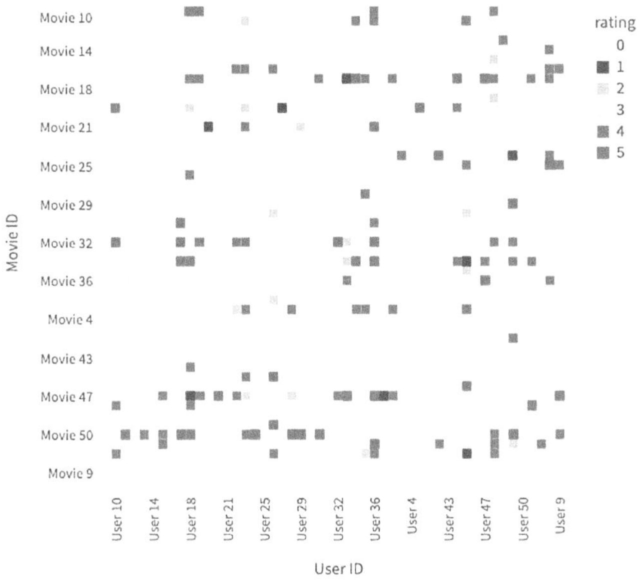


**Fig. 4.** all-heatmap

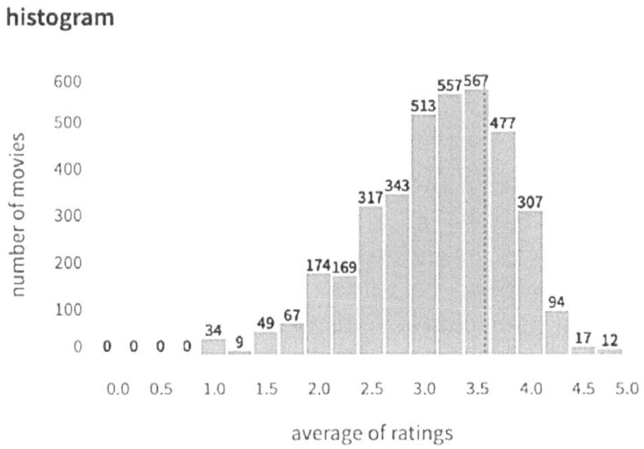


**Fig. 5.** all-histogram (movies)

information using the drill-down function. When a user or movie is specified in the terminal window, the system asks whether to perform a drill-down. By entering "Y," detailed information is displayed. The "det-rating information (movie)" displays the number of ratings and the average rating of a specified movie, or the number of ratings and the average rating of a specified user. The "det-rating counts (movies)" shown in Fig. 6 displays the histogram of ratings of the movie, allowing users to grasp the rating trends of the movie together with the "det-rating information (movies)". Similarly, "det-rating counts (users)" displays a

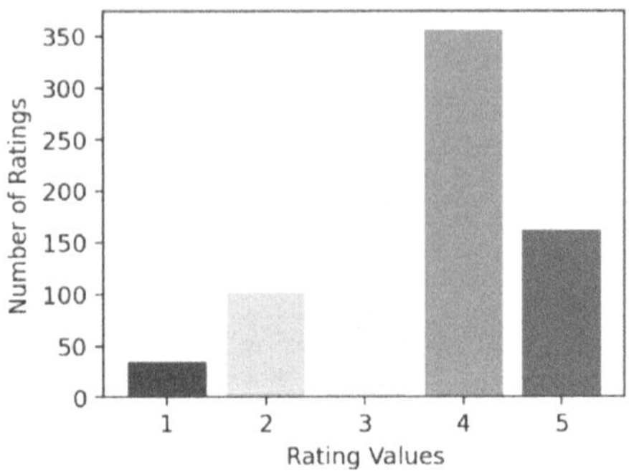


**Fig. 6.** det-rating counts (movies)

1: User ID: User 46, Rating: 5.00

2: User ID: User 63, Rating: 5.00

3: User ID: User 115, Rating: 5.00

4: User ID: User 169, Rating: 5.00

5: User ID: User 281, Rating: 5.00

**Fig. 7.** det-list (movies)

histogram of all ratings given by the user, by combining which with "det-rating information (users)," analysts can grasp the rating trends of the user. In addition, "det-jacket" displays the movie's jacket photo, which is used to check the image of the specified movie.

When the detailed information is displayed, the system asks whether to perform further drill-down for the specified movie or user. If "Y" is entered, the "det-list (movies)" shown in Fig. 7 or "det-list (users)" is displayed. Figure 7 is used to check the list of users who rated the movie highly or poorly. By combining the use of "det-list (movies)" and "det-list (users)," analysts can find movies that were rated highly or poorly by users who have given similar ratings to a specific movie to them. It is useful to discover unknown items that match their preferences.

By utilizing the information presented on the dashboard, analysts can discover rating trends among the majority of users, identify users with distinctive preferences, and investigate items favored by users with specific preferences.

# 4 Case Study

## 4.1 Outline

To validate the effectiveness of the proposed method, this section shows a case study assuming users of a recommender system. In this case study, a rating matrix was generated from the MovieLens[1] 1M dataset and used for the creation of the dashboard. This dataset includes approximately 1 million ratings provided by approximately 6,000 users for about 4,000 movies. In the case study, five users were randomly selected from the dataset as the "system user." Assuming that one of the authors was the selected system user, the author tried to find a user whose preference is similar to the author. To evaluate the validity of the exploration, the similarity between the system user and the identified similar users is calculated using the Pearson correlation coefficient.

## 4.2 Results

When User 5630 is specified as the system user ($u$) , $u$ starts the exploration by checking the "all-histogram" (Fig. 8), from which he found that his average rating falls into a significantly higher category compared to the other users. Therefore, $u$ decided to check the detailed information to find movies $u$ gave low rating, because low rating given by users with high average rating strongly reflects user's preference. Using the drill-down function, $u$ obtained a list of movies to which $u$ gave low rating in the "det-list (users)" (Fig. 9) and checked each movie's average rating in the "all-histogram" (Fig. 10). Among them, $u$ noticed that the average rating of Movie 3793 was higher than other movies in the list. Despite it was highly evaluated by the others, $u$ did not favor it, which strongly reflects $u$'s preferences.

Using the "det-list (movies)" to search for users who also gave low ratings to Movie 3793, $u$ picked up the candidates of similar users by focusing on their interaction to the movies $u$ watched. Among the candidates, $u$ finally identified User 1340 as the most similar user, because this user consistently gave the same ratings as $u$ to multiple movies (Table 2).

The validity of exploration with the proposed dashboard is evaluated by repeating this exploration for five randomly selected users. The average response time of the dashboard to a query was approximately 3 s, and each exploration took about 3 to 5 min per user. Table 3 shows the similarity (Pearson correlation coefficient) and the ranking of similarity among all users. As a baseline, the table also shows the average results calculated from 50 users randomly selected from the half of users in the dataset who have high similarity to the system users.

Table 3 shows that similar users can be identified compared to the baseline for all of the five system users. For User 3389, the identified similar user had a higher similarity than the other four cases. One of the reasons is because there are many users who have similar rating tendencies to User 3389. Figure 11 shows the "det-rating count (movies)" of Movie 50 (rated 5 by User 3389) and Movie

[1] https://grouplens.org/datasets/movielens/

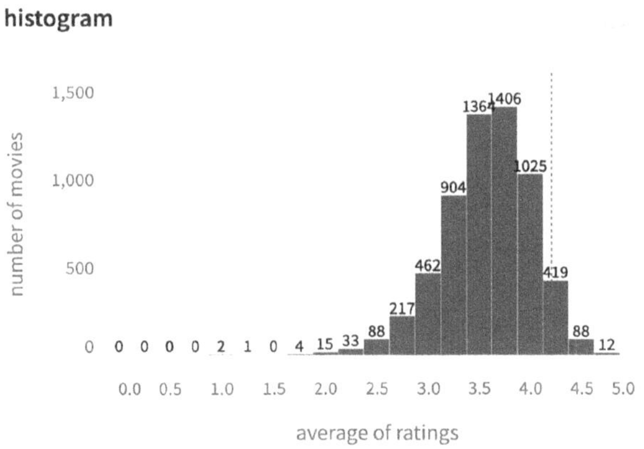


**Fig. 8.** Position of User 5630 in the distribution of average rating

1: Movie ID: Movie 410, Rating: 1.00

2: Movie ID: Movie 3793, Rating: 1.00

3: Movie ID: Movie 1676, Rating: 2.00

4: Movie ID: Movie 2384, Rating: 2.00

5: Movie ID: Movie 2762, Rating: 2.00

**Fig. 9.** List of movies rated poorly by User 5630

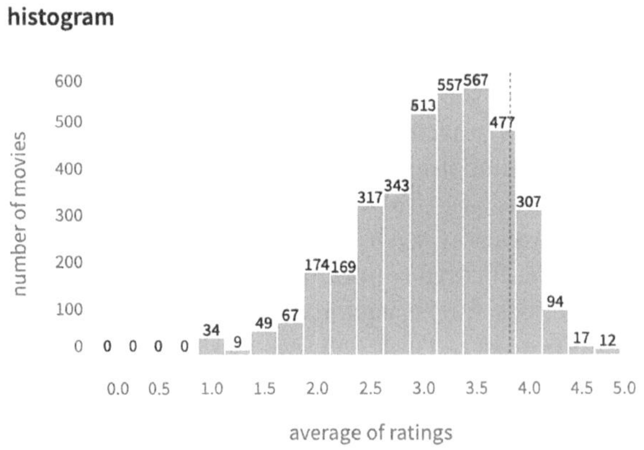


**Fig. 10.** Position of Movie 3793 in the distribution of average rating

**Table 2.** Movies Rated by Both User 5630 and User 1340

| Movie | Rating by User 5630 | Rating by User 1340 |
|---|---|---|
| Movie 318 | 5 | 5 |
| Movie 364 | 5 | 5 |
| Movie 1079 | 5 | 5 |
| Movie 1196 | 5 | 5 |
| Movie 1197 | 5 | 5 |
| Movie 1198 | 5 | 5 |
| Movie 1213 | 5 | 5 |
| Movie 2571 | 5 | 5 |
| Movie 2916 | 5 | 5 |
| Movie 3253 | 5 | 5 |
| Movie 3793 | 1 | 1 |

**Table 3.** Identified Most Similar Users

| System User | Rating count | Similar User | Pearson Correlation Coefficient | Similar User Rank |
|---|---|---|---|---|
| User 163 | 514 | User 337 | 0.3158 | 235 |
| | | Randomly Selected 50 Users | 0.1962 | 1850 |
| User 1943 | **680** | User 524 | 0.4420 | **7** |
| | | Randomly Selected 50 Users | 0.2244 | 1725 |
| User 3389 | 572 | User 543 | **0.4526** | 71 |
| | | Randomly Selected 50 Users | 0.2965 | 1523 |
| User 4309 | 132 | User 169 | 0.2270 | 399 |
| | | Randomly Selected 50 Users | 0.1415 | 2029 |
| User 5630 | 263 | User 1340 | 0.3056 | 205 |
| | | Randomly Selected 50 Users | 0.2189 | 1505 |

258 (rated 1 by User 3389), revealing that many users gave the same ratings as User 3389. Although finding similar users in this case is relatively easy compared with the other cases because there are many candidates as mentioned before, the results still show that the functionality of the proposed system works as intended.

Regarding the ranking of similar users, the identified similar user to User 1943 ranked considerably higher than other cases although the ranking of baseline is almost similar. Possible reason is that User 1943 had the highest number of ratings among the five system users, making it easier to find users who gave the same ratings to the same items as him by repeatedly using the "det-list".

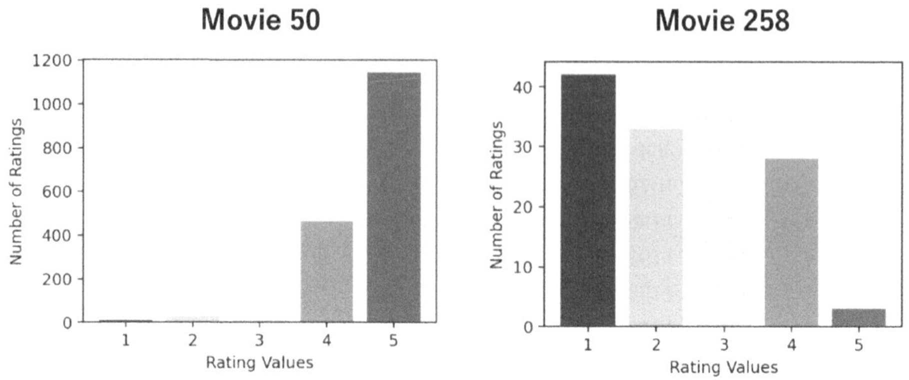


**Fig. 11.** det-rating counts for Movie 50 and Movie 258

# 5 Conclusion

This paper proposed a method for creating a dashboard from a rating matrix. The dashboard consists of visualizations for overviews such as heat maps and histograms as well as for details about specific items such as the list of relevant users/movies and cover images. The visualizations for overviews are interactively linked to the visualizations for the details through a drill-down function. Using the created dashboards, a case study was conducted assuming a task of identifying users similar to oneself. The results confirmed that it is possible to exploratively discover items that strongly reflect user preferences and users with similar preferences. In particular, it was shown that similar users could be identified efficiently.

This paper focused on analyzing rating matrix. Although a rating matrix is commonly used as the input to collaborative filtering (CF), more detailed analysis will be possible by incorporating additional information about users and items, which are utilized in some recommendation systems. Therefore, one of future works is to introduce such additional information. We also plan to conduct user experiments to improve the proposed dashboard based on feedback, and expand its functions to support analysis by recommendation service developers.

Although the proposed dashboard does not impose clear limitations on the size of a rating matrix to be analyzed, improving scalability will be required for handling large datasets or more complex queries in the future.

**Acknowledgments.** This work was partially supported by JSPS KAKENHI Grant Numbers JP22K19836, JP23K24953, and JP21H03553.

## References


1. Resnick, P., Iacovou, N., Suchak, M., Bergstrom, P., Riedl, J.: GroupLens: an open architecture for collaborative filtering of Netnews. In: Proceedings of the Conference on Computer Supported Cooperative Work (CSCW), pp. 175–186. ACM, New York (1994). http://ccs.mit.edu/papers/CCSWP165.html
2. Resnick, P., Varian, H.R.: Recommender systems. Commun. ACM **40**(3), 56–58 (1997). https://doi.org/10.1145/245108.245121
3. Schafer, J.B., Konstan, J.A., Riedl, J.: Recommender systems in E-Commerce. In: ACM Conference on Electronic Commerce, pp. 158-166. ACM, New York (1999). https://doi.org/10.1145/336992.337035
4. McLaughlin, M.R., Herlocker, J.L.: A collaborative filtering algorithm and evaluation metric that accurately model the user experience. In: Proceedings of the 27th Annual ACM SIGIR Conference on Research and Development in Information Retrieval, pp. 329–336. ACM, New York (2004). https://static.aminer.org/pdf/PDF/000/566/823/a_comparison_of_several_predictive_algorithms_for_collaborative_filtering_on.pdf
5. Jawaheer, G., Szomszor, M., Kostkova, P.: Profiling users in online communities. In: Proceedings of the 4th ACM RecSys Workshop on Recommender Systems and the Social Web (2010). https://doi.org/10.1145/1869446.1869453
6. Nichols, D.M.: Implicit rating and filtering. In: Proceedings of the 5th DELOS Workshop on Filtering and Collaborative Filtering, pp. 31–36 (1997). https://www.ercim.eu/publication/ws-proceedings/DELOS5/nichols.pdf
7. Freyne, J., Smyth, B.: Visualization for the masses: learning from the experts. In: International Conference on Case-Based Reasoning, pp. 65–76. Springer, Heidelberg (2010). https://api.semanticscholar.org/CorpusID:934670
8. Satyanarayan, A., Moritz, D., Wongsuphasawat, K., Heer, J.: Vega-lite: a grammar of interactive graphics. IEEE Trans. Visualizat. Comput. Graph. **23**(1), pp. 341–350 (2017). https://doi.org/10.1109/TVCG.2016.2599030
9. Halasz, F.G., Moran, T.P.: Mental models and problem solving in using a calculator. In: Proceedings of the International Conference on Human Factors in Computing Systems (CHI), pp. 212–215. ACM, New York (1983). https://api.semanticscholar.org/CorpusID:17615555
10. Norman, D.A.: Cognitive engineering. In: Norman, D.A., Draper, S.W. (eds.) User Centered Systems Design: New Perspectives in Human-Computer Interaction, pp. 31–61. Lawrence Erlbaum Associates, Hillsdale (1986)

# Estimation of Confidence Level Based on Eye Movement and Temporal Self-evaluations Using CNN with Data Augmentation

Ruka Eto(✉), Shotaro Tanaka, and Eri Sato-Shimokawara

Tokyo Metropolitan University, 6-6, Asahigaoka, Hino, Tokyo 191-0065, Japan
{etou-ruka,tanaka-shotaro}@ed.tmu.ac.jp, eri@tmu.ac.jp

**Abstract.** Self-study with robots has attracted attention in education in recent years. To enhance the effectiveness of the robot's learning support, it is crucial to monitor learners' mental state and situation in real time and provide feedback at appropriate moments. Thus, we focus on confidence levels during learning and estimate them using eye movement and pupil information. Previous research didn't consider temporal changes in confidence levels and physiological data. Therefore, we propose a method to measure the subjective temporal evaluation by considering the temporal dynamics of eye movement and confidence levels, aiming to increase the possibility of estimating confidence levels in real time. Based on the data collected from participants' responses to 30 questions, we used a Convolutional Neural Network (CNN) to classify 'Unconfident' and 'Confident.' The highest classification using all participants' data accuracy was 85.5% in case using saccade and pupil information without data augmentation. The results suggest that these methods are suitable for real-time estimation of confidence levels. The test using all participants' data, which didn't consider individual differences, could not clarify the necessity of data augmentation. On the other hand, from the comparison of individual results, it was confirmed that each feature's effectiveness varies between individuals. Moreover, the ablation test on each participant showed the effectiveness of data augmentation, but it was not significant. This indicates the possibility of improving estimation accuracy, and we need to analyze individual differences such as personality and learning skills and improve the quality of data for future work.

**Keywords:** eye movement · confidence level · CNN

## 1 Introduction

With advancement in Artificial Intelligence (AI) and robotics, Human-Robot Interaction (HRI) has become an important research area. Understanding human mental states, such as emotion, confusion, and confidence level is an essential

© The Author(s), under exclusive license to Springer Nature Singapore Pte Ltd. 2025
W.-T. Chu et al. (Eds.): TAAI 2024, CCIS 2414, pp. 332–343, 2025.
https://doi.org/10.1007/978-981-96-4589-3_24

research field called affective computing , which plays a key role in enhancing HRI.

Additionally, self-study with robots has attracted attention in education in recent years. These robots generally behave as teachers, tutors, or peers and support learners. To enhance the effectiveness of the robot's learning support, it is crucial to teach learners how to solve a problem and provide a hint or feedback to learners. M. Donnermann et al. developed a system that provided hints and feedback to first-year university students through a robotic tutor, supporting their study for exams [3]. As a result, students who utilized the robotic tutor achieved higher scores compared to those who did not use the robot. In addition, Miyauchi et al. reported that having junior high school students learn with a robot that provides hints had higher learning effects than learning with a robot that only teaches how to solve problems [9].

However, some conventional robots provide support regardless of the learner's mental state or situation. Suzuki et al. state that to make the robot's learning support as effective as that of humans, it is necessary to create a mechanism to arouse interest in robots among learners and a way to give hints to them [13]. Therefore, it is essential to enhance their learning experience to monitor learners' mental state and situation in real time and provide feedback at appropriate moments. This study focuses on confidence levels during learning and estimates them using physiological sensor data in real time. Estimating confidence levels in real time may improve the robot's behavior and enable robots to provide more effective learning support. Confidence levels are a key factor in adopting each student's condition; for example, Jimenez et al. focus on an educational robot expressing its sympathy according to a student's condition, such as thinking time and the number of correct answers [5,6]. Additionally, Okawa et al. reported the positive influence of a hint given before a student stops thinking [10].

Therefore, this research employs these ideas and proposes a method that determines the timing of giving a hint depending on students' confidence levels, confident or unconfident. Generally, thinking time is labeled as an unconfident state, so the number of unconfident data is larger than the number of confident data. Then, this paper employs an augmentation method and evaluates its effectiveness, which solves the dataset's unbalance.

## 2 Related Work

### 2.1 Confidence Level Estimation

Many attempts have been made to understand the human mental state . Facial expression is one of the common features to recognize internal conditions. Okawa et al. have developed a system that estimates the state of confusion from facial expressions and decides the robot's action based on it [10]. Some studies adopted voice information as physiological information reflecting mental state. Kasano et al. dealt with recognizing confidence levels by voice information and head motion [7]. However, facial expressions may not alter much when they study.

Also, regarding voice information, learners rarely speak while studying. Therefore, we adopted eye movement.

The approach of using eye movement data to estimate confidence levels has been employed in several studies. Yamada et al. estimated confidence while solving multiple-choice questions based on eye gaze [16]. Cui et al. adopted eye and head movements as features that reflect learners' confidence levels [2]. They estimated whether the learner is confident or unconfident with SVM, achieving a classification accuracy of 81.8%. In our previous study [4], we confirmed the possibility of estimating confidence levels from eye gaze information of learners while answering riddles and a questionnaire about their confidence levels before and after hearing hints. However, these studies didn't consider temporal changes in confidence levels and physiological data. Therefore, we propose a method to measure the subjective temporal evaluation considering temporal dynamics of eye movement and confidence levels, aiming to increase the possibility of estimating the confidence levels in real time.

### 2.2 Eye Movement and Pupil

Eye movements contain various information, such as eye direction, pupil size, and movement . In the field of affective computing , various studies including confidence estimation [2,16], emotion recognition [8,11], confusion recognition [14], interest estimation , utilize the information in eye movements. Some studies have also reported the relationship between eye movement information and human cognitive processes. B. Mathias et al. explored how eye behavior changes when attention shifts from externally directed cognition (EDC) to internally directed cognition (IDC) [1]. They reported that IDC exhibited fewer yet prolonged fixations and more variable pupil diameter and eye vergence, implying diminished visual scanning and enhanced spontaneous eye activity compared to EDC.

In addition, Some studies have reported that eye movement patterns change during tasks involving cognitive processes such as memory recall, idea generation, etc. Carola et al. reported that people intentionally divert their attention away from visual stimuli by looking at empty portions or blinking when looking for a creative idea [12]. Furthermore, Wu et al. used eye movements as indicators of deliberative thinking to predict performance on arithmetic word problems. They reported that RT-TFD (Reaction time minus the total fixation duration), the number of fixations of blank, and pupil size improved the performance of predicting the most [15].

Given this context, we estimate confidence levels while learning from eye movement and pupil information.

## 3 Experiment

### 3.1 Participant

In this experiment, there were thirteen male and female participants, who were all university students in their 20 s (range: 21–24 years, 12 male participants, 1 female participant). 2 out of 13 participants attended the experiment in June 2023 only once. 5 out of 13 participants participated in the first experiment in June 2023, and the second one in July 2024. The rest attended the first one in June 2024 and the second one in July 2024, resulting in 24 experimental sessions.

### 3.2 Materials

Kebbi Air (hereafter referred to as Kebbi) from NUWA Robotics was used as a communication robot to give questions and hints, request answers, and present correct answers (Fig. 1). Kebbi is equipped with AI and is capable of speech recognition, natural language processing, and face recognition, etc., and is used in a wide range of fields such as education, medical care, and service industry. In this study, we used its screen and speech function.

Tobii Technology's Tobii Pro Glasses 3 (hereafter referred to as Tobii) is a spectacle-type wearable eye tracker that can measure eye gaze, head movements, and pupils and record video and audio (Fig. 2). In this study, we used eye gaze and pupil information at a sampling rate of 100 Hz.

The ZenScreen Touch MB16AMT touchscreen monitor from ASUS was used as the input interface for self-evaluation of confidence (Fig. 3). We displayed a web page (Fig. 4) explicitly created for the experiment, and the participants operate a slider shown in the page to indicate their confidence levels. The slider was set to take values from 1 to 1000 from left to right, and the sampling rate was aligned with Tobii at 100 Hz. To reduce eye movements and errors, the screen was covered with a plastic sheet, as shown in Fig. 5.

**Fig. 1.** Kebbi Air

**Fig. 2.** Tobii pro glasses 3

**Fig. 3.** The Zenscreen Touch MB15AMT touchscreen monitor

Fig. 4. Web page displayed to participants

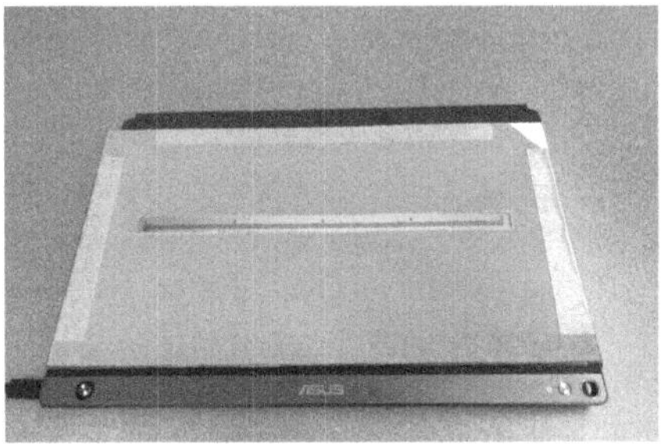

Fig. 5. Touchscreen to be operated by participants

### 3.3 Procedure

In our experiment, we adopted 30 riddles from website[1] . Participants needed to take time to think of the answers until they were given hints. Figure 6 shows the experimental view, and its flow is shown below.

1. Kebbi asks a question, and the participant starts operating the slider until finishing operating on step 4. Between thinking processes, the participant could freely operate the slider .
2. After 15 s, Kebbi gives a hint.
3. 12 s after the hint, Kebbi urges the participant to answer the question by saying, "Please answer." The participant will either answer the question or state that he or she does not know the answer.
4. 7 s after demanding the answer, Kebbi will give the correct answer. The participant finishes the slider operation.
5. The participant repeats from step 1 to step 4 until the last question. The slider is reset to the initial position each time at the start.

## 4 Data Processing

We obtained data from 24 experimental sessions. Some data was removed at the data cleansing stage because the computation of the feature "Fixation of areas

[1] https://nazoq.com.

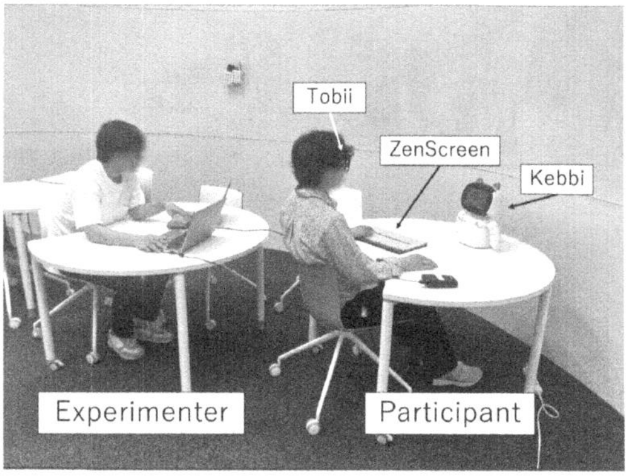


**Fig. 6.** Experimental View

out of Kebbi" using the software Tobii Pro Lab was incomplete, and we could not obtain all the required features. Finally, 9 out of 24 data sets were excluded from the analysis.

### 4.1 Pre-processing

First, missing values were excluded from the raw data (time series data output from Tobii). Then, using the timestamps of the start and the end of asking the question, the start of giving a hint, the start of urging the response, and the start of giving the correct answer recorded during the experiment, we excluded the interval of the utterance of the question and the interval from the utterance of the correct answer to the start of the following question (Fig. 7). The reason for this exclusion is that we considered them to be inappropriate data. During the utterance of the question, the participants often made slider errors, and the period after the start of the utterance of the correct answer did not fit our assumption of what participants were thinking. The data for each question was segmented using a sliding window with a window size of 5.0 s and a shift size of 0.5 s (Fig. 8). 54 sets of data were generated from each question because the available data per question was 34 s long.

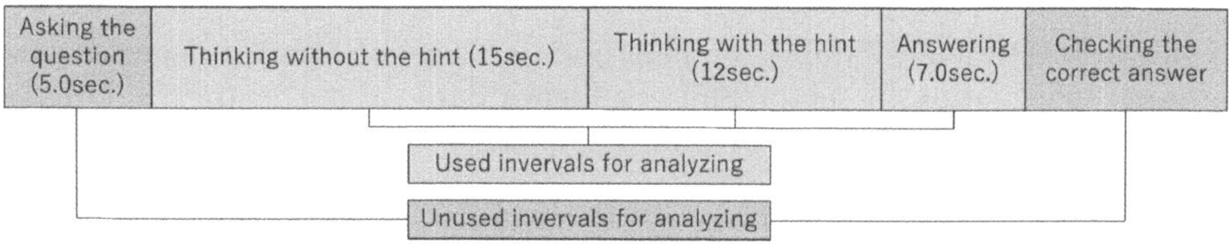


**Fig. 7.** Intervals during one question

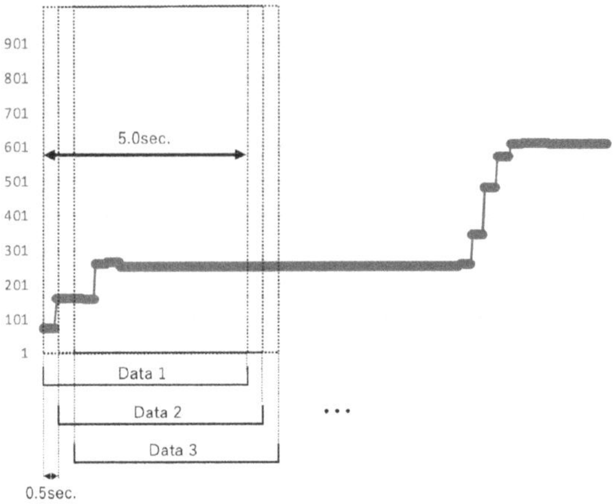


**Fig. 8.** Data spliting methods

Following previous research mentioned in Sect. 2.2, we create 40 features as shown in Table 1 in this study. Eye Movement Rate (EMR) is defined as the number of eye movements (saccade) per unit of time. Eye Movement Amplitude (EMA) represents the distance of eye movements (saccade) measured over the same time unit.

**Table 1.** Features for machine learning

| Category | Features |
|---|---|
| Saccade | EMR(Eye Movement Rate) |
| | EMA(Eye Movement Amounts) |
| | The number of saccade |
| | Fixation Duration{avg, std, max, sum} |
| | Fixation time on areas out of Kebbi |
| Pupil | Pupil diameter left and right {avg, std, max, min} |
| | Pupil position(x,y,z) left and right {avg, std, max, min} |

In constructing our dataset, we incorporated lagged features to consider the temporal information in sensor and confidence data. These features allow the simultaneous input of past and present data points, aiding in time series analysis within machine learning.

The explanatory variables for a single input data consist of the features at time $t$ ($t \geq 5$) and those from times $t-1$, $t-2$, $t-3$, and $t-4$, as shown in Fig. 9. The dependent variable was the confidence level at time $t+1$. We defined Unconfident state as data with a confidence level of 1 to 200 and Confident as data with a confidence level of 801 to 1000. The interval, a confidence level of 201 to 800, is not used in the analysis in this study but is defined as Intermediate.

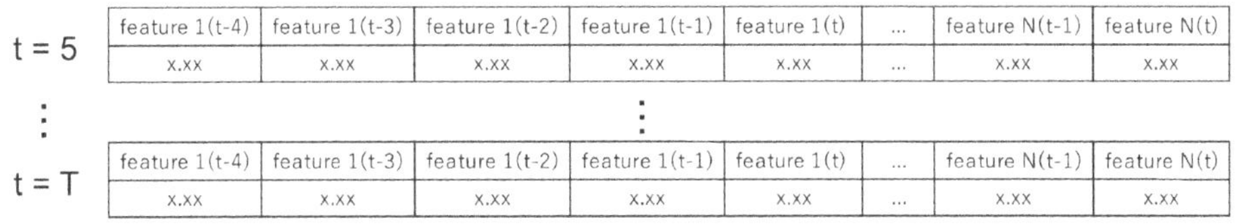


**Fig. 9.** Lagged feature

### 4.2 Estimation Model

In our previous research [4], we estimated confidence levels by using SVM (Support Vector Machine). To extract more effective features from lagged features, we adopted CNN (Convolutional Neural Networks) models as estimators. Figure 10 is the architecture of CNN we used. The stride of the filter in the first convolutional layer is set to 5 to ensure that convolution occurs among the same features in lagged features. The ReLu activation function is used in each hidden layer. This paper classified 'Unconfident' and 'Confident' with this estimation model.

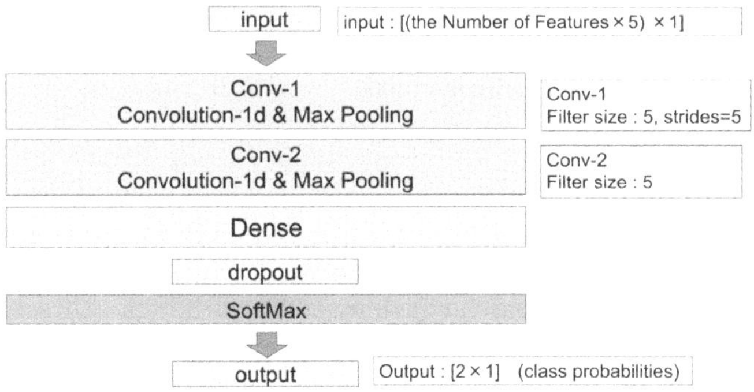


**Fig. 10.** CNN architecture diagram

## 5 Result and Discussion

Table 2 shows each participant's number of Unconfident, Intermediate, and Confident data after generating lagged features. As the table indicated, there is a difference between the number of data points labeled as 'Confident' and 'Unconfident,' with the former being approximately twice that of the latter . To solve data imbalance, we conducted data augmentation with Synthetic Minority Over-sampling Technique (SMOTE).

Additionally, we conducted validation using 3 different patterns: 1)only saccade and fixation features, 2)only pupil information features, and 3)using all features to explore the impact of each feature on estimation accuracy.

**Table 2.** The number of data

| Subject ID | Unconfident | Confident |
|---|---|---|
| A1 | 1073 | 358 |
| B1 | 460 | 582 |
| C2 | 1167 | 219 |
| D1 | 945 | 487 |
| D2 | 876 | 671 |
| E1 | 659 | 694 |
| E2 | 638 | 871 |
| G1 | 1254 | 310 |
| G2 | 1128 | 475 |
| J2 | 1191 | 377 |
| K1 | 807 | 589 |
| K2 | 899 | 515 |
| L2 | 1105 | 414 |
| M2 | 1192 | 441 |
| N2 | 672 | 656 |
| All Participants | 14066 | 7659 |

First, we estimated all participants' data, as shown in Table 3.

The highest accuracy was achieved when SMOTE was not used and both Saccade and Pupil were employed, with an accuracy of 85 This result was better comparing to our previous research which was 60%, although a direct comparison is inappropriate due to differing experimental conditions and features.

When not using SMOTE, the combination of saccade and pupil features yielded higher accuracy and F1 scores than using only saccade features and using only pupil features. This result was also consistent when using SMOTE. Comparing the result of using only saccade features versus only pupil features, using only pupil features resulted in better outcomes regardless of whether SMOTE was used. This result indicates that changes in pupils can serve as a reliable indicator in estimation. Focusing on changes in accuracy due to whether SMOTE was used when using only saccade features, estimation accuracy was higher with SMOTE. In contrast, estimation accuracy was higher without SMOTE when using other feature patterns. However, these differences in results suggest that data imbalance is not a big problem for improving estimation accuracy, and capturing data variability is more important. Furthermore, we estimated using data from only one experimental session for each one. Table 4 and Table 5 show the results of Participants E and G, respectively. The former is an example of a result close to the total results, whereas the latter had no similarity to the total results. As can be seen from Table 4, for Participant E, there was a significant difference between the performance using only saccade information and that using only pupil data, similar to the overall results. On the other hand, for Participant G, the performance using only saccade information is comparable to that using only pupil information. This suggests that the influence of saccade (eye movement) information on estimation accuracy could depend on the subject's personality and learning capabilities.

**Table 3.** All participants Result w/o and w/ SMOTE

| Features | Accuracy | Precision | Recall | F1-score |
|---|---|---|---|---|
| Sac w/o | 0.56 | 0.48 | 0.48 | 0.48 |
| Sac w/ | 0.60 | 0.51 | 0.50 | 0.49 |
| Pupil w/o | 0.84 | 0.84 | **0.81** | **0.82** |
| Pupil w/ | 0.80 | 0.83 | 0.73 | 0.75 |
| Sac + Pupil w/o | **0.85** | **0.87** | 0.79 | 0.81 |
| Sac + Pupil w/ | 0.83 | 0.85 | 0.77 | 0.79 |

**Table 4.** Participant E1 Result w/o and w/ SMOTE

| Features | Accuracy | Precision | Recall | F1-score |
|---|---|---|---|---|
| Sac w/o | 0.54 | 0.55 | 0.54 | 0.51 |
| Sac w/ | 0.57 | 0.62 | 0.57 | 0.53 |
| Pupil w/o | 0.91 | 0.91 | 0.91 | 0.91 |
| Pupil w/ | **0.95** | **0.95** | **0.95** | **0.95** |
| Sac + Pupil w/o | 0.82 | 0.92 | 0.92 | 0.92 |
| Sac + Pupil w/ | 0.94 | 0.94 | 0.94 | 0.94 |

**Table 5.** Participant G1 Result w/o and w/ SMOTE

| Features | Accuracy | Precision | Recall | F1-score |
|---|---|---|---|---|
| Sac w/o | 0.88 | 0.82 | 0.80 | 0.81 |
| Sac w/ | 0.86 | 0.81 | 0.74 | 0.77 |
| Pupil w/o | 0.87 | 0.80 | 0.87 | 0.83 |
| Pupil w/ | **0.89** | **0.83** | 0.87 | **0.85** |
| Sac + Pupil w/o | 0.87 | 0.81 | 0.79 | 0.80 |
| Sac + Pupil w/ | 0.88 | 0.82 | **0.88** | 0.84 |

## 6 Conclusion

In this paper, we estimated confidence levels using eye movement and pupil features incorporating temporal dynamics. As a result, saccade and pupil features achieved high estimation accuracy. In Particular, pupil features are considered to have a strong relationship with estimation accuracy. Additionally, we used a feature incorporating temporal dynamics in this paper, which yielded high accuracy. This suggests that these methods are suitable for real-time estimation of confidence levels. However, from the comparison of individual results, it was confirmed that the effectiveness of each feature varies between individuals. By analyzing individual differences such as personality, learning skills, self-efficacy, etc., there is a possibility of further increasing the accuracy of the estimations. Given the small dataset size, it is a priority to increase the dataset to strengthen the validity of this method. In the future, we are considering using other methods to capture temporal dynamics, like LSTM. In addition, we aim to construct a regression model that can infer confidence levels from eye movement information in real time for future applications in robotic decision-making.

**Acknowledgments.** This study was supported by JST [Moonshot R&D][grant number JPMJMS2034].

## References

1. Benedek, M., Stoiser, R., Walcher, S., Körner, C.: Eye behavior associated with internally versus externally directed cognition. Front. Psychol. **8**, 1092 (2017)
2. Cui, D., Matsufuji, A., Liu, Y., Sato-Shimokawa, E., Yamaguchi, T.: Estimation of confidence in the dialogue based on eye gaze and head movement information. EMITTER Inter. J. Eng. Technol., 338–350 (2022)
3. Donnermann, M., Schaper, P., Lugrin, B.: Social robots in applied settings: a long-term study on adaptive robotic tutors in higher education. Front. Robot. AI **9**, 831633 (2022)
4. Eto, R., Sato-Shimokawara, E.: Analysis and recognition of confidence level based on eye gaze and head movement towards human-robot co-learning. In: 2023 International Conference on Machine Learning and Cybernetics (ICMLC), pp. 495–500. IEEE (2023)
5. Jimenez, F., Yoshikawa, T., Furuhashi, T., Kanoh, M.: An emotional expression model for educational-support robots. J. Artifi. Intell. Soft Comput. Res. **5**(1), 51–57 (2015). https://doi.org/10.1515/jaiscr-2015-0018
6. Jimenez, F., Yoshikawa, T., Furuhashi, T., Kanoh, M.: Effects of a novel sympathy-expression method on collaborative learning among junior high school students and robots. J. Robot. Mechatronic **30**(2), 282–291 (2018). https://doi.org/10.20965/jrm.2018.p0282
7. Kasano, E., Muramatsu, S., Matsufuji, A., Sato-Shimokawara, E., Yamaguchi, T.: Estimation of speaker's confidence in conversation using speech information and head motion. In: 2019 16th International Conference on Ubiquitous Robots (UR), pp. 294–298 (2019). https://doi.org/10.1109/URAI.2019.8768561

8. Lim, J.Z., Mountstephens, J., Teo, J.: Emotion recognition using eye-tracking: taxonomy, review and current challenges. Sensors **20**(8), 2384 (2020)
9. Miyauchi, K., Jimenez, F., Yoshikawa, T., Furuhashi, T., Kanoh, M.: Learning effects of robots teaching based on cognitive apprenticeship theory. J. Adv. Comput. Intell. Intell. Inform. **24**(1), 101–112 (2020). https://doi.org/10.20965/jaciii.2020.p0101
10. Okawa, K., Jimenez, F., Akizuki, S., Yoshikawa, T.: Proposal of learning support model for teacher-type robot supporting learning according to learner's perplexed facial expressions. J. Robot. Mechatronics **36**(1), 168–180 (2024). https://doi.org/10.20965/jrm.2024.p0168
11. Partala, T., Surakka, V.: Pupil size variation as an indication of affective processing. Int. J. Hum Comput Stud. **59**(1), 185–198 (2003)
12. Salvi, C., Bowden, E.M.: Looking for creativity: where do we look when we look for new ideas? Front. Psychol. **7** (2016). https://doi.org/10.3389/fpsyg.2016.00161, https://www.frontiersin.org/journals/psychology/articles/10.3389/fpsyg.2016.00161
13. Suzuki, K., Kanoh, M.: Effectiveness of a robot for supporting expression education. In: 2015 Conference on Technologies and Applications of Artificial Intelligence (TAAI), pp. 498–501 (2015). https://doi.org/10.1109/TAAI.2015.7407119
14. Takagi, H.: Recognizing users' uncertainty on the basis of eye movement patterns: a step toward an effective task assistance system. IPSJ J. **41**(5), 1317–1327 (2000)
15. Wu, C.-J., Liu, C.-Y., Yang, C.-H., Jian, Y.-C.: Eye-movements reveal children's deliberative thinking and predict performance on arithmetic word problems. Eur. J. Psychol. Educ. **36**(1), 91–108 (2020). https://doi.org/10.1007/s10212-020-00461-w
16. Yamada, K., Kise, K., Augereau, O.: Estimation of confidence based on eye gaze: an application to multiple-choice questions. In: Proceedings of the 2017 ACM International Joint Conference on Pervasive and Ubiquitous Computing and Proceedings of the 2017 ACM International Symposium on Wearable Computers, pp. 217-220. UbiComp 2017. Association for Computing Machinery, New York (2017). https://doi.org/10.1145/3123024.3123138

# Persuasion Process from the Perspective of Decision-Making Model in Werewolf Games

Asuka Nakai(✉) and Takeshi Ito

The University of Electro-Communications, Chofu Tokyo 1828585, Japan
n2331112@edu.cc.uec.ac.jp, ito@cs.uec.ac.jp

**Abstract.** This study analyzed players' decision-making process in Werewolf and the success factors of persuasion in a 5-player Werewolf. In Experiment 1, we focused on the villager player and analyzed the process of deciding who to vote for based on what other players say. We proposed a decision-making model in which logical and economic rationality are prioritized, and when they still cannot decide, "empathy" becomes the deciding factor. Experiment 2 focused on persuasion situations and examined how successful persuasion is. The results confirmed that persuasion using logical persuasion materials is successful. This supported the model's validity in Experiment 1 that logical rationality is the overriding criterion for decision-making. However, we could not observe the success factors when both persuaders had logical material. Future research will investigate the aspects of successful persuasion more deeply through complex persuasion situations and games with more proficient players.

**Keywords:** Werewolf Game · Decision-making · Persuasion · Logical Rationality

## 1 Introduction

Werewolf games (hereafter referred to as "Werewolf") are classified as identity-hiding, multiplayer, and incomplete information communication games. They are one of the most popular party games among young people in Japan. Players are dealt their position cards at the start of play. They are informed whether they are in the werewolf camp (werewolves and maniacs) or the villager camp (others) but are not informed of players' positions other than themselves. The objective is to lead one's camp to victory by estimating the positions of others and falsifying one's position. This requires not only advanced communication skills but also logical reasoning. The "Artificial Intelligence-based Werewolf Project" researches and develops AI and robots that play werewolves to realize artificial agents that can play with humans without discomfort [1]. To achieve this goal, it is essential to elucidate the thinking mechanism of human players, and research from a cognitive science perspective is also expected.

In this study, we will conduct a cognitive experiment to investigate the detailed thought process through interviews with players, and propose a cognitive model of the decision-making process of players. We focus on "villagers" and "maniacs" who cannot

© The Author(s), under exclusive license to Springer Nature Singapore Pte Ltd. 2025
W.-T. Chu et al. (Eds.): TAAI 2024, CCIS 2414, pp. 344–355, 2025.
https://doi.org/10.1007/978-981-96-4589-3_25

know the positions of others due to their positions in a 5-player Werewolf game (from now on referred to as "5-player Werewolf").

Furthermore, focusing on persuasion behavior, which is often observed when players discuss with each other, we will try to decipher from the above decision-making model what factors are involved in the success or failure of persuasion.

## 2 Related Works

Fujii et al.'s research can be cited as analyzing the human decision-making process [2]. To verify the reliability of the CVM (Contingent Valuation Method), which measures the value of the natural environment, Fujii et al. conducted a study to examine subjects' decision-making process using verbal protocol analysis, which has been used in cognitive science. Specifically, subjects were given a situation, asked to read a question aloud, and then asked to utter everything that came to their minds up to the answer. The data from the start of the utterance to the point where the decision was made was used as the utterance data, and the contents were categorized and analyzed by item. The results suggest that "bias" cannot be adequately eliminated even by NOAA (National Oceanic and Atmospheric Administration) guidelines. Thus, verbal protocol analysis has the potential to reveal rigorous decision-making behavior. In this study, we want to continue clarifying the werewolves' decision-making process by conducting a verbal protocol analysis.

Crano et al.'s research shows the study of attitudes and persuasion [3]. This research summarizes findings on the formation of people's attitudes through persuasion. Crano et al. mentioned dual-process models such as the elaboration likelihood model (ELM) and the heuristic/systematic model (HSM) as thought-process models of the recipients of persuasion. These models comprise two different processes: conducting based on careful consideration of information and performing based on personal associations with the recipient or simple reasoning. Therefore, persuasive messages are classified according to two elements: logical elements, such as well-reasoned and data-based, and emotional elements, such as peripheral cues and heuristics.

Another analysis of persuasion content in werewolves is that of Zaitsu et al., who classified persuasion in werewolves into three types: "logical persuasion," in which the player tells the opponent his/her viewpoint and the reasons for coming to that viewpoint, "emotional persuasion," in which the player emphasizes the correctness of his/her argument, and "persuasion using meta-information," in which the player uses information that cannot be known within the current game[4]. They also defined successful persuasion in werewolves as "not being selected as the enemy team at the end." They analyzed the effects of the different persuasion contents on the persuaders by examining whether the experimental participants who received the three types of persuasion by the dialogue system trusted the persuasion contents. In this study, we would like to clarify what kind of persuasion content can win trust concerning the three types of persuasion described above.

# 3 5-player Werewolf

Werewolf are generally party games played with many players (9 or more). Still, while Werewolf with many players are as exciting as party games with many roles, many players need roles such as villagers. The game becomes slow in the early stages due to a lack of information, or some players are eliminated without much success or clear reasons, depending on their roles. Therefore, in this study, we will focus on 5-player Werewolf, which are said to be the smallest unit of werewolves.

In 5-player Werewolf, there is a minimum number of roles to be considered in a werewolf game: the werewolf camp of one werewolf and one maniac and the villager camp of one seer and two villagers. The game also retains the essential strategic elements of a werewolf, such as acquiring information through roles and deception. At the beginning of the game, the five players are assigned roles, and Day 1 begins with the seer divining one person. If the werewolf survives until the night of Day 2, the werewolf camp wins. Unlike the multiplayer werewolf game, there is a strategy of deception in all roles. Although the game is settled in a short period, it is a strategically deep game.

# 4 Experiment 1

## 4.1 Purpose

Focusing on the villagers who cannot know the roles of others due to their role abilities in 5-player Werewolf, we analyze how they decide who to vote for based on their utterances during the game and interviews immediately after the game to clarify their decision-making process.

## 4.2 Method

Twelve students (eleven males and one female), well-trained in 5-player Werewolf, were the experiment subjects. To ensure that the participants fully understood the basics of the 5-player Werewolf, they were asked to have played the game at least ten times.

The experiment used the following procedure: Participants were divided into three overlapping groups (each participant could participate in at most two groups), and the following procedure was repeated.

1) The participants were asked to play 5-player Werewolf, and a video of the werewolves was taken. In this experiment, the duration of one discussion at noon was set to 5 min.
2) Immediately after the end of the game, we showed the game video to one of the villagers who had survived until the Day 2 and asked him/her in an interview how he had decided who to vote for.
3) Villagers' statements in the game conversation and the interview were analyzed as follows.
4) The conversations of the game players were transcribed for each player over time and encoded with tags that matched the content of their statements. The tags used were those from other studies, plus those deemed necessary based on the results of preliminary experiments [5].

5) Interview statements were transcribed in the text next to the player's tagged conversation in the game. The starting point for describing these statements was aligned with the in-game video played during the interview.

In the game of Werewolf, players mainly engage in conversation during the game. Therefore, it is difficult to obtain the thoughts of players during the game using online speech protocols. Therefore, in this method, we decided to ask about the thought process in the form of an interview conducted immediately after However, we conducted the interviews carefully, being careful about this point, so we think that the interview contents are generally reliable. As this is a study that examines thought processes, it is an experiment that is difficult to analyze quantitatively due to its nature. We will attempt a qualitative analysis focusing on some typical interview results.

## 4.3 Results

Thirteen games were played, and interviews were conducted for six games that could be analyzed. Among them, we conducted a tagging analysis of the in-game conversation, focusing on games that fit the purpose of this study, i.e., games in which the villagers' decision-making decides the game-winner on the Day 2 of the game. Table 1 is one of the game records of the target game.

**Table 1.** A game record to be analyzed.

| Player | 1 | 2 | 3 | 4 | 5 |
|---|---|---|---|---|---|
| Roles | Werewolf | Seer | Villager | Villager | Maniac |
| Day 0, Night | | Pre>1 | | | |
| Day 1, Daytime | CO:S | CO:S | | | CO:S |
| | Pre>3V | Pre>1W | | | |
| | | | | | Pre>3W |
| | | Sus>5 | | | |
| | | | Sus>5 | | |
| | Sus>2 | | | | |
| | | | Sus>1,2,5 | Sus>1,2,5 | |
| | | Vote>1 | | | |
| | | | Vote>5 | | |
| | | | | Sus>1,2,5 | |
| Day 1, Vote | 5 | 1 | 5 | 5 | 3 |
| Day 1, Night | At>3 | Pre>3 | | | |
| Day 2, Daytime | Pre>2W | | | | |
| Day 2, Vote | 2 | 1 | | 1 | |

First, explain the terms and symbols used in the game record. The game record is a table summarizing the game's flow, including each player's position, main statements, actions during the night, and where he/she voted. Table 1 shows the actions and statements from the night of Day 0 to the vote on Day 2, in chronological order. The squares of players eliminated from the game are blacked out to indicate they are no longer involved. Table 2 shows the meaning of abbreviations and symbols used in the game record.

**Table 2.** Terms and symbols used in the game records and their meanings.

| Terms and Symbols | meanings |
|---|---|
| CO: | Coming out one's role |
| COX | Withdraw the role coming out |
| Pre> | Informing the results of the prediction |
| PD> | Role estimation from the player's view |
| Po> | Possibility of other player roles |
| Sus> | Suspect a specific player |
| Obj> | Objections to specific players |
| Cons> | Consent to specific players |
| Qes> | Question to specific players |
| Vote> | Intention to vote for specific players |
| Pr_Vote> | Call for a vote for specific players |
| At> | Who the werewolf attacks |

Let us look at the progression of this game in Table 1. In this game, on Day 1, a werewolf and a maniac come out as seers in addition to the seer. The timing of the maniac's coming out is a little late, and he is then suspected. Looking at the divination details, the seer in Player 2 suddenly finds the werewolf in Player 1, the werewolf claims the villager in Player 3 as a villager, and the maniac claims Player 3 as a werewolf. The two players, the maniac and the werewolf, disagree about their claims. Villager Player 4 will have to decide who to vote for on Day 1 under these circumstances. Also, on Day 2, Player 1 divines Player 2 to be a werewolf, and since Player 2 has already guessed werewolf, he still needs to mention the other decision results. From Player 4's point of view, both of them have succeeded logically. This situation becomes a situation where one has to decide who to vote for. Player 4 is the player who has to decide based solely on what others have said so far and is the typical research subject of this study. Therefore, we focused our analysis on this game.

Interviews with Player 4 revealed the flow of this game, as seen by Player 4. This is outlined below. (• denotes objective observation, ○ denotes subjective content)

Day 1

- Player 2 claims to vote for the Player 1 based on his own divination result.
- Player 3 insists on voting for Player 5, which is doubtful from any player's point of view.
- Player 1 claims that Player 2 is suspicious because he insists that Player 1 is a werewolf.

  - Player 2's explanation is sympathetic.
  - Player 3's explanation seems to make sense.

Day 2

- Player 1 judges Player 2 as a werewolf.
- Player 2 claims that he is still alive so that Player 1 can say that Player 2 is a werewolf and get Player 4 to vote for him.

  - Player 2's explanation matches Player 3's explanation.
  - Lack of sympathy for Player 1 throughout.

**Table 3.** Statement aggregation results for each player.

| Player | 1 | 2 | 3 | 4 | 5 |
|---|---|---|---|---|---|
| Roles | Werewolf | Seer | Villager | Villager | Maniac |
| Total number of statements | 78 | 91 | 65 | 45 | 13 |
| Illogical statement | 0 | 5 | 1 | 2 | 0 |
| Concurrence | 15 | 4 | 5 | 6 | 1 |
| Refutation | 4 | 4 | 1 | 0 | 0 |
| Statements directed at others | 7 | 17 | 10 | 0 | 0 |
| Statements from the self-perspective | 6 | 12 | 5 | 0 | 0 |

Table 3 shows the total number of statements made by the players. Player 2 has more statements than Player 1. Looking at the content, neither Player 1 nor 2 showed any logical breakdown.

## 4.4 Discussion

### 4.4.1 The Change in Villager's Thinking

Looking at the thought process of Player 4 (the villager) on Day 1, he compares the claims of Players 2 and 3, who were sympathetic, claiming who to vote for. Player 2 claimed that Player 1 was suspicious, while Player 3 claimed that Player 5 was suspicious. Although there is no difference between these two arguments regarding logical rationality, comparing their arguments, Player 2 and Player 3 decided that the latter's argument was better regarding the villagers' probability of winning. As a result, he decided to vote for Player 5, in agreement with Player 3's opinion.

On the Day 2, he reported that they did not sympathize with Player 1 compared to Player 2. Player 2 was suspicious of Player 1, and Player 1 was suspicious of Player 2. In terms of logical rationality, there is no difference between their claims. There is also no difference in the odds of winning other than the logical consequence that one of them is a werewolf. Under these circumstances, the final criterion for the judgment was "empathy." It was impossible to determine from the speech tags alone where the difference in sympathy for these two people came from.

### 4.4.2 Comparison of the Number of Statements

Here, we focused on the number of statements made by the players. Of players 1, 2, and 3, there was a difference in the amount of "attempts to execute other players" and "explaining the situation from one's point of view." These statements were more frequent in Players 2 and 3 than in Player 1, which may have given Player 4 sympathy during the play. This suggests that more statements about the execution target and explanations of the situation from the player's perspective may evoke sympathy for the villager players.

## 4.5 Conclusion

Based on the above, we can consider the decision-making process of the villager players in the order shown in Fig. 1 below.

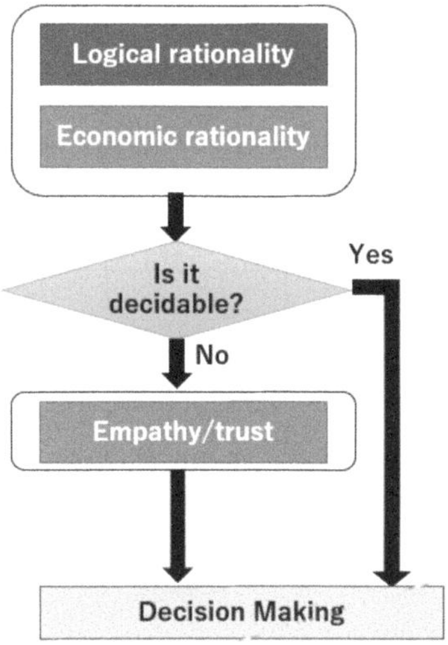


**Fig. 1.** Decision-making process of players (villagers).

First, we focus on "logical rationality" to see if there are any logical contradictions. If there is no contradiction, they consider "economic rationality" based on their camp's winning rate. If no difference is found in either of these cases, the two opposing hypotheses are examined based on the credibility of the previous statements, such as the amount of speech from one's perspective.

Figure 1 shows the hypothesized decision-making model for this experiment. In this decision-making situation, each player is expected to try to persuade the other player about the two conflicting events. Therefore, in the next experiment, we would like to test the validity of this decision-making model by focusing on the persuasion situation and identifying what influences the success or failure of the persuasion.

# 5 Experiment 2

## 5.1 Purpose

This experiment focuses on persuasion situations and examines how persuasion is used in actual in-game discussions. Furthermore, we will discuss the success or failure of persuasion and determine what influences its success or failure.

## 5.2 Method

This experiment was conducted with 16 male students aged 20 or older who needed more experience with 5-player Werewolf. At first, the rules of 5-player Werewolf were explained to them so they could understand the game's content. Then, the participants were asked to play 5-player Werewolf, and the speech data for all 35 games were obtained by capturing the scene with a video camera. Since the participants took turns participating in the games, each participant played about 16 games.

## 5.3 Games to Be Analyzed and Definition of Successful Persuasion

To make it easier to understand the persuaders and the persuaded, the situation to be analyzed was limited to "one person unsure about voting in the Day 2 discussion, while two others are trying to convince him or her. The number of games that met the above conditions was 10 out of 35. Furthermore, among these ten games, we conducted a detailed analysis of the speech of the successful and unsuccessful persuaders and their game development in two games in which the positions of the two persuaders were equal from the viewpoint of the persuaders. These games were relatively complex in determining who to vote for, with only the information given on Day 1 (divination results, Day 1 voting destination, etc.).

## 5.4 Results

The first of the two games analyzed is shown in Table 4. In this game, the maniac, the seer, and the villager came out as seers on Day 1, and the villager withdrew his coming out shortly after that. The divination details are as follows: the maniac in Player 2 claims that the werewolf in Player 5 is not a werewolf, and the actual seer in Player 3 claims that the villager in Player 1 is not a werewolf. As for Player 4, who withdrew his coming out, there were both speculations that he was a villager and speculations that he was in the werewolf camp, so only this player was not suspected. Player 5, who thought Player 4 was a villager, then suggested voting for either Player 1 or Player 5, who was likelier to be a werewolf. However, it was pointed out that at this stage, there was no proof that Player 4 was a villager and that there was a possibility that neither Player 1 nor Player 5 was in the werewolf camp, so it was suggested again to vote for either Player 2 or Player 3, one of which was definitely in the werewolf camp. The result was that Player 2, the maniac, was executed.

**Table 4.** First game record in the games analyzed.

| Player | 1 | 2 | 3 | 4 | 5 |
|---|---|---|---|---|---|
| Roles | Villager | Maniac | Seer | Villager | Werewolf |
| Day 0, Night | | | Pre>1 | | |
| Day 1, Daytime | | | | CO:S | |
| | | CO:S | | | |
| | | | CO:S | | |
| | | | | COX | |
| | | Pre>5V | Pre>1V | | |
| | | | | | PD>4V |
| | | | Sus>4W | | |
| | | | | | Pr_Vote>1,5 |
| | Sus>4 | | | | |
| | | | | | PD>4V |
| | | | | | Pr_Vote>2,3 |
| | | | Pr_Vote>2,3 | | |
| | | | | | Qes>4 |
| | | | | Pr_Vote>2 | |
| Day 1, Vote | 2 | 3 | 2 | 2 | 3 |
| Day 1, Night | | | Pre>4 | | At>3 |
| Day 2, Daytime | | | | | PD>4V |
| | | | | | Sus>1W |
| | | | | Sus>5W | |
| | | | | | Sus>4W |
| | | | | Qes>1 | |
| | | | | PD>1V | PD>1V |
| | | | | | PD>5V |
| | | | | PD>4V | |
| | | | | | Obj>4 |
| Day 2, Vote | 4 | | | 5 | 4 |

On the Day 2, the discussion began with the two players who had come out as seers on the Day 1 gone. Assuming that Player 1 is a werewolf here, Player 3, who divined that Player 1 is not a werewolf, is lying, i.e., a maniac, from the standpoint of Player 1. So, Player 1 doesn't need to attack Player 3. Because if Player 3 remains, a Power Play can be made on Day 2. "Power Play" refers to a play in which a werewolf comes forward and votes against a villager in collusion with a maniac. However, Player 3 was attacked by the werewolf on the night of Day 1. This shows that Player 1 is doubtful to be a werewolf. In this situation, Player 4 and Player 5 must convince Player 1 that they are not werewolves.

Player 5 claimed he was not a werewolf because he had suggested on the 1st day that he be included in the voting list. In response, Player 4 countered but did not offer a logical explanation like Player 5. As a result, Player 1 did not support Player 4's counterargument and ultimately voted for Player 4, resulting in a victory for the werewolf camp.

Next, the game record of the second game among the games analyzed is shown in Table 5.

In this game, the werewolf, the maniac, and the villager came out to be the seer on Day 1. The werewolf and the villager withdrew their coming out immediately after that, and then the actual seer came out late. The divination details are that the maniac in Player 2 claims that the villager in Player 3 is not a werewolf, and the actual seer in

Player 4 claims that the maniac in Player 2 is not a werewolf. Player 4 then proposed to vote for Player 3 based on his perspective, but the other players became suspicious of him because of his late coming out, and Player 4 was executed as a result.

**Table 5.** Second match.

| Player | 1 | 2 | 3 | 4 | 5 |
|---|---|---|---|---|---|
| Roles | Werewolf | Maniac | Villager | Seer | Villager |
| Day 0, Night | | | | Pre>2 | |
| Day 1, Daytime | CO:S | CO:S | | | CO:S |
| | COX | | | | COX |
| | | | | CO:S | |
| | | Pre>3V | | Pre>2V | |
| | | | | Sus>2M | |
| | | | | | Sus>4M |
| | Pr_Vote>1,4,5 | | | | |
| | | | | | Cons>1 |
| | | | | PD>1V, 5V<br>Su>3W | |
| | | | | | Su>4M |
| | | | | Pr_Vote>3 | |
| | | PD>3V | | | |
| | | | Po>3W, 2M | | |
| | | | | Pr_Vote>3 | |
| | | Su>4W, 3M | | | |
| | | | | | Pr_Vote>4 |
| Day 1, Vote | 4 | 3 | 4 | 3 | 4 |
| Day 1, Night | At>2 | | | | |
| Day 2, Daytime | | | | | PD>3V |
| | | | | | Sus>1W |
| | Sus>5W | | | | |
| | | | | | Sus>2M |
| | | | | | PD>5V |
| Day 2, Vote | 5 | | 1 | | 1 |

Assuming that Player 3 is a werewolf here, Player 2, who divined that Player 3 is not a werewolf, is lying, i.e., a maniac, from the standpoint of Player 3. So, Player 3 doesn't need to attack Player 2. Because if Player 3 remains, a Power Play can be made on Day 2.

However, Player 2 was attacked by the werewolf on the night of Day 1. This shows that Player 3 is doubtful to be a werewolf. In this situation, Player 1 and Player 5 must convince Player 3 that they are not werewolves. This development is similar to the first game.

In this game, there was no significant difference in behavior between Player 1 and Player 5 during the Day 1 discussion. However, Player 2 had voted for Player 3, who was clearly not a werewolf, when voting on Day 1. This indicates that Player 2 may be a maniac. Player 5 mentioned this point and insisted that he would not attack Player 2 if he were a werewolf, being aware of this. This assertion won Player 5 the trust of Player 3, and Player 3 voted for Player 1, resulting in a win for the villagers' camp.

### 5.5 Discussion

In both of the two games analyzed in this study, the players moved to the Day 2 with only one of the persuaders having persuasive material from the discussion on the Day 1, and the player who used that persuasive material to persuade logically was successful.

We speculate that the persuaders referred to "logical rationality," which considers logical contradictions in the werewolf player's decision-making process model proposed in Experiment 1. In this respect, the validity of this decision-making model was indicated. However, the examples of these two games showed only arguments that did not fall outside the "logical rationality" category in the decision-making process model.

In general, as players become more proficient at playing, they play various games on Day 1 to accumulate information that might be used to persuade them on Day 2. In Experiment 2, we did not initially see any plays where the villagers played the seers. Still, we gradually began to see plays in which they played the seers. This play is intended to avoid a Power Play situation on the Day 2 if the villagers do nothing. To prevent this, villagers will actively play coming out to complicate matters, gain more information, and leave more persuasive material on the Day 2.

How are decisions made by non-persuaders when players have evenly logical persuasive material on Day 2? To test the validity of the decision-making model in Fig. 1, we need to investigate decision-making in more complex phases.

## 6 Conclusion

This study conducted two experiments on 5-player Werewolf to investigate the decision-making process and the success factors of persuasion in wargames. In Experiment 1, the model showed that logical and economic rationality are essential factors in villagers' decision-making and that empathy can ultimately be the deciding factor. Experiment 2 focused on the persuasion scene and examined the triumphant persuasion phase. As a result, having logical, persuasive materials and persuading based on them is adequate. In this respect, the validity of the proposed model, in which logical rationality is the preferential decision-making criterion in Experiment 1, was supported. However, we could not investigate how successful persuasion is when both persuaders have logical persuasion material and need help deciding which is more reasonable.

Therefore, we plan to conduct future experiments with more proficient players and investigate more complex persuasion situations to examine economic rationality and how empathy is achieved.

## References

1. Artificial Intelligence based Werewolf. https://aiwolf.org/en/. Accessed 17 Aug 2024
2. Fujii, S., Suda, H., Adachi, T., Kitamura, R.: An analysis of decision-making processes under CVM: a cognitive-psychological test of NOAA's guidelines, Journal of Japan Society of Civil Engineers, Ser. D3 (Infrastructure Planning and Management), Volume 19, pp. 91–98 (2002). (In Japanese)
3. Crano, W.D., Prislin, R.: Attitude and persuasion. Annu. Rev. Psychol. **57**(1), 345–374 (2006)
4. Zaitsu, T., Katagami, D.: Persuasion and effects to human players by the AI-based werewolf game player agent. In: The 36th Annual Conference of the Japanese Society for Artificial Intelligence, 4I3-OS-26b-03, pp. 1–4 (2022). (in Japanese)
5. Sugimoto, M, Ito, T.: How do villagers make decision in the game of 5-players' werewolf?. The 34th Annual Meeting of Japanese Cognitive Science Society, P1–26F, pp. 826–832 (2017). (in Japanese)

# Author Index




© The Editor(s) (if applicable) and The Author(s), under exclusive license
to Springer Nature Singapore Pte Ltd. 2025


W.-T. Chu et al. (Eds.): TAAI 2024, CCIS 2414, pp. 357–358, 2025.
https://doi.org/10.1007/978-981-96-4589-3

The manufacturer's authorised representative in the EU is Springer Nature Customer Service Centre GmbH, Europaplatz 3, 69115 Heidelberg, Germany. If you have any concerns regarding our products, please contact ProductSafety@springernature.com

Printed and bound by CPI Group (UK) Ltd, Croydon, CR0 4YY
01/10/2026
02225908-0012